Introduction

At birth I was named Brian Stevens, I am the Man Behind the Mask, and I have a story to tell.

There are many 'rags to riches' stories around, but only a few begin with circumstances so challenging that they seem impossible to overcome.

In 1941, a young working-class woman falls pregnant with a child that is not her husband's; it's likely that only she knows the father. She is sent from her Black Country home to a former workhouse in Shropshire to give birth to her unwanted baby, whom she surrenders into the care of the home and disappears from his life.

The child is adopted by a right thinking, hard working, childless couple, but his adoptive mother dies when he is just seven, and life in the family's council house becomes functional, basic, and emotionally sparse.

His un-addressed emotional needs lead to him being unable to befriend other children, to whom he can't relate, and he finds himself a loner.

School was to feel more like a cruel punishment - he was profoundly dyslexic, which was not recognized or supported in the 1940s. Incapable of reading or writing, he felt even more inadequate; only a life at the very bottom of the labour market awaited him.

It seems clear that this child's future looks bleak...

...but what if he discovers an unexpected but acute talent?

What if he teams-up with an astonishingly colourful range of collaborators and cohorts?

What if he experiences the blood and sweat of competitive combat sports?

What if he ends up travelling around the world and to the pinnacle of British professional wrestling?

What if he emulates his mentors and embarks upon a variety of fascinating entrepreneurial explorations?

How could such a child become a champion for others and involved with a major charity?

With his beginnings, it seems unlikely that any of these possibilities could be anything but idealistic dreams, but if you're interested I'll tell you an unbelievable story, one which has been much sought-after, but never before told – until now...

One of the questions asked about any autobiography is 'Why write it now?' I can admit to two principal reasons.

Firstly, a friend who contracted HIV at the same time as George recently went into full-blown AIDS and died, and it brought back all the memories of George's sad decline and death. Something particular that came to mind was that when he was alive George always wanted to write our story; he'd begun doing this but I'd always discouraged him because I didn't want the glare of publicity focussed on my life. With this other old friend going the same way as George and reminding me of his wishes, I decided that now is the time to tell my story – our story. I'm now in my seventies, and if I don't do it now and fulfil what George had always wanted, whilst at the same time giving the world a glimpse of his luminous personality, it will never be done.

Another motivator to write this book has been the words of my dear departed wife, Yvette. She never spoke much about her time driving an ambulance during the blitz of the Second World War, but what she did say about those she'd lost and the suffering and trauma she'd witnessed mirrors the experiences of modern bereaved forces' families, civilian families scarred by terrorism, and those who deal with the consequences of fighting today's wars. Had Yvette met Lyn Rigby I know she would have put her heart and soul into supporting the work of the Lee Rigby KNFoundation, and this has been one of my own motivations to help them. I am also sure that she would have given this book her blessing because its sales will also support their work.

All the foregoing makes this book important to me in honouring the memories of my own beloved departed at the same time as telling what I believe to be an interesting story for a very good cause. Doing both has given me a sense of completion and fulfilment I could never have imagined; I hope you enjoy it.

Kendo Nagasaki

and the

Man Behind the Mask

By Peter Thornley

ISBN 978-1-908345-45-5

First Published in Great Britain by
The Man Behind The Mask Ltd. 2018

The Man Behind The Mask Ltd.
Moor Court Hall
Farley Road
Oakamoor
Staffordshire
ST10 3BD

www.themanbehindthemask.org

Cover Artwork
& Manuscript Preparation by
Roz MacDonald

ISBN 978-1-908345-45-5

Typeset in Germany by
Paul Foster

Printed by Kindle Direct Publishing.

Acknowledgments

Having never thought that I'd write my autobiography, as time has passed I've come to realise that the ways in which so many people have helped me during my life should be acknowledged and recognised. No man is an island, and no life succeeds without the positive input of others, and while many of those who've helped me are mentioned in this book, like a movie, the limitations of space and time and the need to keep the first telling of my story coherent and concise has necessarily required a focus on those central to that story. In time I will be saying much more, but for now I'd like to also thank the following people for their contributions to my life:

Jonathan Smeed, for his perpetual support and for 'Anthem for Nagasaki', the soundtrack to the culmination of Kendo's career, and beyond;

Rob Cope, for founding 'The Keepers of the Salt', a clan of Kendo's most ardent supporters;

Sylvia Morrison, for her wisdom and insight, and being a very good friend;

Nicola Brooks, for her warmth and support far beyond her legal expertise;

Chris Buckwell, for his friendship and introducing us to tireless typesetter Paul Foster;

Melanie Faldo, for her remarkable media mind and top-notch PR skills;

Chris Gould, for his creativity and flying Kendo's flag in the far east, in fluent Japanese;

James Lumsden-Cook, for his support and advice on turning my story into this book.

For George.

Contents

Foreword

When I began the Lee Rigby Foundation, I was delighted to have a lot of help from a small group of people who immediately lent their support, and everything looked very promising. I wanted to help the families who had found themselves in the same position as mine – those who had lost a loved one but found that they got no support. I was very pleased when my vision began taking shape – the aim was to give bereaved families somewhere peaceful they could go to, away from all the questions and reminders of their loss that they would find at home. In such a place, they could come to terms with their loss as a family, hopefully get a good night's sleep, and begin to find balance in their lives again.

As I began to spread the word about what we wanted to do, I was astonished at how many bereaved mothers and families got in touch with me and said they would really welcome having the chance to have such a get-away, and this motivated me even more to make the Foundation a success.

As things were developing I heard more and more about how forces' Veterans found themselves without the support they needed, not just in adapting to life in 'civvie street' once their service ended, but also those who'd had difficult experiences in combat and may still be coming to terms with them. I heard that many Veterans went through the services provided by the military and organisations like Combat Stress, but they still hadn't found peace. One of them said he really just needed somewhere peaceful where he could get a good night's sleep, which he was sure would help him to heal.

These aims became the basis of the 'Objects' for the Lee Rigby Foundation's Charitable status, and I was delighted to have a clear path ahead.

However, it wasn't long before complications began to arise. As a new support organisation which didn't yet have Charitable status, we had no income and couldn't pay anyone – everyone was a volunteer and had day jobs. One of the people I'd relied upon from the beginning began having difficulties at his work that took up all of his time. Then another found that his work was taking him overseas more and more, and suddenly our ability to make contacts and get more support was really diminished.

Just at the time all this was happening, we were put in touch with Kendo Nagasaki. He already had a charity which supported people through meditation, and they invited our family to go to his retreat for a day out. With things looking ever more challenging for us I welcomed the chance for us to get away from it all, even for just a day.

Before we went I was told that I wouldn't meet Kendo himself, who never spoke, and the man behind his mask was very reclusive so I wouldn't meet him either, but as soon as we walked in to the mansion at Moor Court, a tall, warm, and friendly man with a dustpan and brush in his hand began showing us around and telling us about what the Nagasaki Foundation did. In a glass showcase of Kendo's outfits and swords I saw a picture of a Japanese man who I assumed was the man behind the mask. It was all most interesting and very welcoming but I had no idea who this friendly and well-informed man was...

It wasn't until I got chatting with another member of the Foundation called Yvonne that she told me who he was – it was Peter, the real man behind Kendo Nagasaki! The Japanese man I'd seen in the picture had been Kenshiro Abbe, Peter's judo master. I was astonished! He'd been so chatty, friendly, and amusing – I couldn't believe he was also the legendary wrestler who no-one had met without his mask on. Peter and all of them helped us all to really relax – it was a lovely day out.

Very soon after our visit to the Nagasaki Foundation they got in touch again and said they would help us out in any way they could. When I'd been at Moor Court I'd seen a big former dormitory building nestled among trees and lawns, and it struck me as being exactly the kind of place I'd like for the people I wanted to support to be able to go to – I knew I'd seen exactly what I wanted for Lee's legacy. It was a really moving moment and I cried at having found exactly what I'd been looking for.

When they got back in touch, to my delight, Peter suggested that it may be possible to make the building I'd seen available to the Lee Rigby Foundation. Initially, I'd thought we'd have to raise money and buy a suitable place or buy land and build what we needed, but here I was being offered a building in a lovely setting. It was an overwhelmingly generous gesture, and we began discussing how we could make it work.

Because we'd found ourselves short of man-power, in order to get things moving again Peter offered the full-time support of two of the Nagasaki staff, Yvonne and Roz, and they began helping us with fund-raising events, a new website, social media, email, and even office space at Moor Court. They even came up to our home in Middleton every week to discuss things and keep everything moving forward, and things began to move faster and faster, particularly fund-raising. Kendo celebrated the fiftieth anniversary of an important wrestling match by holding a wrestling tournament at the same venue as the original match, using the event and making a DVD of it to raise funds for the LRF, and he made a personal appearance at a big fund-raiser and promotional event for the LRF, a dinner at Manchester United football stadium, the first big fund-raiser organised by the new team.

While Peter had given us the commitment to use the big dormitory building, it soon became clear that it would be a very expensive project, which meant it would take a long time to raise the money and do the required work on the building, which in turn meant it would be a long time before we could begin offering getaways to the families and Veterans we wanted to support. However, by mid-2016 Peter was most of the way through refurbishing a large four-bedroom house that was just in front of the big building, and in another amazing gesture of generosity, he said that he would make it available to us so we could provide getaways to families and Veterans much sooner. I was grateful beyond words as the Lee Rigby House project was born.

As things were gathering momentum it became clear that I needed to be part of the work in the office, but I couldn't see how we could move from Middleton. I suppose I shouldn't have been surprised when a few months later another house on the Moor Court estate became available, and Peter said we could move in. It was ideal for us all to go to live on the site where the Lee Rigby House and eventually the Lodge would be, and we did, after we'd found a new school for my youngest daughter Amy and Ian could move his job. Coming to live at Moor Court we've had the experience that those we want to support will have – peaceful and surrounded by nature – and it's been the best thing we could have wished for. It's done us all the world of good, and I was really touched when Amy said that for the first time since we lost Lee, 'I've got my Mum back.'

Now things are really moving forward. The Lee Rigby House is open and has lots of bookings, we're planning a special place for Veterans in a wing of the mansion, and more and more wonderful people are coming on-board to support us.

As if I haven't already said enough about Peter's astonishing generosity, he's pledged a million pounds from the sales of this book towards furthering the work of our Foundation. His life-story is a truly fascinating read with many unexpected twists and turns, not to mention the whole amazing story of Kendo Nagasaki. Not only do I highly recommend Kendo Nagasaki and the Man Behind the Mask as an excellent biography, but buying it will also really help us towards helping the bereaved families and Veterans who still need so much support – this book is a win-win for us all.

I know you'll love Peter's life story and I sincerely thank you for buying it because of how much it'll help us. After reading this book I hope you'll get the chance to meet the man behind the mask, as I have. But now, prepare yourself for a truly fascinating roller-coaster of a life story.

Lyn Rigby.

Preface

As I take a subjective view of my life I find it's a somewhat complex position to be in; if I am to tell my own story I must also tell that of the persona who's been such a powerful influence over it, the iconic Kendo Nagasaki. Much is known about him but very little about me, and that separation underpins my relationship with him – he is the public figure, whereas I am the private man.

It would be reasonable to ask, if I am the vehicle for him, how can there be any separation between us? The answer is that it's a state of mind. I genuinely feel that he is more of an inspiration than an aspect of myself, so the easiest way to describe him is in the third person; it's always Kendo in the wrestling ring, Kendo on the posters and bills, and Kendo who has the fearsome reputation, but that's not me.

Kendo's biggest problem is that he does not speak – only I can do that for him, but when I speak of his experiences, they are inevitably mine too.

When I speak of my experiences, they are only mine, and that includes how Kendo inspires me.

When I am acting as the vehicle for Kendo, I seek to forget myself and, as far as possible, express what he stands for, which includes samurai-like focus, discipline, and single-mindedness, qualities which can be applied to all walks of life as well as wrestling.

This interplay of identities is a kind of Zen Koan, and this reveals the state of mind I've mentioned. Zen is about transcending the mind and therefore not being bound by its limitations, and the first step in doing this is to suspend disbelief in radical concepts. This is what I had to do when I began meditating under Kenshiro Abbe, and continue to do as the concept of Kendo revealed itself to me – I couldn't conceive of him or express him in any other way.

So, please bear with me as I describe my experiences as my own, Kendo's experiences as mine too, and Kendo as a separate persona; his energy is what inspires me, and he's been the highly visible wrestling icon who has taken me along for the ride.

...and it's been quite a ride!

Therefore, I invite you to suspend disbelief and join me as I describe an amazing journey from rags to riches, from turmoil to tranquility, and from helplessness to empowerment – all thanks to Kendo Nagasaki.

Chapter 1

Family Ties

My beginnings were extremely challenging. Firstly, I was adopted; as is often the case, I wasn't to find out for a number of years, and as is sometimes the way, I learned of it in an inelegant and piecemeal way. As my suspicions over my origins grew, so did my frustration over knowing nothing of my different parents and mysterious background, and I began to reason that they may be responsible for some of the differences that were to arise between me and my adoptive family. They did their best with me, but their altruism in becoming adoptive parents was to be compromised by a number of serious family complications, which in turn affected my life and shaped who I was to become. Of course, this is true of all families to some extent, but I believe that in my case, a close interplay of wealth and poverty were to create a complex and challenging environment that was bound to teach me some unusual lessons. For all this I have to thank the Thornleys – let me tell you about them.

My father, William Thornley (Bill), could best be described as a genuinely nice guy – level-headed, responsible, and easy-going. He was the middle of three children in a wealthy family which was secure in the knowledge that a huge inheritance would one day make its way to them. They lived on a 300-acre farm called The

Toft at Dunston, Staffordshire, at the heart of which was an impressive mansion where my father spent his idyllic childhood. He was, of course, privately-educated, as were his siblings, but the irresponsibility of their father was to bring about dramatic reversals, which polarised the family, and its influence on me.

As regards maternal influence, this was to be patchy for me, as I'll explain, and perhaps the scarcity of such input had as much effect on me as the complexity of the paternal.

My father's father was called John James Thornley. His mother, Julia, was from the Edwards family, which believed it was in line to inherit part of the 'Edwards Millions' fortune. Legend has it that Robert Edwards, an 18th century Welsh buccaneer, was gifted 77 acres of land in North America by Queen Anne for his services in plundering Spanish galleons laden with treasure from the New World. He leased the land for 99 years, which, on expiry, should have seen it reverting to the Edwards' heirs, but unfortunately, while returning to England in 1762, it's believed that Robert died in a storm and the titles to the land sank with him. Today, now part of Lower Manhattan, the land is estimated to be worth around 650 billion dollars. Literally thousands of heirs have made claims to the fortune, but without the appropriate documentation there's never been a ruling in their favour, and most likely never will be.

John Thornley lived 'the good life' to the full. Secure in the knowledge of his inheritance he drank and gambled without restraint, and managed to get through all his family's existing resources. He took up with a 'fancy woman' and left with her to sail to New York on The Titanic. However, he didn't make it onto that fateful voyage because he turned up at the boat train roaring drunk and wasn't allowed into the port. He took a later passage to America and has never been heard from since.

He left his wife, Margaret, and their children with

considerable debts, and the fabled inheritance seemed to have disappeared; they found themselves unable to run the family farm, and to pay off the debts they had to sell the Toft and almost everything they owned.

My father was twelve when his father disappeared, his sister Ida was eight, and brother Arthur was sixteen. The family scraped enough money together to buy a smallholding, which I believe was about thirty acres, but it didn't produce enough income to feed three children. Consequently, while Ida and Arthur stayed on at the farm with their mother, Bill, in his early teens and no longer at school, was sent to Crewe to live with an uncle, Jim Gibson, who ran the local Bus Company.

Heavily industrialised Crewe was a radically different environment to rural Staffordshire where Bill had spent his childhood. The biggest employer was the railway works, where a great many of the country's trains were made. It was such a big industry that it split the town in half, and unless you worked for the railways and could go through the works, the only way to cross the town was via bridges over the works, of which there were four. It was hard manual labour in a very hot environment, and the employees would drink several pints of beer a day as they worked.

The Thornleys could no longer afford private school for Ida and Arthur, so she would have been sent to a Church school, and Arthur would have immediately had to start working on the farm. As soon as Ida reached eleven, which was then the legal leaving age, she too would have gone straight to working on the farm. For all three children, it would have been very difficult to see their expected affluent future just vanish overnight, but they were of good character and put their backs into making a success of their new circumstances.

Sadly, after a few years, tragedy struck when Arthur fell ill and died. Ida and her mother really needed Bill to return to the farm to help them run it, but he was by now fully settled-in to his new life and work in Crewe and was reluctant to give all that up. The farm was by now beginning to prosper and they could afford some hired labour so they could just about cope without Bill, but it set them back and made things difficult for them once again. Ultimately, I think they decided to battle-on and not disrupt Bill's life if they could avoid it, but they came to feel that he didn't deserve to share in whatever successes the farm might generate.

Rising magnificently to the challenge of a greatly increased work-load, Ida threw herself into things and developed a steely ambition. Perhaps some of her drive was fuelled by resentment towards her father – she later described him as '...a wastrel and a womaniser.' It seemed that, through sheer effort of will, she sought to recover everything that he had lost, and she and her mother built up a very good farm produce business which supplied market stalls in various nearby towns, including Wolverhampton, Stafford, and Rugeley. She was later to branch out and started running a number of cafés – she became quite the entrepreneur.

Through the farm, Ida eventually met the man she would marry, Norman Matthews, whose family lived at Eton Lodge in Rugeley, and which ran a business along the same lines as her farm, but bigger.

Having stayed in Crewe, Bill's life had been very different to Ida's. Growing-up working for the bus company he'd been part of an organisation, with a structured life which ran according to a schedule, and this suited him well. Consequently, he and Ida became as different as chalk and cheese – Ida was all about business, making money, and getting on, whereas he was happy just being a cog in a machine.

Because he lacked her ambition, Ida grew to respect Bill less and less, although he was probably much happier than her. Typical of most ambitious people, she never seemed to feel as if she had enough, and was always looking to be succeeding in new ways. Ida and my father, though very different, were both to be very important in forming who I was to become.

In Crewe, Bill met the woman who would become my mother, Betty Molton. She was from a large working-class family, and her father, George, worked in the foundry at the railway works. When Bill told his family about Betty, they didn't approve – the formerly-rich Thornleys felt that he was marrying beneath himself, so much so that they didn't even go to his wedding.

Ida never had anything good to say about the Moltons – she referred to them as 'spongers'. She told me a story about Bill having had a motorbike, and one of the Moltons bought it from him for an unrealistically low price. It was something that stuck in her mind – that they'd swindled him.

Even though he wasn't ambitious, Bill had had a decent education and could read and write to a high standard. This stood him in good stead when he took an interest in the bus company's social club and became its secretary – it became his main interest outside work. He bought The Daily Mail every day which he would read religiously from cover to cover.

After they got married, Bill moved in with Betty, who was still living with her parents and her younger brothers and sisters. After a while Betty found that she couldn't have children which upset her greatly, so one of her nieces, Marge, came to live with her, and she brought her up as her own.

Then, Grandma Molton became very ill with rheumatoid arthritis and Betty had to look after her. At around the same time, Bill's mother had wanted to set him up in his own small garage, but this would have meant him, Betty, and Marge moving out and going to live in the residential part of the garage premises. Betty wouldn't go because she was committed to looking after her mother, and even though Bill would very much have liked to have gone into the garage, he stayed to support her. For both of them, family was the priority.

Eventually Betty's younger brothers and sisters moved out and her mother passed away, and they then got the option of moving into a new council house at 2, Bowen Cooke Avenue, Crewe. When they moved in, what was left of the old household moved with them, which included Marge and Granddad Molton.

The house was typical of homes built in the early thirties. Upstairs it had three bedrooms, one of which would best be described as a box room, and a bathroom that had no lavatory. The downstairs had two main rooms, one at the front and one at the back, and a back kitchen with a gas stove in one corner and a brick-built 'boiler' in the other, where a fire was lit under a covered cauldron to boil-wash laundry. Outside the back door and across the yard was the standard coal-hole and 'privvy' lavatory. The back room had a coal-burning range which had two hot-plates and a couple of small ovens.

There would have been my father and mother in the front bedroom, Granddad Molton in the back bedroom, and Marge in the box room.

Once Marge was in her mid-teens, Betty felt that she wanted the complete parenting experience, and she decided to adopt. Bill would have done anything for his wife, but by now he was 41 years old, and I think he'd have preferred a bit more peace and quiet than launching himself into parenthood of a new infant! However, to make Betty happy, he agreed to go ahead with the adoption.

The Second World War broke out but Bill wasn't conscripted because he was already nearly forty, and as an experienced bus driver he was needed to drive ambulances, a valued home-front job. This fortunately meant that home-life at Bowen Cooke Avenue was able to continue as it had before.

Bill and Betty made enquiries and found the right

people, which eventually led them to me. I was born on 19th October 1941, and just a few months later, my mother and Marge collected me from a home for poor or unmarried mothers (which I later affectionately thought of as *The Little Sisters of the Poor*!). My mother was devoted to me, and Marge helped her with me and running the house. I think it's fair to say that Bill's laid-back approach extended to parenthood as well; as a child, I didn't see very much of him – he was either at work or at the social club – and this remained the case even in my later life.

My earliest memory was an alarming one. I'd have been less than three years old and I woke up on the settee and found I was alone. Where was my mother? I instantly went into a state of total panic and ran screaming into the street, crying out for her. She'd gone over the road to see a neighbour and friend, Mrs. Evans, who rushed out and scooped me up, and making soothing noises, handed me back to my mother. I'll never forget the feeling of terror at finding myself abandoned; of course, I hadn't been, my mother had just been having five minutes to herself, but that memory is as vivid today as it's ever been.

I have other memories of my early childhood, but I suspect I've put them together from what I was told later. Having been born in 1941 I was, of course, a 'War Baby', and Marge and her husband Eric told me that on a few occasions when German bombers attacked Rolls Royce and the railway works I was taken into the Anderson shelter in the garden. The shelter remained there after the war and I was prevented from playing in it, but while I can imagine myself being taken into the shelter as an infant, I couldn't swear that these images are actual memories. Apart from this, I can't recall any other way in which the war impacted my life.

When Marge married Eric he moved into the house, after which they had the downstairs front room. They stayed until they got their own house, which happened when I was about four, and they moved out to Acton, near Nantwich, so there was then a little more space at home.

When I was about five, out of the blue, Ida visited us, and she brought her and Bill's mother, Grandma Margaret Thornley. In retrospect, I think Grandma knew she was unwell and didn't have much time left, and she'd insisted on being taken to see Bill – Ida would otherwise never have come to our house. Unfortunately, soon after arriving, Grandma was taken seriously ill; a doctor was called, and it seemed that his advice was that she should just be made comfortable and not be moved. A bed was brought into the front room and Grandma was put into it, and, having nursed her own sick mother, my mother capably looked after her.

Grandma really appreciated the care she got from Betty, so much so that she apparently said she'd misjudged the Molton family, and when she got back to Gnosall, she was going to '...put things right.' By this my father thought she'd meant that she'd be more generous to him and his family in her will, but sadly, Grandma passed away about a month after her collapse, so her will, leaving everything to Ida, was never changed. I think my father felt he'd have been in line for at least something, but despite his wife's care for his mother, he and his family ended up being marginalised by his sister.

Ida had more or less assumed control of the farm as her mother's health had declined, so she could only visit briefly because she had to get back to keep it running. My father told me that Ida had been there on the day their mother had died, and immediately afterwards she'd rushed off home to make sure her interests were served first, including taking possession of a bag of sovereigns that their mother had been collecting; she must have taken it because it was never found. I'm sure Bill hadn't been looking to gain from Betty's care for Grandma – they'd just done what had been necessary.

Gradually, my mother became unwell. For a while, her

younger sister, Frances, helped us out and some of the other Moltons visited more often, but it became clear that my mother's health was in decline.

Tragically, when I was seven, she died from kidney failure. My memories of it are vague, but I do recall missing her dreadfully. I was told that she was now in somewhere called 'Heaven', but at home there had never been any talk of such things so I didn't understand what that meant – no-one comforted me and helped me through my loss, as my mother would have wanted – it was an unfair and painful vicious cycle. I clung onto the thought that she would be coming back, but the waiting was unbearable. So was the loneliness; my mother had doted on me, but my father hadn't really engaged with me as a parent, even with her there – now, bereaved, he was even more remote, and I think he was angry and frustrated at himself for being so helpless. All this meant that he kept me even more at arm's length, probably because he feared he might be failing me, but simply didn't know how to do things any better.

There were now just three of us living in the house, my grandfather, my father and myself. My father was at work during the night and in bed for part of the day, and Granddad mostly sat by the range, so I was usually left alone with my grief and confusion. I quickly came to feel that I wasn't wanted. No-one treated me with the kind of affection that my mother had – she'd always forgiven my misbehaviour, but it seemed that everyone except my father held it against me. He never reprimanded me, but no other adults spoke to me except to scold me, and they all seemed to regard me as nothing more than a nuisance. This was worse than mere loneliness – it was an emotional wasteland.

My mother would have been deeply saddened at the environment I'd ended up in – it was such a stark contrast to her loving and nurturing hopes for me. After her passing, her sister and other family members stopped coming to the house, so there was no nurturing female influence nor anyone who would help look after the house and make it more like a proper home. I believe they occasionally saw Bill, but only at his club.

I ended up sleeping in the back bedroom, sharing the old-fashioned metal-framed bed with Granddad, and my father slept alone. By this time he was 48 – middle-aged – and no doubt longing for a peaceful life, but I was turning out to be a real handful and he had no idea what to do with me.

However, he decided to fall back upon a commitment that my Aunt Ida had made. When my mother died, Ida came to the funeral. She later told me that afterwards, the other Molton women had begun talking about how none of them would accept Bill 'palming me off' onto any of them – my reputation for being troublesome had spread far and wide. Ida had intervened and said,

'Don't worry about him – the Thornleys will look after their own.'

There were no immediate changes, but little did I realise that the time was fast approaching when I would be packed-off to her house in Blackpool for the school holidays. It was to be, as they say today, a 'boot camp' experience.

When I was nine years old, a further complication arose regarding my family, specifically, my place in it. I went to school with David, the grandson of one of my Molton aunts, who was a couple of years younger than me. One day at school he told me that my father wasn't my father. Not only was this very confusing, but it cast doubt on who I thought I was and where I thought I belonged. I also didn't understand why he'd say such a thing to me – perhaps he was using a nugget of information he'd heard at home as a jibe at me, knowing I wouldn't hit him because he was family. He didn't push his luck, though, and clammed-up when I took an interest in what he'd said, but I didn't pursue it with him.

I had previously been told that I was nothing like the father I'd always known – was this indeed because he wasn't my real father? If so, was I like my real father, whoever he was? The whole idea opened a chasm of uncertainty in me...

Not having a mother-figure since my own mother had passed away had already created a gulf between me and other children, but now I felt even more of an outsider and unable to relate to them. I wasn't about to make myself appear vulnerable by trying to find any other child in the same situation – I'd just have to tough it out.

Chapter 2

A Loose Cannon

A 'loose cannon' is '...an unpredictable person or thing that could cause damage if not kept in check.' The phrase dates from the 17th century, when wooden warships were armed with cannon. They had to be on wheels because of the recoil when they fired, and they were kept in check by ropes, but if these were ever loose, a half-ton object rolling freely around the deck could be lethal – they had to be either controlled, or avoided. This was how I came to be regarded, but controlling me was not easy...

The first time I remember asserting myself was at the infant school, when I was about six years old.

The teacher had us all making a train out of boxes – a typical early-learning activity, which encouraged children to work together. When we'd finished it, there was a position where someone could get in and sit, and one of the other boys jumped in before I did. I'd wanted to be the 'driver', but suddenly, it had been taken from me. The solution seemed obvious to me – to get him out of my way, I'd make the other boy unable to continue what he was doing. I grabbed something that was left over from the construction of the train and hit him round the back of the head with it. It never crossed my mind to tell him that I wanted a turn at being the train driver, nor to wait until the teacher gave the other children their chance – I wanted what I wanted, and no-one should get in my way.

As you can imagine, my actions caused quite a fuss. I was pulled away and he was taken out, crying. The school sent for my mother, and I was sent home for causing an unnecessary disturbance. This marked the start of a pattern to my behaviour – I was domineering.

When my mother passed away about a year later, nothing made sense to me any more, so I saw no reason to conform to what others expected of me. I became much more disruptive generally as well as in school, and I became more of a loner. I was turning inwards because I found no answers in the world around me to my own inner turmoil.

When my dad was at work, with no mother to look after me at home, Granddad would take me to his working men's club, where he played billiards. He didn't go to my father's club (the Crosville), he went to a nearer one, the West End Social Club, which had two main rooms – a large social area where children were allowed, and another room with two full-size billiard tables. Because I wasn't accompanied by any other family, I couldn't be left in the social side, so I was allowed to sit in with the billiard players.

However, a seven-year-old can only watch the same thing for so long, and eventually boredom got the better of me – I scuttled all the balls across the table in the middle of a match, which infuriated everybody. It was just mischief, but it resulted in me being barred from the club. Granddad was told that he couldn't bring me into the billiard room again, but that's where he wanted to be, so he couldn't take me; this left me with more time to create more mischief!

I was to find that I had a natural flair for getting into trouble, and annoying a great many people. Perhaps I was just impulsive and more than a little 'devil-may-care', because if I saw something that seemed like a good idea, I just did it. My father had never disciplined me, and, probably because of this, I mostly pleased myself without caring about the consequences.

Between the ages of eight and fourteen, I always seemed to be in trouble.

There were a couple of lads that I hung around with, and we would play silly tricks on people. One of our favourites was knocking on people's doors and running off. We'd wait at a safe distance and watch them try to work out what was going on, which greatly amused us. When they went back in, we did it again – it was immature nonsense, but that was what we liked, and we'd do anything that would torment someone else.

My grandfather was pushing seventy, so he was retired. Maybe he was a bit grumpy by that age, but everything I did seemed to annoy him. A typical example involved the greenhouse – I managed to get myself on top of it, which caused him to erupt. He came charging down the garden – as much as a seventy-year old man could charge – wielding a cane, and he tried to bash me with it. Of course, he wasn't anywhere near agile enough to catch me, and I was down from the roof, over the fence, and gone before he'd even realised.

The house was semi-detached and had an outside lavatory and coalhouse. The neighbouring house had a similar arrangement in a mirror image, and they shared a pitched tiled roof. I managed to get up there one day and was sitting on the top, more on the neighbour's side than ours.

The man who lived next door, Mr. Billington, wasn't having me clown around on his roof, so he came out and tried to remove me – he started prodding at me with a washing-line prop. I wasn't having that, so I grabbed the prop and hit him with it. He went to get a pair of steps to try and reach me, but that was a waste of time, because by the time he'd got them, I was nowhere in sight. I'd only left the roof because I wanted to, not because I was worried about him trying to force me off. He complained to my father, but, as was usually the case, it never led anywhere.

There was a woman who lived over the road from us who used to keep chickens in a coup – perhaps half a dozen of them. She ended up round at our house, complaining to my father that I'd forced my way into the coup and murdered her chickens. I don't think I did – if I'd managed to get in there at all they'd probably have died of fright. I can remember her complaining loudly, but I really don't remember actually getting into the chicken coup.

A man called Hatton who lived just around the corner had two taxis, very big old Wolseleys with huge round lights on the front and big mudguards, which he also used as weddings cars. At the back of his house he'd opened up the garden and built a garage so he could park the cars there.

Somehow or other, I ended up on top of one of these cars and was running from the bonnet up on to the roof and back again. Old man Hatton stormed out and was ready to hit me – as anyone would be. I slid down the car and took off along the alley between our street and his, and disappeared into the distance.

About three years after my Mother died, my father came to an arrangement with a woman he knew called Foster, so that she could have the front room of our house in exchange for cleaning and looking after it. I'm not sure if she'd lost her husband or they'd divorced, but I do know she'd had to leave the house she was living in, and that prior to losing her husband, their circumstances had been better than ours. She had a son who was about two years older than me, and she used to put him and me in the bath together to wash the pair of us, probably to save water. I didn't like him, mainly because – once again – I felt he had things that I didn't, including the undivided attention of a mother.

One day I was coming down the stairs and he was in front of me. I was in a hurry, as usual, but he was dawdling and holding me up, so I decided to give him a bloody good shove to get him out of my way. He went flying down the stairs and landed at the bottom, crying and making a scene. She appeared and he told her what had happened, and she was horrified. Soon after, they left; I'm sure she thought that I'd end up really hurting her son.

My father once took me to visit Marge in her new house. It was part of a new housing development, and nearby they were still building. As was usual before the days of Health and Safety, access to the site was barely controlled, so it was inevitable that when I went out to play, I'd end up in there. Unfortunately, with me was Marge's son, Michael, who was a couple of years younger than me.

In the middle of the site there was something that looked fascinating – it appeared to be a room-sized pit in the ground that was full of snow. I decided to investigate, and Michael joined me. We walked onto the edge, which was a hard crust, but a couple of steps towards the centre, it gave way, and we sank up to our thighs. A man on the site saw us and began yelling and scrambling to get us out. It turns out that it was a pit of lime which was used for sand-and-lime mortar, and it was extremely corrosive.

Michael and I were hauled out of the lime, but it stuck to us like mud; we were both dragged to Marge's house to have it washed off as quickly as possible – they actually got the garden hose on us. If we'd got it in our eyes, we'd have been blinded, and if we'd have fallen in, it would have killed us. Such dangers were beyond my understanding, but I was intrigued at how this particular 'good idea' caused such alarm and upset among the adults; they seemed particularly horrified that I'd managed to persuade a younger family member to risk his life!

Another incident that had my name written all over it happened one Christmas. There was a lad who lived further up the street, and he was out riding a brand new bike. I didn't really like him – he was what I'd describe as a 'mard-arse' – a mummy's boy. I suppose he was another whom I despised because he had a life that I envied – two parents and a new bike. My bike was old and well past its prime – it didn't look anything like his, so I, in my infinite wisdom, thought it would be a good idea to make a swap. I knew I couldn't have the two parents, but I could have the bloody bike.

I timed it perfectly so that I unloaded him from his bike and left him with mine, whilst I took off. I don't remember taking it back – that would be far too civilized. Knowing what I was like then, I would have ridden it as far as I wanted to, before dumping it.

It caused a huge fuss. Once again, my father took an ear-bashing, but I never did. Despite me getting into hot water with all these incidents, he never said anything to me – I was never told-off for my behaviour. From what I remember, he used to shrug his shoulders, as if he either didn't believe them or he didn't care what I'd done.

I always felt that he was on my side, though; I remember one angry man complaining to my father about something I'd done, saying that if he wouldn't thrash me, then he'd do it himself. Bill just calmly asked him how he'd got into our garden; looking bewildered, he answered, 'Through the gate...' Bill simply said to him, 'That's your way out, too.' After the man had gone, my father said nothing to me and calmly went back to reading his newspaper.

Come to think of it, I don't think Granddad ever got involved with disciplining me either. What I did to other people didn't concern him, but when it was him I was tormenting that was a different story. However, he did have a surprisingly cruel weapon he'd use to get his own back – when I was being particularly disruptive he'd say,

'You've killed your mother with your behaviour, and you'll end up doing the same to us.'

I sort-of understood that he was probably just hitting back in the heat of anger, but at the time I didn't let his words hurt me because I'd shut all my feelings away – it was only as I got older that I realised how much I'd been affected by my mother's death.

As time passed I seemed to become ever more like the person that Granddad described, but was my behaviour more than just naughtiness? I was later to learn self-control, but I've always been spontaneous and very driven (I still am), and it's been the comments of less-energetic people around me as an adult that have hinted at a possible basis for my childhood problems: attention deficit hyperactivity disorder, or ADHD.

As regards my attention-span I don't think I've ever changed – these days meditation helps me calm down and focus, but without it I'd be overwhelmed by the multitude of things in my head which I wish I could attend to all at once, and there's always a temptation to be immediately drawn to something else that grabs my attention. Then, as now, this does sound like an attention deficit. My explosive energy as a child could easily be described as hyperactivity, and both these qualities running unrestrained in me meant that my behaviour was definitely disordered. However, in the days before such clinical understanding, there really was only one word for me: trouble!

All this time, in the absence of a woman's touch, the house was degenerating into mere function, with no concern for niceties. An image that comes to mind is of a set of curtains – the hems had begun to unravel, but they were never going to be taken down and repaired; come to that, for years, they were never washed. What laundry was done was sent out, but only when nothing else was wearable; we developed a high tolerance for grime on our clothes, so that meant rarely. We did continue to eat at regular meal-times, but cooking had also become rationalised to the most efficient and least inconvenient ways possible, which was, of course, Granddad's 'lobby'.

He used to sit in front of the range, where there was always a big pot on top. It had two handles and resembled a small cauldron – that was the lobby pot. I'm sure I never saw that thing off the range – it was like they were one; you could hear it when you walked through the door, plop-plopping away.

You'd come in, he'd grab a big spoon (not a ladle), slap a dollop on a plate and say, 'Get it down you.' Although it was basic, it was probably very good for you; he just used to chuck things in and keep it on the boil all day. I saw lots of different vegetables and bits of meat go into it – it could easily contain three different kinds of meat, including bits of bacon. I reasoned that he must have taken the cauldron off from time to time to clean it, but I don't recall actually seeing that. But I'm a kid – I don't really care how things work, as long as there's something on my plate when I come in.

Granddad smoked 'twist', which was tobacco, and sometimes he chewed it too. It was in sticks, rather like liquorice. He had this old pipe, and to this day I can still see him poking the twist into his pipe – it had a truly vile stink to it. Sometimes he'd bite some off and give it a good chew. By his chair, he had an old enamel bucket with the edge all chipped and cracked, and he'd spit into it. One little concern used to haunt me – did he ever absent-mindedly spit into the lobby-pot, instead of the bucket? I never tasted anything that smelled like 'twist', and I always wolfed-down my lobby, but I didn't trust the old bugger...

I've since reflected that if I'd lived on a housing estate in a big city, I would probably have done well; my behaviour would have been a perfect fit with the kind of gang culture that flourishes in such places, and I'm certain that I would have been in charge, but fortunately for me, that kind of environment didn't exist in Crewe.

I was never involved in any actual criminality, so I never found myself at the mercy of the justice system, and I suppose I was lucky in that respect. My Granddad always reckoned I would inevitably end up in trouble with the law. One thing that he repeatedly said to me was that I '...would swing' – I believe he meant that I was destined to be hanged – according to him, I was genuinely bad enough.

However, there was one area in which my behaviour was responsible and even productive! Both my father and Granddad were keen gardeners, cultivating various plants and flowers and as many vegetables as they could, both in our home garden and at allotments. They'd begun this during the Second World War – as my father was an auxiliary ambulance driver he was exempt from being called-up and was able to grow vegetables, and they continued doing so after the war ended. Of course, this made ingredients for our 'lobby' plentiful and freely-available, but my father also used to load up a cart with flowers and veg to sell outside the railway works in Crewe.

He'd have available whatever was current in the garden at the time – radishes in bunches of about five, Sweet William, lettuce, beetroot, new potatoes, tomatoes from the greenhouse, and more; we had a vine at one time, which meant we could sell grapes, but it died. He went on Fridays, which was payday – the stall would be sold-out in no time as the workers poured out through the gates at 5:30. He'd also sell from home, on a smaller scale – because people knew he grew veg, they'd call at the house to buy what they needed, even if it was just two tomatoes.

Before I was into my teens he would take me along to help with the cart, for which I'd receive the princely sum of two shillings each week; to me it was generous, as I could go swimming and get a bag of scratchings afterwards for sixpence, so I could go four times a week; consequently, I learned early about commerce and its rewards.

Out of the blue, when I'd just turned fifteen, my father remarried, a woman called Doris. I was delighted that this was going to happen, because I wanted a normal family, but after it happened, I behaved extremely badly towards my new step-mother; I really was awful.

Her situation was very similar to the one Mrs. Foster had been in, because she had two children, Gordon and Dorothy, who both attended grammar school. They were responsible children – nothing like me, the scoundrel! Doris coming into our lives greatly improved our home life, because we moved into her house, which was just over the garden fence. Compared to ours, it was nice and clean and fully-furnished – she had flat-out refused to come and live in our dilapidated shambles. Finally, for the first time in my life, I had my own bedroom – when we moved, Granddad went to live with one of his other daughters, Fanny.

Sadly, Doris was later to remark that if she'd known what she was taking on with me, she would never have married my father. Years later she talked about some of my early misbehaviours, and she told me about her relatives who used to come and visit – they'd remark on how dreadful it was how I tormented the old man (Granddad) so much, and it was a wonder he didn't end up having a heart attack.

Even when I wasn't creating havoc, people never knew what they were going to get with me. I remember a girl from school once telling me that she and other girls thought I was OK, but they were afraid to talk to me because they never knew whether they'd get a nice smile, or 'What are you looking at?!?' I was often grumpy, and always unpredictable.

Ultimately, I think the cruellest thing I ever did was with the lad with the bike, unless you count 'killing chickens', but I swear to this day that I didn't kill a single one, and I suppose old man Hatton's blood pressure almost boiled over as he tried to polish shoe-scuffs out of his immaculate cars' paintwork. Years later when I paid a visit to Marge, she said, 'You used to get the blame for everything – but then, you probably did it!'

So, I was impulsive and extremely headstrong, and I was never disciplined. After my mother died, I saw no reason to please anyone except myself, and I would challenge anyone who tried to do anything with me.

However, all the foregoing applied only to my life in Crewe – from the age of nine, desperate for some respite from the hurricane that constantly surrounded me, my father would pack me off to stay with my Aunt Ida, where things were very different...

Chapter 3

Ida and Norman

They say that everyone has a guardian angel in their lives, someone to watch over them, guide them away from wrong and towards right, help them to make the wisest decisions for themselves, and oversee their well-being. I'd like to think that my Aunt Ida was mine; I owe her so much, but my early impressions were not so favourable.

As I've already said, I'd have been about five the first time I encountered my formidable Aunt. She'd have been very well-to-do – wealthy by our standards, comfortable by her own, and she would have been frustrated at how my easy-going father was comfortable amidst his own modest circumstances. It would never have crossed her mind that my father was happy with his lot – he didn't want or need the trappings of success, he just wanted to live peacefully within his means; Ida seemed to regard luxuries as just rewards for her previous (and continuing) hard work. She undoubtedly loved her brother, but was irritated that he didn't share her fierce ambition and exacting standards.

Ida had a car, and not just any car, like a Ford – she had a Rover, one of those with big headlights and swooping, flared-out mudguards. It was rare to see any kind of vehicle in our street – nobody else owned one, and Rover-driving people were never seen in our neighbourhood. Seeing the majestic carriage swoop up outside our house really made an impression on me – this was clearly a woman of substance.

Being the young ruffian I was, it should be no surprise that I immediately climbed up the car's elegantly-sloping front mudguard, but I was quickly yanked off by my very superior Aunt. There was something about her authority that brought me up short – she was the strongest character I'd ever encountered, and, for the first time in my life, I found myself pausing before reacting as I would normally have done.

I saw my Aunt again within a year of my mother passing away, when my father took me to see her in her new house in Wolverhampton. Apparently, shortly after my grandmother had died, she'd got married to Uncle Norman, and then his mother had also passed away. He and his sister inherited Eaton Lodge, their family's larger market garden, and my Aunt sold her smallholding to buy out the sister, and then the market garden was sold-off. Consequently, they'd consolidated all their assets and were now very comfortably set up – it was typical of my Aunt to have had a shrewd business angle to her marriage...

They bought a nice house in a quiet crescent in Wolverhampton, as well as a generous allotment with a large greenhouse where my Uncle could continue growing vegetables and selling them to farmers' markets. He had staff there, so although it wasn't on the same scale as their previous set-up, it was a significant business.

Their house was immaculate, but the thing that really grabbed my attention when I walked in was the television – wow! I'd seen them in a couple of shop windows, but in 1950, very few people had their own at home. My Aunt didn't let me sit on her beautiful upholstered furniture because I was too fidgety, but I was allowed to sit on the floor in front of the television and watch Muffin the Mule

– it was a magical experience.

As I watched, my father and Aunt talked in the background. I vaguely remember them discussing my poor performance at school; I heard some mention of a friend of my Aunt's who was a teacher and who might be able to give me some private tuition, but it never came to anything, probably because of the distance and my father's laid-back attitude – it was all too much trouble.

After an afternoon there, we returned to Crewe. I had a lot to reflect upon; as soon as I'd seen my Aunt again, I'd had the same unfamiliar sensation of being awed by her presence – what was it about her? She was, as they say, 'big boned', always dressed in conservative hues, and she looked every inch ruddy farm stock; if I'd known the word 'imposing' then, that's how I'd have described her – she had a look that could stop traffic.

The other thing I was mulling-over was her house – it wasn't just that she had that outright luxury, a television, but the house was like nothing I'd ever seen. It was completely organised and ordered of course, but it was elegant, tasteful, artistic; these were concepts beyond my understanding, but I'd just experienced how the other half lived, and I was impressed. My home in Crewe was basic but nothing more, not even clean, and my eyes had just been opened to the contrast in life-styles.

On the advice of her doctors, my Aunt later bought a house in Blackpool as well. She suffered from Angina, and had been assured that the sea air would be good for her, so she and Uncle Norman took regular trips there.

I was nine when my father first put me on a bus to stay with her in Blackpool. It was a Crosville bus, the company he worked for, and this one did a regular route to Blackpool in the summer – probably every weekend. I remember the driver's name was Thornton – it was so close to our family name. He kept an eye on me all the way to the bus station where my Aunt was waiting. She took me back to her home, and that's where I stayed for what seemed like a very long time, but it was probably no more than two months.

My Aunt's regime wasn't an experience I cared to repeat. I certainly didn't want to go again, but my father had found two glorious things – someone who could actually control me, and while that was happening, he was freed from dealing with me. He must have loved his sister in a whole new way for liberating him! I'm sure there was also a part of him which was relieved for another reason – on Ida's anvil, I might actually be forged into something worthwhile.

In Blackpool, I found another home as exquisite as the one I'd seen in Wolverhampton, and more. Mrs. Ida Matthews' manner radiated propriety and authority – people automatically respected her. Nobody would ever call her by her first name, other than my Uncle Norman and my father – not only would she not have allowed it, but nobody would have been brave enough to attempt such dangerous familiarity. To neighbours, even those she was on very good terms with, and even her close friends, she was Mrs. Matthews – never, not ever, Ida. I had to call her Aunt Ida.

She controlled her environment completely and utterly, with an iron will and a rock-solid presence. She was very intimidating, yet also reassuring to be around – the world wouldn't dare come to an end anywhere near Ida Matthews – in fact, in her presence, it would probably stand up straight and smarten itself up.

My Aunt felt that men were naturally troublesome, so they needed to be supervised carefully, and she was absolutely against drink and any activities that involved it. Given her father's irresponsibility in general (but particularly in drink), these attitudes would not have been surprising, and she was determined that the men in her life would not go down the same path.

I needed a very firm hand, but my Aunt never had to strike me – she was so commanding that she simply didn't need to, and answering back was completely out of the question. What she said was simply the law, and I was to learn that her high standards were very far-reaching.

One example I remember very well was cleaning her silver. She announced, 'That's a job for you,' and I was tasked with collecting it all and taking it to the scullery at the back of the house to polish it all. Normally, she would be at home while I did this job, but one day she decided to go out and leave me to the task. In her absence I thought I'd be clever and save myself some work, so I cleaned only the items that I thought needed it, and I put them all back.

On her return my handiwork was inspected, and I was amazed to find that she knew I hadn't done it thoroughly. In fact, she could tell me which pieces I had cleaned and which I hadn't. A look of irritation and disappointment crossed her face. I was made to collect all the silver once more and was told, 'Now you'll clean it all again, and this time you'll do it properly.'

She stood behind me all the time; I couldn't see her, but I could certainly feel her presence. The sound of her breath behind me seemed to press down on me with a granite-like authority – I daren't do anything other than a perfect job this time. It took me about an hour, and she never moved the whole time.

That was an exercise in discipline, to show me that there's only one way to do a job – the correct way. Her attitude was that it doesn't matter how well you do something wrong, it will always be wrong. She had a saying to back up her philosophy – 'Right's right, and wrong is no man's right.' I've never forgotten that, and I've lived my life by it.

I would later find in my working life that this uncompromising standard was also built into Jennings' thinking – no short cuts, no half measures – everything had to be done right.

Another favourite saying of my Aunt's was, 'Neither a

borrower nor a lender be.' Once again, this puritanical approach probably stemmed from her father's irresponsibility, but it was a natural fit with her solid character. She'd back this up with a little story, a fable: 'I had a friend and I had some money. I lent my money to my friend, and I lost both.'

Years later, I wanted to borrow £500 from her towards the cost of converting a house in Wolverhampton into flats. She paused, looked me in the eye, and said, 'I'll lend you the money, but we'll be strangers in this. I'll have a proper agreement with you, drawn up by my solicitors. You will sign it and you will pay me interest.'

And that's exactly what happened. It was all signed and sealed and legally-binding, and I had to pay instalments at regular intervals; even though I was family, in such a matter, I still got the formal treatment.

My first impression of my Aunt had been a dramatic culture-shock to the five-year-old me, and from the age of nine she actually instilled fear in me, and yet, she gave me something I'd never previously had – something to live up to. If I could satisfy my Aunt, I was clearly doing things right, and while I didn't care what anyone else thought of me, her opinion somehow mattered deeply. Looking back, I now recognise what it was I saw in her that I couldn't put into words – she commanded it, and achieving it turned my dim-looking prospects around completely, and into success – it was respect.

Of course, I didn't realise it at the time, but the discipline and obedience that my Aunt required of me would be the making of me – in fact, at the time, they were a most oppressive burden – but there was someone around who greatly lightened my load, possibly because he shared it, and that was my Uncle Norman.

My father once said to me about my Uncle, 'He was a happy-go-lucky fellow until he married your Aunt!' He was recalling when he and Norman used to go to the races together, before he married Betty and Norman married Ida – happy and carefree days, radically changed by marriage in my Uncle's case, and my arrival in my father's!

Uncle Norman was a great guy – he'd been a fireman during the Second World War, and he had a very jolly, amenable personality.

He used to take me to the Blackpool Pleasure Beach, which I enjoyed – he reverted to his true happy-go-lucky nature away from my Aunt. She wouldn't come because she said she wasn't keen on the sea front, and this would have been because of the people who went there. This makes her sound like a snob, but she wasn't – she just didn't do well with ordinary people. She gravitated towards a more genteel way of life, which meant that Stanley Park was more to her liking than the Golden Mile. We'd all go to the Park together from time to time, and shopping in the market was a collective effort.

Uncle Norman and I bonded so well that he felt more like an older brother than an uncle. He looked out for me – I remember Ida once telling me off for something, probably not much by most people's standards, but whatever it was, I was in her bad books. Norman said, 'Ida, he's only a youngster – what do you expect?' She didn't accept that; my age meant nothing when it came to discipline. I was duly instructed, and perhaps I accepted the lesson more because I knew my Uncle understood my transgression, even if he couldn't stop the freezing blast of my Aunt's disapproval.

She was hard on him too. My Uncle had a bad stammer, which was more apparent when he was wound up; I've sometimes seen him hardly able to get a word out because my Aunt had taken him to task.

It began after a traumatic incident when he was a youngster. In the basement of Eton Lodge there was a big safe, something like a vault that you could walk into. Somehow he got locked in it, and the experience caused him to develop claustrophobia. Consequently, my Uncle would never get into a lift – if he went to a department store, he'd always take the stairs. The only lift I ever remember him getting into was the one at Blackpool Tower, and he only did that because it had windows on either side and he could see out.

My Uncle and I both got into serious trouble over what I call 'The Crockery Incident'.

Ida attended Chapel on a Sunday morning – not every Sunday, perhaps once a month – after which she would invite perhaps five or six people back for afternoon tea.

Like most elegant people of that era, Ida had a very nice tea service – cups and saucers, side plates, and a cake stand. On the stand would be a few scones and perhaps a cream cake; it was all very formal – very middle class.

When my Aunt's guests had all gone, all the crockery was taken to the scullery to be washed and dried, after which it'd be put on a large tray before being taken back to the display cabinet where it was all kept – the plates went in the lower section, and the cups and saucers went on top. There was even a place where you could put the tray – it was called the 'siding place'. My Aunt told me that the word 'sideboard' comes from the Victorian idea that you 'sided' a table on to the 'side-board', and the dishes were taken from the sideboard to the scullery by the staff. She was full of such elegant wisdom.

So, my Uncle and I had washed and dried everything and taken it all back on the tray – the cups and saucers were at the front and all the plates were at the back. I can still see it now, so vivid is the memory.

I carried the tray in and put it on the sideboard. Uncle Norman didn't notice that I hadn't put it on properly – it was half on, half off, with all the cups and saucers at the front, sticking out over empty space, balanced by the weight of all the plates at the back.

Uncle Norman picked up the pile of plates from the back of the tray, which caused it to tilt towards him, and everything went up in the air – cups, saucers and plates. There was a furious scramble to try and save all the crockery – my Uncle was doing a high-speed dance to get it all back onto the sideboard – not only to save the tea service, but his skin as well, if anything happened to any part of it.

No such luck – everything hit the floor. It's a miracle that only two cups and two saucers were broken, but this was still a catastrophe. Aghast, he looked up at me, and said, 'For God's sake, don't let your Aunt see!'

I thought, 'He must be joking – she won't miss this!'

Then, our blood ran cold at the sound of her coming down the corridor – she'd heard the clatter.

In she came. Norman was still sliding around, frantically trying to gather everything together; feeling his wife's formidable gaze upon him, slowly, he stopped, like a clockwork toy winding down. Silence fell. My Aunt glanced at the mess, then at us. A less disciplined woman might have sworn, but my Aunt sternly called us a pair of good for nothings, and said we should get out of her sight and not come back.

We ended up glumly sitting on the Pleasure Beach together, gazing out at a horizon as grey as our moods, while she cleaned things up at home. I'll never forget what my Uncle said to me – he said, 'Ee, lad, don't ever get married!' It still makes me laugh today.

My Aunt's disciplined regime was hard going for an unruly child, but it was all made much more bearable by my Uncle's friendly and positive presence. They were both very good examples to me – my Uncle because he was a strong, worthy, and optimistic person, and my Aunt, because I needed that absolutely immovable set of rules for right conduct, which I was later to live by myself.

Chapter 4

Channelling the Aggression

I've said earlier that after my mother died, I was weighed down by my feelings. Of course, as time passed, the loss was less disabling, but my life had been diminished in so many ways – nothing replaced what had been taken away with my mother. Consequently, I remained angry and resentful, particularly towards almost all other children, to whom I couldn't relate at all. I hadn't been great at that to start with, but I wasn't aware of anyone who was feeling the emptiness I was, so other children's happiness felt like a slap in the face to me. I tended to shun them and punish them if they dared invade my space – it didn't take long for most of them to give me a wide berth.

I think this is why I found it so satisfying to seek a sense of control over the things around me, which meant doing exactly as I pleased with them. The resultant disapproval was at least a form of attention, one which I could easily get and which I was completely in control of, and I became quite comfortable with that.

Needless to say, I was a nightmare at school, breaking things and getting into fights, which continued when I went to 'Big School' at eleven.

My secondary education took place at a school which was notorious for being the roughest in the area, Ludford Street Secondary Modern – its fearsome reputation came from the ruffians who attended it. The first day was, unsurprisingly, somewhat intimidating, but I saw a few familiar faces whom I'd scared at junior school, so I wasn't without status.

Initially, I wasn't a threat to the hard fifteen-year-olds, but I still got into fights quickly, sometimes with boys who were older than me. Fortunately, I didn't encounter anyone who was capable of giving me a bashing, and after a couple of years not so many tried.

Some at the school were like me – at the bottom of the academic scale. I'd sat the Eleven-Plus, and as far as I know my score was so low that it wasn't possible to calculate a grade. I remember being asked to read a passage out loud, but I couldn't recognise even a single word; the examiner asked me to find the word 'house', but I couldn't. This wasn't because my junior school teachers hadn't tried – I was, in fact, profoundly dyslexic.

These days, dyslexia is recognised and accommodated, but it certainly wasn't in the 1940s and '50s. I had no idea what was written on the blackboard, nor how to put anything coherent down on paper, and this led to a form of disapproval I was definitely not comfortable with – I was being regarded as stupid. Whenever my form master, Jack Perry, saw me dawdling anywhere, he'd say, 'Get off to your next lesson, cork-head!' Somehow, I knew I wasn't stupid, but there seemed no escape from the obvious conclusion that if I couldn't read and write, I should be ashamed of myself. This only worsened my mood and my need to gain self-esteem in other ways, so I became even more domineering in the playground.

There was a glimmer of light at the end of the tunnel, though – science wasn't a popular subject in my class as few seemed to grasp it, but I did. I was delighted when the teacher recognised this, and his qualified praise meant the world to me – he said, 'I can see it's in there, Thornley – if only you could get it out!' I remember on one occasion, I came top of the class without writing anything down! It has to be said, though, that we're talking about coming top in the lowest stream of the school.

I really did see it – these days, dyslexics are credited with a 'big picture' appreciation of things which keeps research evolving, but my school days came long before such enlightened views. To this day, I still feel the sting of the unjustified shame that I was made to feel back then, which makes it hard to talk about.

To me, school was little more than a waste of my time, so after the morning and afternoon registers were called, I often 'bunked-off', and amused myself in the mean streets of Crewe – well, they were certainly meaner with me roaming them... It was particularly easy to leave during maths, as Mr. Mostin, the ancient teacher, regularly nodded-off, and he'd wake up to find rather more empty desks in front of him.

Fortunately, school did introduce me to another way of getting attention, and this time it was positive – sports.

I found that some sports were of real interest to me. The Assembly Hall was also the location for the boys' gym class, where we were told whether we would climb the frame on the wall, play football, box, play badminton, or do circuit training. I liked boxing, which was basically just sparring. The gloves were very heavily padded, but there was no protective head-gear, and we learned the basics. There were about twenty who were interested in boxing, and I became quite good at it very quickly.

There was a boxing competition at the school every year. All the pupils came, including the girls, so I automatically aimed to be number one. Later on, I achieved that – the gym master, Mr. O'Hare, said my winning the competition was a foregone conclusion. I could hit hard and fast, and I could see where to hit and when, so I must have had a natural ability.

Swimming was also popular at my school, and in the fifties, it was encouraged as a good general exercise. The local baths weren't far away, so every week, our class was marched to the baths – a crocodile of unruly youngsters, marshalled by two teachers.

I found I was really good at swimming, and eventually won medals competing in inter-school competitions. Anyone who was sufficiently capable to represent the school could have extra practice at the pool after lessons finished. We were coached by a couple of the teachers, including O'Hare, and a woodwork and metalwork teacher who helped out with sports teaching.

I enjoyed swimming so much that from the age of eleven, I went to the pool every evening I could, after my evening meal. I'd get there by six o'clock, stay until 8:30 when they closed, and on my way home I'd get a penny bag of scratchings from Mrs. Scott's chip shop.

Thursday nights were water polo nights – the usual attendees would have to get out of the pool by 7:00 for an hour-and-a-half of polo. By the time I was fourteen, because I'd always been around the pool, I was invited to join in. I loved it – in addition to needing fast and capable swimming, it was like an under-water fight, and I was certainly good at that!

I found I could swim quite fast at freestyle. A lad called Michael was the only one of my age who could compete with me in the pool and we became sort-of friends. His father took him swimming outside of school and he'd sometimes take us to swimming galas. Michael and I would swim in relays which we regularly won, and we played junior water polo as well. I later heard that he went on to swim for the national team, but I don't think he ever won any international events.

Swimming also gave me the chance to get my own back on David, the lad who'd dropped the bombshell about my father not being my real father. Once, we were both at the pool, and, unseen by anyone except him, I casually shoved him into the deep end and sauntered away. I was pleased to get my own back, but I didn't know that he couldn't swim – spluttering wildly, he was hauled out by the staff, but he never accused me.

I started putting the shot at about thirteen after I saw a lad who lived down our street doing it. He was called John Foreman but we called him Fogey; I'd seen him at the swimming baths playing water polo, but he went to a different school so I'd not seen him putting the shot. Once I knew he did both, he became a bit of a role-model to me.

I was hanging around on the bit of greenery near my house, and Fogey was there, practising putting the shot. He was hefting an actual shot which he'd got from his school, which was the smaller weight appropriate to the junior shot put. Because I'd spoken to him at the swimming baths I felt able to talk to him about it.

I asked him what he was doing, and he showed me, and said, 'Why don't you have a go?' I tried, and I managed to put the shot some distance, but nowhere near as far as him; he pointed out that was because he was practised at it, so I decided to have a go at school.

As with several other sports, I found I had an aptitude for it and I represented the school in inter-schools tournaments for two years on the trot. In the last year that I did it, when I was fifteen, I represented the county, Cheshire.

The gym master at school was called Mr. O'Hare; he was the one teacher I had any time for, obviously because I was good at his subject, and it was nice to hear a positive response to my efforts, for a change. Sadly, my relationship with him was marred by spontaneous violence.

As I've said, the boys did Assembly and P.T. in the big hall, and it was also where those who stayed for school dinner sat at tables to eat, and the boys from the last class before dinner would put the tables out in the last ten minutes of the lesson. They were stored in the cloakroom, which was quite big, because the school had around three hundred and fifty pupils on each side, girls on one side and boys on the other. I think there were ten classrooms, each of which had at least thirty pupils.

On one particular day, the bell rang, and I went to grab my coat and make my way home for a plateful of Granddad's lobby. As I was on my way out of the cloakroom, a voice shouted, 'Thornley! Take that table in there.' It was O'Hare.

Now, I had about a mile to walk to my house, I'd got to have something to eat, and then get back to school, all within an hour, so I didn't want to be moving tables about – I had to go. I said, 'No, I've got to get off home.' I thought to myself, 'I'm not part of his class, he's got enough people here to move the tables – why is he asking me to do this?' He was insistent; he told me twice to move the table, and I refused twice.

As I was making my way out, he was a bit quicker than I'd thought he'd be, and he grabbed me by the scruff of the neck. He'd decided that if I wasn't going to help move the tables, he was going to drag me up to the headmaster's office, which was on what was known as the headmaster's line, up a set of stairs. That was where we ended up if we misbehaved and had to be reprimanded by the head teacher, whose name was Quine.

O'Hare started pulling me around the corner towards the staircase, and at first, I didn't resist. We got up the first flight of stairs to a landing which turned sharply left and then went up another flight.

By the time we were starting up the second flight, I'd got my balance and my bearings, and I decided that I'd had enough of this. I threw my entire weight of about ten or eleven stone at O'Hare, and sent him flying face first onto the landing. I landed on top of him, and punched him a couple of times on the side of his head.

Quine heard the commotion and came out of his office and yelled, 'You lads – stop fighting on my line!' He suddenly realised that one of the parties was a teacher, and the other a troublemaker. He shouted at me to get off O'Hare, which I did, and then ran off.

When I came back after lunch, I wasn't sure what to expect. Nothing happened in my first lesson and I began to think that I'd got away with it. At the change of lessons, however, two of the biggest teachers appeared at either side of me, grabbed my arms and marched me off to the headmaster's study. When we arrived, he was already inside with O'Hare and one other, so there were five of them – I was well outnumbered.

As soon as they let me go, I grabbed the phone from the desk and threatened to throw it at Quine – they were all horrified. I don't think they'd ever seen such forceful rebellion, and they didn't know how to handle it. They all jumped, but they didn't advance on me – they started making dire threats about what they were going to do with me if I didn't behave myself. Eventually, Quine spoke.

Because he was the head teacher, I had at least some respect for him. He was a bit more awe-inspiring than the ordinary staff because he was the man who stood at the front of Assembly every morning and told everybody what to do, and when – he was the boss. His voice was perfectly measured when he said, 'Thornley – put that phone down now and accept your punishment. If you don't, we'll take it from you, we'll assemble the whole school, and then we'll drag you in front of them all to be caned – the choice is yours.'

Sensibly, after a moment's consideration, I submitted. I expected to be caned – all the teachers could dish-out one stroke, but if the transgression was more serious it was referred to the head, who was the only one who could administer more. I'd had a few single cane-strokes before, but this looked a lot more serious, and I ended up getting six strokes, three across the palm of each hand – it was agony. I was told in no uncertain terms to behave myself, and was then sent back to my class. Fat chance of that – I was in too much pain and thoroughly fed up with them all by then; as soon as they let me out of Quine's office, I buggered off home.

After the punch-up with Mr. O'Hare, it was never mentioned again. I don't remember ever being suspended from gym or games – things just carried on as before. He was a young teacher, and when he tried to make me shift the tables, I suppose he was trying to assert himself – I think he was a little embarrassed that it went so badly wrong.

However, I have a suspicion that he had his revenge. One particular year at the usual time of the boxing tournament, O'Hare told me that I wasn't being entered. As the whole school attended, I had to go along, but I took no part. It seemed that he'd bided his time, and as his personal punishment, he'd taken something that I valued away from me.

One of the last swimming events Michael and I went to was a water polo match in the Potteries. On the way back we were sitting together on the bus, when we had an argument and I punched him. I can't even tell you why, but it was probably because my envy of him and his life just boiled over. He had two devoted parents, and his father was like a good friend and mentor, whereas mine, outside of work and his club, seemed to want only his own company. I hated the way that Michael's life innocently threw my meagre circumstances into such stark contrast; it wasn't his fault, but he was the messenger, damn him.

It seemed that violence was the only way I could express my intense feelings – I certainly didn't have the words, and I was so wound-up all the time. Clearly, despite my Aunt Ida's discipline and finding sport as the vehicle through which I could really express myself, there was more I needed to learn to channel my energy in more positive ways. I remember being dragged to the front of the bus, and him being marched down to the back. It feels strange thinking about it now – sadly, that was the end of our friendship.

I console myself with the thought that there would have been a parting of the ways anyway when we left school, as many friendships fizzled-out at the transition to the big wide world of work. As it happens, Michael and I did go in different directions when the time came – which it was about to...

Chapter 5

Jennings and Judo

'Should do well at manual labour.' That was my school's parting shot about my prospects. It was written in the front of the bible that was customarily presented to all leavers – I threw mine away.

However, it wasn't inaccurate; when I left school, I couldn't read or write – I could barely even write my own name. Before it was properly supported, dyslexia consigned you to the occupational scrap-heap.

For school-leavers, two main employers awaited them in Crewe, both of them with impressive reputations – the British Railways works and Rolls Royce. The Railways was the biggest industry, followed by Rolls Royce, of which everyone was very proud because they'd made the Merlin engines for Spitfires, Hurricanes, and Lancaster bombers during the Second World War. When hostilities ceased, the aero engine side moved to Derby, and Crewe concentrated on making the best cars in the world, Rolls Royces and Bentleys.

Most of the people I knew from school got jobs at the Railways works, but getting into either of these companies meant that you had to pass a written test; there was no way I could do that, so I'd have to look somewhere else for work.

My father still worked for Crosville but he wanted

better for me, and he always told me that I should have a trade. In those days, if a school leaver wasn't going into further education or pursuing a trade, the only alternative was to go into the armed forces – it wasn't a choice. I'd left school a few years before conscription finished so this would certainly have been my path if I'd gone to live with Ida or my father hadn't had higher hopes for me.

He said that with a trade I'd never be out of work, and no-one could take that away from me. He pointed out that anyone could drive a bus and there were lots of people who could, but a trade was more secure and better paid. He felt that plumbing would be something I could do and he knew a plumber but at the time I left school he wasn't taking anyone on, however he'd heard that a coach-building company called Jennings was taking on apprentices so he took me there.

John Henry Jennings & Son, known simply as Jennings, was in a town called Sandbach, not far from where I lived. They built bodies onto chassis, everything from horseboxes to bullion vans, and they had a contract with ERF, a major manufacturer of wagon chassis – in the 1950s, the bodies and cabs of virtually all ERF trucks on the road were made at Jennings. They were made to a very high standard, and widely admired.

We arrived at a very big building which had offices at the front and the factory behind. I was to discover that you could get at least twenty wagons into the factory, and not just small ones – it easily swallowed-up lots of the huge four-axle chassis.

As we approached the offices, a well-dressed elderly man was on his way out. He could have been a lawyer or a city gent, dressed in a suit and a bowler hat, looking as if he'd come straight out of a Dickens story – he turned out to be John Henry Jennings himself. His son and grandsons now ran the company, but Mr. Jennings senior was still pro-active in the business despite his advancing years; he'd have been in his mid seventies, maybe even his eighties, and he looked every inch a true Victorian character.

Mr. Jennings spotted us and said, 'What are you looking for?' He spoke a bit like a Dickens character as well.

'My son wants a job, sir,' replied my father, showing the respect due to such an authority figure.

'Oh, right,' said Mr. Jennings. 'Let me have a look at him.'

John Henry came in really close and peered intently at me. I was later to discover that he had cataracts, so he couldn't see very well; he looked me up and down as if he was searching for lost property. He turned to my father and said, 'He seems like a strong lad. We need strong lads here, we've got lots of heavy things to move around. I'll give him a try.'

He then turned a steely glance at me and said, 'Monday morning, seven o'clock. Don't be late.'

And that was it – I was fifteen years old and I was employed. No test and no writing anything down – much to my relief! I'd start at £2 10/- per week, two pounds ten shillings, £2.50 in today's money.

Come Monday morning, I was up and out by six o'clock to cycle the seven and a half miles to Sandbach – it was to be a baptism of fire.

Jennings was very old-fashioned and very strict. The tradesmen were gods; if one of them told an apprentice to jump, he'd better ask 'How high?', and no-one dared answer them back. It was very much a school of hard knocks – if you did something wrong, you'd likely be clipped round the back of the head – often with a lump of wood. A telling example of their antiquated standards was that they never heated the works, except for the paint shop. Next door was a modern ERF shop, which was heated – Jennings' staff used to love the rare occasions when they were asked to do work in the ERF shop in the winter time...

I was taken through the sprawling, busy works and put with a tradesman called Alistair Birtles. He was a big man – about six feet tall, around seventeen stone, and in his early thirties. He'd come to Jennings and served a full apprenticeship, after which he'd stayed on. I was to serve the whole of my five year apprenticeship with Alistair – eventually, we got on quite well.

At each work area there was a long bench with racks behind it, on which all the tools were hung. The wagon chassis were driven in and parked by the bench, and the bodies would be built onto them, as well as a cab, if the chassis came without one. When all the structure had been made from wood, it went to the panel shop to have the panels fitted. Apprentices were taught every aspect of the job – it was very comprehensive training, in many different skills.

Horseboxes were made in largely the same way as wagons, but with different layouts and much more work inside. They had living quarters like a luxury caravan at the front for grooms, and space for two horses at the back. We made everything, including beds which converted into benches (and some which hinged down from the roof), kitchens, and veneered finishes throughout. They were beautiful things, works of art really, all built from scratch.

My first week, all I did was sweep-up, help Alistair, and closely watch him, because I was expected to learn how he did things. It was daunting to think that I was right at the start of a five-year learning process, but I could see that apprentices gradually became skilled enough to be more useful to the tradesmen, and then it was a matter of experience that saw them trusted with more and more intricate work, and eventually, their own position as a tradesman. However, I could see that it would always be hard work in an industrial environment, and a hint of my Aunt Ida's ambition bubbled up to the surface – I didn't want to be doing that kind of thing all my life; I wanted more and better things, and to be in a better environment.

Apprentices were expected to fetch and carry screws and bolts and such, from the stores on the far side of the works. For newcomers, there was of course the obligatory fetching of non-existent objects, such as 'a wigwam for winding up the sun', or a 'sky-hook'. When you got to the stores and asked for one of these things, the storeman would say, 'Ah, it's just gone out – he's got it over there...' and he'd send you somewhere else for the object, only to be told it wasn't there either, and the man at that location would send you somewhere else, and so on... You'd get sent all round the works after this thing, until someone explained what was going on, and you'd feel incredibly daft. All the newcomers found themselves doing it – the tradesmen had done it many times, and they were very convincing at it.

An unpleasant initiation sometimes took place. If a new lad was a bit on the small side, he'd be picked up and dumped feet first up to his waist into a big barrel of nasty oily water. Hot steel parts from the anvil were plunged into this water to cool them down, which tempered them and made them harder. All the new lads in the smithy got this treatment, and they'd have to spend the rest of the day with squelching shoes and damp trousers, stinking of oil and rust. They never tried it on me, though – I was a bit too big and sinewy.

After I'd been there about three months, I was tasked with my first hands-on job, which was to make a tool box using the skills I'd learned watching Alistair. All the tradesmen had two or three toolboxes which they'd made, and Alistair pointed at one of his and said, 'Make one of those, like that.' It was quite a challenge – firstly, it had to be done when I could grab a few minutes such as when chassis' were changing over, or in my own time after work; and secondly, it was a complex thing to make beyond the basic box and handle, because it had drawers and lids and sections that hinged-out. I enjoyed having a goal to aim for, and having to call on my wits and knowledge, and actually craft this thing, and it took me six months. Needless to say, I learned a lot doing it.

Jennings had very high standards, so everything had to be done in just the right way, so there was no sloppiness, nothing second-rate. Every single action was expected to be performed with absolute focus and precision. This again reminded me of my Aunt Ida, specifically her high standards in all things, so the exacting demands at work didn't come as a complete shock, and while the work was hard, it was enjoyably engrossing.

In addition to their working week, all new apprentices also had to go in every Saturday morning to 'clean up the job'. This meant cleaning and putting all the tools away, and sharpening them if necessary, which we were taught how to do. You had to have everything back in place and ready for the tradesmen when they came in on Monday morning. If it took two hours or ten, you still had to finish the job, and if you didn't do everything just right, the tradesmen would create merry hell. The newcomers were shown what to do by Apprentices who were coming to the end of their term, before they moved on to become tradesmen in their own right.

Unless you lived locally, you never left the factory during the lunch break, you stayed there and ate your lunch – I used to take mine in a lunch box. If you wanted to make tea there were two huge urns to get hot water from, but a few of us would go to the smithy. There was an old smelting pot on a long handle used to boil water in the forge, from which I would fill mine and Alistair's tea cans.

I made friends with another apprentice called Geoff Wheatman, who lived in Alsager. When he'd left school, he'd gone to work in his father's pottery business, but they didn't get on, so he'd ended up at Jennings. During the lunch break, Geoff, myself, and a couple of lads from the smithy played table tennis over a piece of eight-by-four plywood with a plank for the net, and some bats we'd made. We had about three quarters of an hour, so we'd get our meals down us and go for a game.

I'd been at Jennings for several months when, at sixteen, I got a motorcycle. It was a BSA Bantam; they had a notoriously noisy 125cc 2-stroke engine – clouds of blue smoke and pop, pop, popping all over the place – you could hear me coming a mile away. It was a good little bike, and although it wouldn't exactly fly up hills, it made my fifteen-mile daily commute much easier. It also gave me more time to swim, which I'd continued after starting at Jennings.

As soon as I turned seventeen, my father began letting me use his car, a little Austin A30 with an 800cc engine. He'd bought it just over a year previously, but he didn't drive it much because he usually used a works van. It had cost him about four hundred pounds, which was well beyond the means of an apprentice, so it was quite a luxury. However, I really enjoyed riding motorcycles, so at the same time, I upgraded my Bantam to a Triumph 500 twin, which was a lot faster and more enjoyable to ride.

I'd had my Triumph for five months when I had an accident on it. Someone driving an old, black, rusty Morris Oxford suddenly turned right in front of me; I braked hard, but the back wheel came round and I skidded sideways into the car. My bike had a heavy duty crash-bar across the front of the frame, and it speared right through the driver's door panel, which broke away at the top edge. I'd automatically put my left hand out to brace myself against the inevitable side-on impact with the car, and a spike of rusty metal from the top of the door stabbed all the way through the heel of my left hand. I couldn't get my hand off the rusty spike, so I had to sit there, on my bike, pinned to the car, while the ambulance men cut a piece of metal out of the door to free me. They pulled the metal out of my hand at the hospital, and while it healed up well, I still have the scars, and a strange feeling in my hand where the metal went through.

After that, I decided that motorcycles were a little too dangerous, so I sold the Triumph and used my father's car full-time.

Soon after, a man called Jim Chadwick arrived at Jennings. He was about seven years older than me, and he joined in with our lunch-time table tennis games, but something else that he was involved in was about to take my life in a completely new direction.

One lunch hour, Jim started talking about judo. As luck would have it the club that he attended was just around the corner from where Geoff lived in Alsager, more or less at the end of his street. It was a collection of prefabricated buildings panelled in asbestos, which had been the leisure complex for the nearby Radway Green small arms ammunition manufacturing plant. When the buildings became vacant after the war, a man called Ken Hunt managed to acquire the use of one to start his own judo club.

'Why don't you come?' Jim asked Geoff and myself. 'It's in those old Nissen huts round the corner from where you live, Geoff.' We both decided we'd give it a go.

Instead of going home, I went to Geoff's house and had some sandwiches, after which we walked round to the judo hall, where classes started at about seven o'clock.

Jim arrived with a friend called Bernard Platt. He was a burly sort of man, and the same grade as Jim. They'd both begun judo at about the same time, and had worked their way up the ranks through a series of courses.

Jim was a blue belt. The progression through the belts starts with white, and from there it's yellow, green, blue, and brown, which are the 'Kyu' grades. Then you progress to a black belt, which has its own grades called 'Dan' – first Dan, second Dan, and so on. Ken Hunt, who ran the club, was a brown belt – there was no black belt in the Alsager club.

There were about twenty people there that night, so it was reasonably well-attended; they lent me a jacket and belt.

The first thing you do is learn how to fall. You probably spend most of the first evening flapping around on the mat, and then, just to keep you interested, they show you a very elementary throw. Jim and Bernard were the instructors; Ken was much older than them so he wasn't as active, and he tended to teach juniors and the women, who had their own separate class with five or six regulars.

I found the whole evening really interesting and engrossing, and I asked Geoff if he wanted to go again. We did, and after a few meetings, I was hooked on judo.

After a while, Geoff surprised me when he said he didn't want to go any more – apparently he was more interested in going out drinking and socialising and enjoying himself. Those things were of no appeal to me, not just because my Aunt Ida's disapproval of them was now ingrained into my own set of standards, but also because I could see that they were self-indulgent and a waste of time – perhaps that was her influence too... I found judo to be an exciting challenge which I enjoyed mastering and continually getting better at. As I could no longer stop off at Geoff's for a bite to eat before going to the club, I'd take a sandwich with me after work, and eat when I got to Alsager.

After about 5 months at Jennings, Jim left to drive wagons, but I still saw him at judo. I became good friends with him and eventually his wife, Beryl, who was also a judoka. She was quite small but she was pretty good. Before long they'd invited me to their home, a small end-of-terrace house in Alsager, where I'd have something to eat before going on to the club with Jim.

By the time I'd been doing judo for about 6 months, I

had cause to use it at work. There was a man called Pugh, who'd been a regimental sergeant major in the army, and at Jennings he was regarded as a hard man. He was about the same age as Alistair, and as they lived in the same village, Scholar Green, they knew each other. Alistair had built Pugh up as being able to look after himself – he always spoke highly of him – I think they'd been in the army together. Pugh was always very smart, and he walked around the works in a military style, as if he was still on the parade ground. I'd never spoken to him – his station was at the other end of the building.

One day, I'd been to the stores to collect something, and Pugh must have made a wise-crack to me, to which I had a cocky answer. He came towards me as if he was he was going to smack me, but I ducked out of the way and chucked him into a big pile of iron with a crash. I think he was surprised that I'd stood my ground – he'd have expected me to run off, as apprentices would normally do in the face of an assertive, aggressive military type – and even more surprised that I'd dealt with him so quickly and easily. He never followed it up, probably because he was embarrassed at being bested by an apprentice. After that, the atmosphere began to spread that I could handle myself.

However, such a reputation made no difference to the standard of work that was expected of me. When I'd been at Jennings for about two years, I was working on one of the special flat-bed wagons for the Earls Court show, stood on a 'hop-up', which was a small set of steps which we made there, that allowed you to get to the right height to work on the wagons. They used special, well-seasoned high-quality wood for these wagons, and even the bed of the truck would look like a piece of furniture when it was done – they were beautifully finished.

As I was nailing the bed, I accidentally missed a nail and hit the wood of the wagon bed with the hammer. I don't think I marked it, but Alistair saw me do it, and he walked up behind me and kicked my hop-up out from under me. I slithered down the truck, scraping all the skin off my shins on the wagon's mudguard and wheel. The school of hard knocks was always waiting for any misstep, any error – it was bloody tough, but powerful motivation to get things right.

Back on the judo mats after work, I began to follow Jim and Bernard's examples, working my way up through the Kyu grades. I got to the point where I was beating Bernard, and was starting to take Jim to task. He was finding me difficult to deal with, not only because my judo skills were progressing, but also because I had a great deal of raw strength. Of course, you're not supposed to need strength to be a good judoka, but I could combine both, and could haul almost anyone down to the mat – after many of our encounters, Jim would wince and comment wryly on my sheer strength. I couldn't yet beat him (he was a brown belt), but I was definitely catching him up.

One night, Jim mentioned another judo club, which was held on the first floor of a pub called The Mitre, in Burslem. It was a step up from the Alsager club, with better instructors and more challenging opponents, so it was the logical next step and an inviting challenge. Burslem was a long way for me to travel to on a regular basis, but it was worth it, especially to attend courses run by black belt instructors. I was by this time a green belt.

I then suffered my first injury – a common one and not particularly serious, but painful – it was known as 'knocking the top off your shoulder'. I fell slightly awkwardly, which caused my collar bone to pop out of my left shoulder joint. The injury has a classic appearance, of a lump on top of your shoulder – it's quite common in combat sports. It had to be strapped down for a while to make sure it stayed put after being put back, and I was told that the best thing I could do for it would be to strengthen all the surrounding muscles to make sure it remained stable, and the best exercise for that would apparently be training with weights.

I heard that there was a weight training and lifting club upstairs at the Railways works, above the shop floor, under the vast rafters. I went along and found a big, open, rough-and-ready space, nothing like a sophisticated modern gym, with sets of weights for bodybuilding and an Olympic bar on a raised platform. The Olympic weightlifters' equipment was quite new, but the bodybuilders gear was old and worn, but still quite usable. I watched the bodybuilders, and with their help worked out a training and strengthening regime which would be best for strengthening my shoulder.

I'd originally thought that what I needed was weight training, which is also known as body-building. This involves many familiar exercises with weights, including bench presses, various forms of curls with barbells or dumbbells, squats with a weighted bar on the shoulders, calf exercises in a similar way, and more, all of which are gradual, relatively slow strength actions. Olympic weightlifting is very different because of the instant bursts of strength it requires to perform actions such as the clean-and-jerk, press, and snatch. All of these involve moving a heavily weighted bar quickly to a new position, such as up to the shoulders and then above the head, or straight from the floor to over-head. This fast application of strength changes the nature of muscles, and gives them the potential for explosive bursts of power, rather than gradually-applied strength. For throws in judo, bursts of strength is the kind of power that's needed, so Olympic weightlifting is the perfect form of additional training – boxers also favour it for the same reason. I ended up changing to Olympic weightlifting quite by accident...

One day, one of the lads at the Olympic bar asked me, 'Why don't you try this?'

I wasn't sure, so I replied, 'I'm mainly interested in judo, really.'

He said, 'It won't hurt you – it's good for you.'

They were pretty persuasive, and talked me into having a go. I found that I really enjoyed it, and I was satisfied that it had plenty of strength moves, so I changed from bodybuilding to Olympic weightlifting, and was to continue it long after my shoulder had healed.

I didn't miss any work because of my shoulder – I couldn't afford to, nor any judo; I had to scale-back how involved I got, but I kept going to the classes. My shoulder was painful but not fragile, so I began the strengthening weight training within a couple of weeks, and, it healed up pretty quickly. I ended up sacrificing my swimming for weight training, which I did on Mondays, Wednesdays, and Fridays, and judo on Tuesdays, Thursdays, and all weekend.

As I was now established in my apprenticeship, there was less need to do the weekend tidy-up – I was now much quicker on the tools, which would be put away and the job cleaned-up whilst we worked, so my weekends became available. Consequently, in addition to the evening sessions at The Mitre, I was now able to start attending the weekend courses they ran, with special guest instructors.

One particular weekend, The Mitre had a visiting Japanese judoka coming to teach, who was an eighth Dan. I'd never seen anyone from Japan before, and I'd never heard of anyone who was ranked as high as eighth Dan. Jim told me he was the highest-grade judoka ever to visit the UK, and even though it was a foregone conclusion, he asked me if I wanted to go.

'Try stopping me!' I thought.

Chapter 6

Kenshiro Abbe

Jim and I went to The Mitre's judo club expecting great things – we were not disappointed! The higher the grade, the more advanced would be the judo that could be learned and practised, and even though we knew nothing about Japan or the Japanese, with this instructor coming from the home of judo and having such a high Dan grade, we couldn't wait to see this whole new level of skill.

On the mats, I'd thought Jim was good, but this teacher, this sensei, Kenshiro Abbe, was out of this world. In comparison to him, Jim and several other capable judokas looked like they were just playing at judo, whereas he was definitely the real thing. He threw his opponents where and when he wanted to – they couldn't do anything with him nor get anywhere near him. His moves were efficient and precise, they were quick and smooth, and they looked effortless, and he made very short work of all his opponents – it was like some kind of magic. I was fascinated, and I had to learn more.

So, who was he? How did he become this master judoka? He had a most interesting background...

Kenshiro Abbe was born in 1915 on the deeply spiritual Japanese island of Shikoku, where a perpetual pilgrimage runs for 750 miles around 88 temples. The son of a kendo instructor, he started formal judo tuition relatively late at fourteen, but he was both gifted and dedicated and by the time he was fifteen he'd received his second Dan from the Butokukwai. At seventeen he was promoted to fourth Dan, and when he received his fifth Dan aged eighteen, he was Japan's youngest holder of that grade.

He was selected to apply for a place at the Budo Senmon Gakko martial arts university in Kyoto (the 'Busen'), and became one of the one-in-fifteen to secure a place. He studied judo and kendo there, as well as philosophy under the renowned professor Hajime Tanabe, who specialised in 'Ontology', the study of 'being'.

Further memorable achievements came at the age of twenty-two when he won the fifth Dan Championships in the Imperial Tournament, and he became judo instructor for the police in Osaka and the High School in Kyoto, and also at the Special Judo College of the Butokukwai. His sixth Dan was awarded a year later, but another seven years passed before he obtained his seventh.

Abbe's skills were greatly refined and enhanced by a particularly valuable and intensive experience – for ten years he studied under Morihei Ueshiba, the founder of Aikido and a deeply revered sensei.

Abbe developed new judo techniques which were far more than the product of his experience and skill – they were also informed by an inspiration that bordered upon revelation. Over many years, he had envisaged, tested, and perfected an approach to judo which greatly increased the effectiveness of its moves, through the use of skilful positioning and creative use of leverage. It actually had its roots more in philosophy than physicality, by applying a sensitivity towards the dynamics around him. In his view, an opponent could be considered to be a 'system', which, if properly understood, could be easily controlled. Abbe called his system 'Kyu Shin Do', which can be loosely translated as 'The Way of the Circle', and it was devastatingly effective.

Being so accomplished, it is perhaps surprising that Abbe faced problems in his homeland. Having developed Kyu Shin Do for some 25 years, Abbe had attempted to introduce it into the teaching of judo in Japan. Unfortunately, however, an old saying with which we are familiar in the West plagued him – 'A prophet is not accepted in his own country.'

Abbe found his advanced proposals rejected by the Japanese martial arts establishment because they posed a threat to their carefully guarded traditional way of doing things. I was later to learn that there is much about Japan that is very traditional and resistant to change, particularly anything cultural, which is how they regarded their highly specialised martial arts. However, Abbe knew that he'd developed something of real value, so he started looking for an audience that was more open to new ideas, and he found it in Great Britain.

He arrived in London in 1955, with the intention of working with the British Judo Association (the BJA), the official body that chose the people to go to international tournaments, and who ultimately wanted to find candidates for the Olympic Games. However, he soon found that he didn't agree with the way they did things, so he decided to break away from them and form his own organisation with another high-ranked judoka called Otani, which was named the British Judo Council (the BJC).

There are a number of fascinating stories about Abbe's time in London. After an early evening's teaching session, Abbe was returning home through a quiet suburban street when he was confronted by three youths who demanded his money. He glanced at each one, removed his wallet and threw it on the floor between himself and his attackers. He pointed to the wallet and said, 'I am prepared to die for that wallet. What about you?' None of them took up the challenge.

Another incident involved Abbe as a passenger in a car which got held up in a traffic jam. As he peered ahead he noticed a police officer standing beside a red double-decker bus, with a large Alsatian dog at his feet. The dog's back legs had been run over by the bus and it was in serious pain. Abbe walked over and gently stroked the dog's head. The dog stopped howling. Abbe then placed his hand on the dog's neck and with a slight movement, the dog passed over. The police officer glanced at Abbe and said, 'I don't know who you are, sir, but that is the most compassionate thing I have ever witnessed'. Abbe bowed, said nothing, and returned to the car.

I would learn of all these things years later, but they are true-to form – they give a good impression of the quiet power that this man possessed; I'd begun to see it on the mats, but it was clear to me that there was far more to him.

The next time Abbe did a course near to me was on the Wirral, in Ellesmere Port. Jim and I went, and once again we were most impressed, not only with what Abbe taught, but with the stillness and focus he created in the dojo, the judo venue. He had us all stand silently in a circle before training began, and the way he bowed to his opponents had so much more precision than the way we usually did it. His supreme ability seemed to be connected with the care he took over the simplest of things, which made me begin to think that the best judo is more than something you do – it's a way of life.

Jim and I decided to go to as many of Abbe's courses as we could. However, he taught all around the country over a whole weekend, which meant we'd need somewhere to stay overnight, so we got our heads together and decided to apply the skills of our apprenticeships, and build a motor home.

Between us, we bought an old Bedford van with sliding doors – it was a bit of a wreck. We put it into one of the barns at the smallholding that Jim's father owned, and set about renovating it. We used materials from Jennings – wood, screws, anything spare that we could get our hands on. We kept the body but stripped out the interior; we laid bearers across the chassis to strengthen the shell; the wheel arches were rotten so we removed them and made new ones from wood; we made seats that converted into beds, a central table, and we even installed windows, which were elegantly finished with curtains made by Beryl, Jim's wife. It was a very serviceable vehicle, built for very little outlay, and was known as simply 'The Van'.

Now we could drive to courses all over the country and stay in the van overnight, and the only cost of our trips would be the fuel. We travelled around for two years like this, chasing Abbe, our judo skills progressing rapidly under his outstanding tuition.

On one of the Ellesmere Port courses, we witnessed what seemed like a minor miracle. When we got there, one of the course organisers was reluctantly explaining to Abbe that he couldn't take the course because he was suffering with an extremely bad back. He was indeed hobbling around with great caution, but Abbe immediately told him to get onto the mat, after which he got on top of him and seemed to get hold of every extremity, and then he twisted. The man's back suddenly made an explosion of crunching and popping noises and he let out a yelp. Abbe then did the same thing in the other direction to a further chorus of pops and cracks, after which he got up and simply said to the man, 'Ah – now, practise!' The man got to his feet and a disbelieving grin spread across his face as he realised his pain was completely gone. He did indeed do a full practice session of judo. We were all awestruck – I had to learn how to do this too...

Out of the blue, Bernard told me that he was running a judo course at the night-school in Crewe, my home town. On several occasions he said, 'If ever you're at a loose end on a Tuesday night, pop in and see us.' Eventually I did.

It was around seven-thirty when I got there. Bernard had a class of students, which was probably only about ten people, but still a reasonable line-up. Laid out on the floor were about twenty-feet square of sponge mats. I got changed, and returned wearing my brown belt– the same grade as Bernard.

He lined his students up against the wall and introduced me, and then he said something interesting – he told his students, 'Tonight, you're going to see me get beaten.' As I've already said, I'd caught and surpassed Bernard at judo before I'd begun training under Abbe, and he was no match for me. As an instructor, he'd had to fore-warn his students of his inevitable defeat so it didn't come as too much of a surprise to them.

There was another aspect to this, which sprang from the kind of relationships that existed between participants of combat sports. Bernard probably felt he had to invite me to his club because he'd know that if I found out about it and he hadn't told me, I could have turned up and made him look like a fool on the mats. Because he'd invited me, I beat him in a less aggressive way, so it was the best way of dealing with his fear of me; my judo could be described as brutal.

He asked me to do some tuition – he wanted me to show his students how I approached certain throws. I demonstrated a few before we split them into pairs to see how they performed. Then, Bernard and I went around the room to advise them if they were doing things right or wrong, and if questionable, what to change.

After about an hour, Bernard lined them all up again so that, as the visiting instructor, I could take the line-up. The lowest grades stood to the left of the line, the highest to the right. Traditionally, the instructor started on the left with the lowest grade and worked his way across to the higher grades, the idea being that when you reached the end of the line-up you would be tired, so you'd have to work harder to beat the higher grades. Bernard put himself at the far end on the right.

The class was no trouble at all to me. He hadn't been running it long, and the highest grade was only a yellow belt. I finished the line-up with Bernard and beat him – but then, he'd told the class at the start of the evening that I would, so he'd probably defeated himself.

Finally, we went into 'Randori', which means everybody pairs-up and they do free practise with each other, to see who they can beat. On the signal from the instructor taking the Randori, they change; Bernard and I supervised rather than taking part.

At the end of the evening as I left the dressing room and headed for my car, a young guy of about sixteen approached me and introduced himself as Barry. He said the class had been fascinating for him, seeing someone of my skill level there, and he was most impressed that I'd beaten his instructor. He said that his father had a gym where he trained, and he asked me if I'd like to visit it.

This was of interest to me, because although Barry didn't know it, I knew who his father was – he was Geoff Condliffe, who ran the garage not too far from where I lived, the West End Garage. I sometimes got petrol there, and I'd seen Barry on the forecourt a couple of times. I also knew that Geoff Condliffe was 'Count Bartelli', who had been the most famous masked wrestler in the north of England for nearly twenty years, locally known to everybody as 'The Count'. I'd never met him, and didn't know what he looked like. With all this in mind, Barry's proposition was of interest to me, so I agreed to go – more about that later...

Under sensei Abbe, the BJC ran competitions to find champions at the various weights, with whom he would challenge the BJA as the supreme judo organization. The judokas who came out on top would go forward to compete in the Tokyo Olympics in 1964. This was to be a huge honour, as it would be the first year that judo would be an Olympic discipline, added specifically for this year because the games were being held in Japan, the home of judo.

I won The North-West Area Championship for 1961-62, still as a brown belt. During the eliminations, I thought I'd meet a judoka called Brian Mole, whom Abbe had been personally training. I'd seen him at Ellesmere Port, and he was at least a second Dan, but I have a feeling that he didn't take part – I think he might have been injured. He would have been my only competition in that contest, but we would meet on the mats later...

Winning this championship had brought me fully to Abbe's attention, and he began mentioning that there were deeper aspects to Japanese martial arts, which I was ready to believe – the atmosphere around him suggested this. I had already assumed that there must be many things which contributed to his absolute mastery of judo, and if they were part of that excellence, I wanted to know about them too.

When training took us to London, after the classes he would very occasionally invite a student he was considering mentoring to his room at the top of Otani's house. Abbe's presence was in-and-of-itself magical – everything he did was unique, he used cutlery as if he was performing surgery, and the way he walked and sat and drank tea and even smoked a cigarette was precise and even other-worldly; it was impossible to be in his presence without knowing there was real wisdom at his core, and we all wanted it to rub off on us. An invitation to his home promised something extremely special.

His room was quite unusual. It was quite large with a big bird cage hanging on the outside of the window so the birds could fly about inside as well as perch outside in the sun, and there was also an aquarium. On my first visit there, with his typical extreme economy of communication, he said, 'Ah – necessary: look...', pointing at one of the fish. Obviously, when he gave an instruction it had to be followed keenly, so I did as I was told and watched the fish most intensely. He stopped me after about fifteen minutes, and found I had a feeling of being very still, but also very alert. I hadn't realised it, but this had been my first lesson in Zen meditation.

On my next visit, Abbe did the same thing, but after a few minutes, he said, 'Ah – close eyes, still see fish...' I found this quite easy, and before I knew it, twenty minutes had passed. Afterwards, I felt like I'd had a good night's sleep, and was ready for anything.

A few weeks later, he showed me Zazen – formal seated meditation. This time, he demonstrated how to sit in the right position and breathe properly, and he said, 'Ah – necessary, no thoughts...' At first it wasn't easy – things kept popping into my mind, which I automatically began thinking about, but by paying them no attention, they started fading away. Once again, after this meditation I felt calm and strong – a great feeling.

Abbe told me to do this meditation every day if possible, and I did my best to stick at it. I began finding it easier, and I started noticing changes in myself. I seemed to have a calm strength, and I needed to think less about what to do – my reactions seemed to always be the right ones, and they seemed almost automatic.

When I saw Abbe again, he told me that before I meditated, I should think of *Kyu Shin Do*, the 'centre-of-gravity' technique he taught in judo. He didn't explain any more than that, possibly because he didn't have the words, but in hindsight, I suspect that he had introduced me to a 'Zen Koan' – a puzzle that can't be answered with reasoning and thinking. Of course, I had to let this unanswerable question in the back of my mind fall away too, but I suspect that it began to cause invisible changes in my deeper self... Understanding Zen on a conscious level seemed impossible, but somehow it was making me calmer, stronger, and better.

As the weeks passed, I began to find that something Abbe had hinted at was beginning to happen – there were far fewer 'thoughts' in my mind, and instead, I had a confidence that I would always know what to do; was this coming from the 'intuitive self' that Abbe had mentioned? It was almost as if a new part of myself had been switched on. Abbe said that this was why the samurai were so good at what they did – they never had to 'think' about anything – they just did it. With barely a word being spoken, Sensei Abbe had enabled my intuitive self, and it would prove to be very powerful.

Chapter 7

Count Bartelli

After Barry Condliffe had seen me beat his judo instructor and he'd invited me to his gym, I'd agreed to go because I wanted to meet his father, the very successful wrestler Count Bartelli (although I didn't tell Barry that). The gym was behind The Count's garage, which was an impressive place – he sold petrol and there was a car showroom with a constantly changing selection of about fifty cars. He sometimes had some really luxurious and exotic cars there, which I would admire as I passed.

I called round the following Saturday lunchtime. Barry was there, training with a friend, doing bench presses. He didn't know that I already did weight lifting – he thought my only specialism was judo, and I think he was confident that he knew something about weights that I didn't.

The bar was set up for bench press and Barry invited me to have a go. There was about 150lbs on the bar but I could press a lot more, so this was very easy for me; Barry was impressed, and added more weight to the bar. At that point his father walked in and Barry introduced him. Geoff Condliffe was a pleasant guy and naturally approachable, a characteristic he cultivated to be all the better a car salesman – he bonded with people very quickly.

We talked a little and finally he said, 'I'll let you get on...' He never lifted any weights, although I do think he noticed what was on the bar.

I stayed for about another quarter hour before we wound things down. Barry's mate jumped on his bike and disappeared and Barry and I walked around to the forecourt. There were four pumps, and each one had its own attendant on Saturdays because that was the busiest day of the week – but then, the garage was always popular because it sold Jet fuel, which was the cheapest in the area. Geoff was there too, in case anyone came to buy a car. As I was leaving there were no customers so Barry and I went over to Geoff and we started talking again.

Barry was pretty enthusiastic by now and was calling me by my first name. 'Is it okay if Pete comes wrestling with us, Dad?'

Geoff thought about the question for what seemed like ages before replying. Eventually, he said, 'Yes, if he wants to. Next Saturday, I'm in Doncaster.'

I learned that he normally set off for that neck of the woods in the afternoon. There were no motorways yet, so it was quite a trek going through Altrincham toward Manchester and over the Pennines to head for Doncaster; even though it's only seventy or eighty miles, back then it was far from the simple journey it is now.

Geoff didn't like to get to shows too early – he always tried to arrive when the punters were all in, preferably around eight o'clock. He was usually top of the bill, which meant he was on third. He'd go in, do his show, and be back out and in his car and gone before the last match had finished.

So it was all arranged for the following Saturday. I turned up at the garage and off we all went. When we got to Doncaster, Geoff explained that Barry knew the routine; as we went in Geoff went one way to the dressing room and we went into the hall to watch the matches.

That night The Count was on with Billy Howes, which ended in a blood-bath – they both looked like they'd really taken a beating. Looking back on it, I think that Geoff may have been trying to impress me. He would have told Howes that he had a judo lad in the audience, and I suspect that the match was put together to give me the impression that wrestling was a challenge and something to be appreciated. By the time he came out of the hall we were already in the car.

We talked about wrestling and judo all the way back. Barry was still fascinated at how I'd beaten his judo instructor, and he was very keen for me to show him how I did it – I saw that as an opportunity, so I agreed. I got the impression that I was somehow more accessible on this level than his father – had The Count not shared any wrestling skills with his son?

The next time I went to judo I arranged for Barry to come with me, and he came to Alsager and several other clubs that I attended. Geoff seemed pleased that Barry had a friend who could look out for him and help him to focus on something – Barry was, after all, very spoiled and lacking in direction, but I could see why – Everything in Geoff's house was of such high quality that it would spoil any adolescent growing up in it.

He'd made good money wrestling, but he also made a fortune selling Jet petrol, and his car deals always turned in a tidy profit. He was very much the successful entrepreneur, he had a great sense of style, and he was cultured and clever – he always did the Sunday Times crossword very quickly. I admired Geoff and his lifestyle and he seemed to bond with me.

His wife, Muriel, on the other hand, was nowhere near as sensible as him – she was a serious party-girl who caused him many headaches and spent his money like it was going out of fashion. She drank like crazy; at the house she'd always have a tall tumbler in her hand that must have held half a pint of scotch and soda. Sometimes

Geoff would complain that she was drinking too much but in a theatrical voice and with a flourish of her hand she'd say, 'It's just a dash of whisky, filled to the top with saffon.' They were a lot stronger than that, and she'd often have three on the go at various places around the house – I think she forget where she put them down so she just made another.

She was the one who really spoiled Barry, one classic example being when she had him driven to school in a Bentley – more on her later...

I gradually got to know Barry, and therefore Geoff too. He bought and sold and swapped vehicles with several motor dealers. He knew I could drive, and he asked me one weekend if I'd go with him to collect a car he'd bought. I agreed and before long it was a regular occurrence.

That led to more jobs for me – it seemed that he was cultivating me to be a part of his team. It was Geoff, not Barry, who invited me to come to more wrestling shows.

I noticed he'd say things like, 'Show a man a door and he'll open it.' I came to see that he put that philosophy into practise too – apart from wrestling, he was always flitting between car deals, buying and selling high-value jewelry among his business acquaintances, as well as developing properties both here and in Spain, but he was always on the look-out for any possible deal.

He occasionally uttered another pearl of wisdom which also seemed to underpin his approach: 'Most people are too busy earning a living to make money.' I didn't understand it at the time – I thought that 'earning a living' actually meant making money, but I later realised that he meant getting bogged-down in one thing can blind you to other promising opportunities. Looking back I now recognise that his life revolved around maintaining that sharp vision and capitalising on it; to me as a teen-ager, he was an inspiration to watch and be around, because he was a shining example of how to achieve a good life from mastering 'the art of the deal'.

He was very practical too. When I first went to the garage I'd seen a pickup truck with two large barrels on the back. I couldn't work out what it could be for. Geoff told me that after he was demobbed he'd begun keeping pigs on a smallholding and this truck was used to collect food scraps for their swill. I think being a food producer meant he could avoid being called back into the army.

Geoff bought another big house in Wheelock and Muriel had me help her move their things from their house next to the garage. He was preparing to sell the West End garage along with another petrol station he owned by the park, but also he had two more garages. One was called the Lion and Swan which sold petrol and had a small car showroom as well as several warehouses which were let out, and another car showroom and petrol station on the Calveley Straight. I believe he also owned a hotel somewhere in Crewe. He was a fine example of a businessman and he opened my eyes to all sorts of angles, including wheeler-dealing.

I knew very little about the wrestling business back then, but I was to discover that Count Bartelli wasn't an actual fighter – he was what could best be described as a 'show wrestler'. At the wrestling shows, I could see that there were holds being used that simply wouldn't immobilise an opponent nor inflict any real pain, yet the one in the hold would seem to be helpless and he'd struggle and protest, which would fire-up the crowd. I could also see that the audience wanted to see such struggles, and they reacted to it, cheering their champion and booing the 'villain', the bad guy. It seemed that even if the fights weren't real, they had to look real, and that's what the audiences loved and wanted. Viewed on that level, Count Bartelli was brilliant at it – he could keep them on the edge of their seats, even if there was very little serious combat taking place.

Geoff's aversion to actual fighting became apparent

when he was occasionally challenged by a member of a rough family from Crewe. They were scrap metal merchants, and I believe a couple of them did prison time for stealing lead from church roofs. The one who challenged Geoff was a big guy who used to come onto the forecourt and torment him about wrestling. He'd shout, 'Come on Count – I'll wrestle you! We'll have a match now!'

'The Count' had a couple of classic excuses – he said he couldn't wrestle in an unregulated environment because he'd lose his licence as a professional athlete, and he couldn't wrestle a member of the public in case he hurt them. He used these answers for anyone who challenged him that he didn't want to get involved with.

After I'd known Geoff for a while, I was on the forecourt one day when the scrap man arrived in his wagon – I can see it now, brimming with chunks of scrap metal. He started on Geoff again, 'Come on Count, I'll wrestle you.'

With a twinkle in his eye, Geoff said, 'I tell you what – I'll give you a chance. You can have a wrestle with this lad,' meaning me; 'If you can beat him, you can wrestle me.'

The roughneck was up for it – he grinned widely and said, 'Right-ho!'

I was about twenty at the time and this bloke was about twenty-six or seven and he clearly thought he was something of a streetwise hard case.

Geoff said. 'Okay, but we've got to do it properly. Why don't you come up to my house on Sunday afternoon? We'll get on the lawn and if anyone does get thrown they won't hurt themselves – we can't do it here on the tarmac.'

'I'll be there, Count!' shouted the metal merchant. 'I'll be there.'

After the scrap man had cleared off, Geoff said to me, 'Don't let him beat you.'

I said, 'Don't worry.'

Sunday afternoon arrived and so did the scrap man. I had some trunks and trainers to wear, he didn't have anything – he simply took his shirt off to wrestle. We ended up on the lawn. He was quite big, a large, raw, bony sort of bloke, touching sixteen stone.

It was clear that he'd seen professional wrestling on TV, because as we came together on the lawn he went into a stance as seen on TV wrestling – it was what he believed to be the right thing. Of course, he hadn't a clue. I upended him in a crack and had him down on the lawn. If you know what you're doing, once you have them down they're not coming up again.

I mauled him about for quite a while, with a few additional discomforts such as jamming my elbows into his ears. Every time he tried to get up I took his arms from under him and pushed him back down on his face. He didn't last nearly as long as he'd thought he would; if you know anything about ground work, a person who hasn't done any is very soon exhausted.

He struggled and struggled to no avail, and eventually shouted, 'Okay, okay, Let me up, let me up!'

I glanced at Geoff, and I could tell by the way he was looking at me that the roughneck shouldn't be allowed up yet – so I kept him down.

He really didn't like that – he was absolutely helpless, in pain, totally fed up, and hating feeling that way. He shouted, 'Fucking hell, Count! Will you get him off me?'

I mauled him about for another few minutes before Geoff approached and said, 'Okay, okay – let him up.'

I did, and as the scrap man got to his feet he glanced at Geoff and said, 'Fuck me, Count, I'm glad I didn't have a go with you if that's what he can do!'

Of course, the scrap man didn't know that if he'd been on the lawn with Geoff, it wouldn't have been nearly as bad. However, he certainly didn't want to wrestle The Count any more, and I'm sure he never asked again.

At the West End Garage there had been a forecourt

manager who ended up being sacked for stealing. I recalled seeing him when I'd got petrol there before I'd got to know Barry. I heard that he'd been driving Muriel around but the gossip suggested there was more to it than that. He disappeared about a month before I first went there.

With him gone, I took over some of what he did, including occasionally manning the petrol pumps and driving Muriel. I was there whenever I wasn't training, which was some weekends and some evenings.

After I'd been going to the garage for about eighteen months I was offered the chance to do something that sounded like a real adventure – go to Mallorca with Muriel and Barry for a couple of weeks. That would mean taking an aeroplane to somewhere exotic, both things I'd never done before, and I was really excited by the idea. Little was I to know that I would find myself in a head-spinning whirlwind of intrigue.

To get us all ready for Mallorca, first Muriel took us to London. We stayed at the luxury White House hotel, where she had a professional hair-dresser visit her, not once, but twice every day. Then there was the shopping – she really dressed me up. She took us to boutiques, including Cecil G for fashionable casuals and Lillywhites for beach-wear, buying me lots of clothes; she actually threw my own clothes away! We stayed there for about five days and then took a Caravelle to Mallorca, where she went off the rails.

I'd occasionally driven Muriel where she'd wanted to go in Crewe and even picked up the odd bottle of whisky for her, but in Mallorca I really saw what money could bring. They owned a block of apartments in Palma Novo, and two villas with the use of a private beach, one of which they rented-out and they lived in the other, where everything was as luxurious as their home in Wheelock.

She was usually driven to the hairdresser and elsewhere by taxi but while I was there I did it in her powder-blue Fiat Nuova 500 America, the one with the full-length sun-roof. She was out virtually every night at the prestigious Atlantic Hotel restaurant / cabaret venue, where she would consume vast amounts of expensive booze. Her lifestyle was so excessive that she was known as 'The Contessa' (well, she was bound to say that her husband was a certain 'Count Bartelli', wasn't she?). Everybody there believed she really was a countess because of her extravagance.

There was a small bar on the sea front where she bought all her drinks and had them sent up to the villa. As soon as they saw her car pull up the owners would make her a champagne cocktail to be ready as she swept in. When Barry saw her buying wildly over-priced drinks he complained, and Muriel replied, 'These are my friends,' to which Barry retorted, 'Of course they're not – they're only doing that because of the way you're throwing money around.' She bought bottles of Coke by the crate from there, at twelve pesetas each, but they were available from the corner store for, I think, three pesetas.

Her Spanish was very poor, but she showed no inclination to improve it – perhaps that was an affectation too; someone as 'grand' as her didn't need to do things properly because everyone around her would indulge her. When she was warm she'd say, 'Mucho calor para mi', and Barry would say, 'Don't you realise that you're telling everyone you're hot stuff?!?' It made no difference – she didn't care.

After we'd been there for just three days Muriel ended up buying a water-skiing school, which was run by an Australian. She'd booked the ski-boat for us to use every day but on the second day she'd told the owner we wouldn't need it the next day because we were going somewhere. Then she changed her mind and sent us to go and ski, but the man had already booked some other customers. When we went back and told her she freaked out and stormed down to the quay and bought the boat and the hut and the entire business. Then the man disappeared and Muriel was left with the boat and the business. She wanted the boat taken round to Palma Nova and fortunately Barry knew how to drive it. I think it ended up being sold back to the original owner.

She'd been invited to the apartment of some Americans which had absolutely every modern gizmo you could imagine, all imported from the USA, and she decided she wanted to buy it. It was a lot of money but she just expected it to be available.

Sometimes she'd have me carry her into the bar where she bought the drinks, and the Atlantic Hotel. She claimed she had a weakened leg after an injury some ten years earlier. She and Geoff used to go on holiday to Morocco with Arthur Wright. Once, while at the water's edge on a beach, Arthur had boisterously pushed her over and torn her Achilles tendon so badly that it had needed to be grafted. This left her with a long scar on her lower leg, which she really resented. As I carried her she'd say to people who knew her, 'Grande, mucho forte'. It must have been quite a spectacle.

One evening all three of us were dining out at the Atlantic when the cabaret singer started singing *Granada*. Muriel suddenly said, 'Ah! Meine musica!' and she started singing along. Then she stood up and, still singing, she advanced towards the stage until she'd got on it and was uproariously singing alongside the club's singer, who didn't know where to put herself. She made such a spectacle of herself – the diners' reaction was a mixture of amazement and amusement. I was laughing but Barry looked at me with the wryest expression I've ever seen and said, 'This would be hilarious if that wasn't my mother.'

The morning afterwards Muriel woke up and said she had morning sickness (she usually had a hangover, often with sickness), and said she was going to have a baby. She started saying, 'Bambino para mi'. Barry was furious and said, 'Don't be so ridiculous! You're nothing but a drunk!'

It was just another delusion but it was the last straw for Barry – he demanded his passport and made her buy him a ticket to fly back to England that day.

She was upset after Barry had left; she drank even more than usual and that's when it all went wrong. That evening we'd been out and I'd drunk a lot more than I should have. When I went to bed, after about an hour she came into my room and got in bed with me; needless to say, one thing led to another.

In the sober light of the morning after, I was concerned what it would look like if it got back to Geoff. I decided to speak to Muriel about it but I didn't know where to begin. I said, 'I'm a bit worried about last night...'

She said, 'You don't need to be – everything will be fine.'

It wasn't until some years later when I was in Japan with Jim Hussey that I learned the foundation of her confidence. We were out one evening and the conversation wound its way round to wrestling; I wondered what it was like in Manchester when Geoff had gone into partnership with Arthur Wright. I recalled how Geoff had asked Arthur to Wheelock to arrange my entry into wrestling and I wondered if it was because he still had some interest in the promotions. I was surprised at what came next.

Jim said, 'They weren't just partners in Wryton – they lived together. You do know Arthur's a puff, don't you?'

'Yeah, I'd heard,' I said.

Jim said, 'Arthur was beside himself when Geoff was called up to the army for WWII; he was in tears for weeks. And he gave him the money to start his garage.'

I then knew why Muriel hadn't been worried about any indiscretion with me and could deal with anything Geoff threw at her.

But at twenty-one I'd been thrown into this head-spinning dynamic and I could barely believe what was happening to me. From starting off just helping out at Geoff's garage I'd ended up trapped in Mallorca – I couldn't leave because she kept my passport locked away.

What had started as a lot of fun had become a nightmare and I was now desperate to escape. I began telling her that I needed my passport and I wanted to get home. She protested that she was ill and needed someone there, but after about seven days she finally gave me back my passport and arranged my trip home.

As soon as I got back, Geoff asked me what had been going on in Mallorca. Barry had told him about the drinking, her buying the ski school, the singing in the nightclub, and about her wanting to buy the Americans' flat. He asked me if all that was right, and I said it was. Geoff said he was going over there immediately; he said, 'No More! There's no more money going over there!'

Then he asked me if anything else had gone on. I didn't answer – how could I? I had enough sense to know that telling him was unlikely to do me any favours, so I played it down. He didn't pursue it at that point but I knew it wasn't over.

Two or three days later Geoff went to Mallorca to '...sort it out...' and he was gone for at least three weeks; he came back with a tan and behaved as if everything was normal. Not long after that he began seeing Ruby, a wealthy woman who co-owned the Liverpool Road pottery. I met her when we called in one night coming back from Hanley where Geoff had been wrestling; her house in Alsager was even bigger than Geoff's in Wheelock – the door was answered by a maid.

Muriel returned to Wheelock three or four times over the next few months, but only very briefly – she said her leg ached in England but was better in Mallorca. Then she went to Australia for a visit and that's when Geoff made his move. He began again trying to drag details out of me about Mallorca; I'd been very reluctant to talk about it but I said she'd got into bed with me. He asked what happened then and I said just a bit of cuddling – I supposed she was lonely. He persisted and got me to admit that it had gone further. He had me say the same things to his lawyer, who took a statement.

Eventually Geoff and Muriel got divorced. It was relatively amicable and she ended up with all the property in Mallorca, but while she'd been in Australia she'd given Barry power of attorney and he'd sold one of the apartments for £12,000. He and I went to Scotland to collect the money and then we drove straight to London so he could buy a car he'd seen – a dark metallic blue Pontiac Parisienne convertible with a white hood and interior; it was stunning.

When Muriel found out about the apartment being sold she came back to England and was aghast. She came to my father's house with her brother to attempt to claim the Pontiac but I explained that it now belonged to me. She said, 'I thought I had a friend, but I haven't.' She had effectively been cut off. Geoff later married Ruby, who was a complete contrast to Muriel – they got on a lot better.

Then things calmed down and it was back to a more normal insanity!

Geoff knew a motor trader called Charlie Leek in The Wirral. Charlie wasn't a young man, but in his youth he'd been a professional boxer and he thought – with some justification – that he was a hard man. He was apparently a millionaire, which really meant something in 1960s when you could get a house for a thousand pounds.

We used to go over to Charlie's because Geoff did deals with him for cars, jewelry, and gold coins. His house was huge; when you first went to see him he'd show you around, but he didn't bother sitting in the main rooms – he spent all his time in the kitchen, which meant that you did too. The kitchen was big, and when I say big, I mean it was enormous – it must have been thirty feet square.

One night we went over there quite late and the subject wound its way round to wrestling, as it often did. I believe Charlie had said to Geoff a few times that he'd like to give it a go. Geoff did the same thing with Charlie as he'd done with the scrap man.

He said, 'Charlie, if you want to have a go, why don't you try with Pete?'

Charlie was game, but he didn't have a clue what he was getting into.

We shoved the table to one side, and he brought a carpet from another part of the house.

Geoff said to Charlie, 'We don't want you to be thrown on the floor or anything like that. Why don't you let him show you what it's like when you're already on the floor?'

'Go on, then,' replied Charlie, 'Show me a few holds.'

Charlie got down and we had a similar performance to the scrap man. I shoved him around a bit and pushed him backwards and forwards, but I didn't try too hard because he wasn't as young or as supple as the scrap man – I'd have broken half a dozen bones if I had.

Eventually he'd had enough – I let him up. When I did, Charlie had a huge mat-burn across the side of his face where I'd shoved him along the carpet and his elbows were a bit raw as well. He was a hard old bastard, though. He said, 'Bloody hell, Geoff, he's good, isn't he?' We pushed the table back and Geoff and Charlie carried on doing their deals into the night.

When we got back to Geoff's place, he said, 'How many people have had that much entertainment in one night? We've visited a millionaire, we've bought a few cars from him, we've had a steak dinner with him and his wife, and you've had him on the floor and scuffed all his face and elbows. How many people can claim that for a night's entertainment?' It had indeed been a fascinating evening.

Now that I'd demonstrated ground work for a second time I saw why Barry was so hungry to learn. However successful and admired The Count was, he couldn't show Barry what he wanted to learn. Geoff would have had to deflect any such enquiries from Barry, which must have seemed like a dismissal, and that would only have created distance between them.

My relationship with Geoff continued to develop, and we did more and more together. He was much more interested in me than my father was, and he became a mentor in the truest sense of the word. As soon as he knew he could trust me, he included me in his world – he began giving me access to cars on a 'sale-or-return' basis. He'd tell me how much he wanted for a car, he'd let me take it away and sell it for whatever I could get, give him what was agreed, and keep the rest – but, if I brought it back, I'd owe him a fee. He also made me a named driver on his motor traders' insurance, and I found myself driving everything from MGBs to Rolls Royces, Bentleys, and Mercedes Benzes, even a 300SL, the original 'gull-wing' door car, now almost priceless. These experiences reinforced my taste for the good life, as well as my determination to achieve it. I can't remember ever taking a car back to him, except the 300SL.

This was to give me a wonderful opportunity for sweet revenge. I had one of Geoff's Rollses on sale-or-return, which effectively made it mine, and I was having it filled-up with petrol at the garage. Across the aisle I recognised my form master from my old school, Jack Perry, who was having petrol put into a Ford Consul. He did a double-take when he saw me, and when recognition dawned, he looked from me to the Rolls and back and said, 'You've done well for yourself, haven't you?'

I looked him in the eye and said, 'Yes – haven't I just?' That was all we said to each other; when the car was full I got in and disappeared off the forecourt, leaving him fumbling for change. What a great reversal of fortunes – 'cork-head' was clearly doing far better than Jack Perry.

When I went to my last weight lifting championship, Geoff lent me a brand new Mk10 Jaguar to go to Southampton in, and I later got the car I drove to all Kendo's early matches from him – it was the classic '60s villain's car, a Jaguar MkII. Mine had a 2.4 litre engine but it was badged as a 3.8 so it looked like the more expensive version, but I liked the smaller engine because it cost less to run; it was good to look stylish, but do so frugally – my Aunt would have approved!

Geoff's wheeler-dealing sometimes brought him to the attention of the police, a fine example of which was Keith Martinelli's brandy. Keith was a wrestler from Bolton and a friend of Billy Howes. He was part of a gang that broke into a warehouse and stole, I believe, a whole truck-load of alcohol. Keith, not being very wise, decided to take some of the stolen booze to wrestling shows to sell. At one of them he brought in a box and plonked it on the table and said, 'Does anyone want any of these?' In the box were six bottles of brandy.

I bought three bottles, and The Count took Keith on one side and asked him how much he had. He replied, 'How much do you want?'

The Count said, 'Six boxes.'

Keith said he had that much in his car.

Being a man of means and a wheeler-dealer, The Count said he'd take them all.

About three days later at mid-day-ish, two plain clothes policemen arrived at my house. They asked if they could come in and talk to me. They did and said they'd received information that I'd bought some bottles of brandy from a wrestling show. Before I had a chance to answer, one of them looked around and saw one of the bottles that I'd given to my mother. She'd opened it and drunk some. The policeman said, 'There's one there.'

I said, 'Oh, you mean them?'

He said, 'Yes – how many have you got?'

I said, 'Three.'

They told me I'd have to go to the station and speak to them. They took all the bottles.

At the station they said they knew who had stolen the brandy. Then one of them asked, 'What about this Count Bartelli character – did he have any?'

I said, 'I don't know.'

He said, 'Come on, we know you're very close to him.'

I said, 'I just know him as a car trader.'

He said, 'No, there's more to it than that – we know he's one of the biggest fences in the area.'

I said, 'I don't know if he's got any'. They kept me for two hours then let me go.

When I got home I phoned Geoff and asked him if I could meet him somewhere. He said to go to one of the warehouses behind the Lion and Swan. When I got there he asked me what it was about, and I told him what had happened.

He panicked. He had his in a car boot at Wheelock so he had someone drive it to Calveley and we met him there and hid it. I believe that within two days it was on its way to Liverpool.

I eventually heard from the police that I would be questioned again in Manchester. I went there and was interviewed by a high-ranking officer. He said, 'We know who's done it, they've robbed a warehouse and they've taken hundreds of pounds worth of alcohol. The three bottles you bought were for your own personal use, weren't they?'

I saw the cue and said, 'Yes, they were just for my personal use.'

He said, 'My advice to you is not to do anything like this again – if you're suspicious about something, don't buy it. This is the last you'll hear about this matter, unless you do it again, in which case it could come up.'

Geoff never heard anything from the police. He was offended at being called a 'fence', and he was more careful over how and where he bought and sold things from then on.

I can only assume that because I'd bought my bottles in the dressing room and Geoff had got his in the car park, the person who'd told the police had been in the dressing room. Keith got sent to prison for a long time.

Geoff had shown me many interesting and educational things and I was very happy with how my life was unfolding. I was certainly busy, with work, weightlifting, judo, and now feeling like a welcome and useful addition to Geoff, who was showing me a lifestyle that I'd otherwise never have seen. Aunt Ida had introduced me to the 'good life', but Geoff's was another level up, and one that I not only wanted to be involved with, but which was now actively drawing me in.

Chapter 8

Onwards and Upwards

In mid-1961, Jim and I went to Grange Farm in London, where Abbe was holding a big judo course. Almost as soon as we arrived, I was befriended by a man called Eddie. He was about five or six years older than me, and he was graded brown belt. I remember him as being something to do with the military, the Commandos or possibly the SAS.

Grange Farm resembled an Army Barracks. We all slept in bunks in big rooms and drifted into the wash area to clean up. One morning I was brushing my teeth and Eddie told me about brushing your tongue. He'd been in the Middle East in the forces, and the Arabs had taught him that you had to clean your tongue in a morning. I'd never done that before but he told me it was necessary because of the bacteria that built up overnight, and brushing your teeth wasn't enough. I started doing it, and to this day still do.

Jim and most of the others used to go out to the pub at night and partake of a drink or two. I wasn't interested in going to pubs, and there were a few on the course who weren't old enough, so Eddie and I stayed behind with them, talking.

On reflection, I have a feeling that Eddie had been infiltrated into this course for the BJA to find out what was happening regarding the rumours of a new shining light, a serious up-and-coming contender – me. People had begun talking about me because I was beating opponents that I shouldn't have been able to at my grade. I remember Otani, the sensei who'd co-founded the BJC with Abbe, coming to Alsager to teach a course, and he brought his son with him, Robin, who was about my age and a black belt. I was only a blue belt, but I beat him, which impressed Otani senior. When that kind of thing happens, the word spreads. Now, as a brown belt, I was beating second Dans, so my reputation was growing and spreading, and sensei Abbe was taking ever-more notice of me.

During the week, Eddie asked me if I'd like to go with him on the Friday evening to a major judo club in Central London called the Renshidan, to practise. He explained to me that it was a high-calibre club which was attended by all the BJA people who were training to enter international events. I liked the idea, so we agreed to catch the train as soon as the course finished on the Friday.

Friday was the day on which we would be graded, followed on the Saturday by the presentation of certificates. Although there were perhaps a hundred people on this week-long course, not all of them were going for higher grades, but I was among those who were. The lower grades were examined first, followed by the higher grades, and after grading there would be a 'line-up', where the students would face a higher grade.

Abbe's personal student, Brian Mole, took a line-up; he was the judoka I should have faced earlier for the North West Area Championship, but he was absent and I'd won. However, he was here now, and was expected to beat everybody else. He did so for everybody before me in the line-up, and I looked like a foregone conclusion too –

I was still only a brown belt, but he was a second or third Dan.

As we got into it, Mole tried to do a move called 'Hari Goshi', a sweeping loin (now known as a sweeping hip throw). It's a common throw, but Abbe had shown us a special counter to it, known as a 'Transition Loin'; the counter isn't easy, because it requires a lot of strength or a higher level of skill and experience, but my weight lifting stood me in good stead. Abbe's counter transitions the opponent's attack into an offensive move on them; it was Kyu Shin Do in action.

Mole came in and I blocked him, then I took him straight into the air – about as high as you can – before bringing him back down with a crash, right in the middle of the mat.

Abbe jumped up and shouted, 'Ippon!', which means 'win'. Everybody was shocked – what had happened? Nobody on the course was expected to beat Brian Mole – but I had. He was completely startled and well aware that it shouldn't have happened. I was elated but I'd known what I was doing. Abbe had definitely taken notice of me now.

The day wound down and Eddie and I quickly got ready for our trip to the Renshidan, which was in Marylebone in central London – we caught the train. At the time the club had another visiting Japanese instructor called Watanabe who was a fifth or sixth Dan.

The Renshidan applied the rules of the BJA, which meant that if you had a grade from the BJC you had to drop a grade when you went there. Abbe had no such requirements of them, but as a BJC brown belt I had to drop a grade to a blue belt in order to practise on the Renshidan mat.

Watanabe took the class before putting us into a practice situation (Randori), where we were paired up. I started with Eddie, and then we went on to different partners. Because I was a blue belt I was coupled with other blue belts or higher, and I beat them all.

By the time I'd gone through a few of them everybody was discreetly taking notice. One of the top British judokas at the time was there, a Scot called George Kerr. When I'd had the chance I'd studied what he'd been doing. He had a very interesting move where he would go to one side apparently to throw you, but then he'd skip back, taking you the other way, catching you off-balance and throwing you. I watched him do it a couple of times and thought, 'He'll try that on me – but it won't work.' I'd worked out how to counter his special move.

Kerr watched me very closely, but he kept well away from me. I wasn't allowed to approach him to practise because I wasn't a high enough grade – he, the higher grade, had to approach me – that was the protocol; I was surprised and a little disappointed that he never did.

At the end of the night, Watanabe decided that we'd all do sumo wrestling. We put our belts in a circle on the mat and did a knockout sumo competition, where the winner stayed in the circle if he managed to push his opponent out, then someone else would enter to challenge him. We'd taken off our judo jackets but kept the trousers on.

The lower grades would begin and the contest would build up to a final against George Kerr, who'd be the last to go in because he was one of the highest grades. Watanabe didn't take part, but everyone else did. I was somewhere towards the middle because I'd been demoted to a blue belt. I beat opponent after opponent and ended up going all the way through to the final, where I faced George Kerr. I chucked him out too, so although I didn't meet him on the judo mat, I'd met him in the sumo circle, and at least I beat him there.

Eddie and I went back to Grange Farm early. Some of the lads were still at the pub, and we were alarmed to find that the younger ones who'd stayed there had been slapped-around by a gang of local yobs who'd wandered in. They'd moved on to somewhere else on the site, and Eddie said, 'Let's go and see if they're still here...' We found them, and duffed-up four or five of them before they gave up and fled. They were no match for me, and Eddie handled himself well too, knocking several of them down very quickly.

Word spread like wildfire about that incident, and with Eddie telling everybody how I'd chucked everyone out of the sumo ring at the Renshidan, I was getting quite a reputation.

On the Saturday morning, Abbe presented everybody who'd been graded with their certificate. I was last, and was very pleased to find that I'd been graded First Dan – a black belt. This was genuinely a special accolade, because technically, I hadn't been training long enough to be awarded First Dan – beating Mole must have helped Abbe's decision!

However, when it came time for me to receive my certificate, instead of one of the printed ones that everyone else received, for me Abbe produced a much bigger certificate which he'd hand-written in Japanese calligraphy. At the time, I didn't appreciate the magnitude of this gesture – I actually wanted one of the printed ones like everyone else had! It was only later that I came to realise that him doing this personally for me was a great honour; I still have that very certificate, framed, next to my desk. Likewise, what he said when he presented it to me still makes me very emotional to this day – 'For very special student,' and, handing me the certificate, 'I do myself.' The passing years have only deepened my appreciation of what an honour this was.

My reputation began to affect how I was regarded. There was one occasion when I arrived at a judo club and there were about four pairs practising. By the time I'd got changed, they were all seated, because the last thing they wanted was to meet me on the mats! I was asked not to come back to the club, to avoid wrecking the attendance of their membership.

I went on to win the BJC National Heavyweight Championship for 1961-2, the first time ever they had run these championships, so I was their first ever Heavyweight Champion. Following this, Abbe said he wanted me to move to London where he would train me. All he said was, 'Necessary, come to London.'

However, he didn't suggest how I would survive in London. Most of the people he dealt with lived in London, but I still lived in Crewe and still worked at Jennings. Abbe's attitude was very much that of an Eastern master expecting his pupil to drop everything to follow him and 'learn the ways', which just wasn't practical for me, so I stayed in Crewe.

At the same time I'd been going to the British Railway gym, and had become quite good at Olympic weightlifting. It hadn't taken me long to be able to lift much greater weights than the others at the gym could, and now I could press 360lbs above my head. They were all aghast, especially Roy, the guy who ran it – he'd been doing it for about twenty years and he could only press about 250lbs.

Roy told me about how competitions in weight lifting were run. The British Amateur Weight Lifters Association (BAWLA) was the body that sent weightlifters to international competitions, and most of their major tournaments were held in the south. There were no motorways then and car ownership wasn't wide-spread, so people from the north didn't go to the south as often as they do today.

In response to this, a new weightlifting organization was created, The Society of Amateur Weightlifters (SAWL), encompassing mainly the northern half of England. SAWL had their own competitions and their own titles, and I joined because Roy and the others were already members – some were members of both organizations.

Roy told me about a SAWL competition. He said, 'It's in Manchester. We'll put you in as a heavyweight as they're a bit thin on the ground, and we need a heavyweight – why don't you come?'

'Do you think so?' I asked. 'Will I do any good?'

'Course you will – you'll be fine. Come on – it'll be good experience.'

I didn't really want to – I was reluctant to have weightlifting get in the way of judo, which was my priority, but fortunately it never did.

In the end, six of us went. Rather than take two cars to the weightlifting club in Altrincham, they said, 'We'll go in your van...'

It was the first time I'd ever been in a weightlifting competition. There were three other heavyweights, but I scored the highest total and won. The lads were all very pleased, particularly Roy, and he encouraged me to keep at it.

I'll never forget the journey back – it was middle of winter, November or December. It had started to snow while we were there, and on the way back with everyone in the van, it handled well, but when they all got out around Crewe, there wasn't enough weight to maintain traction, and several times I almost lost control of the bloody thing. It was like trying to drive a bob-sleigh home!

After entering and winning several local weightlifting competitions for SAWL, it came to the nationals, which I think were held in Birmingham; having trained me throughout, Roy was delighted when I become the heavyweight champion. At the same time, Dave Prowse, who played Darth Vader in *Star Wars* and was the *Green Cross Code* man on TV, became the heavyweight champion for BAWLA.

I went back for the SAWL championships the following year, which was held in Southampton. I won it again, which made me the Society of Amateur Weightlifters British Olympic Champion, Heavyweight Class, 1962/63.

How things had changed... Despite my early difficulties, by focussing on judo and meditating as Abbe had instructed me, I was finding a sense of identity and purpose, and I finally began to have a sense of self-confidence. My success with weight-lifting was also a huge confidence-boost.

Abbe had mentioned that we should live our lives outside the dojo by the same principles that applied inside it, including always being calm, aware, ready for anything, and always honourably. He called this 'Bushido', the way of the warrior, and it really appealed to me.

In addition to judo and aikido, I'd studied kendo under Abbe, and I'd taken to it quickly. Kendo is the modern interpretation of the sword skills of the samurai, as formalised by none other than Miyamoto Musashi, the samurai who wrote *A Book of Five Rings*. As with judo, there are strict rules about how the sport is conducted, including where to strike an opponent with the bamboo 'sword' (the shinai), to the 'spirit' shown while competing. Also like judo, there are formal 'katas', which are set forms of movement, and these must be mastered just as well as the ability to win. Once again, it was an example of the range of discipline, skill, and focus that's required to succeed in a Japanese martial art, and I took to it like a duck to water.

Abbe occasionally brought a samurai sword to the dojo to demonstrate kendo moves, and every time I saw it, I felt a growing connection with everything samurai. I even found a singing bowl to use at the start and end of my meditations, as Abbe used in his Buddhist home altar, his 'Butsudan'. I began feeling that if the rituals were performed with absolute focus, they acted like another form of meditation, and all this felt completely right and positive to some unconscious part of myself.

From then on, after every session of Zazen seated meditation, I began to feel a connection with something that could only be described as other-worldly. Abbe seemed to know that I was on some kind of journey, and perhaps he had an idea where I was heading, but he never said or did anything, other than say that the answers would come from my meditations.

Coming out of meditation one day, with my mind completely still, I found that two things were in my mind's eye – the first was an image of the kendo helmet, and the second was a word, 'Nagasaki'. I didn't understand what they meant, but I knew they were somehow important; they were eventually in my mind after every meditation.

As they were always together, I began to feel that the image of the kendo helmet grill represented a state of mind that I came to think of as 'Nagasaki'. As it was outside of any conscious thought, I reasoned that it had to be the intuitive self that Abbe said I had. It seemed at its clearest during judo, wordlessly guiding me to exactly the right action. I could make no more sense of it than that, but whatever it was, the clearer it became, the more I found it helped me.

More and more, I felt the need to meditate before I competed; it put me in a very focussed state of mind, which remained until I'd finished what I was doing. I was reminded of a persona which had terrified me as a child – the powerful robot known as 'Gort', in the movie, *The Day The Earth Stood Still*. Gort was dispassionate, all-seeing, and devastatingly effective; this is how I felt I was becoming.

The rewards for all my work were clear to see. My life now seemed to have turned completely away from the bleakness and confusion of my childhood – I was heading towards the Olympics, to which I was looking forward and which I was sure I could master – it almost seemed destined. I was very much at peace with the way my life was moving onwards and upwards, on every level.

Chapter 9

My Hand is Forced

I woke up in a hospital bed, feeling like death. There was a drip in my right arm, my left hand was thick with bandages, and it was being held up in the air by a cord going over pulleys – what the hell had happened?

I had, in fact, damn near died – from septicaemia.

A week earlier, the end of my left index finger had been partially severed. The doctors had re-attached it and patched it up, but, despite my considerable fitness and constitution, it had become infected with a particularly nasty bacterium which had spread and ravaged my entire body – I'd collapsed while waiting for a follow-up appointment. Once the infection had reached that stage, they'd had to amputate the original injury and some more of the finger too, just above the middle knuckle. The septicaemia had really knocked me about – I would be kept in hospital for over a month.

As the dressings were changed and I got to see my left hand, I found it hard to accept the way it looked; obviously, the function of my whole hand was now compromised, but it was ugly too. Hands are virtually always on show, and I hated the idea of people catching sight of this short finger – I wasn't a vain person, but I didn't want people to regard me as incomplete; I certainly felt that way.

The practical aspects were daunting. Without the whole of my left index finger, I would no longer be able to grip a judo opponent's jacket properly, which meant that being competitive at the top level was no longer possible – my Olympic hopes were now gone. I was as disappointed for Abbe's dashed hopes as I was for my own. Furthermore, I would not be able to grip a weights bar as securely, so that would restrict the amount of weight I could lift, and how well I could hold a bar while snatching it. I therefore had to face the fact that my ascendancy in both these fields was at an end. It was actually worse than that – I wouldn't be as good as I was before.

Of course, all amputees have to deal with reduced abilities and having their previous wholeness replaced with an unnatural, diminished ugliness; to me, it felt like grieving, but worse – I would never be able to regain what I'd lost, nor escape from the lessened version of myself that I now had. I couldn't imagine a future like this and under these circumstances, and I sank into depression.

Finally, I was discharged from hospital. I'd lost a lot of weight and felt very weak, and the end of my severed finger was incredibly sensitive – the slightest touch sent white-hot pains searing up my arm – the bit of finger that was left was therefore worse than useless, it was a liability. A doctor had told me that I should try to use it as much as possible, and it would gradually lose this initial sensitivity; it made sense, but every time the pain stabbed at me, I found it very hard to believe.

I hadn't been back to work, and as there was nothing to do at home, I gravitated towards Geoff's place. There were plenty of cars to sell and driving jobs, but I remained generally withdrawn and aimless.

Eventually, Geoff began to come up with ideas for bringing me out of myself. For many years, the Royal National Lifeboat Institution (RNLI) had raised funds by asking people to put their spare pennies onto a lighthouse-shaped stack. When it got to a certain height and resembled a complete lighthouse, a celebrity would be invited to push it over, and all the pennies would be collected-up and cashed-in at a bank for the RNLI. Geoff had been invited to do one such event, but at the last minute, he claimed he had another urgent appointment, and told them he had a weightlifting and judo champion who could do it. They agreed, and along I went, armed with my impressive weightlifting shield.

I was surprised at how good it made me feel. I shoved over a four-foot-high pile of big old imperial pennies – it must have weighed half a ton and it made a huge crash, but when I'd done it everyone in the pub cheered and applauded, and a light went on inside me. I was an achiever again, and it had been appreciated – it was a small start, but it felt good.

Ever the realist, Geoff was well aware that I'd been overwhelmed by my reversals, and he gently began steering me towards being pragmatic about things. He said, 'Your previous plans are not going to come to fruition – you've gone as far as you can with them. You're not going to go to the Olympic Games, and weightlifting will be much more difficult. It's now time to consider capitalizing on your experience, and doing something that will make you some money.' It was common sense, but I'd been stuck in a fog of bewilderment and indecision; gradually, his words got through, and I began thinking...

My old man had always felt strongly that I should do my apprenticeship – he'd really sold it to me, saying, 'You'll always have your trade, you'll always have work and money.' This had made sense when I was fifteen, but after I'd met Geoff and began selling cars my perspective completely changed. I could sell one car and make as much as a whole week of work for Jennings, and I could do that whenever I wanted. I'd actually begun thinking that I should leave Jennings, but I'd resisted the idea out of loyalty to my father's vision for me, although I had begun to skip the odd day – perhaps a part of me wanted to be sacked from Jennings.

I'd finished my apprenticeship and was on my own at what had been Alistair's and my bench. He'd left a few months back and they were talking about giving me a lad to assist me. I lost the finger within days of my twenty-first birthday and I'd effectively become a full-fledged tradesman, but ever since seeing everything that Geoff and Ida had, I'd wanted more from life than Jennings could ever give me. I was now selling cars on a regular basis and it was sufficiently profitable for me to begin making plans to leave Jennings; I'd only hung on there because I wasn't quite ready to make that move.

I'd accepted that judo and weightlifting weren't earners themselves either – Geoff said to me, 'It's all very well winning lots of medals, but you can't take them to the butcher's shop and swap them for meat, can you?' It made complete sense – I knew I'd have to come to some decision over what to do with my life and how to make my own way.

After a couple of months, I'd begun to accept my changed circumstances and I started really thinking rationally. Geoff said that the best thing I could do was to take my previous experience and put it towards learning how to wrestle. By this time the idea felt less like a betrayal of my previous goals, although from what I'd seen of wrestling, it wasn't in the same league as judo. However, there was no denying that it had served Geoff very well.

There was another aspect that appealed to me. Ever since I'd first gone to wrestling matches I'd been impressed that the audiences were so passionate and so big. This was in complete contrast to judo or weightlifting, which only had small audiences and the competitions themselves were comparatively rare; most of the time in those sports you battled away in a gym, with no audience at all. Every wrestling match was a well-attended and exciting event, and every time I went to one I wanted more and more to be a part of it all.

On one occasion I'd been on a judo course in Burslem, and when it finished Jim and another judoka called Bill Reeves asked me if I'd like to go for a drink. Without thinking, I said I already had plans to go and see The Count wrestle at Hanley, and they asked if they could come too. Geoff was wary of letting people into his world, but I said I'd phone him and ask, and he agreed. Geoff said that would be fine and that he'd put our names on the guest list; he also suggested that we meet-up at his house afterwards. I had a key because I was trusted with access there, in connection with the car jobs I was doing for him.

We arrived about an hour before Geoff got back, and Jim and Bill were astounded at how luxurious the house was; after only a few minutes, looking around in wonderment, Bill said, 'If this is how well you can do from wrestling, forget judo!' I'd known for a while there was even more to it than what they could see – Muriel's excesses must have cost Geoff an absolute fortune, and while he complained, he never did anything about it.

It was a dilemma for me; I profoundly respected Abbe's skills as they represented true excellence in judo, and I'd wanted to follow in his footsteps and continue to refine my own abilities, and perhaps eventually teach Kyu Shin Do. Competing at Olympic level may now be out, but that didn't mean I couldn't progress in judo. However, Abbe lived in someone else's house and had no possessions to speak of; regardless of his personal achievements and great ability, his life was virtually that of a monk, and I wanted more than that for myself.

However, could I ever respect the 'skill' of professional wrestling? I'd seen that many holds couldn't actually hold you, and that while others were real holds, they weren't fully applied. It was always an impressive show, but wrestling seemed to require much less actual combat ability than judo, and I was concerned that in contrast to that level of expertise, I'd be selling myself short, so-to-speak. It was a lot to weight up, but ultimately I reasoned that I had more to gain than to lose from wrestling.

Geoff told me that he knew Billy Riley, who was probably the best wrestling coach around; Riley ran his own gym in Wigan, and I could go there to train. Geoff said he'd call him, and see what he could set up. I made the commitment to try it, and it felt good to have an objective again.

I was still weak from the septicaemia and the inactivity of recovery, but I resumed running and weight lifting again to get my fitness back. My finger was still unpleasantly sensitive, but the doctors had been right – it was diminishing, and I worked at it by constantly knocking the end into the palm of my other hand to progressively de-sensitive it more and more.

The one thing I hadn't done up to this point was meditate. I couldn't bring myself to – it was part of a life that was now compromised and which it seemed I'd be leaving, but finally, I shut out my regrets and sat in Zazen. I wasn't sure what to expect; I'd previously done it as part of my self-refinement in judo, and I wasn't sure it could help me outside of that goal, but I was pleasantly surprised.

Coming back to consciousness with a fresh and objective view of my circumstances, my new path felt entirely right. Perhaps I should have tried it sooner, but perhaps I'd needed a direction first; I was reassured by the fact that the image of the kendo mask was still there, as well as the name, 'Nagasaki'. It seemed that even though the judo door was closing, those influences would continue with me in my new direction.

My original interest in wrestling had now developed into my most promising-looking choice for a career – it hadn't been a decision I'd ever planned on making, but in the most literal way possible, my hand had been forced.

The marriage in September 1896 of John James Thornley to Margaret Gibson. His mother (on his right) was from the Edwards family that claimed to co-own Manhattan. She assured everyone that his gambling couldn't possibly impact their 'fortune' - it didn't work out that way...

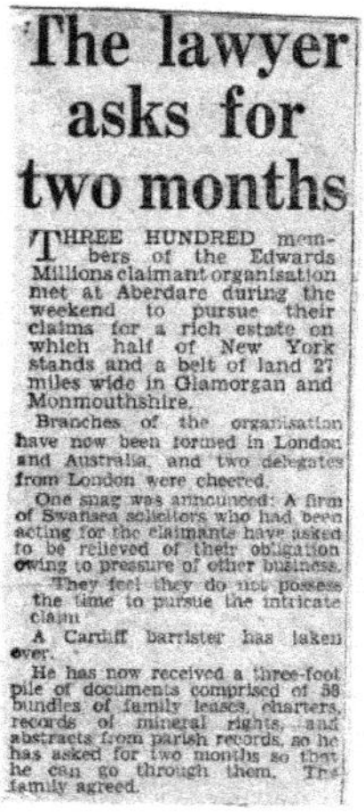

The lawyer asks for two months

THREE HUNDRED members of the Edwards Millions claimant organisation met at Aberdare during the weekend to pursue their claims for a rich estate on which half of New York stands and a belt of land 27 miles wide in Glamorgan and Monmouthshire.

Branches of the organisation have now been formed in London and Australia, and two delegates from London were cheered.

One snag was announced: A firm of Swansea solicitors who had been acting for the claimants have asked to be relieved of their obligation owing to pressure of other business.

They feel they do not possess the time to pursue the intricate claim.

A Cardiff barrister has taken over.

He has now received a three-foot pile of documents comprised of 58 bundles of family leases, charters, records of mineral rights, and abstracts from parish records, so he has asked for two months so that he can go through them. The family agreed.

Oh boyo! We own New York

A £20 BILLION fortune is being claimed by the Welsh heirs of a pirate who once owned 77 acres of New York.

If all the 3,290 claimants reap their share, they will get £6 million each.

But they may have to split it with more of their relatives back home in Wales - if they can prove they are descended from 18th century buccaneer Robert Edwards.

Given a licence by the Crown to plunder Spanish galleons loaded with treasure from the New World, Edwards did such a good job he was awarded a parcel of what is now lower Manhattan.

Cleoma Foore, 64-year-old president of the Association of Edwards Heirs, says profits from her ancestor's legacy now total £20 billion.

A Matthews family gathering outside Eaton Lodge, Rugeley. My father was also present, second from the left on the top row, and my Uncle Norman is far left on the bottom row.

The Matthews family business, circa 1912, loaded-up and ready to deliver to markets in Shropshire and Staffordshire.

Above left, my father and mother as a courting couple, and right, his older brother, Arthur, relaxing in the family's smallholding. Below left, Grandma Thornley and my Aunt Ida among the cattle on the smallhonding, and right, Ida, showing their success by owning a car.

Aunt Ida,
enjoying a little music
out by her greenhouse.

Ida in a typically Victorian
formal and posed picture.

Above, Ida as a 'woman of means' - driving at a time when few women did was typical of her. Below left, she's with the car on which I slid down the mudguard! Below right, Ida and Norman.

Two views of my birth-place, Moorfield Girls' Home at Edgmond, near Newport. Above, the staff are dressed in black. It was described as '...a home for girls from the workhouse and very poor homes.'

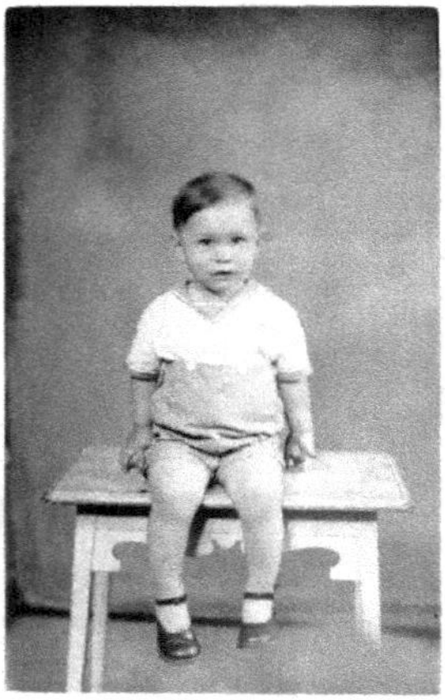

Here I am, as a toddler and with my mother (above), and shortly after she had died (below), with my father. The outdoor shots were taken in Blackpool.

Above, a recent picture of 2 Bowen Cooke Avenue, my childhood home. It used to have a large privet hedge at the front.

Below, Crewe Public Swimming Baths, where my ability with sports first really showed itself.

Above, mid-teens, not long before I would have left school. Below, four of my teachers - the middle pair, Bill Williams on the left and Jack Perry, marched me to the head master for a caning. It was Perry who used to call me 'cork-head'!

Above, me with the Austin A30 and two friends from work, Geoff and Dave. We hadn't yet begun judo.

Below left, Jim Chadwick and me, both brown belts, and me with my first two judo championship awards.

Weightlifters at Birmingham

Left and below left are press cuttings describing successes in weightlifting and judo.
Below is a portrait taken after I'd met Count Bartelli - I was just about to be taken to Mallorca to look after Muriel.

TWO weight-lifters brought honour to Crewe Physical Culture Club with wins in their respective classes in the S.A.W.L. British Olymphic championships at Birmingham.

They are Peter Green (right) of Somerville-street, who won the feather-weight division with a total of 505 lbs. to clinch his second national title in the last three years: and Peter Thornley, of McNeill-avenue, who won at heavyweight with a 700 lbs. total. Thornley's was a remarkable achievement for this is only his second year of competitive weightlifting.

HEAVYWEIGHT JUDO CHAMPION

Peter Thornley, of 14, McNeill-avenue, Crewe, has proved himself successful in the sport of Judo. The

PETER THORNLEY

picture shows Peter, who has been practising Judo for only 20 months, holding the Birkenhead N.W. Areas heavyweight championship trophy and the B.T.C. heavyweight medallion, which he won recently.

Peter, a brown belt holder, can be particularly proud of winning the B.T.C. heavyweight championship in London, for he beat a black belt holder.

Sensei Kenshiro Abbe.

Below, the First Dan judo certificate that Sensei Abbe hand-wrote for me in classical Japanse calligraphy.

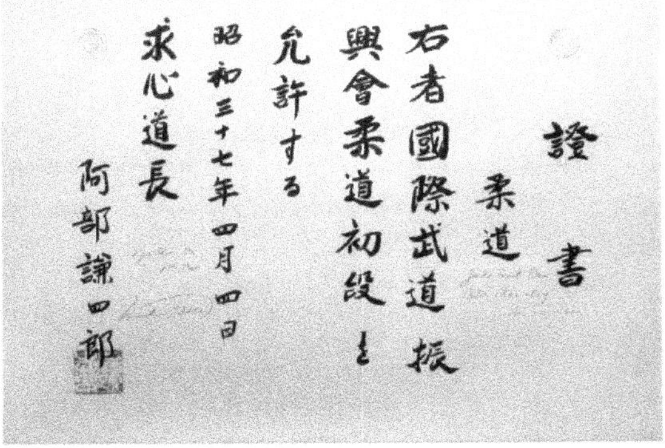

證書

柔道

右者國際武道振
興會柔道初段を
允許する

昭和三十七年四月四日

求心道長
阿部謙四郎

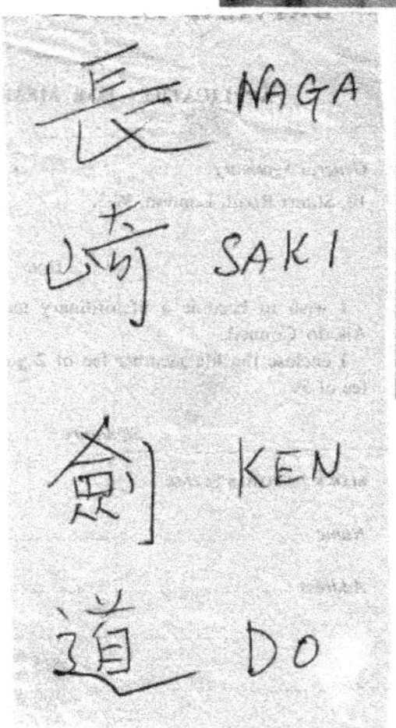

Kendo Nagasaki as he first appeared in the ring, with the original narrow-striped mask.

Left, the piece of paper Sensei Abbe used to show me, in his own hand, how to write the kanji for Kendo Nagasaki. It was written on the back of a membership application for the British Aikido Council.

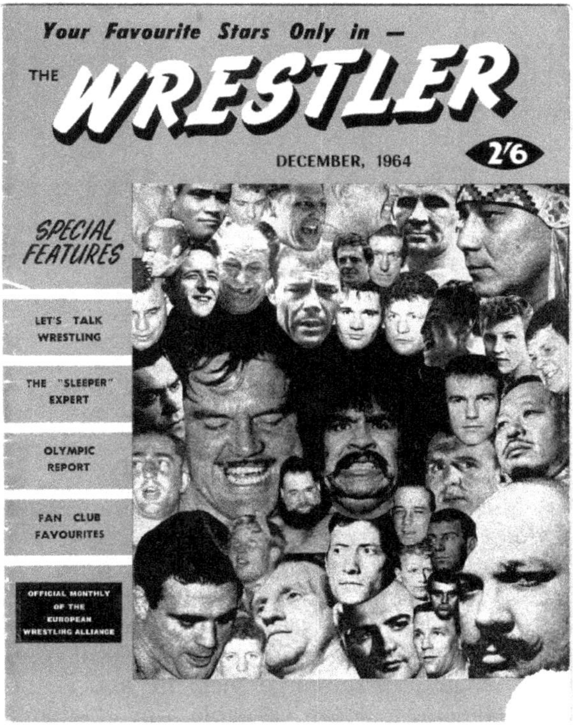

Above, an issue of The Wrestler from the month after Kendo's debut, and below, the promotional feature that appeared in the magazine.

£100 in Golden Sovereigns ★★★★★★

KENDO NAGASAKI

THE 6ft. 1in. 17½st. JUDO EXPERT
FROM JAPAN
OFFERS £100 IN ENGLISH GOLDEN
SOVEREIGNS TO ANYONE WHO
CAN PIN HIM

SUBMISSIONS NOT TO COUNT

Chapter 10

The Snake Pit

Geoff told me that he'd spoken to Billy Riley. I hadn't met him, but I'd seen his son Ernie in the ring as I'd been going round the halls with Geoff; I believe Ernie was the British Middleweight Champion.

Billy had been a wrestler, and a most impressive one. In his home town of Wigan he was originally a moulder, and while still in his teens he decided to train with the local miners at the most popular sport in the area, 'catch-as-catch-can' submission wrestling. He had a natural flair for it, and began going to every possible local contest to see what techniques he could pick up, and he became arguably the most knowledgeable and highly-skilled wrestler in the area. He was notorious for submission holds which could (and sometimes would) break his opponent's fingers, arms, ribs, and even legs, and he won many titles, including a British Empire Championship. He continued wrestling until his late fifties and then decided to promote wrestling shows and teach, opening his gym in Wigan in the 1950s. To use a modern term, it was the undisputed centre of excellence for aspiring wrestlers.

It took about a month before Riley's Gym said they were ready for me. It wasn't until much later that I realised the significance of this delay – I was to discover that normally, new students could just go along, but for some reason they'd made an exception for me...

Geoff said, 'Be there next Monday by eleven o'clock.' He gave me the address and directions.

On Monday morning, I found the street where the gym was supposed to be, but I couldn't see anything that resembled one. Eventually I asked a man walking down the street; he pointed and said, 'There.'

Through a gate, along a gravel path, and in the middle of an allotment I came across a very dilapidated-looking building. It was a wooden structure with a pitched roof, perched on top of three feet of brickwork at its base. The front door needed more than a lick of paint; I opened it and went in.

Inside there was just one person, a lean-looking older man wearing a functional dark suit and a trilby hat – it was Billy Riley himself. On the floor was a rectangular canvas mat about twenty-five feet by twenty, perhaps seven inches deep, with a piece of wood along the front; it went right up to three of the brick walls. Under the canvas was seven inches of sand which, over many years, had become rock hard, like concrete – much harder than tatami or sponge gym mats. The mat was badly stained – it didn't take me long to realise that they must be blood-stains. The floor in front of the mat looked like bare concrete.

To the left side were benches with no backs, two along the wall and a shorter one towards the door, but no chairs.

Over to the right there was a doorway without a door, and a step down to a shower area. It was a very grim little hole, which stank of soap and urine.

At some point in the distant past, the wood inside the building had been painted, but now it resembled an old greenhouse that had been dried out by the sun; some of the paint had fallen off, and the rest was cracked and peeling and barely clinging on. The building appeared to have been very well-used, and generally left alone.

Billy Riley introduced himself and asked me, 'Are you The Count's friend?' I said I was. 'Right,' he said, pointing to a bench, 'Get yourself ready and sit down there.' There was no changing room; you got changed in the same room that you wrestled in, hanging your clothes on hooks along the wall. I'd got myself a pair of wrestling boots, and a proper wrestling leotard, which was like trunks with two shoulder straps.

Riley sat on the end of the bench to the left of the mat; I was to find that he always sat there. He said, 'He'll be along in a minute…', without saying who.

As I was getting changed, the door opened and in walked a man who turned out to be Billy Robinson. At the time I didn't know who he was, but after this day I wouldn't forget him!

The two men struck up a brief conversation; they clearly knew each other well, and I was to learn that Riley had trained Robinson.

Glancing at me, Robinson said, 'Is this him then, Billy?'

Riley nodded.

Robinson said, 'Just a minute, I'll get changed.'

He did so, quickly – everything he did was rushed.

While he was changing, the door opened again and in walked a man called Bob Robinson, who wrestled under the name Billy Joyce. He didn't get changed, but sat down next to Riley and chatted to him; I realised the place was full of people called Billy, except for me.

Robinson finished getting changed and Riley glanced between him and me and said, 'Right. Get on the mat and have a pull-round'. I didn't know what a 'pull-round' was, but I soon found out!

I stepped into the middle of the mat and faced Robinson. It was a matter of seconds before he'd up-ended me and I was down on the mat. He immediately got hold of me and started to maul me around, putting on face-bars and submission holds which were painful and immobilising. When it was clear that I couldn't escape, he let me get up, but he immediately repeated the same procedure. My judo skills were of no help in fending him off – he was only wearing trunks, so there was no judo suit to get hold of, and these moves were completely unfamiliar to me – I was helpless, putty in Robinson's expert hands. Time after time I got back to my feet and he'd instantly out-manoeuvre me and throw me down again, then get behind me for more mauling around; this happened five or six times in succession, and it was exhausting.

Eventually, either Robinson got too carried away or something went wrong. He threw me up in the air and I came crashing down onto the wall. I got several deep scrapes and a cut to my elbow, adding my own contribution to the blood-stained mat. I was pretty shaken up, but no-one else seemed to think it mattered – they expected me to just carry on; I had no choice, so I did.

After a while, Riley said, 'Right Billy – let him get behind you, and let's see if he can turn you over.' Having done judo, I had some idea about how to turn people over, but once again none of my skills were any use against Wigan catch wrestling; almost immediately Robinson was able to turn the tables, and he'd be back behind me, putting on submission holds again.

Eventually, when Robinson had almost completely exhausted me, Riley said, 'Come off the mat and have a rest.' While I sat on the bench and tried to catch my breath, the door opened again and Riley's son Ernie came in. He greeted everybody and changed into his wrestling gear, and he and Robinson then went onto the mat together. That was a real eye-opener because it was completely different to when I was on with him; this time, Robinson was respectful of his opponent and they seemed to work together, whereas he'd just made a fool of me.

They pulled-around for about 20 minutes while I watched their every move, then Robinson said he had to go because he was wrestling that night.

Riley told me to have a shower and get dressed, after which he said, 'Get over here at 11:00 o'clock in two days time and we'll carry on.' I'd got my breath back, but I was completely drained, stretched, and strained practically everywhere, with a cut and some decent scrapes to boot. I'd never experienced anything like it – Robinson had made mince-meat of me, but I was absolutely fascinated by how he'd done it; I had to learn how he did what he did.

The following Wednesday morning I went back to the gym. As I was changing, the door opened and I was expecting to see either Billy Robinson or somebody equally as dynamic walk in, and I wasn't disappointed when a big guy with a ginger beard appeared. He turned out to be Tony Buck, who was the British and Commonwealth Amateur Wrestling Heavyweight Champion.

Buck was a big man, around eighteen-stone, and he looked hard. I found out later that he used to be one of the head bouncers at *The Cavern Club* in Liverpool. As he and I changed, the next person through the door was the man I'd expected – Billy Robinson. I wasn't sure if Buck had ever met Robinson before, but if not, he was in for an enlightening time.

As Robinson was hurriedly changing, Riley said to Buck and myself, 'Get on the mat and have a pull-round.'

Robinson shouted, 'No, no, leave it – wait 'til I'm ready. I'll be there in a minute.' He clearly didn't want Buck or myself to get on the mat without him – I can only assume that he wanted us fresh and lively.

Riley put Buck on with Robinson. He was more of a challenge than I'd been because he was an experienced amateur wrestler, but he hadn't trained in catch wrestling and knew nothing about Robinson's techniques or how to counter them. They spent about twenty or thirty minutes on the mat together, while Riley looked on. Buck never managed to get behind Robinson unless Riley told him to, and then it didn't last long – he was soon out and up.

Then it came to my turn. It was simply a repeat performance of the last time, but without the collision with the wall; for about half an hour, I was thrown around and mauled from one side of the gym to the other. Once again, I was exhausted and stretched and strained, but even more fascinated by the techniques being used on me.

We all came off the mat. I'd certainly had enough, and I'm sure Tony Buck felt the same. Once again, Robinson had to rush off, probably because he had a show somewhere; he jumped in the shower and was changed and gone before we'd even got our breath back.

As Buck and I were leaving, Riley let him go but he called me back and invited me to join him on the bench. He said, 'I know Geoff's sent you here, but what he does is not proper wrestling – it's show wrestling, what the professionals do. That's not what we do here – here, we teach catch wrestling, which is proper wrestling.' This was interesting...

When speaking to me about it, Geoff had only ever referred to 'wrestling', and had never made a distinction between any types – I thought I'd be learning what he did – just 'wrestling' – as I'd seen him do in his matches. Suddenly it was clear to me – I'd experienced such brutality at Riley's because there was no 'show' about it – it was the real thing, a real combat sport. I realised that I'd be learning something serious, with none of the questionable moves and holds I'd seen in Geoff's matches. Riley said, 'Come back next Sunday and I'll show you some wrestling.' You couldn't have kept me away.

I was relieved that I'd survived the initiation and come out of the other side in one piece – and still keen – and that I was going to be brought into the fold with the trainees, rather than be made an example of again. In all fairness, I hadn't been at my best – I was still recovering from septicaemia and had been out of judo for six months, and even though I'd gone back to weight-lifting and running, I was far from fully fit. Billy Robinson was 26 years old and at the top of his game, and I was to learn that 99% of professional wrestlers were scared to death of him. However, I think that even at my best I wouldn't have fared much better against Robinson, especially as he'd been determined to make an example of a judoka trying their hand in his game.

When I arrived on the following Sunday the place had a totally different atmosphere. The lads in there were mainly younger people, about my age, between 21 and 25. I don't think any of them were professional wrestlers, although many of them would make the professional ranks in due course – Alan and Roy Wood were two of my contemporaries that did.

Riley only had two people on the mat at a time. You didn't always start from a standing position – a lot of the time, he would put one person behind the other, because a lot of catch wrestling takes place on the mat. Once there, one behind the other, Riley would run you through moves, show you what you should do, and then he'd reverse the positions and you'd run through it again with your opponent – that was how we learned.

Catch wrestling involves getting a submission on your opponent, either standing or on the mat. Training at Wigan began by learning submissions on the mat, and then learning how to get your opponent down there and putting the submission on. The difference between amateur and catch wrestlers is that amateurs don't want to end up on their backs because they could lose. A catch wrestler doesn't mind going to his, because he can actually come out of it with a submission hold on.

The sessions went on for about three hours, sometimes

more. There would be eight to ten people in the room, two at a time on the mat, with constant advice from Riley (and sometimes he'd demonstrate, getting on the mat and putting on holds himself), and then you'd have a break. He structured it so that everyone had time on the mat, sometimes as much as an hour. There were no winners, but you learned a lot and got a very good work-out!

Riley said I should attend in the evenings as well, and these and Sunday mornings turned out to be the actual sessions where training was given. As I was no longer working at Jennings I made good use of my time and ended up going to Wigan maybe four or five times a week.

Some aspiring wrestlers even found the evening and Sunday classes too much. I recall a well-muscled bodybuilder coming to his first day of training; he thought he knew what wrestling was about and when he went on the mat for a pull-round, he went into the kind of stance you'd see on TV – a pose. He was upended and mauled around time after time, after which he said, 'Man! I've been mis-informed!' We never saw him again. Some never did come back; it was arguably a poor recruiting technique, but it ensured that only the toughest and most determined took up Billy Riley's time.

When I thought about my introduction to Wigan I realised that Geoff had set me up! He must have told Riley about how I'd easily dealt with the scrap man and that I was the British Heavyweight judo champion, so he would have known I wouldn't be a push-over, and maybe even a threat.

So, there was no gentle introduction to training for me – I was chucked-in at the deep end on a morning session. Riley had got the very best 'shooter' in the business to show me how little my judo skills mattered in comparison to Wigan catch wrestling, and they were right – against those skills, I was a lamb to the slaughter. Finally it was clear to me why I'd had to wait so long before I could start at Wigan – they'd had to wait until Billy Robinson had come back from wrestling in Germany and was available to put me through the wringer.

I learned that the Robinson initiation was reserved only for those who already had some skills, but needed to be shown how little they knew in comparison to Billy Riley's techniques. While I was at Wigan I only saw it done with me and Commonwealth Champion Wrestlers Tony Buck and Wally Boothe, who wanted to advance their skills in preparation for selection for the 1964 Olympics.

I also realised that Riley had given me a very important lesson. If I'd just turned up at the regular training sessions, my judo skills would have been enough to keep me out of trouble, and if I'd started and then continued in that way I could have thought I knew it all and got cocky. But, by showing me the vast difference between my judo champion skills and advanced catch wrestling, he'd shown me just how much I had to learn if I wanted to do – as he put it – proper wrestling. Despite everything I'd achieved before, he effectively 'tamed' any arrogance I might have had – he'd properly prepared me to learn.

It turned out that there was a core group of professional and amateur wrestlers who would go along in the mornings, because they would be working in the evenings. They were Billy Robinson, Billy Joyce, Tucker Moore (aka Jack Dempsey) and Ernie Riley, all of whom were Wigan trained, and Tony Buck and Wally Boothe as well. Boothe was also a Cavern Club bouncer and the Light Heavyweight Commonwealth Champion.

I began phoning Billy Riley up to ask him whether he was expecting any of these wrestlers to turn up at the gym the following morning, and if they'd be there I'd go for a pull-round too. It didn't happen every day, sometimes their commitments meant they could manage only once a week, but they went when they could. They were no longer training, that would have been a waste of their time – they were going along mainly for a work-out.

One day, Tony Buck and Wally Boothe were there, and Riley put Buck and myself on the mat. We started from a standing position and were pulling-round, and I threw Buck and got behind him. Riley almost jumped off his bench with excitement, which was rare – clearly a good sign...

After they'd gone he said to me, 'You shouldn't have been able to do that with him. You shouldn't have caught him out.' He went on to tell me where Buck had gone wrong and how I – a newcomer – had managed to get an advantage over an experienced 18-stone champion. Riley's explanation helped clarify what I hadn't been able to see; whatever I'd done, I'd done it automatically, so it seemed that catch wrestling was beginning to come naturally to me.

Soon after this, I found myself being treated differently. Towards the end of one morning's training, Riley put me on the mat with Tucker Moore behind me, and he told him to try to turn me over. After a few attempts, in his broad Wigan accent, Moore said, 'He's too strong for me, Billy!' Riley took him off the mat and I pulled-round with someone else.

After Tucker left and I came off the mat, Riley said to me, 'You know what Tucker's problem is, don't you? He drinks – wine.' I felt that in doing this, Riley was confiding in me, taking me under his wing and giving me what he considered to be sound advice, so that I'd avoid the pitfalls that so many professional wrestlers fell into. He also started calling me 'Peter', rather than just issuing instructions in my direction; I was becoming convinced that Billy Riley had begun to see that I was a cut above the rest – that I had a natural talent that was a bit special.

Soon after that, he tried to encourage me to consider amateur wrestling. He trained in all aspects, from amateur, to catch, to show wrestling. Professional wrestling, which is show, involves moves that look impressive to an audience, and it requires different techniques to catch and amateur wrestling. They had inter-club competitions, and he was telling me that he thought I'd do very well at amateur level.

My actual thoughts on this were something that I don't think Riley would have wanted to hear. I'd already done enough at an amateur level – I'd done judo to a very high level and weight lifting too, but now I needed to earn some money. However, I didn't want to discourage him, so I kept my thoughts to myself and told him I'd think about it.

One aspect of my experience of the morning sessions was particularly interesting, and that was the difference between those I wrestled. Billy Robinson was definitely the toughest; he was arguably the best catch wrestler in the world and extremely strong, but he tended to use more strength than he needed to when putting his opponents into holds – at least, according to Riley. On a few occasions Riley said to him, 'Wrestle him, Billy – stop using strength! Wrestle him properly!'

Robinson would impatiently chime back, 'All right, Billy!', but it rarely made a difference to what he did...

Once when I was wrestling Robinson, it was music to my ears when I heard Riley say to him, 'You wouldn't have beaten him if you hadn't used strength!'

On another occasion I was pulling round with Billy and I saw an opportunity to get him into a submission hold, and as soon as I'd put it on he shouted, 'You bastard!' On hearing this, I let go. We both stood up, and with a furious expression, Robinson put himself right in my face and yelled, 'Never fuckin' let go! Never fuckin' let go!' Robinson wasn't annoyed with me – he was annoyed with himself for letting the hold be put on him, and he wanted to wrestle his way out of it. My letting go had deprived him of that opportunity. Also, he can't have been pleased that this had happened in front of Billy Riley! I believe this incident created a bond between Robinson and myself.

Bob Robinson (Billy Joyce) was a different experience entirely. He had trained Billy Robinson under Riley's supervision, but by the time I got to Wigan he was in his 40s and going there more to keep fit rather than train, so he didn't want to pull round in a rough sort of way. When he went on the mat he'd say, 'Right-oh, no need to get excited!' As a wrestler, he was as smooth as silk, nothing like the forceful Billy Robinson. When Bob got hold of you, it was so subtle that you'd never think it was leading to a hold, but you'd suddenly find yourself in one without realising how it had happened. He was like an Aikido master – smooth and flowing, but devastatingly effective.

After I'd been there for a couple of years, when I pulled around with any of them I was able to hold my own, with the exception of Robinson, which was all credit to Billy Riley and what he'd taught me.

Before I turned professional an inter-club competition came around, and we went over to Yorkshire to a club run by Jack Taylor, former wrestler and trainer and father of wrestler Dave Taylor. I remember that the heavyweight there was called John Cox – 'Mighty John Cox', as he became known in the ring – an ambulance driver from York. He was a good wrestler but when I wrestled him I beat him fairly quickly – later we would work together and we gelled well in the ring and had some really good matches.

Another fellow Wiganer I ended up wrestling professionally was Paul Duval. He was a large black man of about 6'2" and seventeen stone who'd arrived at Wigan after I did. When he went into the wrestling business he knew what he was doing, but he wasn't good at the show side. He was a bit clumsy and other wrestlers found him difficult to work with, so he got a reputation for being stiff and difficult to get a show out of. As a result, he'd get frustrated and stroppy, and he ended up with a bad reputation among wrestlers. However, I could work with him and get a decent show out of him, and all our bouts were good.

Riley's Gym was a baptism of fire for anyone who dared cross its threshold, but those who survived and made the grade emerged equipped with the finest wrestling skills in the world. There's no denying that it was incredibly tough – it gained the nick-name *'The Snake Pit'* for good reason – whatever you thought you knew, however strong you thought you were, that place would render you helpless and in great pain, until you learned what it could teach you. It was a life experience that no up-and-coming wrestler would ever forget, and it certainly sorted the men from the boys.

In many ways, Billy Riley was my second 'sensei', after Abbe. What he taught was similarly specialised and powerful, and head-and-shoulders above virtually all other trainers. As with Abbe, I greatly respected Riley's skills and I felt privileged to learn under his guidance. As time passed, there were fewer and fewer wrestlers who could get the better of me, and yet Billy always seemed to have more to give in continually refining my techniques. I couldn't have dreamed of better trainers in either field.

My confidence was now back. I'd always felt that my successes in sports from boxing, putting the shot, water-polo, judo, weight lifting, aikido, and kendo were leading towards something greater, which was previously becoming an Olympic level judoka. With that taken away, my future had seemed less than bleak – I could see none at all. With the benefit of the Wigan experience I now recognised that professional wrestling was more of a dynamic show than highly-skilled combat, but the success it could bring was most impressive. Not many pro wrestlers had catch wrestling skills, but I now did, which meant that I'd be able to compete with the best, at a high and well-rewarded level.

Having been fortunate enough to have had the privilege of learning from five all-time greats across three generations of the world's best catch wrestlers, including

Billy Riley, Ernie Riley, Billy Joyce, Tucker Moore, and Billy Robinson, I knew I had a future once more, which had been brought about despite (and perhaps even because of) my lost finger – it almost seemed destined.

Chapter 11

Kendo Nagasaki

In early 1964 I began to feel that my life was reaching a plateau where everything was at a high level, and the time would soon arrive to take the next step. I'd been training at Riley's Gym for over a year and was becoming very good at catch wrestling, I'd fully adapted to my shortened left index finger and its sensitivity was almost normal, and my general fitness was as good as it had ever been; I could feel that my debut in professional wrestling was approaching.

However, I wanted it to be very special. I had the skills, but my aim was to bring something never before seen to professional wrestling, something that would lift it to new heights, and somehow, I knew I could.

I'd returned to regular meditating, and was finding it as powerful as I had in judo. It allowed me to feel that all my skills and strengths were fully available at all times, and that when they were needed they could be unleashed precisely, almost automatically – I never needed to feel 'revved-up', and I always just knew exactly what to do and how. Abbe had told me that my intuition would guide me in this way, and while I'd thought this would apply mainly to judo, it now seemed to work with everything I did, but I had begun to feel that I needed something more, so I went to London to see him.

He was as dead-pan as ever, but he welcomed me into his room; it was exactly as I'd last seen it. After the usual greetings we sat down at the table under the window with the bird cage and I told him that I intended to debut as a professional wrestler. I didn't expect him to approve – after all, I'd been his best hope of getting a student from the BJC into the Olympics that year and he still regretted that loss, and he wouldn't respect professional wrestling anyway, as in his eyes, it hardly compared to his precision martial art.

He didn't respond, but he asked me if I was still meditating. I told him I was, and that I still found it very empowering. I believe he sensed that I had a question which I wasn't asking – I'm not sure I knew whether I had any such question or what it might be. He got up and walked over to a table and picked up some papers and brought them over and handed them to me. There was a piece of heavy paper with some Japanese kanji script on it, and several sheets of thin tracing paper. In his usual style he made me understand what I should do with them. They were used in Shakyo, a meditation with focus. He showed me how to do this strange activity, which involved tracing the kanji characters as carefully as possible, while letting all other thoughts fall away, as in Zazen, but there was more to it than that.

I understood that Shakyo supported the Taoist aspect of Japanese martial arts – the '-do' in judo, kendo, and aikido (which I'd also studied under him) were normally understood to mean 'way', but they actually come from the Chinese root 'dao', meaning 'doing not doing', doing in total harmony, doing without thinking. It seemed that Abbe wanted my performance to be this intuitive and free from the need for thought.

He told me to do the Shakyo every second day, and when I could feel the focus it brought, to then approach my training in the same way. I thanked him and said I would; as I was leaving, he said, 'Remember Kyu Shin Do when you meditate.'

I should have expected this kind of thing from Abbe – I wasn't sure what I would get from my meeting with him, and I came away bewildered at what I had got – like so much Zen, it defied explanation, but I felt that my visit would somehow be helpful, so I would heed his counsel and do as he'd suggested.

I also went to Blackpool to see Aunt Ida and Uncle Norman. They had helped me with a little money to keep myself going after I'd lost the finger, and I wanted to let them know that I'd been in training for a new field, and would soon make my debut. My aunt was scathing about wrestling – 'It's nothing more than a fair-ground activity,' she said. I don't think she meant to be cruel, but she probably still had hopes that I'd get into some respectable business or other, and wrestling was probably as far from that as it was possible to be. I'm sure she only wanted the best for me, but then, she hadn't seen what Geoff had got from wrestling; when she did, I was sure she would approve.

So, back in Crewe, I added Shakyo to my regime, and between meditations, I began to ponder who I would be as a wrestler.

In 1964, professional wrestling was generally very bland, except for just a handful who had strong visual images, such as Billy To Rivers, Ricki Starr, The Outlaw, Jackie Pallo, and, of course, Count Bartelli. The majority of other wrestlers basically wandered down to the ring in a dressing-gown and a pair of trunks or maybe a leotard. The audience would acknowledge that they'd arrived, glance in their direction and think, 'Oh yes, that's so-and-so – let's get on with it.' It was generally very workmanlike and more than a little pedestrian – surely the audience should be encouraged to expect great things from the moment that wrestlers appeared? It was those with visual impact who became household names, so I was determined to join that elite.

The Count was different because he wore a mask, and I also wanted to be a masked wrestler, but I wanted to take it much further than that. After my meditations, I'd seen the image of the kendo helmet, which is a practical part of the armour for that sport, but I wasn't heading in that direction so I reasoned that it must be a symbol of something. It wouldn't be possible to wrestle in a kendo helmet, so it came to me that I could represent the kendo helmet with a grill design on the face of a wrestling mask. That would be the face of my wrestling persona.

It dawned on me that all the kendo armour looks impressive, so I decided to include the breast-plate, the gloves, and the 'hakama' (the trousers) as well, but I wasn't so sure about a bamboo 'shinai' (the 'sword' used in the sport) – that would look like I was carrying a stick.

However, I'd studied kendo under Abbe and got quite good at it, and he once staged a contest among the students, the prize for which was a samurai sword – I was delighted when I won it. I'd put it on display at home, but now I could see a use which would honour it – it would become part of my wrestling image. It would be worn on the approach to combat, and brandished in the face of the enemy.

I then realised that because the sport of kendo was so fundamental to my wrestling identity, I should have the word 'Kendo' as part of the name, and this made me think about why I'd had the word 'Nagasaki' in my mind for the last two years. Of course, I knew it was a place in Japan where an atom bomb had been dropped, but when I'd mentioned it to Abbe he told me that it was also an honourable family name there.

Despite my dyslexia I knew that books could broaden my knowledge and understanding, and I'd begun reading (very slowly!) about Japan. I'd been to the library and asked for books about the samurai, which opened my eyes to their history, and in the index of one book to my delight I found the word 'Nagasaki'. They were samurai warriors who had been legendary at the pivotal battle of Kamakura in 1333, where Zen had started. I felt a deep connection with them and understood that their family name was a symbol of strength and excellence, which was absolutely right for my wrestling persona.

Abbe said I should continue to meditate on it, and as I did the image of the kendo mask and the Nagasaki samurai name had become ever-clearer. He'd told me that my intuition would guide me, and it had – Kendo Nagasaki would be the most spectacular masked wrestler there had ever been. The crowning glory, so-to-speak, was to add a cape. It added mystery because it partially hid the samurai sword until it was drawn and suggested that more was concealed beneath it, and it just looked good!

I was guided to approach every match like a Shakyo, with absolute focus, shutting everything else out; that would mean I couldn't speak or even acknowledge anyone, other than my opponent. At first I wasn't sure how that would work, but it was what I'd been guided to do, so I decided to try it.

I found that when I put the mask on, it automatically put me in the right frame of mind – my mission was to remain detached, while my automatic intuitive reactions did their work. It was almost as if someone else was acting through me – I wasn't Kendo Nagasaki – it was as if he was another person, and I was just making sure he could express himself properly. I felt it was more appropriate to refer to the persona I would bring to wrestling as 'Kendo' rather than 'me', 'I', or 'myself'.

The same lady who made the Count's wrestling masks made the signature Nagasaki wrestling mask, and a cape was made by Barry's talented girlfriend. When it was all put together, the result was as I'd hoped – spectacular. Kendo Nagasaki was sensational, riveting – like a Marvel Comics hero exploding into a drab, grey world.

The other remarkable thing about Kendo was the

mystery surrounding him – usually, masked wrestlers were previously-known wrestlers who had decided to put on a mask and use another name, and it wouldn't take long before everyone knew who they were. Not Kendo – he arrived with top class abilities, straight into the top of the business, as if he was a champion from another world – Japan, apparently.

There was already an element of secrecy in professional wrestling anyway – it was called 'kayfabe'. It was mostly used in dressing rooms if someone from outside the business came in. Before matches, there was usually some conversation between wrestlers, and if an outsider appeared, someone would say, 'Kayfabe,' loud enough for everyone to hear. Everyone in the room would have heard it, and then there would be no more talk of trade secrets, such as how a match was being planned. I knew I'd have to talk to the wrestlers, but with Kendo being so mysterious, once all the arrangements were decided and I went into my Shakyo meditation state of mind, I decided that I'd shut the public out completely and never talk to them.

There was one final detail – a promotional flyer. There were two elements to this – the picture itself, and Kendo's signature. I met up with Abbe once again and asked him how to write the name Kendo Nagasaki in Japanese Kanji. It's the most difficult of the three Japanese written alphabets to learn, and it's usually the last learned by students. Inspired by the hand-written First Dan certificate that Abbe had given to me, I'd begun dabbling a little with calligraphy using the simpler scripts, but Kanji was beyond me at that stage. He showed me, and I have since written it countless times. The picture for Kendo's first ever flyer was taken of him wearing the 'full regalia', standing in Geoff's garden, which I felt had a certain rightness, considering all the help he'd been to me.

Events seemed to gather their own momentum, and

Kendo Nagasaki's debut came together, with the help of my mentor, Geoff. He said he'd speak to Arthur Wright of Wryton Promotions about getting Kendo some shows; he was sure he could help, as they went back a long way...

Arthur came to Geoff's house so we could all meet.

He asked, 'What's he like then, Geoff?'

'He's good,' replied Geoff. 'He's played water polo, he's boxed, he's been weight training for years, he's done judo to Olympic level, and he's been going to Riley's for over a year – you name it, he's done it, and he's been very good at them all.'

Arthur seemed impressed, and said that he'd ask his 'pencil' (match booker) Ronnie Jordan to send over a few dates.

That meeting marked the point at which Kendo Nagasaki entered the world of professional wrestling, for Wryton Promotions. It was as simple as a phone call, which goes to prove the old adage – no matter what time you're living in, it's not what you know, it's who.

Of course, Billy Riley knew I was approaching my debut, and he spoke to his promotions partner Jack Atherton who came up with an excellent promotional gimmick – a poster with a picture of Kendo in the full regalia, and a description which said he was a '6-foot 1-inch 17½ stone Judo Expert from Japan', accompanied by a tempting challenge, *£100 in English Gold Sovereigns to Anyone Who Can Pin Him*. Billy was able to confidently assure Jack that his Sovereigns would be safe!

As soon as Kendo's debut had been decided, Jack put these flyers in all of his shows to begin stirring-up the interest in Kendo, and he had me go to several of his shows to be introduced in the ring – audiences were treated to the visual spectacle of Kendo and told that he would be coming to their venue soon... Their interest was very successfully stirred – Kendo's first ever match was sold-out, but no-one ever tried to win the Sovereigns.

As most people now know, Kendo's first match took place at Willenhall Baths in the West Midlands on Friday 13th November 1964. There was nothing glamorous about the place, it was just as it sounded – an old Victorian swimming baths with the ring stuck over the top of the pool, but it was packed.

Kendo's first opponent was Jumping Jim Hussey, Mark 'Rollerball' Rocco's father, a seasoned veteran. I'd seen Hussey – I knew who he was, but I'd had no contact with him. Geoff assured me that he was a pro who worked regularly for Wryton and they wanted Kendo looked after, so he would do the right thing.

Hussey was a true professional and a villain – a bad-guy. Promoters usually matched him against wrestlers from overseas and newcomers who they wanted to promote; Hussey's harsh tactics meant that his opponents usually gained the sympathy of the audience and were viewed as baby-faces, and he was very good at 'working' with his opponents, using that dynamic to make a good show. However, when he faced Kendo, the tables were unexpectedly turned.

I'd always envisaged that Kendo would be very much like The Count, but more spectacular. The Count was a baby-face, someone the audience could gain empathy with and rally behind, especially when he was on the losing end. Everything I'd seen of his matches was positive, as well as the living he earned from it, so it made sense that Kendo would be in a similar mould. However, that didn't happen – the wrestling audience that night didn't associate Kendo and his visual imagery with a baby-face – they were suspicious of him right from the start.

As soon as Kendo first appeared, the audience was struck dumb. As I've mentioned, they'd never seen anything like him and they didn't know what to make of him – I think they were genuinely over-awed. I also think they took an instant decision that even before he'd made a move, they didn't like him.

Immediately after the round-one bell rang, Hussey began using his trademark dirty tricks. These would usually start the audience jeering and booing, but this time they applauded and cheered him. Despite Kendo only trying to hold his own against Hussey's underhand tactics, virtually every move he made was greeted with hostility and resentment; he got the boos and jeers usually reserved for Hussey.

I quickly realized that I was swimming against the tide; the audience felt that Kendo was a villain, so it would be better for the match if he gave them what they wanted. Kendo rose to the challenge, and that night the audience in Willenhall witnessed the birth of a whole new level of bad boy. Kendo hung onto holds long after being told to break, making sure the audience knew that Hussey – their new baby-face – was in pain. Kendo ignored the referee and used a range of underhand tactics of his own, coming within a whisker of public warnings and disqualification.

What emerged was Kendo's absolutely uncompromising warrior nature. The technique and the skills were evident, but the utter dominance, ruthlessness, and a devastating will to win were even clearer. He had risen to the occasion, instantly overturning my aspirations of being a baby-face wrestler.

The records show the final result as a knockout for Kendo.

There is a Japanese proverb that Kendo absolutely typifies: *Deru kui wa utareru ga, desgita kui wa utarenai*. It means, 'The stake that sticks up will be hammered down, but the stake that sticks up more, will not.' The translation of the proverb states that if you are extraordinary, you will be pressured to conform, but if you want to truly succeed and be a leader, then you must really stand out. Kendo's appearance certainly achieved that objective, and once the audience had made their opinions clear, he also excelled at giving them a new, dangerous, and uncompromising villain to hate, and yet admire.

I'd followed my intuition and was sure I'd thought of everything, but clearly I hadn't. I'd been close to Bartelli and watched how he did things, and I was probably guilty of copying him, but that wasn't what the audience wanted from a wrestler that looked like Kendo Nagasaki.

At that first match there was a lot of nervous energy, so the adrenaline was flowing. I was accustomed to audiences because I'd done judo competitions and weight-lifting contests, and even though I'd seen how much more passionate wrestling audiences were, I was still surprised by the intensity of it. Once again, from my previous experience, I knew that the old saying held true: you're only as good as your last show. I'd made sure that Kendo's first performance had been highly spectacular, as well as something to live up to and exceed every time thereafter.

Chapter 12

A Learning Curve

Geoff's relationship with Arthur Wright had been instrumental to Kendo getting his first few matches, and then, following-on from Jack Atherton's 'One Hundred Sovereigns' flyer and taking Kendo round the halls to introduce him, it was time for the shows that he'd promised those audiences.

Jack was truly old-school. From his wrestling days he'd acquired big cauliflower ears, he always wore a suit with a trilby, and he had very bad breath. Everyone called him 'Three-Cornered-Jack', because in his last ten years of wrestling he'd only rarely been thrown – he was like the three-legged emblem for the Isle of Man, with a leg at each corner, stable as a tripod. He was quite a character...

He'd stopped wrestling and begun promoting before I'd begun, but there were some legendary stories about his exploits. One day they found themselves a man short for their match, so he decided to put himself in against Ernie Riley. The match started and they were pulling round; Ernie tried to throw Jack and got blocked, tried again and got blocked again, so he switched his approach and came in from the other side. Jack was caught off-guard and was thrown up into the air, and, while airborne, his shout echoed round the hall for the whole audience to clearly hear, 'I wouldn't do that to a fuckin' dog!'

Another memorable incident with Jack occurred in a match that he and Billy Riley were promoting together. Once again, they found themselves a man short, so again Jack volunteered to wrestle. Billy asked him, 'Are you sure? Sure you can manage?'

Jack said, 'Aye – I'll be all reet!' He was on with a newcomer who was only in his second match. They had the talk in the middle of the ring, and Jack went back to his corner to pull on the ropes and limber-up, with his back to the centre of the ring. The bell went to start, and the newcomer came rushing across the ring at high speed. Jack hadn't turned round when the bell rang, and when he did, his and the newcomer's heads crashed together, knocking Jack out cold.

Billy, who was refereeing, started the count but stopped it when Jack didn't move, then turned and gave the newcomer a bollocking (for doing nothing – it was just to stretch the time). He turned back to Jack and re-started the count, but he was still immobile. Billy did this at least three times but eventually he had to count Jack out. Just as he did, Jack began to recover – he got up and said, 'I'm all reet, Billy, I'll carry on!' Billy replied, 'Carry on ?!? I've already counted thee out three times!' With a face like a puzzled pug, Jack said, 'Well, bloody 'ell!' Once you met Jack you never forgot him.

Kendo's second show for Jack was at Nelson in Lancashire, and it proved interesting, for all the wrong reasons. He would be on with an old hand called Don Mendoza who had been around and was known to be a bit devious. The match had been discussed, and Jack had told Mendoza that Kendo was going to win.

We went into the ring and Mendoza soon realized that Kendo was totally 'green', and could therefore be manipulated. The issue here was ring-craft – the outcome of a match may have been arranged, but how you get there makes all the difference to the appeal of the match.

Until the deciding fall (or submission or disqualification, or even draw), the audience wants to see a contest, a battle of wits and skills, and to see victory plucked from the jaws of possible defeat. A match with a few bland holds and then a couple of falls has no suspense, no excitement, and leaves the audience dissatisfied with both the match and the wrestlers. Unfortunately, this is exactly what Mendoza talked the inexperienced Kendo into doing...

He spoke to Kendo throughout the match, suggesting that he should do this or that hold, and even how and when to get his falls. Kendo did as he was guided to do, and the match ended up being very pedestrian and devoid of energy and excitement – boring, frankly.

When the match was over, Kendo jumped out of the ring and returned to the dressing room where Jack was waiting, waving his hands in the air.

'Awful show! Worst show I've ever seen! Cancel all your work!' said Jack.

I couldn't believe it – only Kendo's second match for Jack Atherton, and it was going to be the last! I went straight back and told Geoff.

'It's that bloody Mendoza,' he said. 'You've listened to him, haven't you?'

I simply nodded. What could I say? I had indeed listened to him. Now I could understand why Jack had been so angry – Kendo had already been to Nelson to be introduced, so the audience was expecting great things, and if the match had been that poor it would have been a big disappointment for them, and Jack too.

Geoff picked up the phone and called Jack. They were in mid conversation when I heard Geoff say, 'You know what it's like, Jack...'

'I know,' Jack had said. 'Of course I know. Bloody stupid – listening to an old hand. Tell him he's on with same fella next week, and make sure he makes a better job of it this time...'

The week after, Kendo was on against Mendoza at Sutton-in-Ashfield. He tried the same thing again, but this time Kendo knew what was expected of him, and he obliged in style – he gave Mendoza his 'pilot's licence', meaning that he found himself up in the air for most of the match. Whatever advice Mendoza offered was completely ignored, so there were no simple holds, no quick and easy falls – Kendo made the match spectacular.

Once again, Jack was waiting for him as he walked back to the dressing room, only this time he wasn't waving his arms about. Smiling, he said, 'That's more like it!' I suspect that even before Geoff's phone-call, he'd known what had happened in that first match with Mendoza, so he was ready to give Kendo another chance – but not without teaching him a lesson first.

Mendoza making a fool of Kendo and getting him sacked was indeed a powerful lesson. It could have happened to any newcomer – but only once, or their career would be over.

A similar situation could have arisen with a wrestler called Ted Beckley (who went on to train The Dynamite Kid). On the night he faced Kendo he was wearing a mask, but I don't know what he called himself. He'd either seen or heard of how Kendo had dealt with Mendoza at their second meeting, and while we were in the dressing room he turned to me and said, 'If you try any of that funny stuff on me, I'll hook-in.'

What he meant by 'hook-in' was to hook one of his legs into yours, preventing you from picking him up. However, Beckley was only a little guy, so I said, 'How are you going to hook-in when your feet are two feet off the floor? I'd like to see that!' In the ring, Kendo did exactly what he wanted, and Beckley never tried anything that might diminish him or the match – fortunately for him!

The foregoing illustrates how good an opponent Jim Hussey had been for Kendo's first match. He was what was known as a 'carpenter' – somebody who could make any other wrestler look good. That kind of approach was good for the business – he did the best he could to work with him as a newcomer. Wryton Promotions knew that Kendo could wrestle, but also that he didn't yet have the professional skills he needed to put on a show. Jim, on the other hand, had all that, and he helped Kendo with the 'show' side. Kendo didn't yet know that there were wrestlers who would not work with him as constructively as Hussey had, so he hadn't been ready for Mendoza; lesson learned, and learned well...

There were quite a few wrestlers who would go out of their way to make life difficult for you, marginalize you, and try and get you out of the business. Their attitude was that the more work you got, the less there was for them, so if they could get you out of the job, they would. Kendo would meet some of them in his next few matches.

Wrestlers like Terry O' Neill, Francis Sullivan, Douggie Joyce, and Ahmed The Turk were all the sort of people who would not help you – all awkward buggers. Billy Howes was a classic example. If you were young and didn't know what you were doing, you were in trouble. Howes was very fit and pretty ruthless – he wouldn't think anything of starting a match with a punch to the nose or a head-butt – nothing that would knock you out, but which would leave you dazed and not knowing what was happening. When you went in with Billy it was always a fight – quite literally a slugging match, and even though he was a dangerous whirlwind, he was always exciting to watch.

Les Kellett was that sort of man. He had dozens of fights where he was toe-to-toe with somebody, hitting them, especially before he became the funny man. He had just that sort of match with Kendo one night, which I'll come to later.

Others included Norman Walsh, Geoff Portz, and Dennis Mitchell who would injure you if the opportunity arose. It wasn't like it is nowadays – it's more of a choreographed performance now where what they do is so elaborate that both parties need the complete cooperation of their opponent. When Kendo started wrestling, such cooperation was far from guaranteed, and you had to be ready for dirty tricks.

If your opponent wasn't really going anywhere, you wouldn't care if you never saw them again, so you'd build your reputation by demolishing them – they would just be a stepping-stone in your career. One such early bout for Jack was in Malvern in March 1965 against a man called Gabriel Kane. I'd never heard of him and reasoned he must be one of Jack's 'knock-offs' – wrestlers that you don't give much to, you make an example of them. These would be 'red meat' situations – Jack would say, 'A bit of blood's in order!', which meant this would be a brutal match specifically staged to build Kendo up; there were quite a few of them, and Kendo always obliged. However, the time comes when it has to look as if your opponents might be able to beat you, and if not at this match, then perhaps finish the job another time.

One of Billy Robinson's biggest failings was that he made everybody look as though they were no good, so there was no edge-of-the-seat excitement over whether he might be beaten. To some extent, in the early stages Kendo did that too – after all, they'd both trained at Riley's Gym, where no-one respected 'show' wrestlers. Consequently, during those early stages, Kendo was likely to beat his opponents without considering a return match. That went on until promoters brought in more established opponents who could challenge him, which led to decent shows and match-ups which could develop into numerous return contests.

Like Robinson, Kendo's Wigan background got him into trouble very early on. Promoters received quite a few complaints that he was dangerous to the point of being out of control, and they began to think he was becoming a problem wrestler. In order to calm him down and lessen the harshness of his matches, in conjunction with Geoff they decided he should be put into a series of tag matches with the Count – it seemed the only way to ensure that he didn't quickly run out of wrestlers who would face him.

The Count did this by keeping Kendo on the apron for quite a lot of the time, and after he'd tagged him in, getting him out as soon as the Count felt he was starting to become dangerous. These matches carried on for quite a while with no problems, until a match in Shrewsbury in April 1965 with Johnny Czeslaw and Leon Arras (Brian Glover) as a tag team. Tag matches don't have rounds – it was generally a twenty-minute period that was only broken by falls or submissions.

I didn't know a great deal about Czeslaw – I couldn't remember having wrestled him. He was billed as 'Johnny Czeslaw – The Polish Eagle' and he looked the part – he was well built and quite stocky with a bald head. I believe he'd been a good amateur wrestler in Poland.

The match started with Leon Arras against Bartelli – he always went in first because he was the showman and would give the crowd a bit of wrestling before letting the wild one in. After a while, Arras tagged with Czeslaw, and shortly after, Bartelli tagged Kendo in.

We moved around a little, linked up, and put on a few holds. Eventually, Kendo ended up with Czeslaw in an aeroplane spin and spun him round a few times. Normally the move ends by bringing your opponent over into a body-slam on the canvas. However, instead of slamming him, Kendo pushed him higher up into the air to full arm's-length and then just walked away, leaving Czeslaw up there. The result was pretty brutal. Looking back, I can only describe his descent as being a bit like a feather – he seemed to come down in a rocking motion, going from one side to the other. The trouble was that he tilted more in one direction, and he came down head-first, hitting the canvas above his right eye.

For a few seconds he sat on the floor rubbing his head,

and when he got up I swear you could see a big lump that had formed in those few seconds.

He put his hand on his head and shouted in a strong Polish accent. 'He try to kill me! He try to kill me!'

With that, he left the ring and went straight back to the dressing room, which surprised and bemused everybody, including Kendo.

The referee, Lou Rosebury, decided that the contest should continue, which meant that Leon Arras would have to jump into the ring to face Kendo – without Czeslaw, he still represented the opposing team.

There was suddenly a heated discussion between the ref and Arras as to whether or not he should go and get Czeslaw back, but that wasn't going to happen, so Arras finally got into the ring opposite Kendo. However, instead of taking up a wrestling position he walked straight over to Kendo, grabbed his right arm and raised it, and in his broad Yorkshire accent he shouted, 'Too strong for me, referee – the winner!' With that, he promptly left the ring himself.

Everyone had been surprised at Czeslaw's hasty exit, but now we were all dumbstruck. Kendo was left in the ring, Bartelli was on the apron, the referee was in the middle, as Leon Arras disappeared towards the back of the hall.

There was a quick discussion and it was decided that the ref would go and find out what was happening. The audience was completely bemused.

Lou Rosebury eventually came back and said that the two wrestlers were not going to return to the ring, so he had no alternative but to announce a double disqualification for leaving the ring before the contest was over.

The audience wasn't happy because our match was the main event, and it was dramatically over in no time.

Bartelli and Kendo had no choice but to leave the ring – sharpish. Back in the dressing room, Czeslaw was complaining bitterly about having been dumped onto his head and threatening never to wrestle Kendo again, and Leon Arras was busy changing – he didn't really care about all the fuss. Czeslaw stuck to his word – to my knowledge Kendo didn't wrestle him again for quite some time.

I later heard that Joe Cornelius, who was quite a big name in the South said, 'If he comes down here, I'm not wrestling him!' – and he wasn't the only one; quite a few big-name southern wrestlers said something similar.

Leon Arras didn't take that attitude – he was very much a jobbing wrestler and wanted the money so he'd get in the ring with almost anyone if money was involved. Arras was actually quite tough (his father had been a middleweight professional boxer), and he'd grown up sparring in a gym, so he was definitely up to facing Kendo. The only time I ever heard him complain about another wrestler was after a match in Hull, where he got a nasty surprise.

The venue was an old swimming baths which had cubicles where people used to take baths – there were two rows of ten facing each other, each of which actually had a bath in it, and this is where we used to get changed. Billy Robinson and I had been top of the bill and on third, and Arras had been on fourth and had just finished his match and was on his way back to his cubicle to get changed. First on the bill had been Mick McMichael who was a baby-face in the ring but loved to torment everyone outside it. This day he decided it would be funny if he lobbed a smelly old industrial mop-head over the top of his cubicle door, at random, into one of the others. Unfortunately, he managed to target Billy Robinson's cubicle, who emerged wearing the mop-head like a hideous, stinking wig. I heard Robinson roar and slam his cubicle door open, and I looked outside to see what was up.

Just at that moment Arras walked into the changing

room area, and his gaze fell on Robinson, who looked a mixture of nightmare and slap-stick, his usual brutal face and wall-eye now wearing an expression of fury, and the daft mop-wig.

Arras involuntarily smirked, which was unfortunate. Billy hated funny-men in wrestling and barely needed an excuse to punish one; Arras simply being there made him a target, and his smirk pushed Billy over the top – he chinned him, almost knocking him out for real. It must have been a hard hit – Arras told Robinson that if he ever hit him again, he'd sue him.

Kendo had no problem with funny men as long as they were capable enough to get a show out of, and Arras was one of the best, in all respects. He was a very interesting and entertaining individual, well-educated and a good talker – by day he was a teacher, and he then became an actor and playwright, and I think he might have studied psychology at some point. In a way he befriended Kendo – we wouldn't go out for a drink together or anything like that, but he made Kendo feel comfortable with him in the wrestling ring, and so avoided any disasters such as happened to Czeslaw.

Arras projected an image of Yorkshire pugnaciousness – cocky, brusque, and full of himself. His catchphrase in the ring was a bolshy-sounding, 'I know the rules, referee!', but he was a genuinely decent man and a most entertaining wrestler.

Kendo never tried to hurt Arras because it was never appropriate or necessary, but practically anyone else was fair game – Max Crabtree had occasionally been heard to remark on the way Kendo battered some less able newcomers; he'd wince and suck his teeth and say, '...it were ugly, kid!'

However, from working with Geoff and heeding the warnings that there were wrestlers becoming reluctant to face him, I came to see the sense of having Kendo calm down somewhat; that was indeed an important learning curve, but Kendo was always to have a fearsome reputation.

One day I found myself booked against a wrestler called Jean Ferre, who later wrestled as Andre the Giant. He was genuinely huge – we measured him in the dressing room and he was a true six foot nine inches tall, and I found I could get my entire foot including the wrestling boot I was wearing into one of his boots – I'd never seen anyone so big. However, before our match he pulled me aside and said,

'Look, I've come here to learn how to wrestle, I don't know a lot about it – if I'm clumsy forgive me, and please don't hurt me!'

I could tell by his manner he was genuinely afraid, but I said, 'Don't worry – you'll be all right...' As I've made clear, I now knew that making a fool of an inexperienced wrestler made for a bad show – he had to look like he might be able to beat Kendo, and physically Jean Ferre certainly did, so I did my best to work with him.

Chapter 13

Controversy in Malvern, Anonymity in Spain

About six weeks after I'd started wrestling, I went with a group of nine, eight wrestlers and a ref, Emile Poilve, to Redruth for a show at a private members club. It was one of the furthest-flung destinations, almost at Land's End, where we'd stay overnight in on-site chalet rooms which they provided.

I normally travelled to shows in my own car, but for a journey as long as this Jack Atherton wouldn't pay travelling expenses to individual wrestlers because the sum total would make too big a dent in his profits, so several wrestlers would go together in a van. This presented me with a dilemma...

Kendo was never seen without his mask in front of anyone, including other wrestlers. There were actually two masks – I'd arrive at the venue in one, and Kendo wrestled in another. After the match, Kendo would shower in the wrestling mask, then take it off and replace it with the other. This secretive regime was carefully worked out and practised.

However, I could hardly do a nine-hour journey there

(and another back), with a break at a cafe, wearing a mask all the time, so I reluctantly made an exception. I only ever did this for two trips to Redruth, three similar trips to Dumfries, and twice to Aberdeen, all within my first two years of wrestling. The wrestlers on these trips were mostly Northern lads, whom I hoped would not betray my confidence. After these few shows, I became a bigger draw so promoters had no problem covering my expenses; I then used my own car, so other wrestlers usually wouldn't see Kendo without the mask.

On the way back from my first Redruth trip, Emile Poilve was driving, and he made a wise-crack about some people coming into the business with a silver spoon in their mouths, getting 'put over', and beating lads that they shouldn't be. Everyone else in the van was a seasoned wrestler, and he knew that as a newcomer I'd beaten Jim Hussey, so he clearly meant me.

There was another dimension to this – Jack didn't have direct access to Joint Promotions wrestlers but he could get them by booking them through Wryton Promotions. Poilve knew that Wryton were looking after me, so he was suggesting that I was only in the job because I was getting special treatment, rather than on my own merits. I wasn't going to have all my hard work, ability, and achievements sneered at, on that basis or any other.

I snapped – I was going to kick the shit out of him. I actually began scrambling over the seats to grab hold of him – while he was still driving. Jim was there though, and he just managed to stop me, and he told him to shut the fuck up – after all, they all wanted to get back alive! It had been an alarming moment, but things calmed down and Poilve did shut up.

We stopped during the journey, and I saw Jim have a quiet word with him, which completely changed his attitude. Jim knew that Wryton were handling me because I could genuinely wrestle whereas Poilve probably didn't know that. After this episode and being informed that I was the real thing, he was extremely polite and he couldn't do enough for me.

Reputation is important, but if not carefully handled it can back-fire, as I was to discover soon afterwards, following a fateful match at Malvern. A look at the records of Kendo's matches shows that he didn't appear there for four years, between 1965 and 1969 – here's why.

Jack had the idea to build up another masked wrestler, who was known as The Professor. He told me what he was doing and that it would end up with a masked challenge match, which Kendo would win. He did a great job of promoting the show – on the night, it was a packed house.

Before we even got to the ring, in the dressing room I'd seen that The Professor was quite a plump man, perhaps around sixteen stone, but his physique didn't seem at all trained or toned. He was dressed entirely in red, mask and all.

Once in the ring we approached the referee for the pre-match talk; on this occasion it was Jack himself. Talk over, we returned to our corners, the bell went, and we linked-up.

It was immediately clear to me that The Professor had no energy. We worked for a few minutes trying to make something of it, during which I hoped he'd be able to step up to the mark, but it wasn't happening.

There was another small problem – because we'd both been villains, it was a bit confusing for the audience, but ultimately, Kendo turned out to be the one they hated the most, so that night The Professor was the baby face.

In an effort to move the match on, Kendo started the villainy and skullduggery. The Professor tried some comebacks, but they weren't very convincing. The audience soon began to get bored with the antics – we were not getting the heat that we should have had ('heat' being audience reaction). If Kendo brutalised a baby-face that the audience could sympathize with, the heat could become quite intense, but on this occasion I don't think they cared what happened to either of us.

Kendo was starting to get annoyed because the match and the crowd reaction were both pretty poor, and he was fed up of having to roll around the canvas with this unresponsive blob.

Eventually The Professor got Kendo in a front headlock. One way to get out of this hold is to grab your opponent by the hips and pick them up so that their feet are sticking out horizontally; Kendo did this and walked towards the ropes with The Professor held aloft. Many wrestlers would then put their opponent onto the apron, over the top rope. If you're a baby-face and you've done that, you'd then part the ropes and help your opponent back into the ring. If you're a villain, the chances are that you'd knock your opponent off the apron once they've let go of you.

The Professor would have expected the latter, but Kendo, being very robust (and perhaps still a little green and new to the business), didn't do either. When he got to the ropes, Kendo launched The Professor out into the audience. You have to remember the strength Kendo has – being able to press 360lbs and bench-press over 400lbs means he's very powerful.

The Professor shot away from the ring feet-first, in an arc as gravity took over. There was a problem, though – the front row of seats had been put too close to the ring, so there wasn't enough space for him to land without hitting them.

I can't remember if the audience had seen what was coming and had moved out of the way or whether he landed on them, but I think he hit the backs of the seats, pivoted off them, and went down head first onto the floor between the seats and the ring. The floor at Malvern was either wood or concrete, so The Professor had a hard landing.

Jack started to count – you could get counted out while outside the ring too. He went quite slowly, and kept glancing through the ropes in The Professor's direction at the same time. Kendo was standing back, as he was supposed to.

Jack reached '...Five...' and saw that The Professor wasn't making any effort to get back in the ring. Quickly, he turned to Kendo, and in a showmanship-type manner, pushed him back and shouted, 'Stand back, Kendo, stand back!' At the same time he leaned-in and said. 'Go and find out what's happening. Get him back in the ring!'

We were only in the second round at this point – the contest had barely begun. At Jack's direction, Kendo jumped out of the ring and tried to coax some life into the prone body that was still motionless on the floor. Being a villain, Kendo tried to pull The Professor up with the aim of heaving him back into the ring, but he was a dead weight. It crossed my mind that he'd bumped his head hard enough to have knocked a bit of life out of him, and he may be only semi-conscious.

After a fruitless struggle, Kendo climbed back into the ring and said, 'I don't think he's coming back.' Jack re-started the count, and tried again to salvage the match. He theatrically pushed Kendo back once more. 'Stand back, Kendo!', shouted Jack, then he urgently hissed, 'Get thee out there get him back!'

Kendo tried again, but still no joy – The Professor remained slumped in a heap. Kendo jumped back in the ring and said, 'Jack, he's not moving.'

The count was started yet again. This time, when he reached five (for about the fifth time!) Jack stopped, looked at Kendo for a moment, then turned to the audience – and started the count yet again! He'd tried everything but to no avail, so this time he counted The Professor out. He called in the MC, who announced that Kendo was the winner.

Kendo returned to the dressing room with no real

concerns, and The Professor was eventually brought in on a stretcher by the Red Cross, or St. John's Ambulance staff. About five minutes had passed, and he was no longer unconscious but was wincing – they were giving him the smelling salts treatment.

He came round fully and asked what had happened – Jack told him he'd bumped his head. He wasn't too happy about it, but he never blamed anyone. Jack made sure he was okay before we all went home.

Some time later, I was working again for Jack. He said. '...Kendo...' (he always called me that because he couldn't say Nagasaki – when he tried, it came out as 'Nagasity!') He was stalling quite a bit; he said, '...er, Malvern...'

'What about Malvern, Jack?' I asked.

'I think we've made a bit of a mess with Malvern. You can't go there again.'

'Why? What have I done now?'

He didn't seem to know how to tell me something...

'Well...' said Jack. '...you do know that The Professor passed away a week or two ago?'

I had indeed heard. I'd understood that it wasn't wrestling-related – I believe he'd had a heart attack.

But Jack, being a bit show-business savvy, had (somewhat unwisely) decided to capitalise on the sensationalism, and at the earliest opportunity he'd announced – in Malvern – that The Professor had died from injuries caused by Kendo Nagasaki at that show. The result was pure hatred in Malvern, but because of the nature of the business back then, it didn't cause a problem anywhere else.

It's important to understand that each show ran in isolation from the rest of the wrestling world. What happened at one show wouldn't necessarily become known at any other – you could do something in Hanley or Wolverhampton, and nobody at any other venue would know anything about it. So if you wanted, you could get away with doing the same sort of thing night after night at many different venues. There was no Internet then so results were not shared around for all to see, and what happened in one venue only spread from there if it was on TV.

This illustrates another of the problems of being a wrestler back then. If you hadn't worked on TV, you could be a big name in one small area only – Count Bartelli was a prime example of that. He was a big star in Wryton Promotions' sphere of influence, but once he was out of their area, in Yorkshire for Morrell & Beresford, or London for Dale Martin, they had no idea who he was – his name meant nothing in those regions.

The only exception to this was if you were a jobbing wrestler who had worked for all the promoters for about ten years – then, as a result of long and wide-spread exposure, people would know you. But it took forever; you could achieve it far quicker on the TV.

Malvern was one such isolated venue. That particular hall was owned and run by the council, and the audience took the whole Professor episode very seriously – so much so that they raised a petition with the council objecting to Kendo Nagasaki ever wrestling in Malvern again – and it succeeded! Jack received a letter from them stating that Kendo had been barred.

'How long is it going to last, Jack?' I asked.

'I've no idea,' he said, 'But I'll keep asking...'

As the records show, it turned out to be four years.

However, in the summer of that year (1965), Kendo acquired a good reputation from an unexpected quarter. For his first appearance at Blackpool Tower Circus, I invited my Aunt Ida and Uncle Norman along. Neither of them had been to a wrestling show before, but my Uncle was really taken with it, and from then on, they both went every week. After this, my standing with them went up considerably – it was as if my Aunt's scathing 'fairground activity' put-down had never been uttered.

There was also an occasion where I stepped completely away from Kendo's reputation, as a favour.

Count Bartelli's son, Barry, admired his father very much and wanted to be a wrestler too, but unfortunately he just didn't have what it took. He was only about five feet nine, he didn't have an athletic build, he was prone to putting on weight, and he simply didn't have the natural flair required. Even though Geoff knew Barry wasn't going to make it beyond getting a bottom of the bill job here and there, he encouraged me to help him so that his hopes weren't prematurely dashed, but he quietly accepted that regardless of what I did, Barry was never going to be a 'name'. He'd been around the wrestling business all his life so he knew what it was about and he could mimic it; he went a couple of times to wrestling training (never at Wigan) and I trained him a bit, but he was never more than average.

In 1965 on his way back from Mallorca, Barry had arranged to stop off in Barcelona to do some wrestling. However, the Spanish lads had given him a hard time; they didn't mock him, but they didn't work with him or give him anything – they made him look like he didn't know what he was doing.

He came back to the UK and told me all about it. He asked me to go over there with him so we could tag – I could be 'policeman' and look after him, like I'd done with his father when the scrap man had wanted to wrestle him.

We arranged the trip for mid-1966. Barry decided to take his glamorous girlfriend Ros, Rosalind James. She was from a wealthy 'county' family near Crewe; she was beautiful, intelligent, well-spoken, and well-educated. Despite all these advantages, she rebelled against her parents and their expectations of her; she drove a purple Mini with her phone number on the side, which drove her father nuts. Barry saw the car and called the number, and he went to meet her driving the Pontiac. They became a couple.

Before we left, we went shopping in the West End, including in Carnaby Street, the centre of high fashion in the '60s. Someone spotted a dashing lightweight suit in lavender, which both Barry and Ros thought would look good on me. I wasn't at all vain, but I thought I might as well look stylish when we were relaxing in Spain, so I bought it – Ros in particular liked how it looked.

All three of us and our luggage crammed into a Spanish-registered, left-hand-drive, convertible MGB. In between the wrestling jobs we did quite a few touristy jaunts, which were a lot of fun, and the MGB, rare in Spain at that time, was widely admired.

I also found that my lavender suit had a dramatic effect – when I walked down any street in Barcelona, all eyes swivelled towards me and gazes remained fixed on me – I felt like a movie star. Little did I know that in 1960s Spain the colour lavender was associated with shame, and here I was, strutting around swathed from neck to ankles in it. They must have thought I was completely debauched, and proud of it! I only discovered this nugget of information years later, by which time the suit was fortunately long gone, or I might even have burned it.

For the wrestling shows, Barry and I were a tag team, and I used the name Paul Dillon for the tour. We didn't go for long, only about a month, but there was plenty of wrestling in Spain in the summer. We did bull-rings in the big cities like Barcelona, and they also had rings in the middle of swimming pools – wrestlers walked across a ramp to get to them. Needless to say, one of the highlights of those events was chucking someone over the top rope into the pool.

The Spanish lads tried it on with Barry again, trying to make us look incompetent, but they came unstuck when they faced me. I showed them that there wouldn't be any liberty-taking and the atmosphere changed quickly – the

Spanish wrestlers looked at each other as if to say, 'We'd better be careful with this pair, that one knows what he's doing,' meaning me. They all behaved themselves, and Barry didn't get the same treatment this time.

Towards the end of our time there, the Barcelona promoter asked us if we would do a couple of shows for the promoter in Valencia, to which we agreed. One was in a holiday resort and the other was in the bull-ring on a Sunday evening. We were billed with what the promoter claimed were his tag-team champions, and the orders were for Barry and myself to lose.

All the time I'd been there, I'd never lost to anybody, so I wasn't going to do it then either. He argued that we were just visiting wrestlers – we would go home, but his wrestlers would have to live with the result, so they should win – he felt that our job was to build his wrestlers up. I was conscious that although I was wrestling as Paul Dillon, it might leak out that I was actually Kendo Nagasaki, and I wasn't going to allow even the possibility of a rumour that Kendo had been beaten. I told them the best they were going to get was a draw – or I could beat their lads, of course! Reluctantly, the promoter agreed, but he said that we would never work for him again. I wasn't concerned because I wasn't at all reliant on working in Spain, and, in fact, I never wrestled there again.

A funny thing happened while we were over there, which showed how effective my secrecy with the mask was back then.

Jackie 'Mr. TV' Pallo was a big name, one of the major stars on television, and he was in Spain on holiday while Barry and I were there. He'd worked in Spain before, and he came into the dressing room in one of the venues to say hello to a couple of Spanish wrestlers whom he knew. Jackie said hello to them and shook their hands, but he didn't know Barry so he went to walk out.

I shouted after him, 'What about me, you old bugger?'

Pallo turned and the realization hit him like a brick. 'Fuckin' 'ell – Naggers!'

'Naggers' – that's what all the wrestlers used to call me.

He came over and said, 'I've never seen you without a mask on – I didn't know who you were 'til I heard your voice!' It may seem surprising, but despite having been in the same changing room as Kendo several times, like all the others, Jackie Pallo had only ever seen him in his mask, so he'd had no idea who I was.

Barry and Ros stayed on in Spain, but because I'd been there a month it was time for me to go home so I caught a flight back. It was to be a sad homecoming – my father came to collect me in his car, and he broke the news that my Uncle Norman had died and had already been buried.

My Aunt said she couldn't get in touch with me, which was actually quite understandable; communication to Spain in the '60s was difficult – Franco was in charge, and even if you had a telephone number you couldn't always get through. Ida had simply done the practical thing and had gone ahead with my Uncle's funeral.

I was taken aback at how matter-of-fact she was. Instead of sympathising with my sense of loss, her attitude was, 'He was dead and there was nothing else I could do.' Once again, her strong and pragmatic character shone through, but at the time it felt a little cold-hearted. I had very fond memories of Uncle Norman and I was saddened that I wouldn't see him again and hadn't had the chance to say goodbye.

Chapter 14

Norman Morrell, Joint Promotions, and Skulduggery!

In Kendo's early days, in addition to working for Wryton Promotions and Jack Atherton, he also did some shows for Billy Best in Blackpool and Liverpool and a few for Relwyskow & Green, but initially none for Morrell & Beresford, who were based in Bradford and operated in the North, East Midlands, and Scotland.

Norman Morrell had been an accomplished amateur wrestler and had set a record by winning the British Featherweight title four years in a row, from 1932 to 1936. He represented Great Britain at the 1936 Olympic games in Berlin but came away without a medal. He did, however, see the notorious opening speech of the games given by Hitler, and he came away very impressed with how everything was organized; he was to use that inspiration later in how he managed wrestling in the UK.

After World War II, Norman saw that wrestling in Britain needed to change, and he got onto the committee with Lord Admiral Edward Mountevans which created a new set of rules that subsequently became the basis of *World of Sport* wrestling.

He teamed-up with Ted Beresford, a retired light mid-heavyweight, to form Morrell & Beresford, and was later instrumental in forming Joint Promotions, an alliance of promoters which shared talent and shut-out the competition by controlling bookings across the UK. Norman remained central to its operation, which was often characterised by manipulation and behind-the-scenes arrangements, pitting one promoter against another and using the wrestlers against them. I was to have first-hand experience of this.

Norman was never seen at matches, and even if he was there somewhere, he never came into the dressing room; other than the old-timers, I don't know of anyone who'd ever seen him at a show. I heard that a lot of the time he would be there, watching from the back of the hall, then he'd go home without speaking to anyone. In contrast, his partner, Ted Beresford, was a jovial chap who always came into the dressing room if he was at the show.

Every month Joint Promotions sent their wrestlers a date sheet which was divided into weeks showing dates, times, venues, and the promoter. I first got bookings for Morrell and Beresford in November 1965, and my eighth show for them was to be an important one; I'm pretty sure it was at Middlesborough on 11th February 1966.

I arrived early because I wanted to get in before the punters. I went to the dressing room and saw the referee, Lou Rosebury, and Ernest Lofthouse was there; I think it was him who said that Kendo would be on second, which was ideal because I could leave before the end of the show. I'd be up against Ernest Baldwin who hadn't arrived yet. I knew that he was notorious for being a hard man and had a reputation for being a bit awkward, but I wasn't worried – Kendo had come across awkward people before.

Eventually, he arrived; he was about five foot ten, around sixteen-stone, and he looked like an old-fashioned strong-man, the kind you'd see in a fairground or carnival. He had been the British Heavyweight Champion – when I met him, I think another of the Wigan lads held the belt, either Billy Joyce or Billy Robinson.

Matches for Morrell & Beresford used to have four ten-minute rounds; they were the only promoters in the country to do this – the others had eight five-minute rounds. I'm not sure of the orders on the day of this match, but the result would be that Kendo would win.

Eventually, Kendo and Baldwin were in the ring. The announcement was made: 'Ernest Baldwin, the former British Heavyweight Champion, against Kendo Nagasaki, an unknown warrior from Japan...', and with the formalities over, the bell went and we met in the middle.

Immediately, Kendo found himself on the receiving end of a very short elbow right on the chin – full force. This causes a terrible pain because your jaw goes up almost into your ear and nearly bursts your eardrum. Baldwin was no lightweight, and when he cracked you one he did it with his whole body weight behind it. It went down well with the old-timers in the crowd.

Kendo stepped back, wondering if it was an accident – maybe he didn't mean to do it. We moved around a bit and the ear was still tingling. We came back together and immediately, he did it again. The crowd lit up once more. Second time around it clearly wasn't a mistake.

We came together for a third time, and I made sure I was ready if he tried the same move again – there was no way he'd get away with it a third time.

As he came in, Kendo did an arm-drag and crutch-hold, lifted him into the air, and power-drove him into the canvas straight onto his left shoulder, and then put a face-bar on him and mauled him around for a while.

Eventually, Kendo got up, expecting Baldwin to follow, but he didn't – he remained on the canvas. The ref was counting him, also expecting him to get up. The heat began to drop away and the crowd quietened down – they were watching closely. Lou was an old-time referee, and he must have sensed that something was wrong – he stopped the count. Kendo was standing back, somewhat surprised at Baldwin's immobility, and Lou pushed him and shouted, 'Stand back!' – he was trying to give Baldwin time to get up.

Rather than resuming the count, to stretch the time even more Lou started it again, then stopped and once more told Kendo to stand back.

Lou quietly said, 'He's not getting up; I'll see what I can do.' He bent down to Baldwin, who must have said something that only he could hear. He came back over and pretended to push Kendo back again, as if he was growing impatient and trying to get to Baldwin.

Under his breath, Lou said, 'He says he's done his shoulder – you'll have to do a finish.' The only option was for Kendo to put a hold on him for a quick submission. Strategy agreed, Baldwin got up and Kendo did the finish. It was all over very quickly – we were only about a minute and a half into the first round, though it might have been two minutes, including all of Lou's antics.

Kendo was declared the winner and we went off to the dressing room. Once there, Baldwin said, 'I did my shoulder in, I couldn't carry on.' We got dressed and went home.

It had been a poor show – Kendo had injured Yorkshire's former British Heavyweight Champion in the first two minutes of the first round of his first match with him. Obviously Baldwin wasn't happy, and the audience had booed – I thought, 'That's it – Kendo won't get any more work from Morrell & Beresford,' but, to my surprise, I was wrong. Next day, I got a phone call – I didn't recognise the voice.

'Hello, Norman Morrell here.'

I thought I was in for a bollocking...

However, he said, 'I liked your show.' It seems I was going to get more work after all.

It came as a complete surprise – how could you like a show like that? It could only have been because Norman had set it up. He'd have seen Kendo in shows with good professional wrestlers but then he'd sent Baldwin in to see what he was really made of. Kendo had passed the test, and this can only have impressed Norman...

On the other hand, Baldwin may have felt set up – he may not have been told the full story about how capable Kendo was, and once he'd found himself getting a hard time, he may have faked his shoulder because he wasn't prepared to carry on under such circumstances. He probably would have been pissed off with Norman for putting him in this position...

Kendo never wrestled Baldwin again, but he did referee some of his matches – not without incident.

Five months later Kendo was in a match at Cleethorpes against Dennis Mitchell and Baldwin was refereeing – this was the first time I'd seen him since the Middlesborough match. The orders were that I was supposed to win, 2-1, but after we'd got a fall apiece, Baldwin gave Kendo two public warnings in short order, and then disqualified him. This was completely contrary to the orders and he had no right to make such a decision. Kendo ended up trapped in the middle of the ring surrounded by an audience demanding that he unmasked, as was required when a masked wrestler lost. I knew what was going to happen so I jumped out of the ring and fought my way back to the dressing room, and Baldwin arrived there soon afterwards.

I said, 'What are you doing? You nearly got me fuckin' lynched there!'

He said, 'You'd gone too far...'

I grabbed him and said, 'It's not your job to make those decisions – your job is to do as you're told!'

Then King Ben, who'd been trained by Baldwin, jumped on my back, so I had to get rid off him and I chased him up the stairs into the hall. By the time I got back to the dressing room Baldwin had gone; I don't remember seeing him for quite some time after that.

But – once again – Norman must have been at the foundation of this situation; Baldwin would never have done the disqualification without his authority, so Norman must have just been interested to see what would happen when he caused more mischief. It was no laughing matter – in those days, if an audience felt they'd been cheated, they virtually believed that they had a licence to kill – rings have been pulled out from under wrestlers, who've then got into serious trouble and had to be rescued by other wrestlers... You had to be ready for anything, and expect the unexpected.

Norman's mischief was seen and admired by Max Crabtree, who went on to use such tactics on many occasions at his own shows. I've been at venues where riots have almost broken out because of the upsets Max has caused. He and Norman ensured that wrestling continued to be controversial, but at times it could genuinely put people in danger.

Another example of Norman's skulduggery involved a wrestler called Peter Preston who came in through Morrell and Beresford, and whom I think had been trained by Baldwin. He was a bit tubby and thought he was better than he really was – a lot of them were like that. His cockiness came about after appearing on television against Mick McManus somewhere in the London area.

Norman tutored Preston to double-cross Mick, who had never lost on television. Mick, being the pencil (he gave out the dates for Dale Martin), wouldn't lose – nobody would go against the pencil because he'd make sure you'd get no bookings and you'd be out of the business. Norman sent Preston down to London and he sprung the double-cross on Mick as soon as the match started.

Preston said, 'Do your best.' In the business that means,

'It's off – it's a shoot; we're not going to work together, so if you think you can beat me, try it. I'm not going to give you a fall, so if you think you can take one, take it.' To use Billy Riley's phrase, Mick wasn't a 'proper' wrestler, he was a professional, a showman, and by now, being in his mid-forties and up against Preston who was in his mid-twenties, he was no match for him.

But Mick wasn't stupid – in fact, he always was a clever little bastard. Instead of wrestling Preston and trying to beat him, he took control another way – he threw out a couple of punches and said to the referee, 'Disqualify me,' so he did.

That was the first time Mick had ever lost on television, but he'd rather suffer a disqualification than let Preston throw him around and make a fool of him; besides, it was good for him as a villain. Mick used to put the fist in behind the ref's back quite often, and by rights he was overdue a disqualification, so it wasn't that controversial.

Preston got the sack from Dale Martin, but that didn't worry him because Norman Morrell gave him more than enough dates to make up for it. Norman even had posters ready – 'The only man to beat Mick McManus on television' – Peter Preston, top of the bill, which was good for Norman.

Unfortunately, Preston let the incident go to his head.

Not long afterwards, I was in Middlesborough for Morrell & Beresford, either at the Guildhall or the Town Hall. It was a very old Victorian building with ravaged old furniture, and the dressing room was just a room with some ancient tall school cupboards in it.

I was sitting in a corner, out of the way, facing the door. Everybody was changing in the one room, and I had the mask on as usual. I unpacked all my gear and laid it out ready to put on, and went to use the toilet first, which wasn't in the dressing room.

When I came back, Preston had arrived and was sitting

in the chair I'd been using, even though there were others he could have chosen. There was no mistaking my bag – it was so big you could have slept in it. There were four other wrestlers in the room, one of whom was Jackie Pallo. If memory serves me correct, Pallo was top of the bill with Preston, and I was the main supporting bout, on second. Preston, having just beaten McManus, was the big draw.

I said, 'I'm getting changed there, Peter. All my gear's there.'

Preston glanced around, and said, 'There's plenty of other seats.'

I repeated myself; 'I'm getting changed there. My gear's all there.'

'Well, go and sit somewhere else,' he said.

'No, I'm not sitting somewhere else. Get out, now!'

He refused; enough was enough – time to teach him a lesson.

I grabbed Preston and slammed him in a front headlock, which he wasn't ready for. I dragged him up out of his seat – Pallo had to jump out of the way. I hauled Preston up on top of the cupboards, with his feet and body across them. I was leaning back on his neck, which meant he was in a lot of trouble, and he was screaming the building down.

Ernest Lofthouse came running in; 'What the fucking hell's going on? I can hear this right through the hall!' His voice was an octave higher than usual.

Pallo shouted. 'It's them pair – they're falling out.'

'Leave him alone!' Lofthouse shouted at me. 'For God's sake let him get up!' I did.

Preston managed to get to his feet, and he turned to me and said, 'I bet you think you're a big guy now, don't you?'

I snarled, 'I'll fucking show you what a big guy can do,' and I went for him again. Lofthouse intervened and said to Preston, 'Shut your mouth and come with me. Bring your gear.' He took Preston off to another dressing room out of the way; he never came back.

Norman's skulduggery over McManus had gone to Preston's head, and he'd made a mistake by trying his attitude with me. I was kept well away from him for a long time – in fact, I don't think I ever saw him again.

That's the way that Pallo tells it in his book, 'You Grunt, I'll Groan'; he said he'd never seen a man dragged out of a chair so quickly and violently in his life.

Another situation concerning Norman's control developed with Kendo and Billy Robinson.

Billy was so tough that a lot of the lads were scared of him – he thought nothing of making fools of the top professional wrestlers. Albert 'Rocky' Wall wasn't keen on working with him because he was such hard work, John Lees refused to work with him unless he was paid double wages, Steve Veidor simply wouldn't work with him, double wages or not.

Out of the blue, a string of dates for Robinson and Kendo came through, about four in quick succession, along the East Coast. Being Morrell & Beresford, they'd be matches of four ten-minute rounds, somewhere during which we'd get one fall each so the result would be a draw. They were long, gruelling shows, and once again, it's my opinion that Norman put them on for his own entertainment.

They weren't good for either of us. Robinson was the former British Heavyweight Champion, and Kendo was the masked man – neither of us could lose a match, so what did that leave? Thirty minutes of wrestling with one fall each, or a double knock-out, or a count-out outside the ring.

After the first show, Billy said, 'We'll just pull round for the first round,' which means doing what you do in the gym, but it wasn't show wrestling and was not at all exciting for the audience.

Billy had an advantage because he'd only got a pair of

trunks on, but Kendo had all the gear on – a wrestling leotard, tights, and the mask – which restricts you to some extent because it alters your breathing and your vision. You can end up blowing like a wounded buffalo, and a lot of what you see in wrestling is out of the corner of your eye, but in a mask, you've lost that advantage – any hits can come as a surprise, and therefore more of a shock. Against an opponent as uncompromising as Robinson, it was very hard work, and of no entertainment value whatsoever. They weren't shows, they were just an ordeal – you wanted to get it over with.

If Norman had come up with the right ideas we could have made something of it, but he didn't. I'm sure that he just wanted to see these two hard men wear each other down, and I'm bloody sure Norman would have been at the shows, even though no-one saw him. I think he'd be watching to see if Robinson got frustrated and did something to Kendo, but he wouldn't – he made things hard, but he wouldn't take liberties with me. We weren't friends, but he respected Kendo, which went all the way back to The Snake Pit.

These are just three examples of Norman Morrell's skulduggery, but it went on all the time – he was brilliant at 'divide-and-conquer', using that technique to empower himself and disempower others. Once you'd experienced it, if you had any sense you started to look for the hidden agenda, but it was often hidden beneath other layers of intrigue. Most of Joint Promotions' wrestlers and promoters had a hard time knowing where they stood, but it has to be said that Norman's antics usually ended up being good for the business.

Chapter 15

Professional Wrestling vs. Professional Sportsmen

As I've said before, there were some in the business who were very skilled at wrestling, but that didn't mean they were any good as professional wrestlers. The other side of that coin is that many of the wrestlers who enthralled audiences were not skilled at catch wrestling but they may have been very hard men.

Les Kellett is an interesting exception – he was popular with audiences because he was a comic, but behind the antics was a very hard man who was also a capable wrestler. He was actually feared by most wrestlers (and other hard men), and while they would work with him, they'd be scared of him the whole time! They had to let him get away with his comic antics, which often made them look like fools, because they knew he might do something dangerous if they didn't. He would almost invariably hurt his opponents and he was difficult to retaliate against – it was as if he felt no pain.

He came into wrestling through Norman Morrell

before Joint Promotions existed, and he played an important – if dubious – role when Norman wanted to bring promoters together to form the organisation. There was resistance to this because it meant losing their independence, so Norman recruited a couple of hefty lads to force their hands. He'd send Les and Ernest Baldwin to rival promoters' shows where they'd jump into the ring and completely disrupt matches, as well as making their top-of-the-bill wrestlers look like cowards because they wouldn't take them on – Les especially. Many promoters gave-in because it was better to knuckle-under and work with Norman rather than have their shows wrecked by a dangerous and uncontrollable nutcase.

Before I'd ever seen Les I'd heard of him and his reputation. Apparently, once, in Germany, his opponent did something that he didn't like, so he bit the top of his ear off. It could have been just a myth, but I heard it often enough for it to have some credibility.

Another story described how hard Les was; in a match with Norman Morrell, he grabbed Les's finger, intending to use it as a submission hold – his choice was to submit or have his finger broken. Norman said, '...finger, Les...'

Les replied, 'Break it!' He would do whatever it took to avoid defeat.

Kendo's first appearance against Les was on the South coast for London-based Dale Martin promotions. When I first started working for them I used to go for a week at a time and, along with the other Northern lads, I'd stay at a place called Martinez, until it became so regular that I got my own bed-sit. I didn't meet Les in the ring until I'd worked for them for about two years.

When I got to the show, Les was in the dressing room; he was well-built and had hands like dustbin lids. Mike Judd, one of the officials there, told me that Kendo was on with Les, who nodded. We started talking and he said the match wasn't a good idea; Kendo was a serious wrestler whereas his shows were based on comedy, and he felt it would be difficult for Kendo to sell him, but not the other way round. He said, 'What do I do then? My comebacks are all comedy. I'm not a baby face in the usual way – I'm a comedy-maker.'

I thought for a moment and replied, 'We'll just have to make the best of it.'

Match time came and we went into the ring and started working, and everything went okay for a short while. At one point Kendo was kneeling on the canvas and Les put him into a headlock and whispered into his ear, 'Trust your uncle Les.'

He did one of his comic runs-around which ended with a boot in Kendo's back. The kick was so hard I thought I'd swallowed my tonsils. I thought, 'Fucking hell – you old twat!'

Kendo didn't sell it. He was so livid that he jumped up and hit Les with about the same amount of force as the kick, which surprised him. Les hit back, then Kendo hit him again, and it spiralled out of control into a virtual street-fight. We were hitting each other so hard that it became a matter of who would give in first – neither of us did.

We reached the second round and were still raining blows on each other, but it wasn't getting either of us anywhere; eventually Les said, 'Throw me into the ropes – I'm going home.'

That finish was Les's usual trick – he'd fall back against the ropes, try to catch them with his upturned feet, miss them completely, and fall through onto the floor of the hall. This time he landed on his head and never got back in the ring.

Kendo went back to the dressing room and Les arrived soon after and said to me, 'That's how I like it – hard!'

'Don't worry, Les,' I said. 'That's how it's going to be!'

I called in at Dale Martin's gym the following morning and went upstairs to the office where I saw Tony. He was a nice guy and very camp; looking at me with eyes like saucers, he said, 'Oooh! What have you been up to, then?'

'What do you mean?' I asked.

'Well, we had Uncle Les in first thing this morning and he's had Mick across the desk and he told him that if he ever puts him on with you again, he'll come down here and drag him round the fucking office!'

'Where's Les now?' I asked.

'He's buggered off home – he's booked for us all week, but he's told Mick to stick it all up his arse!' Mick McManus was the 'pencil' for Dale Martin, and not a hard man at all – he wouldn't have welcomed being roughed-up by Les! A serious masked villain against a comedian had actually been one of the most ill-advised match-ups ever –Les had probably decided to smack Mick as soon as he'd found out he was on against Kendo.

Kendo didn't get in the ring with Les again for quite some time (certainly not for Dale Martins), even though we both ended up on many of the same bills. He was respectful towards Kendo and always spoke highly of him – he didn't give that sort of credit lightly.

As a wrestler, Les was genuinely very tough and he was highly skilled, but he was also very engaging to watch; it's a surprisingly uncommon combination. Most wrestlers as skilled as him felt that the professional scene was simply beneath them – they wanted to show their real abilities, as opposed to playing to an audience with what amounted to acting.

A fine example of this was arguably the most capable wrestler I ever faced, the man who gave me such a hard time on my first day at Riley's Gym, Billy Robinson. Not only did he have a background in boxing and was extremely strong, but he was arguably the best catch wrestler in the world – I truly believe he was unbeatable. However, he confided in me that having such a reputation was a burden – it was hard to maintain a high enough level of fitness when on the road, eating bad food, not getting enough sleep, not being able to maintain a training regime. The top lads lived by their reputations and couldn't afford to have them diminished by any defeats in the gym – the top shooters stayed that way by staying away from each other, but they would face each other in the professional scene, usually with agreed compromise finishes as the result.

He'd started at Riley's Gym around ten years before me so he had a huge head-start on me, and even though I could probably beat him in judo, his considerable natural ability and long study under Riley himself made him formidable in catch wrestling. Wrestlers were afraid of him, but in a different way to other hard men like Hans Streiger (Clark Mellor), who would wait for you in the car park if you messed him around in the ring, whereas Robinson would have you in the match.

Of course, in professional wrestling, Robinson and I would do draws or double knock-outs, both ending up outside the ring and both missing the count.

Big Bruno Elrington, a six foot six inch professional wrestler from Portsmouth, once burst into the dressing room and bellowed, 'I'm a giant!'

Someone shouted back, 'What about Billy Robinson then?'

Slightly subdued, Bruno replied, 'He's a giant killer...'

Robinson expected his superiority to be respected. There was a time when Kendo was working with The Count and Robinson was on the same bill, and he told me that Kendo was giving the Count too much, making him look better than he really was. Robinson didn't like that because he felt the Count wasn't in the same class as him, and if he could hold his own against Kendo, it made Robinson look less capable when he fought Kendo.

I tried to justify my working relationship with Geoff by telling Billy that I owed him a lot. I was surprised at the ferocity of Robinson's reply; he snapped, 'You don't fuckin' owe him anything – you're here on your own merit!' I was taken aback, but there was real depth to his words. Not only was he advising me not to sacrifice myself to relationships with men he considered less able, but he was giving me this heads-up as opposed to dealing with it how he usually would, by making an example of someone. It seemed that he didn't want me to make a mistake that wouldn't look good for either myself, or him – very few got such advice from him.

What's evident here is Robinson's professional pride, but it got in his way. It's all very well being able to tie up any opponent with skill, but professional wrestling has to engage the audience, and all the shooting technique in the world simply won't do that.

Unfortunately for him and for what he could have brought to professional wrestling, Robinson's reluctance to engage properly with 'show' techniques meant that he wasn't entertaining, so it was more difficult to get a show out of him. Consequently, he wasn't a household name, and there was a risk that he would actually make his opponents look bad; being slick and efficient at winning simply wasn't what audiences wanted, and on that level, The Count was indeed much more successful as a professional.

Robinson's ability served him very well in other ways, though. He went to Japan in late 1966 and they really liked him. He came back to the UK for two or three months but was quickly lured back to Japan after being offered the job of training Japanese wrestlers. Over there, one main promoter worked with American wrestlers and televised wrestling, and Dutch shooter Karl Gotch (another former Wiganer) trained their Japanese wrestlers. Then a competing promoter emerged, supported by a senator who was also an executive for a TV company which wanted to broadcast wrestling as well. They also needed a top shooter to teach their lads, and Billy Robinson was the man. In that field, he was very successful, and most British professional wrestlers breathed a sigh of relief when he got the job! No-one missed the ordeals of matches with Billy...

Another Wigan man, Bob Robinson, who wrestled as Billy Joyce, was similar, but subtly different. He too had trained under Billy Riley, and had been there for fifteen years when a teen-age Billy Robinson arrived, who then trained under the senior man.

In comparison to Billy's prize-fighter style, Bob was more like an Aikido expert. He was very smooth – you didn't know when a submission hold from him was coming. I recall when wrestling him, we'd be pulling-round, and I'd suddenly find that I was a hair's breadth from being in a submission hold – he'd manoeuvred me into it with such stealth that I'd barely noticed; he had, though – he'd giggle slightly when he saw that I'd spotted the trap, almost too late! Clever bugger!

Sadly, Bob was also a poor show wrestler. He had a flat Wigan accent and a very dry sense of humour so he was very entertaining to be around, but his wrestling, while brilliant, was as dry as his manner.

Bob was one of those who came to Riley's to watch Robinson smack me around on my first day, and yet a few years later when we were booked together for Dale Martins, he asked me to make sure he went over well so they'd give him more work. What a reversal of fortunes! From novice to top-of-the-bill, putting over Billy Joyce, in five years – I'd come a long way...

There were plenty of wrestlers who had reputations for being tough when they weren't particularly; an example of this was Billy Torontos. To audiences, he was a bit of a joke – not funny, like Kellett, but in the gym he was capable of screwing people, as we say. I'd heard that one of his boasts was that no-one could make him submit.

During my second stint in London for Dale Martin I went to the gym on the ground floor at their offices (which had a wrestling ring), and while I was training on the weights Torontos came in to wrestle with a newcomer who'd been brought in to be assessed by Jack Dale. Jack came down from the office to watch the proceedings – he seemed to take note that I was there – and I watched how Torontos did things.

From what I could see he was quite strong. Once he had his partner in a front headlock he'd drag him down to the canvas and maul him around. However, he was quite short, maybe about five feet eight, so when he put the headlock on, he went up onto his toes – a weak point as far as I was concerned. I was ready if (and probably when) he tried the same thing on me.

Eventually I jumped into the ring. He tried his move but didn't succeed; I teased him three or four more times until he wanted it really badly, and, sure enough, he went up onto his toes and I had him. I shot him straight up then took him into a reverse souplex; his head caught the low ceiling and I brought him down and landed with him, then I mauled the living daylights out of him for about ten minutes, while Jack watched intently.

The opportunity eventually came for me to end his boast of never being made to submit. We were training one day and I put him into a submission hold and kept the pressure on. He shouted, 'Okay, okay!'

I said, 'No – say the words, 'I submit.''

He resisted so I applied more pressure, to the point where I would have broken his arm – I made sure he actually said it. To give him his credit, he did tell everyone that Kendo Nagasaki was the only man who'd ever made him submit.

Finally, there were the dedicated show-men. Professional wrestling really is all about the show – forty minutes of drama, where a good guy and a bad guy do battle, there's a to-and-fro of advantage, genuinely painful and immobilising holds are not fully applied but are made to look like they are, and there's often victory snatched from the jaws of defeat – or denied, to be hoped for next time. Next time is what really matters – the drama skilfully woven, hungrily devoured by an eager audience.

This has been exposed many times now, but there's more to it than fakery – succeeding in professional wrestling requires its own set of finely-honed skills. I've mentioned Count Bartelli many times as an example of a successful professional wrestler, so how did he do it?

The Count was intriguing because on the limited circuit of venues he wrestled at, he was the only masked baby-face – all other masked men that Wryton employed were villains. As far as I know, only he and The White Angel (Judo Al Hayes, who only worked for Lincoln Promotions) were masked baby-faces.

The Count was good at getting the sympathy of the audience because he was good at taking punishment; Billy Howes, for example, would really smack him around, which worked well with his image – the more punishment he took, the more his victories meant. He would get bloodied and terribly pasted and then make a valiant comeback and win, to the delight of the audience.

As a show-man, The Count had a certain exaggerated and dramatic style of doing things. He had no spectacular moves, but he posed in his moves and held them in a way that gave them drama and tension – a forearm smash wasn't just a hit, but he'd wind it up with several swirls before landing it; when he fell, he'd bounce and 'sell' it; when he put on a hold, he'd flex his muscles as if he was in a bodybuilding contest; he telegraphed his moves, making it clear what he was about to do, which made them more accessible and engaging to the audience because they could see what he was doing and where it would lead. As a result of all this, his ring presence was star-like, and wrestling fans would talk about what they'd seen him do so spectacularly.

There's no single reason why a wrestler becomes a good show-man – The Count's ring presence, as well as his mask and being a baby-face, were the foundation of his success, which shows that in addition to being able to 'perform' well, it's usually those with a strong visual image that succeed in professional wrestling. For example, Billy Two-Rivers did a war dance; Big Daddy had the theme song and the glittery top hat; Adrian Street was originally a Hell's Angel and then very glam-rocky; Jackie Pallo was a typical cocky cockney, swaggery and over-confident and they hated his arrogance. Each individual's image became their trade-mark.

Jim Hussey was a great villain because he'd never been a catch or amateur wrestler! He had no sporting pride to get in the way – he wasn't trying to protect any cherished reputation. This characterises the best showmen – they're not wrestling sportsmen, they're often other kinds of sportsman, and they go into a gym and learn professional wrestling from scratch, which is what you see in a wrestling ring – it's a far cry from catch wrestling.

Marc 'Rollerball' Rocco came into the business as a professional wrestler from day one – it's my understanding that when he was young he'd been a show-jumper and after he finished in that sport he trained-up specifically as a professional wrestler, and he made an excellent villain.

The foregoing shows that in terms of professional wrestling, straight wrestling actually becomes baggage that gets in the way. Straight wrestlers aren't working for the show, they're working to protect their image of themselves – they need to prove to themselves and everyone else that they're better than the other man. Because in professional wrestling many holds are held-off and posed-in to sell them to an audience, to many real wrestlers it's just an embarrassment.

An example of this is George Gordienko who would do villainy as a professional, but he couldn't really pull it off because he'd been a Canadian champion and was good at proper wrestling. Because he was a true wrestling champion, he was badly conflicted – his genuine skills were at odds with what he found himself having to do, and he only did it because it made him a good living.

Likewise Karl Gotch, who came to Wigan and didn't leave for 4 years – he just kept on learning under Billy Riley. Combat sports are addictive – continuing to refine your level of expertise is compelling, and the continuing achievements are personally empowering.

However, a great many real wrestlers ended up doing professional wrestling because there was no money in the real thing (Amateur Wrestling), but if they could bring themselves to set their pride aside they'd be able to make a very good living from professional wrestling. But most couldn't, or at least not do it convincingly, and fully commit to the theatre of professional wrestling.

Last of all there was a unique group of wrestlers who came through Lincoln Promotions, including Wayne Bridges, Ray Hunter, Mike Marino, and 'Judo' Al Hayes; I met them when I went to work for Dale Martins. Their approach to professional wrestling was based on what they would call being a 'loose worker'. This consisted of being extremely light, meaning they didn't put on any holds in a strong or 'stiff' way. This even extended to when they shook hands with you – it was like getting hold of a wet fish. They would tell you that working with them you could go home from a match feeling like you'd had a day off – they treated that as a badge of office. They often used the term 'lover' to speak to each other and other wrestlers, which Gorgeous George later seized on and he nick-named them the 'Lovey-doveys'.

Some of them had done movie and stunt work and they brought the techniques into wrestling, such as looking like they're throwing a punch but not actually hitting the target. It wasn't easy to work with because are you supposed to fall down when someone in the audience might have seen that the punch hadn't actually made contact? But if no-one had seen that and you don't fall down, will you make the other wrestler look like a fool? – I found it all quite alien.

On my first encounters in the ring with these wrestlers they complained that I was extremely 'stiff', and they tried to induct me into their ways – Al Hayes was one of the prime advocates. If he was matched against me I'd do a throw called a 'hype', which involved locking his shoulder and sweeping him into the air with my right leg and bringing him over onto his back, and in his perfect Received Pronunciation he'd charmingly say, 'Peter, old boy – do I have to go quite so high, and do I have to have two?'

I'd say, 'Well, we'll see how it goes, Al...'

With refined dismay he'd reply, 'Oh, no....'

He'd make me laugh, so I tended not to be so hard on him.

When I got to know him better I asked how Mike Marino got his enormous cauliflower ears. His face had also been so battered that whilst he was very much a 'loose' worker, he looked like a hard man. He actually had been a hard wrestler once, but had then whole-heartedly adopted the 'loose worker' approach.

Al told me that Mike had been on at Aberdeen against Bert Assirati, who was genuinely dangerous. He'd been a tumbler in the circus so he was very agile, and he was very strong. He wasn't very tall, perhaps five foot six, but he was very broad. As a wrestler he was a monster and earned himself a terrible reputation for doing vicious things to his opponents.

In the Aberdeen match, someone in the audience shouted to Assirati, 'Come on, Chico – you're just playing about with him.' Assirati went crazy and beat Marino very, very badly. Until that day, he'd been a handsome young man and a capable wrestler, but when he came out of the ring he had permanent cauliflower ears and his face was so smashed up that he was unrecognisable. Apparently he was really disoriented too – he didn't know where he was for six weeks. The word was that he was never the same again.

By the time I faced Marino it was many years later and he'd developed a style that I found hard work. When the bell went for the start of the round he would stand away from his opponents and do a kind of lurching-grabbing move that looked like he was about to weigh-in, but he always took a step backwards. It worked well, because it meant the villains who faced him always had to go after him, which made them look more aggressive – I used to call him 'Come-and-collect-me Mike.' When you were in-close he also had a way of hanging on to you so it looked like you were punishing him more than you actually were. All these behaviours had a devastating effect on a show in Croydon just before George joined me.

It had been a hot match. He was going after the mask, making it clear during the match that he wanted to get it off but never quite managing it. At the end of the match Kendo slithered through the ropes and he was supposed to go after him, still chasing the mask. There was a gangway between the ring and a side-door that went through the audience seats, and the plan was that he would chase Kendo to the door and finally grab the mask off and Kendo could then disappear through the door. It would be a double count-out (a double KO had been ordered), but with added danger and excitement.

When Kendo got to the door Mike was still at ring-side, doing his jumping-grabbing thing, waiting for Kendo. For the finish I had to go back and collect him, dragging him towards the door, making it look like we're fighting, and at this time all the audience was becoming more wound-up – they were getting to their feet and wanting to join in.

When we reached the door Kendo virtually had to hand the mask to him then rush out, away from an audience that wanted to lynch him by then. Kendo rushed into the corridor that led to the dressing room with members of the audience chasing him while Marino was a hero with Kendo's mask in his hands.

I was so wound-up that I missed the dressing room door and rushed up some more stairs and through a door that led straight onto the roof. Fortunately there was a bolt on the outside so when they banged on that door they thought it was locked and they looked for me somewhere else.

I was stuck out there on the roof for twenty minutes while the crowd dispersed – other than that door there was no other way off it and I was relieved that I didn't have to confront angry audience-members up there; it could have been genuinely dangerous for me.

When the noise subsided I made my way back to the dressing room and found Marino calmly taking a shower. He said, 'Where've you been?'

I said, 'Stuck on the fuckin' roof for twenty minutes thanks to you! That was fuckin' dangerous!'

He said, 'Yeah, but it was a good show, wasn't it?' He'd cleverly put himself over, which he was always good at doing, but this time it had been at some risk to me.

Kendo was never going to be just a show-man, or one of the 'lovey-doveys'; I'd originally thought that Bartelli was a real wrestler only to have the truth revealed after training at Riley's Gym, and then by experiencing what my opponents were and weren't capable of. After that, I could have suffered the same disillusionment with professional wrestling as any catch wrestler, but I'd been fortunate enough to have seen Bartelli's example of what could be gained from the show aspect, and I had the skills to ensure that I could look after myself.

For Kendo to be the best he could be, it was very much about being objective about professional wrestling and bringing all the elements together in an inspired way. I also knew that with all my training, I could bring a new dimension to what was seen in professional wrestling – new and more impressive moves and throws, and a new style of aggression and attitude.

Now that I was established I occasionally had some gratifying reactions to my success. I was still living at my father's house and I had the lovely blue convertible Pontiac Parisienne parked in the drive – it was the car that Barry had when he'd met Ros; he'd pranged it and I'd bought it from him for a song and repaired it, and it was such a nice drive that I kept it.

As I was getting into the car one day, walking past was Mrs. Evans, my mother's friend who'd come to my rescue as a panicked infant in the street so long ago. She saw the car and saw me and said, 'Oh, it's Peter isn't it? What a lovely car! You've done so well – your mother would have been so proud of you!'

I don't recall seeing much of her since my mother had died. I was pleased at her warm reaction to how things had turned out – she must have been amazed, as it had hardly looked likely back then.

Chapter 16

Japan, Chelsea, Stockwell Rd.

By 1968 I'd moved into my Aunt Ida's house in Riley Crescent, Wolverhampton. Between wrestling commitments I'd begun helping her with her properties, and was overseeing the conversion of this one into flats and would later look after renting them out.

In fact, whenever I'd had time, I'd driven my Aunt when she needed to go to see family in Staffordshire. We once stopped at a service station on the M6 for a cup of tea which my Aunt insisted she'd pay for, as 'her treat'. I tried to refuse but she was insistent, and demanded to know how much it was. I told her it was three shillings, or one shilling and sixpence per cup.

She was horrified! She spluttered, 'I've never paid more than sixpence for a cup of tea in my life! We shan't stop here again!' We did stop there again, but she brought her own flask of tea...

Soon after moving to Wolverhampton, I got the opportunity to wrestle in Japan.

As I've already described, there was a new 'opposition' promoter in Japan called Kokusai Pro Wrestling, also known as International Wrestling Enterprise, which established itself by bringing top-notch British wrestlers to the country for televised matches, along with a few from other countries who also had prominence in the UK. They contacted Relwyskow & Green and I was booked for some shows about six or seven months after they'd first brought wrestlers from Britain – Billy Robinson and a few others among them.

On this tour, Jim Hussey, Al Hayes, and myself went; we flew from Heathrow in a Boeing 707, which couldn't fly all the way to Japan, so we went 'over the pole', stopping in Anchorage, Alaska, to re-fuel, and there we picked up Canadian George Gordienko. When we got to Tokyo, we were joined by Ray Hunter who'd flown in from Australia. Ray had been a partner with Paul Lincoln in Lincoln Promotions, which then sold out to Dale Martin, so he decided he'd carry on wrestling.

Jim Hussey and Al Hayes were fond of playing pranks on people, which they did all the time, and once we'd taken off from Anchorage they decided that it would be fun if I arrived in Japan and got off the 'plane wearing the Kendo mask; I wasn't particularly keen on the idea but they talked me into it. There were no boarding bridges back then, they had steps which were brought to the 'plane which you walked down to the tarmac, so when we got off, I dropped the mask on and walked with the others to the terminal building.

We were met by one of the directors of the TV company (who was also a Government senator called Hata, I believe) who took us straight to the VIP lounge where immigration came and collected our passports. They didn't talk to us or ask me to take the mask off – they just stamped our passports, so I entered Japan masked, with no-one comparing me to my passport picture or checking who I actually was!

From there a limousine took us to our hotel, which I also entered wearing the mask, and I also did this whenever I was coming and going to and from shows.

In the hotel we found that a box had been left for Jim

by his friend Roy 'Bull' Davis, Skull Murphy's father, who'd been on the tour before. He took it up to the room, and found that it was full of crepe bandages and plasters and liniment and all sorts of other things to treat injuries, so the first thing he thought was, 'Bloody hell! The boys must have had it rough!' It seemed we were in for a hard time from the Japanese – they were all quite young and very fit whereas Jim and Al Hayes were in their forties. I would have been around 27, so, concerned about what might be awaiting him, Jim pulled me on one side and said, 'Don't let these fuckers run all over us!'

One of the first matches was a three-man tag with Jim, Al Hayes, and Kendo, versus three Japanese wrestlers. Jim came out complaining that his opponent had been very 'stiff', unresponsive and hard work to get a show from, so he tagged Kendo in. As that happened, the other side tagged another man in too, and Kendo found himself up against someone different, whom he started heaving about. Jim suddenly shouted, 'Oi! What the fuckin' 'ell are you doing? That's the boss you're chuckin' around!' I hadn't realised it but my opponent was the promoter!

It had been Jim who'd told me to go in hard, and here he was bollocking me for doing it, so I told him, 'You can fuck off and all, Hussey!' He grizzled away in his gruff voice, but he didn't try to tell me off again.

I found Japan fascinating, and my ability to see more of it was enhanced with the help of George Gordienko. We used to go out late at night because George used to like going around all the little back-streets to take in the culture. He used to paint, and he liked going to all the places the normal tourists didn't, so he could breathe in the atmosphere and use it in his paintings. He'd knock on my door and say, 'Come on, Peter-boy, let's go for a walk,' and we'd have a midnight stroll around the streets of Tokyo – or wherever else we might happen to be.

George loved the places where the natives went after

they finished work, catering to the tourists – truly ethnic places, such as bars and eateries which could only seat ten people, where there would be nothing western on the menu, none of which were in English. He was a fascinating and cultured man, very much a loner and hard to get to know, but we bonded well on that tour which was to help me later in Canada.

Jim Hussey, on the other hand, was mischievous with the culture. At the hotel one day, he bowed to a Japanese man, who bowed back, as is the cultural norm, to show respect and humility. It's like their hand-shake, but they bow instead, and like a hand offered to be shaken, it would be rude to refuse. The two parties normally stop bowing more-or-less together so they can move on, but as soon as the Japanese man finished his bow, Jim bowed again, which precipitated another bow from the man. The rest of us were watching and it seemed to go on and on as playful Jim bowed.

While we were in Tokyo I went to the Kodokan, the world headquarters of judo, to practise. It felt a little like completing an unfinished circle, using Abbe's skills in his homeland. I practised with several of the judokas who were there, who ranged from Kyu grades upwards; most of them weren't really a challenge to me, but my catch wrestling techniques gave me an edge which they found difficult to deal with. After a while I was privileged to be invited onto the mats with higher grades who'd watched me, and practising at that level at the heart of judo was a challenge and an honour.

I told a couple of the judokas there that I'd studied under Abbe, and one of them said he knew about him. The promoter, Hata, also did – he actually came to me and mentioned that he knew I'd studied under Abbe, which seemed to give me some extra credibility. He took us all out to dinner two or three times, and we were taken everywhere in limousines; they really looked after us well, but I heard that as the tours went on, the wrestlers who went later got more down-to-earth treatment. It seemed only those of us on the earliest of the tours got the VIP treatment, until they found a working balance.

We had an interpreter for the tour who was always with us; we called him 'Freddy', but I never knew his Japanese name. About a week into the tour he brought a fan's wrestling magazine into the dressing room and asked Kendo to autograph it. I started signing his usual Kanji, but Freddy stopped me and told me to sign 'Mr. Guillotine'. I asked him why – he told me that Kendo had been billed as Mr. Guillotine for the whole Japanese tour, even though all the other wrestlers had retained their usual professional names.

This was news to me! My knowledge of kanji was limited to Kendo's autograph so I hadn't noticed that he'd been billed differently on the posters; it seemed that the promoter had taken the decision to do this. I asked Freddy why this had been done, and he told me it was because they thought the Japanese people wouldn't understand why a wrestler from Britain would have a name like Kendo Nagasaki.

It wasn't a sensible decision because even in Japan they got the British wrestling magazines, so they knew who Kendo was; Freddy even said that he'd heard that the fans thought I may have a Japanese father which was why I had a Japanese name.

Needless to say, I refused to sign as Mr. Guillotine – it would be Kendo or nothing.

During the final match on the tour Kendo faced Japanese star wrestler 'The Great Kusatsu', for the 'Western Great Britain Heavyweight Title'. The story went that Kusatsu had won the title belt from another British heavyweight some time earlier and Kendo challenged him to win it back, but, according to the Japanese wrestling press, Kendo lost to Kusatsu by virtue of his signature figure-four leg-lock. The facts of the matter are that Kendo did not lose a match to any

Japanese wrestler, not even Kusatsu, but in a gesture of patriotism, the Japanese wrestling press sold the story that way. The title itself (and the belt) had also been manufactured in Japan for the challenge matches in order to raise the stakes, which it did – they were very compelling shows which the audiences really enjoyed, but we had no control over how the results were reported.

As Kendo never returned to Japan, Kusatsu's alleged win never really mattered anywhere outside of that country, but I am bound to set the record straight, whilst still giving Kusatsu his due – he was a very able professional wrestler, fully deserving his star status in his homeland, but he never beat Kendo.

I loved my brief time in Japan; the tour didn't encompass the whole country, but we saw quite a lot of the Eastern half, and I appreciated the chance to experience the serene, disciplined, and excellence-oriented culture and land that Abbe had come from, and I vowed to return one day.

I was delighted to hear that we would return home not by re-tracing our flight over the pole to the UK, but by flying East to Hawaii, then San Francisco, then New York, and then home. Tremendous – wrestling was allowing me to see the world!

As we took off from Japan, we hit the back end of a typhoon that had hit the southern island, Shikoku. The 'plane shook quite violently for at least an hour, which really upset Al Hayes, who didn't like flying because he'd previously been in quite a serious accident. He calmed himself down before take-off by getting very drunk – too drunk, as it happened, because he ended up throwing-up during the flight and losing an essential item.

When we landed in Honolulu, I noticed that his two front teeth were missing. I'd known that they were false and that he normally wore a plate, so I asked him, 'Where's your teeth, Al?'

His hand shot to his mouth and he said, 'Oh, fuck!

They must be somewhere in the Pacific! Why didn't you take them from me before I got drunk?!?' Clearly he'd have liked me to have looked after him a bit better!

In Hawaii we stayed in a 5-star apartment which overlooked the stunning Waikiki Beach – in fact, you walked out of the front door and straight onto the beach. Our accommodation there had been arranged by local promoter Peter Maivia; there were two bedrooms, one of which I shared with Al, and Jim shared the other with American wrestler Pat Barratt who was already there.

I enjoyed Al's company because he was very amusing and really quite cultured – he spoke several languages and could write fluently in French. In fact, before the Japan trip I'd wrestled with him in France and Switzerland, promoted by Dave Morgan, a friend of Al's, who had been great company throughout.

In Hawaii I found myself the subject of the charming attentions of the promoter's daughter, Ata, who was my constant companion – we were together all the time I was there. She took our group to many of the most beautiful places around Honolulu and she was very good company. My five days there were genuinely like visiting paradise, and Ata came to the airport to see me off. She gave me a lai made from seashells and told me I would return to the island, and I've often thought I would have liked to. Ata would eventually marry professional wrestler 'Rocky' Johnson, and her son was to become a wrestler and movie star – Dwayne Johnson, 'The Rock'.

We then flew to San Francisco, which was only an overnight stay but I had the chance to see a couple of the sights. Then it was on to New York, and when we went to enquiries at San Francisco airport and Al started speaking, the girl behind the desk was bowled-over by his refined English accent. She shouted across to other nearby desks and said, 'Hey, you guys, come and listen to this guy!' About six girls came over and were completely awe-struck at his voice; it turned out to be a watershed moment, as Al later went back to the USA to wrestle as Lord Alfred Hayes and eventually became the commentator for the WWF.

When we got to 'The Big Apple', the others insisted that I kept all their money with me in a money belt, because they couldn't trust themselves with it in the city that never sleeps! I even had to sleep with the 'mazuma'... We were there for about four days and saw the sights, including walking along Broadway, going to Jack Dempsey's bar, going to the top of the Empire State Building which that day was swathed in low clouds, and spending some wonderful evenings in music clubs. New York was a tremendous finale to our tour.

When we got back to the UK Al stayed in London and Jim and I caught a domestic flight to Manchester. When we landed Jim's wife and son met us and he introduced them. He also said, 'This is my son Marc who's coming into the job' That was the first time I met Marc 'Rollerball' Rocco; he'd have been about sixteen years old.

At almost the same time as I came back from Japan, Billy Robinson went to work there, and in America. I heard he occasionally ended up in Hawaii where, unbelievably, he'd had a fight with Peter Maivia. They'd fallen through a plate glass window and Maivia had bitten the top off Robinson's ear – the word was that Maivia got the upper hand. I found this most surprising – how could the upstanding Wigan-trained 'super-shooter' whom I'd always so admired have become a drunken brawler? Billy Riley would have been deeply shocked.

When I got home to Wolverhampton there were orders waiting in the letterbox and it was straight back into British Professional Wrestling.

Away from the wrestling business, I bought the house next door to my Aunt's in Riley Crescent, Wolverhampton. She arranged a mortgage for me, which a young wrestler would normally never have got – she went into the Stafford Building Society and was so respected that they just granted it on the spot. I used the money I'd earned from the Japan tour to convert my house into four bed-sit flats, with a view to renting them out except for the bigger ground floor flat where I lived. My old school-friend Peter Latham came to Wolverhampton to help me with the conversions and to look after the flats when I wasn't there.

Then, out of the blue, I came home one day to find Ros there; Peter had let her in. She and Barry had broken up. She told me that she'd decided she wanted to be with me, and when she'd told Barry he'd literally dumped her on my doorstep and gone back to London.

When they came back from Spain they went to a special college in London where he did a butlering courses and she did a house-keeping course, after which they ran a restaurant and then went on to work for a titled family near Bolton. They wanted the qualifications and experience to get a Green Card and go working in the United States and all this was part of that process. Their agency put them in touch with American Stanley Picker and they went to his new Thames-side house as house-keeper and butler – they thought he might take them to America.

I'd seen them occasionally throughout this time – it must have been a year and a half since Spain. It seemed that Ros had a thing for me. I went to see them at Picker's while he was away and stayed over. Barry had awakened one morning and found Ros entwined around me, which made our attraction pretty clear, so I suppose it was only a matter of time before their relationship ended.

Ros moved in with me, but after only a month she found Wolverhampton boring and wanted to move to London because I was spending quite a lot of time there.

I'd stopped going to Martini's and had a very small bed-sit on the Fulham Palace Road and Ros moved into it. It was really far too small for two people so we agreed to get a bigger one. We found a nice one-bedroom flat in

Chelsea but the cost of the flat and our life-style was more than our disposable income could sustain so she decided to get a job. I wasn't surprised when she walked straight into a hostess job at the Churchill, an up-market gentlemen's club, at which she did very well. We spent a lot of time together out on the town and it was a lot of fun; she had a way about her that even the staff in Harrods would take notice.

Barry got a new girlfriend called Elaine, after which he started speaking to me again, but it was a bit frosty. Elaine was nothing like Ros, and any time we were all together she seemed to want to rub it in that he hadn't been able to do as well as her.

Ros's mother made several visits to London to see her, and after she got to know me better we were invited to spend Christmas at the family home. Late on Christmas Day her father invited me outside to see their extensive greenhouses and whilst there he asked 'Are you going to make an honest woman of my daughter?' I wasn't! Marriage was the last thing on my mind. This was to be an omen of things to come.

On Boxing Day I went to Blackpool to see Ida. I decided to take her for a drive around Stanley Park, and as she was getting in the car she saw a hat that Mrs. James had left on the back seat after we'd been to a country club on Christmas Day. It was genuine leopard-skin, but Ida thought it was a cheap copy, and she said, 'I know the sort of woman that wears a hat like that!' She didn't! Mrs. James was as respectable as they came, but I didn't bother replying – Ida used to throw controversial quips like that around.

Over the next few months I spent as much time as possible in London with Ros and we'd hang out with George – she thought he was great fun. Her work was pretty flexible; she wasn't needed every night and the three of us would hit the town and have a great time. When she did have nights on we'd go shopping – she was a shopaholic and she dressed herself – and me – very well, although I didn't always go along with her because she had very expensive tastes.

As time went by and Ros's mother began visiting more often the idea of marriage seemed to be hinted at more and more. Mrs. James liked me and her father couldn't wait for his daughter to stop 'living in sin', so all three of them wanted things to move in this direction. I really liked being with her but I certainly didn't want to make that kind of commitment. More than that, marriage would bring about a complete change to how I lived. There were things in my life outside my relationship with Ros, all of which I could keep in balance as things were, but I wasn't prepared to sacrifice them for marriage. I kept trying to play the idea down.

Then Ros met someone called Denis through her work and he asked her to marry him. She gave me an ultimatum – if I didn't marry her, she'd marry Denis. I wasn't going to be pressured so I said she'd have to do that – we gave up the Chelsea flat and she moved in with Denis.

Two or three days before her wedding she rang me up and asked to see me; we met up somewhere and she told me that she'd made a mistake, she didn't want to marry Denis but wanted to be with me, and we wouldn't even have to get married. I said she couldn't do that – her father would go mad. She said she didn't care, but I said she had to go through with it. We hugged and said goodbye and I never saw her again.

I later heard through a cousin of hers that she and Denis had gone to Portugal and opened a bar, but just a year after getting married she'd run off with a bull-fighter.

After Ros and Barry had split up he'd gone to work at specialist car dealers Chequered Flag in Chiswick, where he had a flat above it. With the Chelsea flat gone, the next time I was in London I stayed there. As we chatted we decided to get a place together and took a lease on a 2-bedroom flat on Kennington Park Road.

With the income from the Wolverhampton flats and my wrestling work I had more than enough money to start a business which would use the knowledge and experience we'd gained from selling cars. We teamed-up and opened a car site on the Walworth Road, South East London. We called it Serviced Vehicles, implying quality and reliability. It was a relatively small concern, a fenced-in storage yard that could accommodate around 15 cars, and from there we sold family cars. As I was wrestling quite a bit I depended on Barry to run it.

Soon afterwards a small car showroom became available nearby on the Stockwell Road; we bought the lease, and as it was under cover, we sold sports cars from there.

We got to know many of the local south London motor traders, who were a fascinating lot – real personalities, all with razor-sharp wits and tongues, with a killer instinct for a deal. They'd all troupe into the West End for salt beef sandwiches, have their hair cut on the Kings Road in Chelsea, and buy their clothes there and in Carnaby Street boutiques. Barry became more like them – very slick and good at his job. Both our south London car sites did extremely well, affording Barry and myself a comparatively extravagant lifestyle.

For our showroom in Stockwell Road we bought a red Pontiac GTO from Chequered Flag where Barry used to work, When we went to collect it we were having a look at it in the showroom and I opened the door. A salesman came in from the yard and said, 'What are you doing?' and he slammed the car door shut. I didn't like his attitude so I back-handed him. He dropped like he'd been pole-axed and lay on the floor, moaning.

A couple of people ran out from the office saying, 'What have you done?' Then Graham Warner, the owner, appeared and asked Barry what had happened. One of the first two came back and said, 'I've called the police!' and Graham said, 'Fuckin' hell! Just leave! Don't come back – I'll get the car delivered.'

We went back to our showroom in Stockwell then popped over the road to a large car site owned by David Black. One of the salesmen was a tall guy called Innes; we called him the 'Jolly Green Giant'. He was about six foot four and a friend of Freddy Sewell, and he too had a shady past. He was playing cards with some others and I told them what had happened at Chequered Flag. Innes immediately said, 'Couldn't have been you boy – you was playing cards with us all afternoon. Must have been some other cunt that looks like you.'

Instant alibi.

The Freddy Sewell connection was about to make life very difficult for us all. After Sewell shot and killed a police chief inspector in a Blackpool jewelry raid, the northern police came to London and spurred the 'Met', the Metropolitan Police, into vigorous and extensive action. All the car dealers were arrested and hauled-in for questioning, including Barry, to such an extent that our sites were virtually shut down. Eventually Freddy was found in north London after 45 days – he may have been 'shopped' by a car trader who couldn't stand the pressure any longer.

Barry and I used to buy cars from Freddy; he had a nice site in Peckham and we'd drop round to see if he had any part-ex cars that were below the level of his stock but were right for our site. He was always charming and softly-spoken; as a car trader I knew he'd be a 'Jack-the-lad', but the lengths he went to in the Blackpool heist was an absolute shock.

Chapter 17

The Route to TV

Another masked wrestler on television? They said it would never happen. It did – but it took Kendo to achieve it.

In the early 1960s Canadian wrestler Gordon Nelson wrestled in the UK – he was a good amateur and an able 'shooter'. I believe he'd wrestled in North America under his own name and in a mask as 'The Outlaw', and it was in this guise that he persuaded Joint Promotions to put him on television. Prior to that there had been numerous masked wrestlers such as The Ghoul, Dr. Death, and others going round the halls, but none had ever appeared on television.

Joint promoted Nelson as 'The Man Nobody Can Pin', or get into a submission. His job was to challenge the audience, to see if someone would like to try, but he was good enough to look after himself so no-one ever did. The problem was the mask; it's an easy thing to imitate, so in a short period of time, all the opposition promoters (outside Joint) ended up with their own masked Outlaws, wrestling all over the place.

As a result, Joint Promotions' experience with masked men on television had been bad, so they decided – no more masked men.

This directly affected a particular well-known masked

wrestler who had higher-profile ambitions, Count Bartelli. He aspired to greater success and wider appeal, and he knew this could only be achieved if he got onto television. He was aware of the problems that Joint had over Gordon Nelson, so he knew this would affect him too.

Bartelli sold his big garage in Crewe and earned himself a lot of money, sixty or seventy thousand pounds – a King's ransom back then. If you won that much on the Pools, you'd be comfortable for the rest of your for life. He kept two smaller garages and he had some other properties, but the big garage had been quite time consuming, and selling it meant he'd have more time to devote to his wrestling career.

At that time, Bartelli only worked for Wryton Promotions; Arthur Wright gave him shows which meant he didn't have to travel very far – the furthest he ever went was Doncaster. Generally, he worked in Birmingham, the Potteries, Liverpool, and Blackpool, distances he could commute to quite easily, but he didn't venture any further.

His biggest problem was he was unknown outside of that circle – he was a big star on a small stage. He wanted national recognition and he knew the only way he could achieve that was to go on television. This meant he'd need to work for other promoters, and because of the blanket no-masked-men rule he'd have to lose the mask.

He came to a decision to unmask at Hanley in a match against Kendo, who would win. That match is still talked about today – Bartelli was the local hero, and in order to show how valiantly he fought against the villainous Nagasaki, he took a huge amount of punishment; his mask was bloodied early in the match, and there are pictures of him after he'd unmasked, and his whole face is battered and swollen. The victorious Kendo kept his mask on, but the valiant baby-face Bartelli remained the darling of his adoring local fans.

Unfortunately, as regards being the doorway to national

success as the non-masked Bartelli, the plan backfired. He was booked for televised shows, but he never became a household name.

If you watch the documentary, Masters of the Canvas, Bartelli says in his interview that Kendo Nagasaki was 'a usurper', had 'usurped' his position. That wasn't the case, because Bartelli had engineered it all himself – it seems he resented the fact that Kendo ended up benefitting more from the plan than he did.

Contrary to what's written in Simon Garfield's The Wrestling, that match had nothing to do with Max Crabtree. At that time, Max promoted only in Scotland, specifically through Morrell & Beresford as opposed to the totality of Joint Promotions, and before he unmasked, Bartelli would never venture as far away as Scotland, so he would therefore have had no contact with Max.

Of course, I was ambitious for Kendo and I wanted him on TV as soon as possible, but I knew he'd also encounter Joint's mask ban.

Surprisingly, however, it was Max who had a hand in Kendo's first television appearance. He came up with an intriguing idea...

Andy Robin was a big draw for him in Scotland. He was built up as the Scottish champion, and I believe he'd said he was the Commonwealth Belt Holder. Max decided that he wanted a Commonwealth championship in Stirling, but he wanted the challenger to come from another member of the Commonwealth; he approached me about the idea. Every time Max saw me he spent a lot of time trying to convince me to be a part of his plan, but I kept refusing. Eventually he wore me down (with money!) and I agreed.

I decided that I would wrestle as Paul Dillon, the alias I'd previously used in Spain. I don't think that Max had known anything about that, but I told him I'd use it this time too; I don't know whether that name actually appeared on a wrestling poster, but I'm pretty sure he billed me as a French Canadian.

Max told me I should arrive in Stirling at a pre-arranged time and place. He would then collect me and tell everyone that I'd come straight from the airport, on a flying visit to the UK. I'd be straight into the ring to do a challenge match with Andy Robin for the Commonwealth title.

I don't actually know whether Andy was the Commonwealth Champion and I'd come in to challenge him, or whether the title was free and we were wrestling for it – I was just doing a job.

When Max picked me up he was a bit anxious. He said, 'Kid, don't talk to anybody – don't sign any autographs. You're French Canadian, you can't speak any English. Get straight in, get the show done and I'll drop you back at your car.'

When he said 'don't talk to anybody', he meant the audience, of course – I'd talk to Andy Robin to work out the match, as usual.

Andy did all his cocky stuff, like he always did – parading around the ring with his arms in the air, pointing and shouting about what he would and wouldn't do – the Scottish audiences liked that. Paul Dillon wrestled as a clean, straight wrestler.

It turned out to be a long one – it was scheduled over eight five-minute rounds, and we went the full distance. When promoters pitched a title match they preferred to keep it very straight. There was no villainy – it was all wrestling, all the way through.

Andy won the match in the last round and either became the Commonwealth champion or he retained the title. The Canadian guy had lost, and it was quickly out of the hall and back to the airport for him.

The next time I worked for George Relwyskow he said, 'I've heard good things about your show in Stirling for Max. Well, what I need is a new baby face who can really wrestle.' I think what George was after was for me to do a double – to wrestle as Kendo, and as a baby-face.

When I'd wrestled Andy, I'd used a different style than would be normal for a Kendo match. I wrestled him from start to finish and gave it everything. Andy was notorious for making fools of his opponents, but he couldn't – and didn't – do that with me. I made him work a lot harder and wrestle more professionally than he would normally have to, and word had reached George Relwysco.

I said, 'George, there's loads of baby faces. Why don't you use one of them.'

'I think you'd be different,' insisted George.

'No,' I said, firmly.

So it was his turn to hound me; it went on for probably six months – every time he saw me he brought it up, but I always refused.

Eventually it fed back to Joint Promotions, and they decided to call me in to a meeting.

It was unusual for a wrestler to be invited to Kirkgate Chambers in Leeds, so when I was asked to go there I knew something big was being considered. The 'big nobs' were there, which consisted of Norman Morrell, Ted Beresford, George Relwyskow, Arthur Green, Ronnie Jordan for Wryton Promotions, and Jack Dale represented Dale Martin's. I'm pretty sure Jack Atherton was there as well.

It was like an interview; I waited in the outer office before being asked in to where all the big cheeses were sitting round a table; it felt like going into a meeting with Mafia Dons.

Someone said to me, 'We're thinking about putting you on television...'

I liked the idea, but I wasn't giving anything away. Kendo was already top of the bill almost everywhere, but hadn't yet been on television.

The spokesman went on, '...but there's gonna be certain conditions put on it.'

Then George Relwyskow took over. They'd got it all

worked out – he explained that they were going to put Kendo on with Wayne Bridges, and Kendo would win. Then there would be a second match against Billy Howes, whom Kendo would also beat, and that victory would lead to him challenging Billy for his Light Heavyweight title.

'But I'm not a light heavyweight, am I?' I replied. 'I'm about sixteen stone.'

'Doesn't matter,' said George. 'You can challenge him for his title anyway.' It didn't seem to matter.

They said the matches would be heavily promoted in the TV Times, and Kent Walton would build it all up in the intervening televised wrestling shows, stating that – crucially – Kendo Nagasaki was going to take his mask off and wrestle for the title belt.

After hearing what they'd had to say and how they'd build me up, I agreed to it there and then. Kendo Nagasaki was finally going to appear on TV – not once, but twice.

It was only on reflection that I realised it was a conspiracy to destroy Kendo Nagasaki – to create a new unmasked baby-face who would be the puppet of the promoters. The prospect of television had been so alluring that I hadn't noticed the warning voice in the back of my mind, which was actually Kendo's.

The matches went ahead. Everything went as planned in the first two – Kendo beat Wayne Bridges, and then in a sensational second match he beat Billy Howes, so it was on to challenging for the title, and unmasking in order to do that.

About a week after the second match, the phone rang. Now, anybody who'd ever met Norman Morrell knew that he had quite a high-pitched voice. Such a voice spoke, saying, 'Norman speaking.'

'Oh, hello Mr. Morrell,' I replied.

He said, 'I don't think Kendo would be Kendo without the mask,' and he put the phone down. That was it.

I thought it was weird. Norman had been sitting in the

meeting in Leeds when the unmasking was discussed.

I spoke to Geoff. He said I should talk to Jack Atherton, which I did, and Jack said, 'Take it from me, if Norman says it's OK then it's OK.'

'Well, won't I get the sack, Jack?' I asked.

'Not if Norman says not,' said Jack.

Clearly, it was time to carefully consider the situation.

I thought, 'If I do what Norman says, I'm going to cause an upset with George Relwyskow; if I don't, I'll be going against Norman's advice, and he's very influential...' But George had been so very keen on the idea – he'd said, 'I've got this big show at Catterick and I want that unmasking on my show. I want to be the man to present all this.' I had a lot to think over.

The time for the third and final match arrived, for George Relwyskow, in Catterick – the big one: Kendo unmasked.

However, I had an epiphany. I saw the truth in Norman Morrell's words that Kendo wouldn't be Kendo without the mask, I saw that certain elements in Joint Promotions wanted things their own way, but I also saw that Norman Morrell would win a power battle against George Relwyskow by overthrowing his big idea. Norman had carefully selected his words – he never told me not to unmask, and he could always say so. But he'd planted a seed which could lead to an upset from which he could gain an advantage. This was more of Norman's well-documented skulduggery, cleverly manipulating things without a care for anyone else's hopes or wishes; under him, the politics of Joint Promotions were ugly and complex.

Ultimately, however, I would only do what was best for Kendo.

I came to the conclusion that I wouldn't do it – Kendo would not unmask. An alternative vision came to me – I'd allow the mask to come off right at the end of the match, but then I'd be out of the ring and disappear into the night.

I arrived at the show and George came in and he said, 'How are you going to do it?' He was quite excited, like a kid with a new toy. 'We've got Kent Walton – he's really gonna build it up. It's the championship, so you'll take the mask off. Kent will tell everybody...'

I interrupted him and stopped him dead. I said, 'No – it's not going to happen, George.'

'What do you mean?' he asked, alarmed.

In a matter-of-fact way I said, 'Kendo will not take off his mask.'

George hit the roof with a certain amount of velocity – he was like a Catherine Wheel. He remained up there for God knows how long, then he told me I'd never work for Joint Promotions again. He said he had a good mind not to let me go into the bout, but he was committed to it because it was in the TV Times. There really was no way he could prevent Kendo from appearing – it had to go ahead.

'How the hell are we going to get away with it?' George asked. 'Everybody thinks you're doing it. It's been promoted everywhere.'

'Get Ken to announce that I couldn't get down to the weight so I can't wrestle for the title, but I'm still going to wrestle Billy Howes.'

'What will Billy say about it?'

'Let me deal with him,' I said.

I discussed it with Billy and he thought it was great – he'd keep his belt and pull Nagasaki's mask off on television.

It went exactly as planned. In those days it went out live, it wasn't recorded, so people couldn't look back on it and analyse it again. What they saw was a brutal match – we did smash each other up. Howes would hit me in the face and I'd hit him back, and there was blood everywhere because that's the type of match you had with him. It was one of the rare occasions where we got away with it in front of the cameras.

Right at the end I moved myself into a position so that I was facing the exit. I fed the mask up to him, he ended up with it in his hands, he pulled it off, and I was gone. All anyone saw was a glimpse of the face and the back of the head as I ran out of the hall.

It was sensational. All the punters watching the match on television wanted more – a lot more. They'd seen a brief view of a masked man that they'd only seen twice on television anyway, and he'd lost his mask but they still didn't see his face. Billy and I wrestled around the halls for a year-and-a-half on the strength of that match.

When I came out of the ring, George Relwyskow cancelled all the dates I'd got for him, and said he'd see to it that I never worked for Joint Promotions again. That didn't turn out to be the case – the other promoters picked-up the shows he'd cancelled, and they offered me extra shows as well.

Around two weeks later, George rang me and said, 'Let's let bygones be bygones – I want to start booking you again'.

He never tried to persuade me to unmask again.

That turned out to be the beginning of Kendo Nagasaki as a household name. However, I was looking for a way to take things to a whole new level, where no other wrestler had ever gone before, to fascinate and intrigue the wrestling audience, and I had something in mind...

Chapter 18

George Speaks...

The following is an extract from 'My Outrageous Biography' (unpublished), written by George Gillett in the late 1980s.

'In early 1967, at the age of 26, after leading an intriguing but somewhat sheltered provincial existence, I decided to have a taste of the good life and fully engage with all the riotous colour and sounds and attitudes of London's 'Peace and Love' generation. I had a small flat in South Kensington, but had found that a few streets to the south was another world – Earls Court.

Outside of the West End, it was the gayest place in town – and with very good reason. There were no less than three clubs and three pubs within a hundred yards of each other that catered exclusively for homosexuals. This was no twilight world of sad gays, it was a constant non-stop orgy of fun and frolics, entered freely into by a most homogeneous cross-section of society. Funnily enough, the centre for all this activity was none of the afore-mentioned places, but the all-night Wimpy Bar in Earls Court Road.

The place always looked like a recruiting hall for drag queens, there never being less than half a dozen in attendance either coming from or going to some scene of decadent debauchery. Then there would be the odd hustler or ten, having strayed from Piccadilly's meat-rack in search of the 'odd' pop-star bold enough to sample the delights of 'hamburger 'n' camp'.

From time to time the Law would look in, shake their heads and walk out backwards in a sadly macho fashion. The place wouldn't have come into the top hundred of smart places to be seen in, but it had a life all of its own. The locals, bless them, didn't seem to mind too much, but as most of them were themselves rejects of one sort or another and therefore inclined to be tolerant, that was possibly to be expected.

What the owners thought must have been another story, but wherever we had been, and however much liquor was sloshing around inside us, it's where we all landed up to swop gossip, news, and scandal.

To my delight I soon began bumping into 'the great and the good', as well as the controversial and the stylish. Rounding a corner one evening onto Earls Court Road I found myself face to face with someone who appeared to be camouflaged as a wolf – it was Rudolph Nureyev, wearing a huge and gorgeous fur coat. It turned out that we were both on our way to the same watering-hole, and after a few pirouettes in the street we went on our own merry way!

A little while later in almost the same place I met playwright Joe Orton. I'd long admired him, from his artful defacing of library book covers to his astonishing plays, and as he was a regular on the gay scene meeting him had only been a matter of time. When homosexuality was de-criminalised and we could all find love, Joe was tragically murdered only two weeks afterwards and he never got the chance to enjoy that freedom. We were all devastated at the loss of such a bright light and brilliant talent.

One night in early 1968 a very distinctive guy walked

into the Wimpy Bar. He looked like a cross between an up-market brick-layer and a straight 'gigolo', well-dressed and obviously well-muscled, and he seemed self-possessed and self-sufficient – the eyes of everyone present magnetically swivelled in his direction. He certainly stood out from the usual denizens, but no-one either accompanied him or joined him, and I wondered, 'What could he be looking for?'

About a week later he came in again, and then again the following night, and my curiosity got the better of me – I thought, 'Fuck it! Let's see who he is!', and I went to sit at his table.

I was surprised at how softly-spoken he was – he had a northern accent, but then, most of the people you meet in London aren't Londoners! It turned out that he travelled a lot, and was in London for a week at a time every so often, and that he liked the unconventional atmosphere of the Wimpy Bar. I thought to myself, ' I can show you a lot more fun than this!'

*I took Peter to the next best place in town, which wasn't a pub or club, but someone's lounge. That someone was Mike McGrath, one-time pop writer, fashion designer, child star, gossip columnist, publicist, and photographer. He's still going strong as well, name subtly changed to Mike Arlen, and the genius behind a string of photograph studies entitled '*Mike Arlen's Books of Guys'. *He tried to talk Peter into doing a photo session for the 'Book', which would have meant a naked photo-shoot, but he wasn't up for that! Mike also consistently dips his pen in vitriol and '...rushes his nasties into print' for a string of magazines the world over.*

In those days, Mike seemed to collect all the oddities that one could put a name to, and very much in the same way that a millionaire might collect paintings, he collected people. They dropped-in on their way to the Scotch of St. James, or the Ad Lib, and a few hours and several drinks later they dropped back in again, complete with their fantasy of the night.

A typical late night Session there might well include Lionel Bart, wildly rich and famous composer of 'Oliver', who had single-handedly put a whole new meaning to the expression 'how to go broke without even trying'. It didn't seem possible that a man who was earning such phenomenal amounts as he could ever manage to spend it all, but eventually he did.

Tony Toon might drop by. In those days a simple journalist, fresh from the country, but soon to latch on to fast city ways, he clawed his way into the unenviable position of Rod Stewart's very own personal assistant. Exactly what that job entailed he has been able to reveal to the public via the more sensational press on at least two separate occasions to date, therefore proving that he never lost his eye for a good story.

Lolling in an easy chair – which wasn't that easy if you were 6' 7' – would be Long John Baldry, dispensing witty, bitchy lines in that delightfully educated voice of his. John was a very big star in those days, but nothing seemed to faze him, least of all his own drinking habits which were nothing short of prodigious.

For my money, John was the most likeable of that particular group, and is still today a friend. I bumped into him in a West End Club a few months ago on his return from a successful American trip, and he proceeded to quickly drink us all under the table then egg us on to dismantling the premises, chair leg by chair leg. He as usual succeeded.

I subsequently met a number of International stars, but I have never ceased to be amazed at the total candour and lack of pretence that John consistently displayed while at the top. Sadly, this also probably explains why he never really capitalized on his success – he didn't really care enough.

Nevertheless, when 'Ada' Baldry was around, you could always be certain of a rollicking good time. They say that Rod Stewart used to refer to him as 'Mother', and this was in fact his own term of 'endearment' for me!

If it hadn't been for John, there would probably have never been Brian Auger, Julie Driscoll, Steam Packet, Elton John, or Rod Stewart. They all at one time or another came up through the Baldry school of entertainment, and much of their subsequent successes can be laid at his door. John has very nearly drunk himself into an early grave on more than one occasion, but he's also had far more than his own fair share of troubles. It's really no co-incidence that he could put his feelings so dramatically into his No.1 hit 'Let the Heartaches Begin'. For the moment however, lets leave John lolling idly in his chair, he'll surface from time to time later.

Rather prim and neat in another corner, discreetly sitting so that the light masks any wrinkles or other signs of impending middle age might well be Peter Wyngarde, on a very big high in those days with his success on TV's 'Department S' series. Peter was very much a fashion plate, given to flamboyant dress, busy hair styles, and if my memory serves me right, he owned an asthmatic Afghan Hound. That hound once entered my flat very early one morning dragging an extremely beautiful young man behind it, leaving me no prizes for guessing where he'd spent the night.

As a conversationalist Peter wasn't exactly in the Ustinov class, unless you happened to light on his favourite subject – himself. However, he did add a touch of class to an otherwise rather untidy and somewhat drunken bunch of dilettantes.

Mike Mansfield of 'Cue camera three!' fame might arrive with his steady date in tow. Mike hadn't then reached the heights which were to follow, but his distinctive head of white hair was already his most saleable feature. There must have been an awful lot more going on in that brain than most of us would have at that time allowed, for he was another who wasn't exactly known for statements worthy of posterity.

Today there's hardly a top class pop video or TV Rock Show, complete without Mike's deft touch with a smoke machine or bubble-blowing contraption, and where Adam Ant would be without his touch of class, God only knows, but in those days it was still firmly entrenched in his head.

Others present might well include a selection ranging from Billy Gaff, then John Baldry's Manager and soon to repeat the performance with Rod Stewart, Tony Stratton-Smith, founder of the Charisma Records empire, and prolific racehorse owner, Jonathan King, Marc Bolan, David Essex, and many other aspiring starlet of the time. But the picture was never quite complete without the 'friends' they brought with them. The majority were dragged up to be shown off once only, never to be seen again, either by us or their patron of the night.

Most of them were completely at sea in such rarefied company, and could no doubt dine out on the snippets of showbiz chat they picked up between snores for weeks ahead if they arranged their 'bookings' carefully enough. A sensible person might well be tempted to ask at this point what on earth I was doing there amongst this motley crew of stars and future stars. The answer's quite simple – I haven't got a bloody clue. It certainly wasn't for my looks, but facilitating Peter's tall, dark, muscular presence secured me some measure of caché!!

When he was in town, we visited all the favourite haunts of the gays, including the Masquerade Club, now sadly closed. The funniest character I remember from the Boltons was a local named Charlie, who did a very passable 'Old Mother Riley' impression. He once took it to such extremes that he bicycled right through the pub and down the stairs from the top bar waving his arms and legs about, straight out into the street.

As the acknowledged haunt of the macho image, the Coleherne abounded with leather persons, clanking and creaking their way around the bar in a predatory fashion. With their hushed tones and covert glances they always reminded me of leather clad ghosts. What always amused me even more was the great queue of them at the end of the night waiting for the No. 30 bus! Peter and I went there only infrequently, but I managed to get myself barred from there in due course for '...bringing the pub into disrepute'!

It happened that in 1971, the Sunday People decided to do a series of articles on the wickedest streets in Great Britain. For some reason they decided that the first article should be devoted to Earls Court Road, and their opening blurb was a gem of mis-information: 'A girl needs strong nerves and a sense of humour to walk down Earls Court Road alone in the daytime. If she did so at night, she would need her head examined, or an armed guard'. *Five paragraphs down however the article went on,* 'Homosexuality abounds in the most blatant ways – there are more men carrying handbags than women!'

Now, I can well believe that a girl would possibly need a sense of humour, particularly in view of all those handbags, but her head examining? ...an armed guard? ...in a street full of gentle queens?

This mixture of paranoia and paradox continued right up to the time that the intrepid reporter, no doubt armed with tin Y-Fronts and a can opener, dared to put his frail hetero nose through the door of the Boltons, a place frequented by 'those pathetic people'.

There, he immediately picked up a young man, who told him: 'If you're looking for chicken (sic), you ought to meet Mother George...' *(no prizes for guessing that John Baldry's nickname for me had spread somewhat).* 'He's an old queen...' *(wrong on both counts, I was a mere 30, and trying out a butch image that week!)* '...I never knew him not to have a crowd of kids around him...' *(the only true bit of the lot – I couldn't help it if I'd had four years in which to develop a sparkling, attractive personality!)* 'Anyone in trouble used to go to George, and it was nothing for him to have two or three chicken (sic) staying at his flat.' *(Yes, people did come to me if they were in trouble – it was usually financial, or questions related to the aborting of their girl-friends' babies, or how to kick drugs – I was not running my own unofficial borstal.)*

This garbage ploughed on, mentioning me three times more as it trailed off into its own slime. I was indeed the only person to get a name-check in the whole article. There was nothing I could do about it – they would quickly claim it was 'another' George to whom they were referring, and could no doubt provide some little scrubber to claim it was he.

...but the damage was done.

By the Sunday night of publication, people had already arrived in the Boltons from Manchester in order to see this extraordinary provider of trade, and as I say, the Colherne, a place never high on my list of 'in' places, barred me. I think it was unfortunate that 'the People' chose to include a photograph of their clientele doing what appeared to be a leathered Gavotte in the street immediately above the paragraphs relating so scurrilously to me.

It goes without saying that the whole article was written by a regular – and gay – customer of the two pubs concerned, who also claimed to be a friend of mine! Peter thought it was hilarious!

As a change from the giddy heights of Earls Court, there was of course always the West End. In the late sixties London was full of kaftans, mods and rockers, and pill-poppers.

There was, in D'Arblay Street, a club called Le Deuce, open all night on Friday and Saturday, it quickly became a haunt for a veritable motley bunch of people.

It hadn't got the class of the Scotch, or the Ad Lib, or any of those other star-riddled havens, but it had an air of excitement about it. A trifle seedy, full of suburban ruffians popping purple hearts and doing their thing, it was just the place to sit and drink and view the scenery. The club proper was in the basement, and various of my friends were Managers from time to time. There was a restaurant on the ground floor, which usually had to be reached internally however, as illicit after hours drinking meant that the Management wisely kept the street door firmly barred.

I was once sitting in the restaurant as dawn broke, still imbibing freely with John Baldry and another sixties personality, David Garrick. John at the time was No. 1 in the charts, though David hadn't been so lucky for a couple of years.

The Police must have thought that our drinking hours were being extended a little further than even they could allow, and so decided to raid the place. They couldn't gain access from the street, so marched downstairs into the club, and began to chop down the door which connected the club, via an internal stairway to the Restaurant. As the sound of axes grew louder, David, still very much aware of his position as a pop personality kept muttering 'Oh dear, my fans, what'll they say?', while I distinctly remember John Baldry looking me firmly in the eye and saying, 'Fuck it dear, let's have a drink ready for the buggers when they arrive.'

And there he sat, large drink in large hand, a benign smile on his face, totally oblivious to the carnage being enacted around him. As I've said, John just didn't care.

You couldn't say the same for David Garrick though. He'd had a couple of relatively large hits in the mid sixties – both with Stones compositions – and even five years later was enjoying great success in Germany, having at one period five records in their Top Twenty in the same week. However, in England his career had, as they say, gone down the pan.

He was a really generous person, and for some unknown reason had struck-up a close friendship with a young guy who had most unfortunately been run over and lost a leg as the result. David used to go to visit him in hospital and entertain the whole ward with impromptu snatches from his musical repertoire. Even though he was going to a hospital whose wards were in the main full of scruffy kids, David would never have dreamt of dressing down for the occasion. He always looked like a million dollars, even if at times they weren't his own.

Occasionally David would take me to the Hospital in a Bentley which would mysteriously appear at his front door. I didn't even know that he drove let alone have a car, but as I was on a scene that fascinated me, and it wasn't costing me money, I wasn't about to jeopardise matters too much by asking awkward questions. At the end of our visits, or after one of our nights on the town, David would drive along to Sloane Square, stop the car, and ask me to wait for him for a couple of minutes or so. Sure enough a very short while later, he would re-appear on foot, and we would grab a cab home.

The mystery was solved one day in a very unusual way. Peter and I were sitting in David's flat when the 'phone rang. As he was unavailable I answered it. A female Scottish voice then proceeded to berate me in language that could never have been learned at a charm school – not this side of the Gorbals, at least! The one thing I did understand was that she thought she was talking to David, and gave me no chance to inform her otherwise. The few non-obscene words that I managed to catch were: car keys... Bentley... Barry... Maurice... ...and then she slammed down the 'phone.

I sat back and thought about it. On a glass table in front of me was David's very own scrap book, with pictures of him and many other stars. I leafed through it and suddenly the answer dawned on me: there staring me in the face was a whole selection of photos of David with none other than Barry Gibb of the Bee Gees.

Now, Barry and David were – or had been – friends. Barry had a lovely wife, Linda, a Scottish beauty queen, he lived, if my memory serves me right, in Sloane Square, and most important of all, he owned a Bentley. How David had (a) got a key, (b) known when the car was available, and (c) managed to keep doing it for so long remained a mystery, and I never mentioned the phone-call to him. I think he must have had at least one other though, because I don't remember any more trips in the Bentley after that.

One Sunday night after our regular hospital visit we came back to his flat, both somewhat depressed. We both needed a good laugh to cheer us up.

I had been in the habit of going to a pub named the Union Tavern every possible Sunday night for well over a year, to watch what we considered to be one of the funniest drag acts in the country, the late Lee Sutton. It was, for about five or six hundred people, something of a weekly pilgrimage, and when he was in town, Peter came along. We decided that we should go with David to the Union to see Lee, and I even went to the trouble to book a table to ensure our being able to get in – it really did get that busy in those days.

The Union Tavern is styled as a late-Victorian or early Edwardian pub, typical of many, especially in South London. Internally it was very large, and the one room was laid out very much in the manner of a mid-Victorian music hall. There was space for about two hundred to be seated at tables, and standing room for probably another three hundred. On a busy night, which was most nights, the atmosphere was both electric and hot, and I was pleased to see that our reserved table was centre front. David pretended to go coy on us at that stage, but it goes without saying that there wasn't really anywhere else he would rather have sat.

There were two tables likewise reserved to our right, but there was no special significance in that. Many passing celebratory popped in from time to time, and that was their regular corner.

Just before Lee Sutton was due to start the first of his two spots there was a flurry and a buzzing from the back of the pub. We turned round, to witness a path being swathed through the crowd by a group of people. There were a number that I didn't know, but I recognised the late character actor, Richard Wattis, the choreographer Paddy Stone, Danny LaRue, a somewhat dishevelled lady who I would have sworn to be Veronica Lake (it was), and finally – incredibly, considering the location – Liberace.

The buzz didn't really settle until the night's entertainment began but then we all got lost in the magic of Lee Sutton's risqué routines. Sometime during the evening, one of the guys in Liberace's company came over to our table and spoke to David. It appeared he was an A & R man with EMI and they had obviously met before. We were invited to stay after the show finished and be introduced to the bejewelled pianist. Naturally we accepted with a certain amount of alacrity, I for one had always been fascinated by his mixture of charm, schmaltz, and high camp, and was dying to find out what sort of a person he really was.

As the pub emptied, we were introduced all-round. At first, Peter and I got entangled with Miss Lake, who considering the vast quantities of booze swimming through her system was most aptly named. She didn't last very long however, finally slipping discreetly to the floor quietly muttering vague obscenities. I could see that David was certainly hitting it off with Liberace (whom I shall from now on refer to as 'Lee', that being his common nickname). Eventually we were beckoned-

over to join in the general conversation.

The evening was terminated with Peter, David, and I being asked by Lee to join him in a very late supper at a well known Italian Restaurant in Dean Street called the SPQR. We dashed home so that I at least could effect a quick change, then it was off once more to the West End.

Both the restaurant and the company were equally enjoyable, and for a while we were joined by Lee's Manager, Seymour Heller. It was obvious that Lee had taken a great 'patron'-like shine to David, and at the end of the night we had all had a great chatty evening.

Lee was over here to record – I think – ten spectaculars for TV which would not only be shown nationwide over here, but which would be networked in the States. Obviously there could not be much of a greater boost to David's flagging British career than a spot on one of those shows.

We were invited to join Lee at Borehamwood Studios early the following morning to watch him rehearse one of his weekly shows. Being whisked by a studio limousine to ATV, and meeting Eva Gabor, Frankie Vaughan, Moira Anderson, and the Sandpipers was all a little overwhelming for someone like me, unemployed and rapidly approaching bankruptcy. However, game to the last, I soon joined the spirit of things, feeling very much livelier after a rest in a private dressing room that Lee had thoughtfully provided for us.

The night of Tuesday April 15th 1969, was to be the occasion of the recording of Lee's final show, and as David was one of the guests, Peter and I were naturally invited along. David had previously recorded his 'operatic' segment (a snippet from Aida, which had apparently been accomplished in something a little under thirty takes), and his live performance of 'Land of a Thousand Dancers' went down extremely well.

After the show it was all down to party time once more, but not this time in the VIP Suite, it was a very private little do back at Sloane Square, with just Lee, David, Peter, myself, and Momma!

Now, Momma cooked a mean meal at 4.00 am let me say, and for a lady who was then 75, she was very much a live wire. She obviously enjoyed discovering new talent every bit as much as her son did. In fact their personalities were generally very similar. Surprisingly, Liberace was yet another of those great big Stars that I found to be very lonely people indeed.

My final memory of Lee however is a very funny one. He told me that on one of his trips here, he decided to attend a large meeting of his British Fan Club in a northern theatre. As he explained, with them being, in the main, middle-aged ladies, he didn't foresee any screaming mobs of twin-setted hooligans trying to tear him limb from limb. So sure of his safety was he that he even took 'Momma'. How wrong he was.

He decided to enter the theatre from the back stalls and walk down the centre aisle with Momma on his arm. He swore that by the time he reached the stage, Momma was bereft of a sumptuous fur coat, and he had lost half his jewels and clothing. As he said: 'Gee, George I never would have believed it, but you know...I never did it again!'

By this time, I'd known Peter for about two years, and it had taken me all this time to find out what other name he went under. All I knew at first was that he drove flash Yankee cars, was good company, seemed to live the high life, and that he had a constantly-locked glove compartment.

We only met each other from time to time, and I gathered that he travelled a lot, and sometimes went abroad. It took a little while to dawn on me that I didn't really know anything about him.

The mystery was cleared up however when one afternoon he arrived unheralded on my doorstep and asked me if I'd like a run down to – I think – Southampton.

Being a man of few ties I agreed and off we sped.

It must have been around 7.00pm when we drove into Southampton's City centre, and he leant over, unlocked the magic glove compartment, and withdrew... ...a black and white striped face mask. I'll never forget that my immediate reaction was, 'Oh goody, we're going to rob a bank!'

Not so – we were going wrestling.

'Peter' turned out to be Kendo Nagasaki, top of the bill professional wrestler, one of the most competent and highly paid of them all. He was one guy who could really wrestle. I later discovered he'd got medals for judo, weightlifting, wrestling, water polo, and just about every other sport that I'd never been anywhere near.

After that first time, I accompanied him to a number of his bouts whenever he was in the London area, and was there to see him make his TV debut at St. Albans. I didn't realise then that I had met the person who was going to so drastically change my life so as to make it almost unrecognizable, and who was – very literally – just about to take me away from it all.

Following my sudden 'exposure' in the Sunday People I couldn't rid myself of the paranoid feeling that it wasn't only the nutters in Earls Court who were interested in my activities. Don't forget – just because they're not there, it doesn't mean to say they're not watching you!

Anyway, my bed-sits became drabber, cheaper, and more fly-blown almost by the week, until eventually the only home I could call my own was the good old Wimpy.

Now, although I didn't know it at the time, Peter – in his Kendo persona – had wrestled as far-afield as Japan, and with increasing success back home, he was encountering an unusual problem. Kendo didn't speak, and was finding himself in ever-greater need of a 'side-kick' to navigate the venues, deal with fans, and wind up the crowd to fever pitch in order to be sure of a 'lively' response to his less than humane approach to his opponent.

So, what simpler than a Manager to air all his many grievances for him, and generally make a damn nuisance of himself; the only problem was – who?

By this time, I was not only living in the Wimpy Bar, but had actually moved one of my cases in there with me, the rest being scattered from one end of Earls Court to the other. There I was to be found, tearful and suicidal, firmly convinced that my four years of freedom had been at least three too many, and I didn't have any idea of where I went from there.

Fate, however, was there to kick me in the pants. In walked Peter, out went my bags, with me being dragged behind them. It would be unfair, though hardly inaccurate, to say that he kidnapped me, as I didn't put up that much of a struggle, but bags were collected, clothes organized, and the next thing I knew I had said goodbye to the good life, London and all, and for the next six years viewed the world from the somewhat more slow-paced atmosphere of Wolverhampton...'

So – how did I end up in the Earls Court Wimpy Bar? I'd done several shows for Dale Martin Promotions and had just done one in Slough which is out west of London and was travelling back to Martinez in Brixton. The route from the west took me through Earls Court and on the way I was hungry and decided to look for somewhere to eat. I saw a brightly-lit Wimpy and decided to stop there and found myself face-to-face with a whole new world.

In the Wimpy I found a collection of people I had no idea existed. They were for the most part all very glamorous, theatrical and aspiring pop-star types, but as they hadn't yet 'made it', most of them were a bit threadbare; George has ably described them.

They were using a kind of slang that I later found was

called Polari. Like Cockney rhyming slang, it was essentially a coded language so that gay people could talk amongst each other without straight people knowing what they were saying. Homosexuality had only been decriminalised about a year previously so this sub-culture was still alive and well, but its members were beginning to express themselves much more freely. George was right at the core of the gay scene and was fluent in Polari – I didn't realise that I was a 'bona omi'.

I found the scene fascinating – it was such a contrast to my very ordinary roots in Crewe and a great many of the people seemed to be cultured and engaging. George and I seemed to have a great rapport and he was very good company; I was made very welcome and enjoyed being on the 'gay scene'; my life was never to be the same.

To the next question you might ask – the answer's no, we never did.

Chapter 19

George's Baptism

On the first morning after I'd got George to Wolverhampton I told him what I had in mind for him.

The idea of a manager went back to when I wrestled in tag matches with The Count. It dawned on me that we should have a 'second', an assistant devoted to us, rather than someone provided by the venue. Maybe that second could wear a jacket with the names Bartelli & Nagasaki on the back. Today it's known as branding, but back then no-one did it.

Originally, Bartelli's son Barry had been the first choice. We wanted someone young who was familiar with the business, but he still had ambitions to be a wrestler, so he was out. Another problem arose, which was that even if we found someone suitable, Bartelli and I didn't always wrestle together – there were times when we had solo matches, so a question would arise over which one of us would use the second. Such practicalities and the shortage of suitable candidates meant that the idea never really developed.

As I continued to wrestle and went to more and more halls, it was becoming increasingly difficult for Kendo to maintain his silence. I'd arrive at a new venue, wearing the mask and being mysterious and unspeaking, and if I had no idea where the dressing room was, I couldn't just ask someone. It was obvious I was a wrestler because of the mask, so the staff would try to communicate with me, saying hello, asking what I was doing, whether they could help, but I couldn't reply. Eventually they'd realize that I wanted to go to the dressing room so they'd take me, but it could take a while and be quite awkward.

Ideally, I needed an extra person to assist me with these basic tasks, such as carrying the bags and communicating with the venue staff, and as my friendship with George developed, I began to think about how I could make that work with him. He had the biceps of a sparrow so he didn't fit the bill as a second, so I briefly considered the concept of him as a valet, but I couldn't really see that working either – George's manner was amiable, but a little too superior for that.

He could, however, be my interface with people, and it followed that if you take it that far, it's not a huge leap from the dressing room to the wrestling ring, and from friend, to second, to manager.

George becoming Kendo's manager had nothing whatsoever to do with Max Crabtree. Prior to his descent into chaos in Earls Court, George used to work for a cinema chain called Essoldo. Due to falling revenues they decided to convert some of their cinemas into bingo halls, and George was in charge of overseeing these conversions. George once told Max that he did one in Halifax and Max said that his family had a nightclub in the town, and that they'd probably met there – George had no such recollection. Max seems to have put these possibilities together as a colourful but false memory of knowing George, followed by claiming that he came up with the idea of George as Kendo's manager and performing his introduction to me. I can categorically state that neither happened – it's just one of many examples of Max stealing other people's thunder, when he is, in fact, far from being the Svengali at the core of all good things.

When I mentioned the manager idea to George, he was sceptical; he looked at me with one eyebrow raised and said, 'I don't think I could do that, dear.'

'Course you can. You're already doing everything it would need,' I said.

He protested in typically dramatic style: 'What if I get hurt? I could be maimed for life!'

'You won't,' I assured him.

I finally managed to persuade him that it would work and that he'd survive the experience.

We hit the shops and dressed him as a businessman, in a suit, shirt and tie, and patent leather shoes, which made him look most respectable – it was a very sober start to a career which was to become highly flamboyant.

Originally he was billed as George E. Gillett, which evolved into Gentleman George, and he finally became Gorgeous George, having taken his name from a wrestler in California in the 1940s. I've always thought that the name suited this George far better.

For his first match, I told him not to camp it up – I said, 'Don't let them know you're gay.'

His eyebrows shot up in disbelief. 'You must be joking!'

'No – just play it straight.' I couldn't be sure of how an audience would react to his theatrical personality, George's default state, and that wasn't what I'd envisaged anyway – I wanted him to represent an additional level of serious professionalism concerning Kendo's presence. Ultimately, of course, George's personality could not be suppressed, and the journey towards high camp gathered its own unstoppable momentum.

I called Jack Atherton and described the idea to him, as well as seeking his advice on where we could try a debut match with George. 'Can you put it on somewhere out of the way so as we can give it a trial run?' I asked.

We ended up in Dumfries, Scotland – over to George...

'My debut in the wrestling world as Kendo Nagasaki's Manager was to be at Dumfries in November 1971. I hadn't a clue what I was letting myself in for, and bearing in mind that I – like millions of others – had previously watched it on T.V. (and I'd been to a few live shows with Peter), I must, in retrospect, have been completely off my rocker. I could be maimed for life, or even worse, and yet there I was, serenely trotting two hundred odd miles in order to get my block knocked off. Peter had years of training behind him, but I, what did I have? Nothing but four years of complete idleness.

As it turned out, there were some ways in which I didn't need to worry half as much as I had been, whilst on the other hand there were far more things to worry about than either Peter or I had ever dreamt of.

I remember that on the way to Dumfries we stopped off at a pub, and over a very large whisky Peter told me that wrestling was not altogether what it seemed to be. A great deal of it was 'choreographed' and while wrestlers quite often went out to win, they certainly didn't go out of their way to hurt each other – after all, it was a profession, and all of them had to make a living; if you got a reputation for winning consistently at the expense of your opponent's bones, you'd soon run out of opponents, and therefore work. The idea was to entertain, to give the public what they wanted.

Now, whatever the public may tell each other to the contrary, what they really want – and what they have always wanted – since the first two cavemen hit each other over the head with rocks, is a bit of good old fashioned blood and thunder, preferably more thunder than blood, one hopes, but goodies and baddies, cowboys and Indians. There was never any doubt that Kendo and I came into the latter category – we were the biggest, baddest injuns of 'em all.

A lot of what I was told helped to put me at my ease,

but unfortunately Peter had to go and spoil it by reminding me that British audiences had never before seen a loudmouth Manager extolling the virtues of his protégé at the expense of the heroic, and no doubt local, hero. Neither of us knew exactly what sort of reaction we'd get, though Peter at least had a shrewd idea that it was going to be a hot one.

As luck would have it the opponent of the night was one Andy Robin, Scottish Heavyweight Champion, a title bestowed upon him mainly on the grounds that he was such a wild-man and that there were very few other heavyweights around foolish enough to fight him. Actually, Andy is quite a nice guy, and has taken to living with a bear called Hercules, who has a thing about Kleenex. However, one can gauge the caution that an invitation to wrestle with him should engender, from the following tale.

From time to time, Andy would promote his own wrestling show, with himself naturally as the top of the bill. As an increasing number of wrestlers were decidedly dubious about getting into the ring with such an unpredictable tartan terror, he occasionally added Hercules the Bear to the bill. On the night in question Andy had actually succeeded in persuading Klondyke Jake, a rough and tough fighter from the Midlands, to join battle with him, and Andy said to him, 'Jake, I'll tell you what, you fight the bloody bear, an' there'll be another tenner in fur ye.'

Jake turned round contemptuously and replied 'Fuck off, I'll do the Bear for the same fucking money, it's you I'll need the extra tenner to fight!'

That was what I was walking blithely into on my debut.

The bout itself was not particularly remarkable, and I thought my opening speech went down quite well, considering only a couple of beer cans bounced off my glasses – yes – unbelievably, I had omitted to remove them. In the second round Kendo got a fall, and I quietly encouraged the timekeeper to start the third round promptly, by looking at my watch and shaking my head.

Now, if you've never actually 'felt' a thousand hostile Scotsmen standing simultaneously and moving as-one in your direction, it's something that defies description. The next thing I knew was that I was trying to get into the relative safety of the ring, aided and abetted by both Kendo and Andy, whilst those same thousand Scotsmen were trying to pull me out!

After one or two of them received 'accidental' kicks in the head from both wrestlers, the crowd suddenly let go of me, and I fairly catapulted into the ring with the velocity of a bullet. I was bereft of great chunks of clothing, and missing one shoe. It says something for Peter's careful upbringing that when I told him this – in the ring – he just replied 'Well, go out there and bloody get it!'

Somehow we managed to get through the rest of the bout, though truthfully I remember very little of it. We decided there and then that we had a product – me – that would have to be marketed very carefully if I wasn't going to get lynched on an almost nightly basis.'

George worked on his routine and got better and better at it. He was a unique and highly charismatic character who brought a great deal of colour and personality to the world of wrestling – but he sometimes got himself into trouble with the more reactive members of the audience.

We came up with a rescue plan if he ever found himself being threatened by the audience – which, considering the combination of his costume, his physique, his camp banter, and his proximity to the often-unpredictable masses, was quite frequently; the plan was that he should always make for the ring.

We had an entertaining show at Nantwich one night.

As Kendo defeated Billy Howes, George fled into the ring seconds ahead of a screaming mob – he'd found himself the focus of their anger and frustration, and Howes chinning George would have delighted them. Any other wrestler and George probably wouldn't have been too bothered, but not Howes with his fearsome reputation. He approached with his fist raised, giving George two options – a definite serious thump or a possibly light mangling by the mob. George chose the mob which was probably the wisest option.

Sometimes however, he'd be in trouble right after the introductions, even before he'd left the ring. The next time Kendo met Billy Howes was in Halifax, where the ring was on a stage. After the introductions George went and stood in the wings where he was attacked and dragged-around by a woman, and frankly she was getting the upper hand. The referee suddenly noticed this, leaned in close, and said to us, 'There's a woman attacking the manager.'

Billy glanced over and said, 'By 'eck it's the wife!'

He jumped out of the ring, ran over and snarled, 'Get in the bloody car, you daft sod!'

It turned out that whilst she'd known for years what wrestling was really all about, George's camp and condescending remarks about her old man had really got to her... which ably illustrates the impact that George's pithy wise-cracks could have.

Some months later Max Crabtree double-crossed George at Edinburgh, which was a terribly rough venue. While I was in the ring he gave George a torch, to make out that he could use it to control me – and he was daft enough to do it. George flashed the torch and all the audience looked to see where it was coming from. We had another riot, and he had to run again.

After a while I realised that my TV appearances had stopped, and I found that it was because George was too radical for the promoters – they wanted to marginalise him. There was no denying that George alongside Kendo was controversial – never before had there been a 'camp' man associated with the pure violence of a villain wrestler – 'camp' was usually associated with far less villainous wrestlers, such as Adrian Street and Bobby Barnes who frankly weren't taken seriously, but George was far from 'cuddly' – he was a cutting and bold homosexual and straight people felt intimidated by him, and he and Kendo both un-nerved and fascinated people; some promoters genuinely feared a back-lash.

An incident involving George, myself, and a man called Martin 'Chopper' Conroy occurred at Wryton Stadium in Bolton for a TV show – the first since George had joined me.

When Kendo first started wrestling Conroy was a referee but he went into the office and became the pencil when Ronnie Jordan left Wryton. When this happened, Conroy changed; in the early days he was generally amenable but he then became quite cantankerous.

When we arrived in Bolton I told George, 'We're going on – get ready.'

Conroy came in and saw George and said, 'What's he doing getting changed? He's not going on.'

My response was, 'Of course he's going on!' to which Chopper replied, 'No – he's not.'

I said, 'What's it got to do with you – you're just a jumped-up referee!'

Conroy said, 'Well, I'm telling you – he's not going on.'

I grabbed him and shoved him up against the wall. He was very shaken-up but managed to say, 'It won't do you any good hitting me – if he goes on, they'll pull the plug on you.'

I let him go and talked it over with George, who thought it would be better if we didn't push things and cause a fuss at that early stage.

By the time we got the next TV show Joint Promotions must have had a change of heart. It was months later, during which time Kendo and George had done a lot of shows and they'd obviously put 'bums on seats' – it wouldn't make sense for Joint to fight that tide, but before the match I was still half-expecting another challenge to George appearing. When we arrived I said to George, 'This time we're going on – fuck them!'

The show was for Dale Martin in London and although he wasn't wrestling, Mick McManus was there as the pencil – he went to all their televised shows; he was a natural networker and always had the future in his sights. As George was getting ready Mick came into the dressing room and asked, 'What's happening?'

I pointed to George and said forcefully, 'He is going on!' There was no way I was going to back-down on him appearing a second time – I regretted letting it happen the first time.

Mick said, 'That's fine,' and we went on to discuss the show. I initially thought that he'd backed-down because word had reached him about what had happened to Conroy and he didn't want to risk getting the same, but on reflection I believe that Joint Promotions had yielded to the demand for Kendo accompanied by George.

However, as we did more shows, I began to detect resistance to George's presence. We discovered that his in-ring speeches were being edited; anything George said before the MC did the introductions and anything he said at the end after the MC declared the result would be cut from the broadcasts. I noticed that the MC would sit at ring-side with the mic in his hand, ready to do the introduction and get the result out at the end, so I told George to grab the mic after the introductions and then say his provocative piece. Likewise, at the end of a match George was initially at the back of the hall, so I made sure that he'd make his way to the ring in time to get in and grab the mic from the MC and get his speech out, before the result could be delivered. Working this way meant that George's inflammatory proclamations were fixed into the broadcasts.

I firmly believe this resistance was homophobia – as far as certain macho elements in Joint Promotions were concerned, George was highly risqué, and these 'men's men' wanted to maintain wrestling's tough image in all respects. They wouldn't mind Adrian Street's camp antics because they knew he wasn't really gay, but George was the real deal, and he therefore posed a pernicious threat as far as the homophobes were concerned.

I'm sure that Jack Dale wouldn't have liked him, nor would Norman Morrell, and Martin Conroy had already made the position clear for Wryton Promotions. Max Crabtree thought George was great because he was good for business, but Kent Walton, the voice of World of Sport, was very sniffy about George and played him down whenever he could. However, despite this resistance, we went over very well and people talked about us, and whatever degree to which they did manage to marginalise George, it only seemed to increase demand for him. The old anecdote proved true once again – less was more...

Perhaps the clearest indication that the British wrestling hierarchy cared nothing for George was a financial one: Joint Promotions never paid him – he was regarded as my responsibility. In Canada he was appreciated as a part of the show and a contributor to Kendo's draw which was why he got his own wage packet. This never happened in the UK and I believe that once again it was because of the homophobia of the promoters and their wish that a character like George would just disappear. Had it been any ordinary wrestler they would have succeeded because very few of them could have afforded to have a character like George alongside them.

My Aunt Ida had been a wrestling fan and followed my career ever since I'd invited her and Uncle Norman to a show in Blackpool in 1965, and although she never went back to a live show after my Uncle died, she had seen me on TV, with George too, as soon as he'd joined me.

Kendo's first live show in Blackpool with George was on the Sunday afternoon immediately after the Saturday my Aunt had first seen us on TV, and after the show I took him to meet her for an overnight stay. Her reaction, though uncomfortable for George, was entirely in keeping with his role – she disliked him quite intensely. Having seen him on television in his loud-mouthed, arrogant, and provocative guise, she seemed unable to see past that – very much a punter's viewpoint, and arguably a good yardstick.

We sat down for a cup of tea and I asked her what she thought of my Manager; she replied, 'I cannot tell a lie – he's no more use than an ornament..!'

George laughed it off, but I think he may have been frustrated at being unable to swipe back with some stinging camp banter.

The following morning my Aunt again left George in no doubt about her scant regard for him; before breakfast he sat in a chair by the fireplace, but my Aunt flatly told him that that was my chair, implying that he had to sit elsewhere. She made breakfast for us, and whereas I got two fried eggs, he only got one. I don't think she ever engaged him in conversation; he tried to engage her, but that only resulted in him suffering further condemnation – he was accused of being '...far too familiar.'

Of course, George did indulge in his own covert retaliation; he called her 'the Bism', an old word which the Urban Dictionary states is someone who is deliberately irritating or annoying but not quite as bad as a 'bitch'; no doubt it was a mutual sentiment!

George would also hiss quietly when out of her ear-shot, suggesting that she was some sort of viper, and then smile sweetly on her return; I could quite understand him letting off steam in these little ways – it was actually a lot of fun watching these two antagonists making the best of their dislike for each other!

The Kendo and Count Bartelli tag team, prior to the March 1966 match in which Kendo defeated and unmasked him at the Victoria Hall, Hanley. Also in Hanley and in 1966, here's George Gillett at his then job of converting failing cinemas into bingo halls. This one was the Essoldo.

Some still images from Super-8 movies, taken in Japan in 1968. Top, I'm doing my western strong-man impression, centre is me pictured with our interpreter 'Freddie' (no-one ever knew his real name!), and below, Freddy and me at Osaka Casle.

Another Super 8 still, from Honolulu, where we stayed for a week on our way back from Japan. Here, American wrestler Pat Barratt clowns around with a palm frond, fanning me and Ata Maivia, the daughter of the promoter who'd arranged our stay. Then, after one night in San Francisco we spent a few days in New York - below, a shot of a rainy Big Apple.

A couple of images from the top of the Empire State Building, before coming home. Below, I'm with Ida in Blackpool, petting her beloved Boxer, 'Snootcher'.

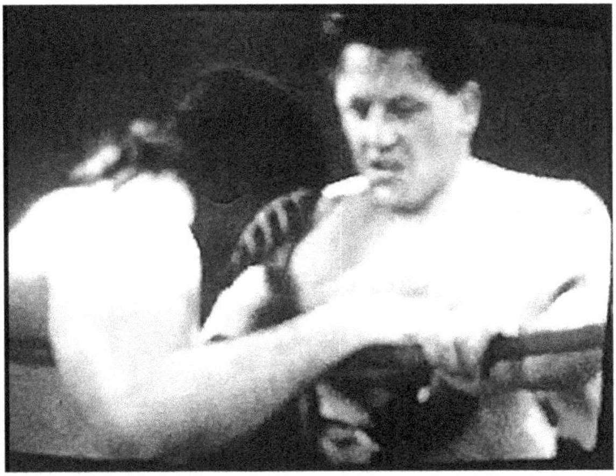

A recording from before the days of video recorders (it's Super 8 film), of a crucial match in Kendo's history... Arranged by all the top promoters, Kendo ended up against Billy Howes to be unmasked in this final match in a trilogy to get him onto TV. However, Kendo retained his mystery while giving them what they wanted - just!

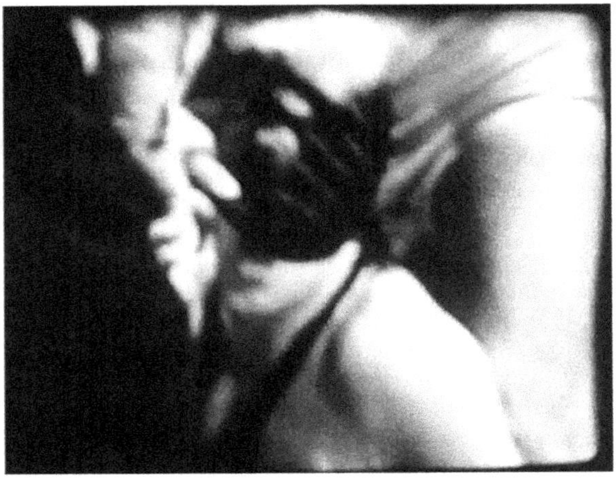

By 1969 I'd met George and been introduced to his 'hamburger 'n' camp' and star-studded lifestyle, including a megastar of the day, Liberace. The above picture was one of George's most cherished possessions, given to him by 'Lee' that year, and displayed with pride and affection for the rest of his life.

Above, Kendo and George in Canada, with Stampede Wrestling's commentator, their version of 'Kent Walton'.

Below, Kendo and George after being presented with 'Teddysaki' and 'Gorgeous McGeorge', teddy-bear tributes made by fans.

*'Old Red-Eyes' - Kendo's fearsome mid '70s image.
This mask had clearly seen a lot of action, showing
fraying around all the openings.*

The unmasking - a silver-haired George lifts away Kendo's mask, unshering-in a new era. It was a solemn moment before a television audience of over fourteen million, which belied the frantic activity which preceded it!

A snap of Kendo as The Death Angel in Granada TV's 'The Wild Bunch', an episode of the 'Send In The Girls' series. Brian Glover not only appeared as the MC, but he wrote this episode, which meant that the wrestling back-drop for the main plot was completely convincing. Kendo's voice was 'heard' on TV for the first time, which caused much debate! The Death Angel's love-interest stands behind him in this picture, Floella Benjamin. The show was aired within weeks of moving into Gladstone Street.

Chapter 20

Calgary Stampede

In August 1972, Kendo and George spent some time in Calgary, Canada, as many other British wrestlers had done before. Whilst there, apart from facing Canadian wrestlers like George Gordienko and Danny Kroffat, there was also the Mexican masked-man Supahawk, and other well-known British grapplers such as Geoff Portz and Lennie Hurst.

As it was such a big country, matches were booked in a 'tour' format around a 1,500-mile loop which was known as 'the circuit'. Myself and four other wrestlers took it in turns with the transport, using our own cars; it was quite lucrative because you got extra money, so we all wanted to do it. I'd bought a Buick early in the trip, and the promoter, Stu Hart, liked me to drive because he felt I was 'steady' and safe, not least because I didn't drink.

During the tour, George Gillett underwent a transformation, re-Christening himself 'Lord Sloane of Kensington Gore'. Gore is of course a theatrical term for blood, and blood and wrestling were synonymous in Canada, so it was a good moniker.

George loved Canada – it was him who'd really wanted to go and I decided to indulge him. Speaking in haughty Oxford English, he dismissed the whole country as bunch of colonial nit-wits that needed teaching an unforgettable lesson, and he had just the man to do it – Kendo Nagasaki. This went over a storm!

The biggest character we encountered over there was Stu Hart, the promoter. He'd had a very successful career as a Canadian amateur and professional wrestler, promoter, and trainer. He established Klondike Wrestling in 1948 in Edmonton, which metamorphosed into Big Time Wrestling and then Wildcat Wrestling, before finally becoming Stampede Wrestling, the promotions we now worked for.

Stu was in his early fifties; he was a big man and had been rated as a 'shooter'. He admired people like George Gordienko, Billy Robinson, Karl Gotch, Lou Thez – all the top shooters, wrestlers who could really look after themselves.

A little before Kendo arrived in Canada, Billy Robinson had been over, and I believe he'd told Stu that I was a 'Wiganer', which, as far as Stu was concerned, was a badge of office.

He'd purchased a mansion in Patterson Heights, Calgary, which closely resembled 'The Munsters' shambolic pile, and it became known as The Hart House. In it there was a notorious basement which had been christened 'The Dungeon'.

George and Kendo were invited to the house to have dinner on two occasions with Stu and his wife, Helen, a Greek-Irish New Yorker who apparently very much ruled the roost. George and Helen got on very well, not least because George was theatrical and Helen loved all that sort of thing, particularly Woody Allen whom she admired very much. They could talk theatre all night, leaving Stu and myself to talk shop – wrestling.

Stu was basically a bully, but he didn't want to wrestle any more. In 'The Dungeon' he had a wrestling mat, and he liked to get unsuspecting wrestlers in there and 'screw' them; he'd convince his guests to go onto their hands and knees, and then he'd maul the living daylights out of them. He tried to get me into that position but fortunately I'd been fore-warned.

I'd heard that Stu's children thought it was funny when he made someone in the Dungeon scream. They were old enough to understand what was going on, and they worked with him to get people into the basement and let the old man loose on them. Stu enjoyed this – he had a sadistic streak.

Once, when George and I were at Stu's for an evening I did go down into the basement with one of his lads, who'd asked me to show him some moves. While we were there, Stu appeared – he'd obviously had his card marked.

He watched for a while. He had this strange habit of making indescribable noises, a bit like a small grunt that almost formed the word, 'hey'.

Eventually he said, 'Maybe, Kendo...' he always called me Kendo, '...I could show you a few tricks here.'

'Go on, then,' I replied.

He got on the mat and said, 'You get down and I'll get behind you.'

I said, 'Oh, no – you show me your tricks from here – you can wrestle them on.'

'No,' he said. 'I'm kind-of an old fart nowadays. I don't really wrestle, but if you get down I'll show you.'

I stood my ground; 'I don't think so. If you want to show me some tricks, show me them from here.'

With that, he withdrew, apparently deciding that his 'tricks' wouldn't be all that good. Eventually he went away and his son and I carried on. His son couldn't do anything with me, but I wasn't going to let the old bugger get behind me and maul me. It had been Eric Cutler, another Wigan wrestler, who'd warned me about Stu's little games...

Stu had quite a big family, twelve children as I remember, some of who came into the wrestling business. Those who did, especially the older ones, played tricks on other wrestlers and got away with it – there was more than a little of the old man in them. I didn't have a lot to do with the younger ones, from Bret downwards – I only had contact with the three older ones, Smith, Bruce, and Keith.

Bruce and Smith forged out very good careers for themselves, and Bret 'The Hit-Man' Hart became the most recognizable. Whilst Kendo was there, Bret was only about fourteen so he hadn't yet started wrestling, but older brother Bruce debuted about half way through that tour.

On arrival in Canada, I joined a functioning team of wrestlers, the members of which regularly changed, not only to fit in with their respective individual commitments, but it also helped keep the matches fresh for the audiences. I was the new villain, and baby-face Geoff Portz was leaving Canada for three months work elsewhere. Accordingly, he dropped the North American Heavyweight Championship belt on Kendo, with the idea that he'd get it back when he returned.

After Portz left, Dan Kroffat arrived as the new baby-face, and he immediately started being billed with Tor Kamata, a heel who'd been there forever – their villain-versus-baby-face battles were invariably at the top of the bill.

Several weeks into the tour, George Gordienko pulled me aside and said, 'Do you realise that Kendo – who is, of course, the belt-holder – is being marginalised? He's supposed to be up against Kroffat and at the top of these bills, not Kamata. It's not right – I think you'd better go and tell Stu Hart that you're not going to put up with it.' I was astounded – I'd thought that the tour was running as it was supposed to – I had no idea this was going on.

I did indeed confront Stu, and he explained. He told me that Kroffat was actually scared of Kendo – apparently, he'd been badly mauled around by Billy Robinson quite recently in Texas, and when he'd heard I was from the same stable, he was very wary of me. He'd told Stu that he really didn't want to work with Kendo, and he more of less insisted that the villain he confronted was Kamata instead.

Clearly, common sense had to prevail. I met with Kroffat and assured him that I was prepared to work with him and not maul him around as Robinson had. He accepted this, and from then on, the top of the bill was indeed Kendo against Kroffat.

I have much to thank Gordienko for – only Kroffat and Stu Hart had been party to this arrangement, but the old hand George had spotted it, and acted in my best interests. His counsel put Kendo where he should have been – at the top of the bills, and earning more money. It's strange to think how Kroffat's fear had completely skewed things for Kendo, behind the scenes...

After a few singles matches against Kroffat, Kendo (partnered, believe it or not, with Lord Sloane of Kensington Gore) met him and Bruce Hart in a tag match for the weekly televised show from Calgary. Because he was from the venerable Hart family and new to the business, he really wanted to make his mark, so he asked Kendo if he could make sure that he bled – that wasn't a problem! Apparently he had some friends in the audience, and if he was going to lose, he wanted it to look good.

It was billed as a 'Hair vs. Mask' tag match; I can assure you that Kendo didn't lose the mask, so someone must have lost some hair. Toward the end of the match, Kendo had Bruce in a corner, and this was the opportunity for blood to flow. He was young and hot, and it wasn't a bit of blood – it was an awful lot. He also had blond hair, which, when covered in blood, really helped him look the part – it ended up looking like a slaughterhouse.

When we got back to the dressing room, Bruce was on one side and Kendo was on the other. Stu walked in and stood in the middle and started to make his characteristic grunting noises. When he did speak, the only word you could make out was, 'Goddamn!'

Then he walked over to where Bruce was sitting and smacked him across the face, saying, '...stay away from your fucking mother!' and then he stormed out. It seemed clear that he was very apprehensive over what Helen would have to say about one of her brood being so badly bloodied.

Kendo wrestled the Mexican 'Lucha Libre', Supahawk, and before their first encounter, in the dressing room he told me about his speciality – after he'd done a double-handed chop to his opponent's neck, he would do a 'Hawk Dive' off the top rope. So, after his chop had knocked his opponent down, he would climb the ropes and strike a pose like a hawk waiting to pounce on its prey. The crowd loved it – it was very theatrical. Unfortunately, when he tried it on Kendo, it didn't go well...

After the neck-chop, Kendo was indeed knocked to the canvas, and Supahawk went into his routine, swooping around the ring before climbing the corner-post and posing theatrically. However, he spent so much time lapping-up the audience reaction that he gave Kendo way too much time to recover.

By the time the leap from the top rope came, Kendo was ready and waiting in the middle of the ring, and as the Hawk leapt, he simply stepped aside. Supahawk crashed into the canvas in a heap, getting bashed and bruised in all sorts of painful places – it took him a while to get up, which he did, groaning.

Back in the dressing room, Supahawk asked me, 'Why you move?!? You supposed to catch me!'

I replied, 'Well, I got bored waiting!' He wasn't amused!

It was while I was in Canada that I finally used a move I'd been developing – the Kamikaze Crash. There were plenty of 'aeroplane spins' used in matches, usually culminating in a body-slam, but I'd envisaged a much more spectacular move which would be a knock-out finish. I'd wanted a way of combining a throw and a slam, but incorporating my weight coming down onto my opponent, knocking the wind out of him. When it came to me I knew it would be a crowd-pleaser, but it wasn't for the faint-hearted – a great deal of fitness, strength, and agility was required. I sprang the move on Frank Butcher, an unsuspecting minor-league opponent, and everyone was astonished. The other lads were scared of having it used on them but that didn't save them!

After his three months away, Geoff Portz had now returned to the tour; as I've already mentioned, he was a bully, of which he gave us a prime example one night.

We were on our way back to Calgary from Regina. It was a 450-mile overnight trip on which Bob Pringle and I were the transport, and we were about half way when we stopped at a roadside cafe. There were a group of lads already there who'd obviously had too much to drink, and when we came in and sat down, one of them recognized us as wrestlers and started making the usual sceptical taunts, such as, '...it's all fixed!' They were only silly teenagers, not a challenge to anyone.

Eventually, Bob got up and told them off, and he back-handed one of them, after which they all shut up.

It was winter so it was pretty cold, and Bob went outside to keep his eyes on the cars because we'd left the engines running to keep them warm. As soon as he left, Portz decided to have a go at these lads. He'd already seen that they were no challenge, but instead of just ignoring them and leaving, he dragged one of them out of his chair and smacked him a couple of times. He ended up on the floor where Portz kicked him.

I jumped up and stopped him. It was bullying for its own sake, against a soft target. I'm sure that if there had been repercussions after Bob had slapped one of them, Portz wouldn't have done anything – he could be quite despicable.

One night, Portz was on with Gordienko, who could be

difficult – it wasn't easy to get a show out of him if you were a baby-face. In the dressing room, Portz started complaining about how the match was going to be hard work, but he didn't realise that he could be heard. There were some coat-hooks on the wall with clothes hanging from them and Gordienko was tucked out of the way behind them. Portz suddenly realized that he was there and he clammed-up straight away, but we all knew what would happen next.

When they got in the ring, Gordienko seriously mauled Portz – he almost never got off the canvas. He didn't injure him, but he wanted him to know he was being punished. Portz was quite right – it was hard working with Gordienko, but it wasn't wise to say so in his earshot.

Towards the end of the tour, I got some disturbing news from home. My father rang me up and said, 'You'd better come back because I don't think your aunt is going to live much longer.'

Smith bought the Buick from me – he'd lost his licence and couldn't get insurance, so he drove it on my details and insurance plate after I'd left, and George and I got the soonest possible flight back.

After we'd left Canada, I heard that Dan Kroffat had studied and copied the 'Kamikaze Crash' move, and then passed it off as his own. He would have been among the first I'd ever used it on, and while they say that imitation is the sincerest form of compliment, I was somewhat pissed off that my innovation had been stolen by a much lesser wrestler. It didn't end there, either – I later heard that Ricki Fuji had copied the move from Kroffat; both of them still called it the 'Kamikaze Crash', but without ever mentioning that it was my creation. There were to be other imitators of the move too...

We arrived back in the UK on New Year's Eve, 1972. I was saddened at the thought that I was going to lose my Aunt, as I deeply admired and respected her strength, discipline, and single-mindedness, and I was grateful that she'd taken the time to instil them in me.

About a year before I'd gone to Canada she'd been diagnosed with breast cancer and she'd been successfully treated for it, and as far as I knew she was all clear. I didn't know that she'd developed secondary cancer that had spread into her bones; shortly before I'd left she'd started to complain about backache, and while I was away she'd slowly got worse. No-one had told me.

When I arrived at the hospital she was in bed, and looked seriously ill – very pale, face drawn. It was the first time I'd ever seen her vulnerable and it suddenly hit me how important she'd been to me; even now I get very emotional about it.

'Oh, I'm so glad to see you,' she said. 'I didn't think I was going to see you again.

I held her hand. 'What's the matter?' I asked.

'I've been a very naughty girl,' she said.

I thought to myself, 'This isn't my aunt – it's like she's someone else.' I said, 'I don't think that for a minute. Everything's going to be fine, you've no need to worry.'

'No,' she said, 'You'll find out what I've done.'

I didn't take it too seriously as she didn't seem entirely lucid and she was heavily medicated – I think she may have been having a flash-back to her childhood. I reassured her and promised I'd keep coming to see her, but that night she passed away peacefully.

I was deeply touched by her loss. She'd slipped away, and no matter how many mountains I thought I could move, I couldn't do anything about it. I hated the feeling of powerlessness, and it made me feel vulnerable as well.

I'll never forget my Uncle Norman and Aunt Ida and I'll always be grateful to them – they were, respectively, a dear and supportive friend when I'd most needed one, and the most excellent mentor anyone could wish for.

She left me several properties and a large amount of money, but her convictions about my father being an undeserving case were evident to the last – she'd only left him £100.

My Aunt also left £100 to my step-mother, Doris, which was paltry compensation for all the time she'd devoted to looking after her until she'd died. She was indifferent about her own legacy, but she was very annoyed on behalf of my father, saying 'How could she? He was her brother!'

I told her not to worry about it, and I gave my parents a lot more, out of what had been left to me.

I decided to sell my Aunt's bungalow and hotel in Blackpool and use that money to buy a bigger house in Wolverhampton called White Lodge, in a nice area called Goldthorn Hill.

I also decided to expand my car-dealing business, selling the London site and showroom to set up a bigger garage in Wolverhampton, for which Barry came up with the name – Chequered Flag. It was in a good position, almost in the town centre and on a main road leading to and from Birmingham, the Birmingham New Road. The core business was based around selling sports cars – E-types, Scimitars, Jensens, Triumph Spitfires and TRs, MGBs and Midgets, Frogeye Sprites, Austin Healeys, and Porsches – all the sports cars of the day. We also had American cars, including Pontiacs, Galaxies, Camaros, Corvettes, Cadillacs, and Mustangs.

We also bought a workshop between Wolverhampton and Willenhall to have repairs and servicing done on the cars we sold. If a specialist car needed work it could be bought at a significant discount, and with in-house facilities to do that work, a lot of money could be made when the car was sold. Our turn-around was so good that the workshop was busy all the time.

For some time I drove around in a Rolls Royce Mulliner Park Ward 2-door coupe, which was the identical predecessor of the Corniche, but as soon as the blue Jensen Interceptor came in, after one drive I loved it, and it became my daily driver. The only car I found with a similar super-grand tourer feel was the Porsche 928.

Chequered Flag did very well, until a hole was found in the accounts, and I was very saddened to find that Barry had taken ten thousand pounds out of the company for his own use. Our business relationship ended at that point; I hadn't ended our friendship and I kept the door open for bridges to be re-built, but sadly it never happened.

Chapter 21

The Faith Healing Incident

I need to return to some of the fundamental aspects of Kendo Nagasaki and how they evolved into something I hadn't anticipated – a mystical presence.

I've already described how Kendo came into being and how I didn't consciously 'think' about how he should come across in the ring – I let mindfulness take its course, forgetting myself, so that everything I'd learned could come together intuitively for Kendo to express himself. I was there, of course – I was the physical vehicle – but I didn't interfere or really even pay attention to how it happened; I stepped back and let it happen of its own accord.

Since George had joined me, this process had been much easier; not having to talk to people or deal with anything other than the match ahead meant that I could go completely into a mindful state, and react as a samurai would – automatically. Whilst it was true that professional wrestling was a form of combat that needed to please an audience, it mirrored the sword-sport kendo, where samurai sword skills are expressed in structured ways, but both skill and 'spirit' were needed to be the best.

I'd been meditating for over fifteen years and practising mindfulness for over ten, so the way Kendo came across was completely natural by now, and even though I'd heard some comments about how people felt he was 'mystical' and had a 'quiet power', I hadn't realised that for some people Kendo was genuinely inspiring.

It crossed my mind that because there was no human face to Kendo, only his mask, people looked more closely at the things they could see to get an impression of what he was really like. It seemed that his hands were very much a focal point, not least because of the missing left index finger, but Kendo could use them to inflict great pain as well as write his signature in elegant and flowing Kanji, and I'd found that my hands had been remarked upon for another reason as well.

For some time I'd had my own small physical therapy room at my home in Wolverhampton, a brick-built garage added on to the side of the house, carpeted and made comfortable, which I'd initially set up to treat my own strains and sprains. Wrestling takes its toll on muscles, joints, and tendons, and as you grow older you start to feel the effects of such wear and tear more and more, so I'd studied the latest treatment techniques and had acquired, among other things, an electronic interferential muscle treatment machine, an ultrasound machine to help cartilage problems, a therapy couch with a large infra-red array above it, and an orbital massager. Separately, I also had a sauna cabinet and a thermo-pool.

After a few of my acquaintances had reported their own physiological problems – back pains, shoulder problems, stiff necks, sciatica, and so-on – I'd volunteered to help them. I combined the use of my 'new technology' with what I'd learned from Abbe – 'Katsu', or 'Judo Healing' – into a form of chiropractic treatment. I was pleased to be able to help people when other treatments seemed to have failed, and it was after a few such sessions that I'd received comments about the 'magic' my hands could work at fixing sometimes quite debilitating problems. To me it wasn't magic – I was just mindfully practising what I'd learned, and doing what felt intuitively right.

After quietly doing this for quite a few years, it was as if a cork popped out of a bottle, and interest in Kendo's 'healing' was suddenly everywhere.

It began at a match in Chesterfield in February 1976 – it was Friday 13th, coincidentally; of course, a previous Friday 13th back in November 1964 had been highly ominous for wrestling when Kendo had his debut match, and this one was to prove equally influential in its own surprising way.

The day proceeded as normal to start with (although I'd always felt slightly heightened senses on any Friday 13th), and we'd arrived at the hall, gone to the dressing room, and were waiting for the first match on the bill.

Suddenly, having had a scout-around before the match, George burst into the dressing room in a slightly more flamboyant way than usual and announced, 'Tonight, dear, you're going to be a faith healer!'

I was most surprised at this and cautiously enquired, 'Where have you got that idea?'

He said, 'I've got this lady outside who has a son with a pain in his stomach. He's about six or seven years old, and she's had a vision that Kendo Nagasaki can either help it or heal it.'

I didn't know what to say; George continued, 'She says he's had the pain for quite some time. He's been to doctors and seen specialists, but it's persistent and they can't get rid of it. She's convinced that Kendo can cure it, just by placing his hand on his stomach.'

I was sceptical; I said, 'That sounds a bit odd to me, George. I need to know a lot more about this. What's she like? Is she strange? How does she come across to you?'

'She seems fine, actually. I can't see it doing any

harm,' he said; 'Why don't you give it a go?'

I cautiously agreed, and George went back to see the woman and make the arrangements.

The venue had a backstage area with a corridor leading to the dressing room. George told her that after Kendo left the ring that night (he was on third), if she made her way to the corridor, he would meet her and do what she wanted.

Eventually the time came and the lady arrived with her son as arranged. George came into the dressing room and said, 'Right, dear – let's go and do it.'

Mother and son were standing in the corridor, looking very solemn. The mother explained to George what she wanted while we listened carefully. Her son then sat on a chair and Kendo placed his hand on his stomach, leaving it there for several seconds, and I briefly went into a mindful state visualising the boy being free from pain. When Kendo removed his hand he bowed to the mother and went back to the dressing room while George ensured they were satisfied and bade them farewell. He said that the woman was very grateful to Kendo, and as what he'd done seemed to have been what she'd hoped for, I thought no more about it.

A short while later, a reporter from Psychic News contacted us and said that he'd been told of this 'healing' incident. He explained that the lady had called the magazine and told them all about it, that she'd claimed that her son had been cured and had stopped complaining about the stomach pain. She'd taken him back to the doctor and the specialists who had examined him, and they couldn't explain his improvement.

This was exactly the kind of fantastic story that Psychic News wrote about, the spirit world and episodes of healing, and they wanted to meet Kendo and 'interview' him. It was arranged, but Kendo never spoke to them, of course – it was all done through George.

After we'd confirmed that the events at Chesterfield

had indeed happened they wanted to know if we had ever done anything like that before, but, of course, we hadn't – it had been a first. We dealt with it the best way we could and they ended up printing a big article about it.

Soon afterwards, journalist David Nathan came over and spent a full day with Kendo. He watched him conduct a therapy session and asked what some of the wrestling holds felt like. Of course, he was astonished at the power of the holds, as well as the contrast between them and how Kendo used his hands to 'heal', and he made a feature of this in the four-page article he wrote for the TV Times magazine; it was published in December 1976 and led to a further dramatic increase in Kendo's reputation for the mystical.

News of the articles kept spreading, and word reached a woman called Bertha Barr. She lived in Mitcham, Surrey, and she and her husband, Tom, who was one of the 'Fathers' in the printers' union, were friends of Mick McManus. Bertha asked Mick if he could put her in touch with Kendo to help her with the osteo-arthritis she'd suffered with for thirty years. She'd seen doctors and visited hospitals and had even had consultations in Harley Street, but no-one had been able to help her.

Mick spoke to George and myself at a show and asked us if we would see Bertha. Once again we were a little reluctant – George explained that while it was good that what had happened at Chesterfield seemed to have worked, we didn't consider ourselves to be 'faith-healers.' However, Mick eventually persuaded us to see Bertha at my home therapy room.

Once again, another sensational article was the result – Bertha reported back to Psychic News that she too had been 'cured', after which interest in Kendo as a 'healer' exploded. People began writing to us to request treatment and I was happy to help as many as I could.

It began to feel like a roller-coaster – an aspect of Kendo I'd never imagined, but which had just appeared out of nowhere. Letters flooded in from all over the country, and some even came from the USA and Australia – the demand was so great that I could have ended up giving therapy every day of the week, but it felt best to keep it to just the Sunday sessions at my home. I couldn't hope to treat everyone who wrote, but George answered every letter, scheduling an appointment for those who could come and at least encouraging those who couldn't to be inspired by the strength they sensed in Kendo.

I began seeing small groups of people every Sunday at my home for therapy sessions, and as more and more people came I noticed that many of them were insecure, or confused, or both. As I treated their physical problems, I could feel tension and weakness and indecision in their bodies – it was a complete contrast to the strength, rock-solid confidence, and focus I'd gained from my studies under sensei Abbe. I was surprised to feel the difference between my 'energy' and theirs, and when I manipulated them, I mindfully visualised them becoming as strong and self-assured as I was. Everyone I treated did seem more confident and clearer-headed afterwards. I also started recommending that those I saw try to meditate, and those who did said they'd begun feeling better sooner.

It had always been clear to me that meditation led to better physical health, and I saw this being proved again and again. Obviously, a trapped nerve or a muscle in spasm needed manipulation to start the healing process, but once recovery from a problem had begun, looking after the inner self seemed to mean that the outer physical self stayed in better shape and continued improving quicker.

When Kendo 'healed', perhaps he was simply breaking a cycle of tension and anxiety but it certainly seemed to work, and his aura also seemed to inspire people to deep calmness, and from that, strength. Through George, I began trying to put across Zen and KyuShinDo principles to the people I was helping, in as few words and in as simple terms as possible.

There was a lady who was a fine example of the positive thinking I was able to encourage. A friend of Bertha's ran a shop in the same parade as Bertha's flower shop, which sold nick-nacks. Her husband had died and she'd lost her confidence and retreated from the world to the extent that she'd given up her shop. She owned the building and still lived above the shop premises but she'd felt unable to run it and had let it to other people who also sold novelties. She came to Kendo for treatment of a bad back and I felt great confusion and powerlessness in the way she reacted, so as I treated her physical ailment I visualised her strong and confident once again, and told her to see herself in that way too. She did, and soon afterwards she told me that she'd felt calm and clear and strong after seeing Kendo, and she'd felt that getting her shop back was what her husband would have wanted her to do, so she did. She wrote several letters thanking us for her new-found strength and optimism.

People who were spiritually-inclined also started to visit me. One day a woman came along who I think was part of a spiritual healing church; she was quite a well-known character in her local area and may even have had some national recognition. She said that she had a spirit guide, and that her spirit guide was talking to my spirit guide. I'd never really thought that I had such a guide, but I reasoned that it may be possible to think of Kendo in that way; however he never 'spoke' to anybody – not even me. Whatever wisdom he may possess, I realised that I'd taken the old maxim for granted, which is that 'He who knows does not speak'.

She began talking about what her spirit guide was telling her; she said, 'He's told me that you're not going to continue doing this (healing) work – you're going to stop and take up something completely different. But you will come back to it. It's going to take a long time but you're not going to leave it altogether. It will always be in your subconscious. He's told me that it will be very big.'

She also said, 'You're going to stop wrestling as well.' This was a strange thing to hear; at the time, I had no intention of stopping wrestling...

She continued, saying, 'You've seen a man prior to my visit that you can't help – he's going to pass.' By that she meant he was going to die. 'But don't worry about it – you're doing good by seeing him. You mustn't turn him away even though you ultimately can't help him. You must not alarm yourself by becoming emotionally distressed by his condition.'

How did she know this? The week before she came I had indeed seen a man who'd arrived in a wheelchair. He'd looked very ill and could hardly move, and he'd asked me to do whatever I could for him. I hadn't been at all sure what I could do, but I did some manipulations and visualisations, for which he was grateful.

After the man had left I mentioned to George that I'd felt somewhat helpless – there was nothing I could do to prevent the inevitable, and I was concerned that anything I did might seem self-serving, but I never charged anyone for any treatment and I did what I could. I hoped I hadn't given the man or his family any false hope.

I never made any assumptions about spiritual or psychic energies; I know people have always believed in them, and if that works for them I respect that, but I only ever adhered to the principles of Zen and Buddhism. If you still your mind you'll prevent its nagging and worrying from undermining you, your stress levels will be lower, and your health will inevitably be better. Also, stilling the mind switches off the noise that can prevent your own intuitive self from guiding you, and I have always believed that it can make better decisions than the mind alone, which is actually a rather simple thing; intuition is far closer to nature than reason and rationalising, and it can guide you how to be the best you can be as a part of the big picture of the whole of nature. This is, of course, sensei Abbe's Kyu Shin Do in action, as a philosophy for life.

However, I still reflect on what the lady from the spiritual healing church had said to me, about things she had no way of knowing. What she'd said did turn out to be true – I did stop wrestling, I gave up the therapy except for my own personal joint problems or helping people that were close to me, and I did move into a completely different field, the music business. As regards '...coming back to it...', I can't imagine that her words turned out to be a self-fulfilling prophesy, but I was later to be involved in a company which supported people with learning disabilities, and there's no way she could have known that Kendo would eventually have his own meditative retreat, again to help people.

If I had to try to explain such 'vision', I would envisage it as being a part of the natural world which – like intuition – has many aspects that are beyond reason and rationality. Buddhism states that there's no need to ponder such things, but instead to work benevolently with the whole of nature, seen and unseen, reasoned and intuitive, within us and around us, to be the best that we can be.

Another way of viewing Kendo's 'healing' might be to think of his 'aura' as having the power to unleash deeper energies within ourselves, which are capable of bringing about positive outcomes in ourselves; I like to think that he's always done that for me.

Kendo had always had a strong image with more than a little mystery about it, but the explosion of interest in his 'healing' had taken his mystique to whole new levels, and it had all sprung from one Chesterfield woman's vision. Quite how and why she'd seen that Kendo could help her son was a mystery, but what she'd seen had revealed an inspiring energy that even I had no idea that Kendo possessed. Perhaps all these things are indeed evidence of higher forces which are around us and can be tapped-into, but, as I've said, while I didn't dwell on such things I was then and still am happy to accept and work with them as a part of the big picture of nature, to help anyone I can to be the best that they can be too.

Chapter 22

Brian Dixon, Big Daddy, and Max Crabtree

I was approached by a promoter called Brian Dixon, who had managed to become one of the largest independents. He felt that Joint Promotions was losing its grip and it might be the right time to get hold of the biggest villain draw in the business – Kendo.

I'd first became aware of Brian some years earlier when he was a teenager, through a fan-based magazine he ran. He was from Liverpool and used to come to the stadium. He eventually fell in with a man called Orig Williams, a Welsh promoter, after which he started to take wrestling more seriously. Initially his role was to go around the venues handling publicity for Orig – one of his jobs was putting up the posters, and from there he progressed into the office. Orig ran shows in Ireland as well, so when he was away from the Rhyll headquarters, Brian would take the bookings and pass the information on to him when he returned.

But something odd happened, and my understanding was that Brian took a call in the office one day concerning a request for a spot show, which is a one off show – it could have been for a fete or something similar. I could imagine Brian in his enthusiasm thinking to himself, 'Why don't I have a go at this myself? I know all the wrestlers, I know who has a ring – I can do it.' – so he did, behind Orig's back.

However, I believe the second time it happened, Orig found out. He wasn't pleased because he felt the shows had been stolen from him, which led to a parting of the ways, but Brian now had a taste for the wrestling business and he wanted more.

He didn't run many shows to start with, just the odd one here and there, and he soon realized that he needed someone to take care of the wrestling side of the business. This was how he came to be involved with Monty Swan. Monty was from a big family, one or two of whom were known for being hard lads who could look after themselves. Brian felt that there was a certain amount of safety by being associated with them, so that if anybody came to interfere with his shows they might think twice because they weren't dealing only with him.

Brian met up with female wrestler Mitzi Mueller; she became his big draw, and effectively launched the Brian Dixon phenomenon. He eventually made her the British Ladies' Wrestling Champion. Even though they never made it as far as television, Mitzi made Brian and Monty quite a lot of money – if someone booked a stag party or something similar, they wanted female wrestlers on the bill. Joint Promotions wouldn't have anything to do with them – I believe the council wouldn't allow women wrestlers in London.

Brian has since done very well for himself – to this day he's still promoting wrestling under the banner *All-Star Wrestling*. On 16th March 2018,before moving his shows to the King's Hall, he invited Kendo to make a commemorative appearance at his last ever-show at The Victoria Hall, Hanley, which marked my fifty-fourth year of appearing there. Lyn Rigby appeared on stage beside

Kendo as we used the occasion to announce my autobiography, pledging all the proceeds to the Lee Rigby Foundation. Brian also presented Lyn with a cheque for her Foundation. It was all very well received by the audience.

Brian and I had a chat back-stage when he reminded me of a funny incident from a few years back. It would have been 1988 at the DeMontfort Hall in Leicester. In the dressing-room Brian and I had ended up having a blazing row over something to do with the show, and eventually he decided to storm out. His dramatic exit failed miserably when he ferociously grabbed the door-handle and it came off in his hand. Sheepishly, he turned to me and said, 'Now look what you've made me do!' There was still a hint of panic in his eyes at being stuck in a room with an irate me, but it was so funny that the argument evaporated immediately – which was fortunate because we had to bang on the door for quite a while before someone opened it from the outside!

So, back in the early seventies, Brian came to talk to George and I. He'd put together a very tempting proposition where he offered us not only work, but also a full partnership in his business. At some stage in their lives, nearly all the wrestlers ended up as promoters – it had become a pattern. Wrestlers don't necessarily make the best promoters but it was how the business went – it was an appealing and powerful role.

The idea appealed more to me than to George – he liked being on television, and we knew if we went over to Brian that would cease. However, despite that, we decided to join Brian.

His partner, Monty, didn't like the idea because it meant that they only had half the business between them and George and I had the other half. Monty was the nuts-and-bolts man who put the rings up and wrestled, whereas Brian was the brains behind it all who booked the shows and paired-up the fighters, so Monty ended up being overruled.

We went over to All-Stars and worked with them for quite some time, but eventually Monty decided he wanted out and he resigned, leaving it to the three of us. That created a new problem, particularly for Kendo.

When George and I went to a show, Kendo had to stay in the dressing room. If there were two shows running, you had to be there early enough in the day to collect the advance bookings, because sometimes they were not done at the hall, but at newsagents or similar establishments in the town.

Two shows meant that Brian was at one and we were at the other, both of which had to be organised from start to finish. After collecting the bookings we had to get to the hall and oversee the arrival of the ring and the wrestlers. This usually meant being there from around three pm right through to gone ten at night, until everybody else had left.

Eventually the pressure began to tell on both George and myself, so we went over to sort things out with Brian. The meeting was pretty stressful – when we came away, we realised that we didn't know where we stood or what was happening with the business. This kind of uncertainty really upset George.

He and I had a pretty volatile relationship at the best of times. On the journey from The Wirral back to Wolverhampton we were arguing about what we had and didn't have with Brian. It was all so unclear – he'd set us off, and we ended up bickering with each other. We were on the M6 and had got as far as Knutsford services when George really started to rant.

'I've had enough of this,' he snapped; 'Stop the car and let me out!'

I drew straight into the services and did as he'd asked; 'Go on, then,' I said.

He jumped out and slammed the door, and I drove off, all the way back to Wolverhampton.

As soon as I got home, the phone rang. I didn't answer it at first but it was pretty persistent. Of course, I knew who it was; eventually I picked it up and George said, 'Are you coming to pick me up, dear? You've left me on the motorway and I haven't even got my coat.'

'No,' I said.' You got out of the car, you can stay there. Hitch a lift – do whatever you have to.'

Thankfully, we weren't doing a show that night. By the time he'd phoned me it would have been around five or six o'clock.

Time passed and the phone rang again; reluctantly, I answered it.

'I need to get home, dear...' said George.

'Haven't you tried hitching?' I asked.

'I have tried! I'm freezing cold, with no coat, and I'm not pretty enough – nobody wants to know!' he wailed. I relented, slightly.

At the time, Barry, the Count's son, was staying in the house. I said to him, 'Will you go and pick him up? I'm off to bed – I've had enough.'

What did Barry do? He removed the receiver and went to bed himself, leaving George on the motorway.

Next morning I was up around nine o'clock and I noticed the phone off the hook so I replaced it. It rang straight away.

'Hello dear!'

It was obvious who it was. I said, 'Where are you?'

'Where do you think I am? I'm on the bloody motorway, where you left me!' wailed George. 'I've been here all night, I haven't got a pot to piss in or a window to throw it out of, I'm on first name terms with all the lavatory attendants, and the women up in the café are all giving me cups of tea because I've told them what a bastard you are!'

They'd recognised him from TV. He'd told them that he'd been thrown out of the car without any money by Kendo Nagasaki, and they'd taken pity on him.

'Are you going to come and pick me up?'

I had no choice – he had been there all night.

So I picked him up. On the way back he wasn't in the best of moods and was clearly still consumed by the problems with Brian.

'I've had enough. I really can't stand much more of it. Brian's getting on my nerves – everything's getting on my nerves. I want out. I've had enough, dear.'

Then, of course, he started to cry – George was very good with tears. When we got back home I made him go to bed and recover – I reckoned he'd be fine later that day.

That evening we had a show, but after it he still wasn't okay. He said that we were much happier when we were doing shows for Joint Promotions, and he was right. I've always battled through problems, but for him, the Brian Dixon partnership was just too chaotic and stressful.

Over the next couple of weeks we decided that we were going back to Joint's. We had a meeting with Brian, and we broke the news.

'It doesn't fit in with who Kendo is,' I said. 'I can't be a promoter and be Kendo Nagasaki, it's an impossible job – it just can't be done. If I was an ordinary wrestler, I could go out there and mix with the others and organise things, but I'm not, so everything has to be brought to me in the dressing room. I can't move when I get to venues, and George has to do everything.'

Brian panicked. 'What the hell am I going to do? Monty's gone – if you go, I won't have a partner at all!'

I reassured him; 'Brian, you don't need a partner – you run the whole thing anyway. This business is Brian Dixon.'

As a matter of fact, he carried on and did very well, and he gave me the credit. He began to call me 'The Godfather', and often said, 'The Godfather put me on the right track.' I sometimes wondered what kind of chaos lay behind his continued success, but I was relieved that it was no longer mine and George's problem.

After we'd bailed I spoke to Wryton Promotions – returning to them was quick and easy.

When I went back to Joint's, Shirley Crabtree was wrestling for them as 'The Guardsman', while his brother Max was still running his own 'opposition' promotion in Scotland. Max was young and vibrant and doing very well up north where he'd built up Andy Robin to be a great draw (in which Kendo had a part), and they all thought he was a new breed of promoter.

Max hadn't been alone in seeking independence – Jackie Pallo, Adrian Street, and Kendo had all gone over to the Opposition. Pallo thought it was a good idea and he left to work for Max in Scotland before starting his own promotion, and Adrian Street worked for Max, Pallo, and other opposition promoters, but I don't think he ever had his own promotion.

Interestingly, when he was on the 'opposition', Max never once offered me work – I think this was because he was a control freak and recognised that I was too so he'd have known we would clash; he couldn't control me with money either – I didn't need it. I have to say that I wasn't particularly keen on him and his manoeuvrings either – I didn't trust him. Because of all this, if Max had been at Joint's before me, I would probably never had gone back to them.

Then, Morrell & Beresford had an offer from the Hurst Park Syndicate who bought them out and put Max in charge, which brought him into Joint Promotions, and he'd soon be in charge of Wryton as well.

Max's dynamism stood him in good stead because wrestling was actually stagnating. The trouble with Wryton, Morrell and Beresford, and Relwyskow & Green was that all the men in charge were old and they'd lost their spark. They were rich and comfortable, so they'd put someone else in charge and didn't really bother with the business any more. As a result, wrestling wasn't being run in a hungry sort of way – until Max came along.

Having seen a ladder match in Canada, I'd never set one up for Brian Dixon's All Stars, and I knew that Martin Conroy at Joint's couldn't be bothered with innovation, but now with Max there, I knew I'd have a receptive hearing – being new to the job he wanted to make a big impression, and he welcomed new ideas. He loved it – it would be the first ladder match in the UK. He even suggested that he'd put a few pound notes in the top of the prize bag which could be taken out and thrown to the audience, but with customary prudence he said, 'Make sure you don't throw too many, kid!'

Max suggested that I use Eddie Hamill who had wrestled for Joint's for years under his own name, but when the television show 'Kung Fu' became popular, he decided to give himself that name and wrestle in a mask. It worked well and he was a decent show-man, and the match was sensational. Another wrestler, Gwynn Davies, saw the show and said he couldn't believe how effective it was. He said we'd had the crowd in the palm of our hands right from the start.

For the weekend of the 1976 FA Cup Final, The TV company wanted something spectacular to show in competition with the football, so instead of showing a match from any regular venue they decided to televise an already-scheduled match at the Royal Albert Hall. It was already set up and billed, with Kendo and George as a tag team against Mick McManus and Steve Logan, but this posed a problem for Mick – he never wanted to be seen to lose on TV, which he would against Kendo.

Mick came into the dressing room and tried to steer things in his favour. He said he wanted the result to be 2-1 with him and Logan winning, and both their falls being on George and me getting one on Logan.

I said to Mick, 'Oh, no – it'll be 2-1 all right, but I'll get the first fall on Logan, you can get the equaliser on George, and I'll take the winning fall on you.'

He said, 'Erm – that's not what I had in mind.'

I said, 'Well, that's what you're getting!' Logan didn't care, but Mick did – this would be one of the few occasions where he would lose on TV.

It was bound to be a popular match, but George prepared for it by making sure he looked particularly eye-catching. He had it in his mind that he wanted to wear a big afro wig, and one evening in Earls Court Road he came across a friend of ours, Mick, who was with a friend of his – a 'lady of the night' called Lisa. She just happened to be wearing precisely the kind of wig George wanted, and as soon as he saw it he said, 'Ooh, that's just what I'm looking for!' and he plucked it off Lisa's head.

Much to everyone's surprise this liberated lots of cash which had been carefully secreted away, and it fluttered into the air! Lisa went bonkers! She didn't know whether to chase the cash or George to give him a kicking – the cash won! However, when she'd calmed down she still lent George the wig, and he certainly looked striking in it when we met McManus and Logan. Kent Walton idly mused over whether it was George's real hair, as many others no doubt were too, but the audience hooted with laughter when he took it off with a flourish!

A few months after returning, a series of matches began which led to one of the big questions surrounding Kendo Nagasaki: did Big Daddy really manage to take Kendo's mask off? Well, here's a little background and insight...

As Max had become more influential, he'd introduced Shirley as Big Daddy and begun to build up his image. I believe that Shirley had mentioned to Max that he could work well with Kendo, and Max needed to change Shirley from The Guardsman as a villain to Big Daddy, a baby face, and Kendo was the ideal vehicle. He approached me and said, 'Kid...' That's how he always spoke – whenever he spoke to anyone, he called him 'kid'... 'Kid, I've got Shirl, and I see a great future for him and Kendo. What

I'd like is for Shirl to pull the mask off on television...'

A number of discussions followed. His idea was to build up Big Daddy and get lots of television and the whole thing would simply get bigger and bigger. After giving it some thought, I agreed – anything that kept Kendo prominently in the public eye was not going to be bad.

Kendo and Daddy became top-of-the-bill attractions, and it soon evolved into the mask-removal feud. In the ring, Daddy seemed able to bounce back – literally – from Kendo's assaults, and ultimately he'd stun Kendo to the point where he began untying the laces to the mask, and despite Kendo fighting back Daddy eventually pulled it off. It was a battle royal in which audiences loved seeing the villainous Kendo subdued and then unmasked – they loved it. Kendo still didn't lose the match, but the people's champion, Daddy, got one over on the big bad villain, much to the crowd's delight.

On the strength of that television show Kendo and Daddy toured all around the country, going back to most of the halls three times. In every one of those shows it looked like the mask could come off again, which had the audiences at fever pitch all the way through. I believe it went on for well over a year.

Ultimately, by putting him over so well, it was Kendo who made Big Daddy into a household name, not the manoeuvrings of brother Max, other than setting it up. Others helped him later on, but it was in the ring that Kendo laid all the groundwork; in real terms, Daddy couldn't have pulled the mask off without Kendo's co-operation, but it made for spectacular drama and put us in great demand.

As Daddy became bigger, Max grew more powerful. It wasn't too long before Dale Martin was also bought out. Jarvis Astaire, the man in charge of the Hurst Park Syndicate, liked what Max was doing because he was now getting the wrestling business back into shape and making money. Kendo and Daddy were attracting full houses every night – you couldn't get a seat – they were all sold out.

Shirley wasn't just a big attraction, he was also a character. Every wrestler I've ever met has a favourite story connected to Shirley Crabtree. George and I had more than enough to last a lifetime.

Once we were on at the Tower Circus, Blackpool. After George made his speech, Shirley grabbed the microphone and informed the startled audience, 'Ladies and Gentlemen, you do realise that tonight we're in direct competition with the Beverly Sisters at the North Pier?!?'

I remember a match when Kendo was relentlessly pounding Big Daddy in a corner. Daddy leaned over the ropes and, staring some poor old dear straight in the eye, he said, 'Not for the squeamish – get the women and children out first!'

Another incident occurred at the end of a match, which was in fact one of George's favourite moments. Daddy was supposed to charge across the ring, slightly bent over, as if to give Kendo a shoulder tackle. Kendo would jump up so that his knee hit Daddy on the head, leaving him unconscious. The problem was, Daddy bent himself over so much that he was barely two feet from the ground. He launched himself across the ring like a lunatic pig. Kendo jumped up, walked two steps over Daddy's back and jumped off behind him, only to find that Shirley had gone straight through and into the ropes, landing in a heap.

Another finish was managed, and after the bout Shirley came up to us and said, 'Kid, if I do that again, stand aside and wave me through!'

Shirley was such a loveable old rogue both in and out of the ring that later on, George and I were more than happy to join Eammon Andrews in tricking him onto 'This is Your Life'.

Having your kid brother as the promoter couldn't exactly

be considered a hindrance, though. Max had one of the shrewdest and most ruthless business brains that I ever came up against in wrestling, and his handling of Shirley's career was a masterpiece of timing and audacity.

Max has made – and broken – more careers in wrestling than anyone could count, and around him he built a tight little group of men who owed him total allegiance, as well as their livelihoods.

On his bills Max always had one or two wrestlers who could really wrestle, to deal with anyone foolish enough to attempt a challenge, or a national newspaper putting up some mug to try his luck. Just because a business is entertainment, it doesn't necessarily follow that there aren't some people who are capable and know exactly what they're doing.

Max once said, 'Kid, we don't want them that study the game – we want those that believe in magic! Magic is an illusion – a trick, if you like – but nonetheless clever, breath-taking, and entertaining – wrestling *is* magic!'

Chapter 23

The Ceremonial Unmasking

I took stock, and I wasn't happy with how things measured-up. I felt that wrestling was degenerating into something lesser and poorer than it had ever been, and I was having difficulty seeing a future for Kendo. Sure, the halls were being filled by the Big Daddy versus Kendo battles, but they had become mundane and predictable; with Max Crabtree running Joint Promotions, Daddy was practically his sole focus, and he directed everything he controlled into feeding that phenomenon.

Anti-heroes were used to keep making Big Daddy more and more popular. Haystacks had never been keen on wrestling Kendo because he felt that Kendo would diminish his own standing as a villain or beat him (of course, he didn't want either), whereas being matched against Daddy allowed him to maintain his super-villain status. The Canadian, Mighty John Quinn, was also to follow this route.

So we ended up with Kendo as the biggest 'heel' villain and Stacks as the biggest physical villain, both being used as foils for Daddy as 'The People's Champion'. Max's control was becoming ever-more limiting and frankly claustrophobic, and I could see that it was bad for the business – if everything was geared around one phenomenon and all else was allowed to stagnate, there would be nothing to take its place when interest in it faded. Under Max, wrestling was becoming a 'one-trick pony'.

It was such a contrast to the time he was taken on at Joint Promotions – he'd actually rescued wrestling then, when the business really was on its arse. Before his dominance you could play one promoter against another, but now there was nowhere else to go; without any serious competition, the scope of wrestling was bound to suffer – you either went along with what he wanted or you could be taken off television and marginalized until you'd find yourself out of the business altogether. Such absolute control was ultimately short-sighted.

I'd begun to feel that George and I were in a similar situation to the one we'd been in with Brian Dixon – far from ideal. Once again it began to seem that our lives would be better off this particular merry-go-round, but this gave rise to an even bigger question – would we be better off out of wrestling completely?

There were rumours that Kendo had been injured, and he had, but not seriously enough to leave wrestling. He took a crack to the head which left me with a mild version of vertigo, and I did choose to reduce the number of matches while it settled down, but I think my general dissatisfaction with wrestling was an equal factor in stepping back and taking stock.

This led to another consideration; I was still busy every Sunday with therapy sessions at my home, helping people in ways that were at odds with Kendo's reputation in the ring, and I'd become concerned that it may not be appropriate to be both a villain wrestler and a 'healer'. I definitely intended to continue the therapy for people, but was it too incongruous?

George and I discussed it all at great length, and we

gradually came to the decision that we'd rather withdraw from wrestling and put our energies into something else that had been gradually gathering momentum for some time – the music business.

As George has already mentioned, he'd been meeting show-business people since practically his first day in London back in 1967, and he'd become friends with several musicians and entrepreneurs whom we'd often encounter while out in the West End. In Wolverhampton, George became the magnet for interesting people, including aspiring musicians and song-writers, and in him they saw an opportunity to advance their careers – which wasn't easy as a starving artist in an unremarkable Black Country town.

It's been said that anyone can spot talent but it takes talent to spot genius, and I believed that George had that talent. Sadly, he'd always had to tell the aspiring hopefuls that he couldn't help them. I knew he'd have loved to, and as wrestling had become so unrewarding, it began to seem entirely sensible to explore an intriguing-looking field which had basically come to us.

George was interested in a number of local bands in Wolverhampton that wanted us to manage them. We had plenty of organizational experience and we knew our own show-business niche very well, and in many ways, music didn't seem that dissimilar. Our idea was to use our skills to bring some groups from obscurity into the limelight, and, as long as we chose the right ones, capitalise on the success we could deliver.

Once the decision had been made, the question arose of how we'd step back from wrestling – how, where, and when we would do it? Having had an intuitive connection to Kendo for the past 14 years, I waited for guidance and, sure enough, it came.

It had to be ceremonial, spectacular, and unforgettable. As I continued to meditate, everything came to me; it would be classic Kendo Nagasaki – he would ceremonially unmask on television. This would be the first time a masked wrestler had ever voluntarily unmasked, as opposed to being required to do so after losing a match – instead of that, Kendo's unmasking would be spectacular.

One of the bands George and I wanted to work with comprised singer/songwriter Geoff Southall and guitarist Jim Crosbie, and as the official unmasking would be televised we decided to promote their band on the back of it. Their image was as-yet undecided, and we hoped that they'd come up with a presence that worked with Kendo's mysticism, as doing so would have a promotional synergy.

We decided to use Geoff and Jim as acolytes in the ring with us, and we spent quite some time choreographing their roles. George would officiate, and Kendo would unmask and be seen as he'd never been seen before, and as no-one could have expected.

We decided to do the unmasking at Wolverhampton Civic Hall, which was close to the Willenhall venue where Kendo had debuted thirteen years earlier.

Geoff and Jim made their own way to the hall; they had the necessary clothing for it – monk's outfits. George had hired his robe from Burman's in London and Kendo wore his normal wrestling attire.

George and I arrived at the venue in our street clothes. We had our own dressing room so we could all spend time together. There were no other wrestlers present, but Max Crabtree was there. He popped in from time to time to see how things were going, and he reassured us that he had the cauldron and the flammable liquid ready for the burning of the mask.

The time came for us to dress as required. George changed into an elaborate blue gown with drapes everywhere – he resembled a priestess. He applied his own make-up and sprayed his hair silver, making himself look appropriately unique and gorgeous.

Kent Walton came into the dressing room to ask how

the show was going to run; I explained to him what was going to happen and he listened without making any comment. I decided to make sure that he didn't undermine the unmasking; Walton had never liked Kendo or George, and while he had never been unprofessional enough to say anything that belittled us, I'm sure he would have done if he thought he could get away with it. I certainly didn't want him seizing his chance as Kendo bowed-out.

After I'd explained everything, he said, 'OK, that's fine.'

Before our gaze broke, I looked intently at him and said, 'Don't fuck it, Kent.'

He said, 'OK,' and left.

Then we were ready and the introduction music started; as we made our way to the ring the atmosphere was very solemn. The enormity of what was about to happen seemed to suddenly hit me; I'd spent a long time with Kendo, and this would be the end of it. Questions came to mind – I'd ask myself, 'Are you sure you're doing the right thing? Should I go ahead with it?' I could always get into the ring and have George announce that I'd changed my mind...

But by then it was too late – it was advertised; I was committed. Even at that very late stage I was apprehensive – I had no way of being sure that what I was doing would work out.

Norman Morrell once said to me, 'Kendo won't be Kendo without the mask.' That thought suddenly haunted me. Max Crabtree had advised against the unmasking – he'd said that the audience would be very disappointed if the mask came off and they saw that Kendo looked like an ordinary bloke. I'd never have allowed that, but his sentiments only reminded me of Norman's...

However, Kendo without a mask still looked different to any other wrestler. My head was shaved apart from a ponytail at the back. The tattoo was clearly visible on my head (it had in fact been there for some years), and there would, of course, be the red eyes...

Once in the ring, the atmosphere was almost religious. The audience was very quiet. We didn't have the usual comments – 'Get on with it, Nagasaki! What a load of rubbish!' – there was none of that. People almost seemed to rise to the occasion – they showed respect.

George went into his speech as Kendo and the two acolytes stood side-by-side by the ropes. When George finished, Kendo threw his cloak over his head and took off his sword and the kendo helmet, handing them to a Second. Then he took the unsheathed sword and drove it into the ring. Kendo knelt in front of it as the acolytes poured salt into George's hands as he stood behind Kendo. The acolytes then knelt either side of Kendo and threw themselves onto the canvas, towards the sword. George cast the salt over Kendo's head, blessing the ceremony, and he then began untying the laces of the mask.

The mask came off Kendo's bowed head, revealing the hexagram tattoo with the Third and All-Seeing Eye at the centre.

George placed the mask in the cauldron, drenched it with the flammable liquid, and set light to it.

Kendo stood up, pulled the sword out of the ring floor and raised it in the same challenge as he'd used to face so many opponents, and he stared outwards with a solemn, dispassionate expression. He then turned and faced the opposite way, once again pausing at that compass point, with the sword lowered.

There was virtual silence in the hall. There may have been the odd comment or someone shouting out, but other than that – fascination; they were watching intently.

Then, someone started to applaud, and before long the whole audience had joined in.

George placed a hooded cloak around my shoulders and we left the ring.

It was a very moving experience which appropriately honoured all Kendo's achievements and what he stood for.

Once it was over there was a feeling of anti-climax, but as it turned out, right up until the present day, it was the right thing to do. We later heard that the unmasking generated one of the biggest ever television audiences for a wrestling event – fourteen million viewers.

The real Kendo may have unmasked, but that didn't mean he wouldn't still wrestle. George and I had decided to explore the music business but I didn't want to completely give up a career I'd enjoyed for thirteen years, and George was fond of being in the lime-light and he was very good at what he did, so he welcomed being able to keep his hand in too. Wrestling wouldn't be our primary focus but the unmasked Kendo would be able to determine the shows he'd do, so he'd need a new storyline.

Many of Kendo's traditional feuds had revolved around the mask being pulled off, but with that now out of the picture I was inspired that he would become a 'Super Baby-Face'. There were plenty of villains whom Kendo could challenge and overwhelm, and I decided that teaming-up with Kung Fu would work well. He was also a baby-face, and there hadn't yet been such a hard baby-face tag team.

A stunt was set up – Kung Fu was on against Mick McManus, who got him into a vicious hold which he refused to break, even with the ref's intervention. Kendo jumped into the ring and rescued Kung Fu from McManus, and it went over very well. That event was intended to set up the start of a series of matches featuring Kendo and Kung Fu as the super-baby-face tag team.

I'd decided that the unmasked image would include what had been seen at the unmasking – the cloak, the bald head with tattoo and the pigtail of hair at the back, with sunglasses and an attitude of total superiority. I decided I would walk into a hall like this and the image would be seen in the street as well.

By now Max Crabtree was running the Dale Martin office in London. He'd only recently been promoted by Jarvis Astaire and had ended up in charge of virtually the whole wrestling business. Even though he'd said the unmasking would be a bad idea and that Kendo would end up as just another wrestler, I'd already made sure that wouldn't be the case; there was still a strong demand for Kendo and Max asked me to drop in to his office to discuss the way forward.

I went there dressed in my new gear (and the accompanying attitude) and we started talking about the next phase – Kendo and Kung Fu as a tag team. It was all clear to me and I laid it out for Max, but I sensed that he wasn't happy. He was the promoter, the man who was supposed to control the business, but here he was being told what to do by a wrestler. He'd always been a control-freak, but unlike other wrestlers he had no control over me – I was essentially a free agent who would only do what was best for Kendo, and Max must have felt that was a problem.

About an hour later I got a phone call from him and he said he couldn't work with me. He said, 'Kid, you come in my office laying down the law, but I'm the promoter. I think we'd better call it a day.' With that I realised he'd got the wrong end of the stick – I was just trying to describe how I saw things happening but he'd taken it that I wanted to rule the roost. I calmed him down and I stressed that my attitude was part of the character and we could still work together, and he said he'd give it a go.

However, there are ways in which a promoter like Max will try to screw you – he'll put you on with wrestlers that you can't get the best out of, and the match ends up being mundane and boring. He put Kendo on with Bronco Wells who was poor to say the least – nothing Kendo did could make him look like a credible threat.

I certainly didn't consider this 'working' – Max had given Kendo an awful match; I wasn't going to stand for that kind of treatment and I suspected this was likely to be the pattern going forward, so I thought about it and decided it was time to withdraw from what the business had become and concentrate instead on the music.

As it turned out I was right – Max's focus ended up entirely upon putting his brother over – he even used the super baby-face tag team idea, including Kung Fu and various other wrestlers to make Big Daddy into 'the people's champion'. Practically every other wrestler was sacrificed on the altar of Daddy's success, but that definitely wasn't for Kendo.

After retiring properly a new phenomenon immediately appeared: Kendo rip-offs – other wrestlers copying his image and using the name.

The first was Bill Clarke. Right from the start he called himself Kendo Nagasaki and he used every aspect of the original image, including the kendo helmet, sword, cape, and striped mask. Sadly, everything about his outfit was cheap and tacky, much of it poorly home-made, so he was hardly taken seriously. However, I certainly wasn't going to tolerate a direct rip-off so I launched legal proceedings against him; he changed his ring-name to King Kendo but he carried on using his tacky version of the original Kendo's visuals. Quite some time later, the real Kendo was occasionally to face King Kendo for a few matches for Brian Dixon's 'All Stars', and he'd go on to work for Joint's too.

Then there was Japanese wrestler Kazuo Sakurada. Before I left Canada Stu Hart had already opened discussions with American promoter Vern Gagne who wanted Kendo and George to appear in Texas. I couldn't go because I had to get back to see my Aunt, after which I never returned to North America. I don't think it started immediately but Sakurada used the name Kendo

Nagasaki for shows in the USA and Puerto Rico. He didn't wear a striped mask but he painted his face instead, and as I stayed in the UK and he mostly stayed out of it, we didn't clash. Eventually he ceased to be a problem when he changed his ring-name to The Dragonmaster.

After Bill Clarke retired another King Kendo came along, this time fronted by Dale Preston. Lloyd Ryan managed him, which was an unsuccessful attempt to add credibility. He made a weak attempt to re-enact several of the real Kendo's earlier battles but they weren't as inventive or exciting as any of the originals.

Several other wrestlers used the word Kendo or Nagasaki, or even Nagazaki, in their names, all of which imitation could be regarded as compliments to the original but their inferiority was actually more of an insult. Having taken casual looks at them I remained confident that Kendo could return at any time he wanted to with his reputation intact.

There was another side to the Nagasaki phenomenon that the public didn't see – fortunately – and that was the kind of hilarious nonsense that often occurred behind the scenes. It was arguably an inevitable consequence of having someone as outrageous as George on the team, because around him, almost anything could – and often did – go awry. I've already described some of his funnier moments, but he almost threw the unmasking itself into chaos.

Ten minutes before we were due to go to the ring for the unmasking ceremony, George decided that his hair wasn't quite right so he asked me to help him.

'Would you mind just touching me up down this side of my hair, dear?'

I took the aerosol and sprayed – catastrophe! Unfortunately for us both, he hadn't properly protected himself from any over-spray, so I instantly made one entire half of his face silver. Had he turned around he would have resembled Tommy Cooper in a routine playing two people, each one revealed when he turned sideways-on. If it hadn't been disastrous for the image he wanted to portray, it would have been side-splitting.

He went into a complete meltdown. I can't remember what he called me but it wasn't very complimentary. The tears started, which George could turn on like a tap. There was a mad scurry round the room to grab all the wipes and anything else we needed to clean it off, and then he had to start again – frantically. It was amazing that we managed to look so composed by the time we had to make our way to the ring.

There was something else too, right in the middle of the ceremony – if you watch the video, George struggled to remove the mask – it took him quite a while because he got it stuck around my nose; he was a little clumsy like that. I was becoming a little apprehensive, thinking, 'Is he going to manage this or not? Am I going to have to remove it myself?' Of course, I sincerely hoped I wouldn't...

Such spontaneous comedy arose again and again, a classic example being after we'd moved to London when we had to make our next television appearance following the unmasking, for a show at The Fairfield Halls in Croydon.

George wore the same gown as he had for the unmasking, the one that made him look like an Egyptian priestess, and so that he could arrive in all his splendour, he decided to change before we set off – ever the drama queen. However, this made us late, and we set off for Croydon like a bat out of hell in a little black Mini Cooper.

Kendo and George were notorious for arriving at venues at the last possible minute, and under those circumstances Kendo had a reputation for being a tad intolerant of anyone who got in his way.

Within ten minutes of our appearance before the cameras, we reached the artiste's car park at the rear of the Fairfield Hall, only to find the gates closed. George got out of the car, robes flowing all over the place, and started to open the gates, which were ten feet tall and fifteen feet wide and made of wrought iron.

There were already ten to fifteen cars in the car park, plus a huge outside broadcast truck, which took up a lot of the space, but there was still enough room for our Mini. There was a security kiosk overlooking the car park, and, on seeing George, a 'job's-worth' rushed out shouting, 'The car park's full!' He started to push the gates closed again, but George, still trying to push them open, said, 'We've got to get to the show!' The gates had begun to close, but George pushed them partially open again, only to be met by 'job's-worth' shoving them closed again. George realised that he was going to have to make an almighty effort, so he pushed the gates really hard, and caught 'job's-worth' off-guard and off-balance, and he got the gates about three-quarters of the way open.

I was watching from the car, and thought the gates were open just far enough to get the car in; I could see that 'job's-worth' was making a recovery, so I decided to drive in quickly. 'Job's-worth' was facing the approaching car so he saw it and jumped out of the way, but George has his back to it and didn't; as I flew through, part of his robe got caught in the wheel, which ripped half the side out. I drove in and parked the car, and ended up hunched over the wheel helpless with laughter. What had just happened was hilarious, but I knew George was about to explode.

The dressing-rooms were two floors above the car park and the commotion had alerted the other wrestlers, who were now at the windows hooting in disbelief at the spectacle below. George gathered up what was left of his robe and, with a flourish, threw it over his left shoulder. He stood opening and closing the other remnants with disbelieving pathos, revealing spindly legs wearing ladies' stockings held up with garters, the look completed with men's Cuban heels. He walked up to the car and said to me, 'You couldn't wait, dear, could you? You just couldn't wait! Here I am, arriving like Demis Roussos, and within seconds you've turned me into Gypsy Rose Lee!' He then said, 'That's it – I'm not going on – I'm off!', and he ran through the gates, up the bank, and off in the direction of Croydon town centre with me in pursuit.

The robe and shoes got the better of him, so he stumbled and I caught up with him, stopped him and tried to reason with him. 'Look at you! Where do you think you're going to go?' He was crying and he told me to piss off, but then he had a moment of clarity, pulled himself together, and we made our way back to the venue.

Never one to be defeated, the old maxim that 'the show must go on' held true that night. Kendo's own 'street' clothes proved pretty effective for George in a Quixotic Dracula fashion, but as he was somewhat smaller-built than Kendo, that night he resembled a sort of cavalier Worzel Gummidge. Neither the audience in the hall nor the television audience had any idea about the slapstick that preceded our appearance – on that occasion or many others – but it regularly befell us...

A week or so later, a story was relayed to me by John Harris – he told me that Dickie Davies the 'World of Sport' presenter had been talking to Max Crabtree. He said, 'Max, tell me about Nagasaki and his Manager – they seem a weird pair.'

Max replied, 'Don't talk to me about that pair! There I am wi' millions of viewers waiting, cameras rollin', and he's out in the car park wi' manager stripped off!'

Dickie Davis told another story about Kendo and George, in which an innocent action turned out to be sensational. After doing his speech before a match, George would get out of the ring and make his way back to the dressing room. Kendo would come to the ropes to make sure he was safely on his way, ready to intervene if a member of the audience had a go at him; Kendo being there usually kept things calm.

On this occasion he paused on the apron and it seemed like he wanted to say something, so Kendo leaned across to listen – and George kissed him! As Dickie Davis told it, the phone lines for London Weekend Television were jammed for hours – but then, the country had just witnessed what had almost certainly been the first ever men's kiss on national television – another first for Kendo and George!

Chapter 24

The 'Death Angel', the 'Healer', and Nagasaki Management

After the unmasking, George and I decided that we would move back to London. We'd kept a flat there and had regularly been back and kept in touch with friends, and we looked forward to returning to where our friendship had begun ten successful years earlier. Also, as we were looking to promote the band we'd decided to manage, we had to be in London.

Before we could move south, I had several properties and two garages to sell – like my mentor Bartelli, I'd been buying and selling cars for years.

I found a large house in Gladstone Street, London SE1, that had loads of character and plenty of space – there were 5 floors and off-street parking for 6 cars – very rare in central London, but it needed a lot of work – essentially a full refurbishment.

We began sorting out the house at the start of 1978. It was a huge task and it needed facilities for George and I, including an office for him and a new therapy room, all done to the right standard. The building work was entrusted to Percy Guire, a man who had regularly been coming to Wolverhampton for treatment on a sprain injury.

As demand for treatment had never diminished throughout all my time in Wolverhampton, one of the first places that needed sorting out in the new house was the treatment room. It was during this work that Percy mentioned a lady for whom he'd done some building work, who he felt would benefit very much from some treatment; that lady was Yvette Hanger.

Yvette came for treatment in early 1978 for early-onset arthritis. Over her following appointments I learned that she was living in a big, old, somewhat decayed house in Clapham with a housekeeper, Edith, who had originally worked for Yvette's mother. Since mother's death around 1967 nothing had been done to the house; all the grand old rooms were shut up and Yvette and Edith only used the kitchen and a sitting room.

I heard that Yvette's family used to have a paints business which did well. Yvette had been a young adult when the Second World War broke out, and she volunteered for the Women's Auxiliary Army, learned to drive, and then drove an ambulance during the Blitz. Her father didn't drive, and when his driver was conscripted she drove him. Because the family business made industrial paints they had to continue during the war, particularly because their paint for ship hulls resisted barnacles better than any other.

Sadly, soon after the war ended Yvette's father died; he'd been around thirty years older than his wife so he'd had a good innings, but her mother's health started to deteriorate soon after, and Yvette had to look after her for the next twenty years.

I enjoyed listening to Yvette tell me about her life. The family had travelled widely and she had some very interesting tales to tell. One of the sadder ones was about the only time in her life she'd come close to finding love;

it had been with an Australian airman who had died during the war. With every visit, as she continued to speak her mood improved, and she was soon happy and smiling and very good company – which George used to enjoy very much as well.

Within a short time of meeting Yvette I seemed to know a lot about her, and there was always more to hear. She had a car and still drove, but she wasn't comfortable doing it and had no-one to go anywhere with, so at her invitation I began picking her up in Clapham and taking her for drives, sometimes to see her friends in Brighton. I found myself looking forward to seeing her again – I began to feel that we were becoming good friends, and we saw more and more of each other.

As the refurbishment of the house progressed, on 1st March 1978 a television programme aired which I'd filmed a few months before the unmasking. It had been written by Brian Glover as an episode in a series for Granada TV called 'Send In The Girls'. Each show revealed more about the girls' lives and relationships, set against various different backdrops; Brian's episode was wrestling-themed, and was called 'The Wild Bunch'.

Most of the story unfolded back-stage at a wrestling venue as the girls promoted a new brand of nicotine-free cigarette. True to the wrestling theme, it was filmed entirely on location at the Kings Hall, Belle Vue, Manchester, and the intensity of a 1970s wrestling bill and an enthusiastic audience made it interesting and really quite involving.

The star of the series was Annie Ross and the cast included Floella Benjamin and Michael Elphick (later of 'Boon' fame) as the cigarette promotional organiser. You can't have a wrestling-themed show without wrestlers, so, among others, the cast included Jim Breaks, Brian Maxine, Brian Glover as the MC / referee, and Giant Haystacks and – apparently – Kendo Nagasaki.

Brian had written a character called 'The Death Angel'

who was based on Kendo, and he told me that he'd recommended to the producers and the director that they should definitely use him for the part. This character was top of the bill, against another formidable wrestler called 'The Juggernaut', a part Brian had written around Haystacks. He'd said the same thing to the directors about him, that no one else should play that part either.

Any other wrestler in a mask could have been cast to play 'The Death Angel', but Brian convinced Granada that if they wanted a credible show, particularly for the wrestling sequences with the Stacks, Kendo really was the only man for the job because of his extensive experience in the ring with Haystacks.

After a number of interviews at Granada they gave Stacks and myself the parts, which they must have felt was quite a coup. We may not have been the best actors for the parts we had to play outside the ring, but as far as the wrestling sequences were concerned, we were the best you could get.

The story-line included a long-standing rivalry between The Death Angel and The Juggernaut which had become a vicious vendetta – the wrestling scenes didn't hold back and definitely added to the realism and involvement of the whole show. The contrast of the girls and their lives set against genuine professional wrestling in an established wrestling venue worked very well, and 'The Wild Bunch' was well-received by audiences and critics.

Of additional interest to wrestling fans was seeing Kendo as they never had before – The Death Angel spoke, he was seen unmasked, and he ended up with a love-interest with Floella Benjamin. Many questions were asked, foremost among which was, 'Was that his real voice?' Some argued that it was and others insisted it was an overdubbed voice, and I can now reveal that it was both – there was some overdubbing, but I did it, just to make some of the dialogue clearer.

However, I have to clarify this. This wasn't Kendo – it

was me acting the part of 'The Death Angel', wearing a Kendo mask. Kendo never speaks, but I could, and I did so with the kind of blunt aggression that wrestlers reserve for each other. I was happy to help Brian by playing the part he'd written based on Kendo and I was pleased that it was well-received, but I was also comfortable that as an 'actor', I didn't really give anything away about Kendo, or myself.

It had been as 'The Wild Bunch' was being filmed that I'd found myself beginning to think about what an unmasked Kendo might be like; I'd felt that he may be more accessible. The filming had taken place while George and I were considering leaving wrestling, and although Kendo would never speak, perhaps having a visible face would allow him to be perceived in a new way. It was almost certainly Kendo's idea that he'd given to me intuitively, so I'd meditated on it, and it definitely contributed to the decision for Kendo to unmask, as opposed to simply bowing out of wrestling.

Whilst George didn't have a part in 'The Wild Bunch', he did of course accompany me for all the filming. For him there wasn't much to say about the wrestling side – he described it as '...short and sweet...' compared to any real match, but he was completely at home with all the showbiz types, and he later wrote-up those experiences in his diary:

As the final shots were being taken, on a Saturday night and partly in front of a real, live wrestling crowd, Annie Ross – like the rest of us – allowed herself one drink more than usual and gave us a personal, stylised, and electrically-emotive rendering of Send In The Clowns. By the time she'd finished about thirty to forty people had crowded into the small room we'd been in, and she received a rapturous ovation.

The post production party, held at the house of the Director, Alan Grint, was another occasion for Annie to simmer her way through a couple of numbers. Now, Annie had her own very special way of phrasing and timing, and during one number, she paused, seemingly out of time, but her pause was designed to heighten a creative effect. However, there was one poor female extra in attendance that obviously didn't realise that, and slap bang in the middle of the pause, started to sing the following phrase, as if to help Annie remember the words. Annie stopped dead in her tracks, leant forward, hands on hips, and said, 'Thank you for teaching me the words, but I was just taking my fucking time,' *and then blithely completed the song as if nothing had happened.*

It's quite possible that the extra was a mere pawn in the game, as behind-the-scenes, both at the party and throughout the entire production, the 'winder-upper'-in-chief was the late, highly mischievous Michael Elphick.

Michael was already an actor of note, having started out as an electrician, and through sheer hard work and quite natural talent progressed very nicely into being a star. Michael enjoyed a drink and a chat, and you'd often find him and I propping the bar up every lunchtime.

Michael was a man who could, and would, talk to just about anybody. He was full of fun and witty anecdotes. Most of them were unprintable, and not a few of them probably slanderous, but all told with such a mixture of cheek and innocence that the victims would be the first to laugh at themselves.'

As we worked on the new house, it was interesting to see 'The Wild Bunch' – it reinforced our new direction away from wrestling and into the show-business field, giving George a new creative outlet and bringing all our previous knowledge and contacts into focus. For myself, The Wild Bunch had been something of a stepping-stone, into show-business and away from Kendo.

Coincidentally, ten days after the screening of 'The

Wild Bunch', Psychic News did another big write-up on Kendo's 'healing'. They described my new therapy room in London and wrote at length about the therapy I gave, as well as describing testimonials that had been given by an assistant matron and two nurses. The article re-kindled the interest in Kendo's 'healing' and mysticism that had been at its height some fifteen months earlier when David Nathan had written his extensive piece for the TV Times. It mentioned the recent unmasking but politely continued referring to me as 'Kendo', without disclosing my name. Once again, I was able to describe how meditation was the source of my intuitive guidance for helping others.

When musicians had first approached us in 1977 to manage them we'd decided to call ourselves Nagasaki Management, and George designed a striking letterhead logo. From his new office in the basement of Gladstone Street, he became its charming and eloquent face and voice, and he seemed to really enjoy the role.

We'd picked up quite a lot about music through the various entrepreneurs and musicians we'd been getting to know throughout the seventies, and it was clear that success in that field had a lot in common with wrestling: skill and talent were essential, but the other main requirements were a unique and strong image, and the right connections. We wouldn't have been interested in any band who didn't have the first three, and George had been casually making such connections since long before I'd known him. Having become good friends with many music entrepreneurs and told them what we had in mind, they were intrigued at our plans, and said we should go for it.

We'd worked out how we would progress the careers of Geoff and Jim, who had moved south with us. George had great faith in their writing and performing abilities, so we supported them in every possible way. At that time we were joined by a capable young man called Lawrence

Stevens; he was already an ardent Kendo fan and worked as road manager for the band. He went on to support Kendo and all our future music projects on the road – he's assisted me, Kendo, and all my businesses to this day.

George recalled the start of our music business venture as follows:

We had by this time taken over the management proper of the duo from Wolverhampton, and they in turn had expanded first into a quartet, then a quintet.

After suffering the heart-searching of a number of name changes, they finally settled on 'Burnt Out Stars' – most prophetic, as events turned out.

At first it all seemed almost too easy. Rehearsals went well, and we were at least blessed with a group of people not afraid of theatrics and trying the outrageous, including the use of a rat, 'Jemima', who appeared in the set's opening number.

In answer to an advert in a music paper, one of the band-members had sent in a rough 'demo', and they must have been impressed because they arrived at a rehearsal with a guy named Danny Morgan, who had discovered, and then became co-manager of, the band 'Japan'.

This was a remarkable coincidence, as we had earlier been asked by 'Japan's' record company to do a publicity stunt to promote their current album. As Kendo Nagasaki had been a wrestler garbed as a Samurai warrior, complete with sword and all trimmings, it was felt fitting to send he and I around the music press together with copies of 'Japan's' Album, and copious supplies of 'sake', the Japanese 'firewater'.

The other half of 'Japan's' management team, Simon Napier-Bell, then appeared on the scene. He already had a track record as long as your arm, both as manager of the Yardbirds and Marc Bolan, and as one of the wheeler-dealers-cum-'hype'-merchants of all time. We thought it was a good sign that he was interested in 'Burnt Out Stars.'

Before the band had a single gig under their belts, we'd signed a publishing/production deal with one of Simon's many companies, Chadwick-Nomis, and a recording contract with Ariola-Hansa.

Many trials and tribulations went into the production of the first (and last) single, 'In Vain' (another apt title, if ever there was one), and a promotional video was made. The director was Mike Mansfield, who was one of the people I'd met some ten or eleven years before, and whom I was to meet again through the music business.

Finally, the band got around to actually doing the odd gig, and when we first supported the all-girl band 'Girlschool' at the 'Music Machine', I discovered the weird and wonderful way in which the music press conducts itself. At the gig were representatives of the allegedly omnipotent music press, also on this occasion, all girls. A couple of them interviewed our own little lot of loonies, though one of them later chose for reasons known only to herself to write up the interview as seen through the eyes of Jemima the rat. Jemima obviously had very little time for the band who fed her, and when the article appeared, she very nearly got the sack!!

Unfortunately for all concerned, I don't really think all the purple prose and printed abuse heaped so generously upon the heads of 'Burnt Out Stars' made any great difference in the long run. The old adage that 'the band that plays together stays together' may be true, but only if all the participants don't actively hate each other. Neither can it work if the lead singer has an ego the size of the Empire State Building, even before he has any successes under his belt.

Of course, musicians in general have egos, and singers in particular always seem to have more than their fair share. An ego is necessary, but it should be in some sort of proportion to the successes the performer is at that time currently having. It's no good swanning or ligging around, laying the foundations of an enterprising career, if the whole thing is built upon sand, the sand in the case of 'B.O.S.' being an unstructured, undisciplined, and undecided talent.

Managers can advise, book gigs, buy clothes and recording time, arrange photo sessions, devise publicity stunts, and make sure that everything but everything hangs together as it should ... apart from one vital thing: the actual sound of the music and writing and delivery of the lyrics are almost always solely in the hands of the Band.

In the case of 'B.O.S.', there were perhaps only the germs of ideas floating around, and Peter and I were probably not experienced enough at that stage, nor ruthless enough to be able to make them grow. We left it in the hands of the Band, and the germs subsequently withered and died, smothered in a morass of clashing personalities, and a self-preening, over-fed ego that finally had nothing other to feed on than itself.

Ariola-Hansa had decided not to renew Burnt Out Stars' recording contract, and we felt there was little point in continuing with the Band as a unit. We did however think – wrongly – that we could still do something with the singer – he had after all been responsible for the bulk of both the music and lyrics, and we felt we could build up a better relationship with him as a solo performer, and also be in a position to control the general situation more easily. It didn't quite work out that way, but indirectly we created a situation from which everything that subsequently happened to us, and from which most of our subsequent musical involvements, grew.

In the basement of Gladstone Street, we set Geoffrey up with everything he needed to write and record 'demos' of his new compositions, but sadly, while the new songs sounded good when played first-hand on a guitar or keyboard and sung in one's presence, the recordings were, frankly, dreadful – they sounded thin and distant and weak, and we'd have no chance of impressing any A&R man with them.

Geoff then mentioned an old school-friend, who had some experience of music recording – perhaps he could help to convincingly commit the magic to tape? The complication was that the friend had a settled life in Wolverhampton, and we wondered whether we would be able to persuade him to come to London for long enough to have a result with Geoff, who was still pretty temperamental.

However, an opportunity presented itself, albeit a somewhat tragic one. Geoff's friend, Roy Rowland, had apparently had a serious motorcycle accident, and would be unlikely to be able to return to his work as a salesman for some time, so he might be available for at least a while to help Geoff. His father was a huge wrestling fan, watching it on 'World of Sport' every Saturday, so we decided to 'drop-in' at Roy's parents' Wolverhampton home, and treat them to a full charm-offensive...'

I didn't know it then, but Roy was to become a long-term member of the team – I think it's appropriate that he explains why...

Chapter 25

Roy Speaks

I am so grateful to have met Peter Thornley when I was twenty years old. Even at that young age, my life was in ruins and I was in dire need of guidance and direction, the absence of which as I'd grown up had arguably led me directly to my immediate difficulties. It was quite some time before I learned that Peter had also had challenging origins, albeit of a different nature to mine, but a part of me recognised that his strength and vision trumped the consequences of unfairness and hardship in early life, and on meeting him I was immediately intrigued and, for the first time ever, optimistic about my future.

I came to know of Kendo Nagasaki when my father would stamp his feet and go purple in the face and yell at the TV when he watched him on World of Sport in the 1970s. He hated Kendo, particularly when he was mercilessly demolishing a 'good guy' opponent, and distracting my father when in the midst of his outrage seemed almost dangerous! However, if I could make myself invisible, I'd watch the wrestling too, and find myself mesmerised by the dispassion, the brutality, and the utter dominance of this masked lunatic! I wished I was as powerful.

My father was a doctor, a General Practitioner who

loved his whisky. He would get seriously drunk twice a day, every day, and he crashed almost every car he owned; he was prosecuted for drink-driving on two occasions, which was miraculously few considering his copious daily indulgence. More seriously, when drunk he would be either oafish or, like a switch flicking, fly into drunken violent rages when he'd attack my mother, my brother, and I. Behind the veneer of what appeared to be a respectable middle-class home, terror reigned on a daily basis.

Christmases were the worst – it was unbearable being stuck for several days in a house with a violent and sarcastic man whose behaviour was the absolute opposite of 'Peace on Earth'. One of my most vivid memories from my teenage years was being thrown out of the house on Christmas day; my father was drunk, stood at the front door with a twelve-inch carving knife in his hand, telling me to fuck off and never darken his door again. My mother stood behind him crying bitterly at my enforced departure, not daring to intervene. I left, hating the thought of the environment she'd have to endure later. Christmases make me deeply uneasy to this day.

At primary school I emulated my father – I was confrontational and quick to threaten and punch and kick, so I ended up with very few friends, but I accepted the fear of other boys as an acceptable substitute. I knew that at my core I wasn't a bully – it was simply that such behaviour was all I knew of social interaction. When I saw other children just peacefully getting on with each other, I simply didn't understand what was happening or how they did it.

Another serious problem I had was that I suffered from a form of learning disability (which wasn't to be properly diagnosed for many years), so my school reports were always terrible; their arrival was inevitably a cue for a serious thrashing from my father with a three-inch leather belt, as well as ongoing sarcasm, belittling, and humiliation from him about how stupid and lazy I was. He wanted my brother and I to also be doctors – to him, no other profession or occupation measured up to medicine. As far as he was concerned, for us it was that or nothing, and he was furious that my every school report seemed to indicate that I had no chance of achieving it. He was constantly surly, unpredictable, and threatening, the worst presence any home could have and a terrible example to children, so I grew up thinking that all relationships were based on harshness, violence, and bullying.

When I went to secondary school I met a contemporary called Geoff Southall, who invited me to his home. The contrast to my home was a profound shock – everyone at Geoff's was friendly and sociable with each other, laughing and taking an interest in each other's lives. The entire feeling was so alien to me – in my home I was always wound-up and defensive, perpetually afraid of the arrival of my drunk and violent father and steeling myself for yet more humiliation and being smacked-around when he did; my enduring memory of him is arriving at the top of the stairs, purple with rage, gritting his teeth and clenching his fists, looking for me.

That went on until I was fourteen, when I decided that the violence had to stop. One evening, trembling in my bedroom, I waited for him to appear, and when I heard the approach of his usual curses and stamping feet I came out of my room and said, 'Are you looking for me?'

He stopped at the end of the corridor, gritting his teeth and purple-faced with clenched fists, as usual. Terrified but determined not to show it, I walked up to him and looked him in the eye and said, 'Are you going to have a go? Well, let me start, for a change,' and I punched him on the jaw.

I held my breath, waiting for a reaction – and that's

when I knew he was a coward. Like most bullies, when faced-down he just stood there, doing nothing other than glare at me. Still looking him in the eye, I smiled at him and said, 'I thought so. I'll be ready if you want to try again,' and I made sure I was a picture of composure as I calmly turned and walked back to my bedroom and quietly closed the door, behind which I shook violently at the intense hostility of the encounter. I heard my father walk back downstairs, not saying a word.

For my part, I sat on my bed and cried. I hated what he'd made me become – he'd brought me down to his level, which had been the only way I could deal with him. I was also afraid that he'd focus his violence more on my mother and brother, but fortunately that didn't happen. The old man was a lot more surly and shouty after that, and I noticed that more furniture tended to get smashed, but he never hit any of us ever again.

The contrast that Geoff's household held up to mine made me begin to realise that I was already past the point of being able to participate in normal, healthy relationships, such as they had. I could see that confident, out-going Geoff was a product of his environment, just as I was of mine, and I was now aware that I was entirely dysfunctional – among civilised people I felt thoroughly unworthy, like a leper at a banquet. None of the Southalls realised I was so damaged, and they invited me to drop in whenever I felt like it, so I did, feeling like a pariah every time. Each visit was like a holiday to a lovely place, but they also depressed me because I had nothing like it, and I knew I'd inevitably have to return to my own domestic hell. Under a black cloud of depression, resentment, and hopelessness, I simply endured life, day after day after day, hoping that one day, something would change for the better.

Because of the nature of my home life as a child, I'd become an atheist – I'd prayed and prayed for the violence to stop, but it never had, so I'd concluded that

God didn't exist and the whole Christian myth was a cruel joke. I had absolutely no experience of a loving God, and the unfulfilled promise of the myth had only made me feel betrayed and even more hopeless.

I'd found that I had an ear for music and had begun hanging around a hi-fi shop, and at fourteen, the manager offered me a Saturday job there. I realised it was an opportunity to try to learn how to interact with people, which I attempted, but failed, and I was sacked. However, about a year later, after I'd learned how to fake social interaction, I was offered the job again, and I took it. I knew by then that being a perpetually anti-social outsider didn't pay, so I leapt at it and forced myself to appear confident and helpful – fundamentally, I was neither.

Eventually, Geoff left school after his O-levels to pursue a music career, and he told me that he was being handled by Nagasaki Management, but beyond that he wouldn't be drawn; it sounded like a powerful connection to have, and I was awed.

I ended up being asked to leave school because education was flat-out not working, and I hadn't been bothering to attend anyway. I did almost two years of manual labour before a full-time position at the hi-fi shop came up, and I leapt at it. I bought a motorcycle and loved the sense of freedom that riding temporarily gave me.

One day, an acquaintance, an aspiring music business type, told me that he knew Kendo Nagasaki, who'd told him that he would 'make it', and that affirmation had given him huge self-confidence – I was so envious! However, his cousin whom I knew better had said something entirely different – he told me that Nagasaki had deep knowledge of the occult and was 'dangerous' and should be avoided; that intrigued me even more. As I'd felt so powerless in my adolescent life I'd taken an interest in the occult, and I wondered what the supremely successful and evidently powerful Kendo Nagasaki might know that I could learn, to finally give me some control over my blighted life.

As I seemed to know about sound, I began being asked to help with making recording of musicians who occasionally came into the hi-fi shop. I did what I thought sounded right, and it worked – at last, I could be confident in an ability I actually seemed to have.

However, I wasn't to hear anything more about Kendo until after I'd had a serious motorcycle accident when I was twenty. A drunk car driver had pulled into my path and I'd suffered multiple serious injuries, including a smashed pelvis, an almost-amputated foot, and several damaged discs in my back and neck. I'd been hospitalised for two months and discharged early because my father was a doctor, but that was no help – I'd have been better off staying in hospital as some of my fractures still hadn't united, so I couldn't walk, and I was acutely isolated at home.

Once I'd been there for six weeks and going crazy from boredom, out of the blue one evening the doorbell rang, and it was Geoff asking if he and some other people could come in and have a chat with me and my parents – he was accompanied by Kendo Nagasaki and Gorgeous George Gillett!

Introductions were performed and my parents were more than a little star-struck! I'd never seen such a quick reversal in my father's attitude towards someone! 'Kendo' insisted that we all called him Peter, and he seemed nothing like the mad-man we'd seen on World of Sport – he was friendly and thoroughly engaging, which just bowled my parents over even more. Fortunately, my father hadn't yet got drunk, so he was 'present' and affable, and they got enough chairs into the front reception room for us all to talk.

George explained that Geoff's group hadn't had their recording contract renewed so they were managing him as a solo artist, but they needed help with his demo recordings. Before my accident my recording experience had moved on to include some work in actual studios, which had gone well and Geoff had heard about it. He'd visited me in hospital and knew I had no chance of returning to my sales job, so his need for help with his demos would also provide a new opportunity for me. After finding my life in ruins after the accident, I agreed immediately, and my parents were satisfied that I was strong enough go to London to at least see what the set-up was; I left with Geoff the following Monday, 17th December, 1979.

I had no idea what to expect of the London house, but it was exquisite. It was the largest house in a long black-and-white Georgian terrace, beautifully decorated and meticulously clean and tidy, and in the basement there was a four-track demo studio in one room and a 'therapy room' in the other. I instantly spotted several problems with the studio and directed a full re-organisation, from equipment positioning to electrical and signal connections. Geoff played me some of his new songs – they were very impressive and I looked forward to recording them.

As regards the household and its inhabitants, it was something entirely new for me. Peter and George lived there and so did Geoff and another guy called Lawrence. I was soon to find that Peter ran things with ruthless discipline and very high standards, and George was the master of the kitchen. I knew that he was gay and Geoff was straight, but nothing about anyone else, yet I began to wonder if this would be the place where I could begin to find myself...

When I was having emergency surgery immediately after my accident, my heart had stopped on the operating table and I'd had a near-death experience. It had been indescribably surreal and compelling and I had no idea what to make of it, not least because it had shown me that there was a great deal more after death. When I was finally allowed onto crutches after eight weeks in bed in hospital, the first place I'd gone to had been the hospital's chapel, to see if there was any echo of what I'd experienced – there wasn't – absolutely nothing; orthodox religion was definitely dead to me now.

There was something else though, that had seriously blighted my whole life – I had been born into the wrong body. I'd deduced the problem at age four in kindergarten when I kept being put with the boys, whom I'd found coarse and rough, instead of the girls, with whom I identified completely. I always knew I should have been a girl, but when I'd mentioned it to my mother she just told me I'd grow out of it; I'm sure my parents desperately hoped for that, because this was during the 1960s, which wasn't the most enlightened time for transgender issues, and the last thing they'd want would be an embarrassing child. I knew my mother had told my father because he became even more surly towards me. I very much wanted to grow out of it too, because it was extremely unpleasant being regarded as something I wasn't and having expectations imposed on me with which I had absolutely no affinity.

However, I never did grow out of it, which was another reason I'd begun to doubt God during my childhood, as so much more prayer to resolve my awful situation had once again led to nothing. I clearly remember the day when I realised that things weren't going to fix themselves and I was going to be stuck in my horrible situation with no prospect of it ever changing – I was seven years old, stood alone in my primary school playground. After that point, I sank into a deep, black depression.

I muddled-through life in a dysfunctional fog, pushing this biggest of all my problems away, quite literally (and very reluctantly) acting-out the male roles that everyone else expected of me, gritting my teeth just to get through it one day at a time; suddenly I was twenty, and having had no help, advice, or support, I had no idea whether I was deluded, or, if not, how I would ever become who I really was. Ironically, because this had always been a bigger problem to me than the violence at home, it had somehow made that easier to deal with. Not that I was at peace with anything at all – I'd grown up so stressed during every waking hour that I was amazed that I hadn't had a heart attack or gone insane.

So – this lovely Georgian house in London where I'd suddenly found myself appeared to offer a quite unbelievable range of promising possibilities. It appeared to be at least a predominantly gay household so my gender identity wouldn't be judged prejudicially, there was the prospect of a new vocational direction through working with music, and there was a strong man at the helm who had a reputation for special skills and deep wisdom – a proper father-figure, at last. I hoped he might be able to help me understand my near-death experience, possibly help me with my disabling injuries, and perhaps even shed some light on my personal identity. I'd suffered so much long-term negativity that I no longer allowed myself the luxury of optimism, but in this magical new environment, I cautiously conceded that there just may be a glimmer of hope for my future...

The first priority was the music. Geoff's songs were really good – unique, imaginative, and catchy, and his singing and playing of multiple instruments were all very skilled, but the recordings weren't capturing them at all. Geoff and I decided a schedule and began recording, and we looked forward to playing the results to Peter and George.

They were both always busy at something; George had an office just outside the studio, and he could be heard talking mellifluously and occasionally roaring with laughter on the phone or clattering away on his typewriter, or he'd be in the kitchen at the top of the stairs. Peter came and went, often with various cars to which I'd wished my father had even aspired, let alone acquired.

Occasionally there would be a lull in everyone's respective work, during which I'd try to pluck up the courage to speak to Peter. The first thing I tentatively asked him about was his reputed occult knowledge, and I was hugely surprised by his answer. He told me that people said all sorts of things about Kendo that he didn't discourage because it was good for the public image, but the truth was that he steered-clear of anything like that – he said his strength came from Zen. He told me that the occult could be genuinely dangerous as it disturbed the balance of life, forcing it instead of working with it; he said that nature had a way of snapping the balance back, undoing any artificial changes and probably leaving you worse off. That did sound like deep wisdom and I was glad I hadn't already done anything extreme with the occult, and that there was a better way to work things out. It seemed, to use a Dennis Wheatley metaphor, that Peter was more Duke deRichlieu than Mocata – someone with all the knowledge, but only used in a good, holistic way.

He told me that he'd learned his path through life from literally sitting at the feet of a master, sensei Kenshiro Abbe. I didn't fully understand, but I was delighted that Peter was telling me these things and I looked forward to learning more – could he be my sensei? He told me that the most important thing I had to realise there and then was that true wisdom was a gradual thing that came from within, but you had to know how to open the door to it.

I told him about my NDE, my near-death experience, and he said he'd spoken to several people who'd also had them. He said that once you'd had such a revelation, you had to treat it with great care. He said that it was easy to over-analyse such an experience, but it was important to remember that when it happened my conscious mind had been switched off so it wasn't a conscious thing, which meant that the mind wasn't the right tool to use to understand it; he said it had to be meditated on, and he could show me how.

Having had sensible responses to two somewhat surreal questions, I felt sufficiently confident to ask him the big one – I told him about my gender identity problem. Once again he told me that clarity would come from meditation. He said it was a big decision to actually change genders, so I had to be certain that it was the right thing to pursue, so, once again, as the problem didn't originate in the consciousness, it had to be set aside so that 'intuitive understanding' could be my guide. He told me that there would be several levels of myself that I'd need to discover and understand before I could even approach any kind of decision, and it was imperative to take all the time that process needed.

It had been my first in-depth encounter with Peter, but we all had things to get back to so he rounded it off by saying that no-one could tell me how to think or feel – I'd need to find things out for myself, perhaps with a little guidance such as he'd had from sensei Abbe and from Kendo himself. He said that some types of understanding could take a life-time, which was why we had a life-time, and that the only safe and sure way to reach that wisdom was through meditation.

The conversation had been a revelation and I'll never forget it. As a result of the reputation that Kendo had in Wolverhampton, I'd originally thought that I might be able to get to know an occult master who could show me how to work some magic to make things better in my life, but the reality seemed far more profound and to come from a different kind of strength. Surprised and brimming with expectation, I looked forward to learning more.

Peter did 'therapy' for various people who would occasionally come to Gladstone Street, one of whom was a lovely lady called Yvette Hanger. She had a wonderful smile, an infectious laugh, and sparkling eyes, and everyone felt happy to be around her warmth – she reminded me of my mother. I looked forward to her visits as she brought a wonderfully good-natured atmosphere to the house, and she always brought fresh fruit for everyone!

After a few weeks Peter said he'd help me. I was in constant pain, not only from my non-united ankle fractures but also from nerve damage and my damaged back and neck discs, and he said he could use some 'judo healing' techniques on my injuries to release the pressure and ease the pain. I was astonished at how well they worked, and my ankle fractures even united – the doctors had given up hope of that happening, and I was about to be fitted for calipers. It would still be many months before I could walk unaided, but this was a big and unexpected improvement in my prospects.

However, I couldn't wait for Peter to start showing me Zen, whatever that was – I was impatient for some clarity on my NDE and my own identity. I hadn't realised that getting my physical discomfort to more manageable levels had been part of his plan. Finally, it was time. He showed me what I now know to be Zazen, formal seated Zen meditation. He warned that it would take time and practise, which is the last thing a twenty-year-old wants to hear, but he was so positive that it gave me confidence, and I began. At first I wasn't sure that anything at all was happening, but I found myself with an unfamiliar calmness and everything seemed clearer and less impenetrable. It hadn't been a wham-bam experience – it was quiet and almost imperceptible, but it was working, which was fantastic, and I committed myself to pursue it.

Gladstone Street was a fantastic place to be for other

reasons too. George was amazing! Twice a week he and Lawrence walked to the Elephant and Castle shopping centre for provisions, and George always came back with a hilarious litany of camply-outraged complaints about the experience. He was great company and always took an interest in everybody around him; he'd listen to what everyone had to say and always offer considered counsel; he was a like a wise mother-figure – literally Mother George, bless him. Also, in addition to those coming for therapy, there were always people coming and going to and from the house, often musicians and sometimes Peter and George's friends, so it was very much a social hub too. They were golden days, full of promise, the magic of which all flowed from Peter.

I found him fascinating but also intimidating – around him, absolutely everything seemed possible, but his gaze always contained a fierce, innate challenge to be as dynamic as he was; I was seriously pessimistic that I had the confidence to do so. He'd already 'made it', emphatically, and deservedly so, but he always conveyed a fantastic generosity of spirit – he wouldn't give anyone a hand-out, but he was always open to working with others who also aspired, and I hoped that if I could measure-up, Peter would be instrumental to revolutionary changes in my life too.

Meanwhile, the demos, while a big improvement, still weren't knocking the management's socks off, so-to-speak. One big limiting factor for Geoff's recordings was that we couldn't accommodate a real drummer, and drum machines in 1980 were very primitive and un-natural-sounding things. Also, we'd heard that the music business was changing. The phenomenon known as 'Production Companies' was taking-off, which would essentially make finished-product music and then sell it ready for pressing to record companies, without suffering deductions from recording costs and yielding a bigger share of sales royalties to the owners of the art. Our 4-track demo studio was far from able to make such product, so we began to consider upgrading the facility.

Chapter 26

Nagasaki Studio and the Music Biz Roller-Coaster

George continues the story:

On balance, we decided that even though we had limited space, building a professional-quality studio facility would be a sound investment, both for Geoffrey's and our own futures, so we set-to.

The dust! For almost eight months, there was tons of it, which floated up all five floors of Gladstone Street and got everywhere. I lived on the top floor, and I found myself having to clean surfaces I'd long since abandoned, apart from an annual once-over. Even Geoffrey was giving practical help, in a hap-hazard and artistic way, fetching nails and timber and such.

However, when we were three-quarters of the way through and with our goal in sight, he threw a wobbly, and said he didn't want to do any manual labour any more. He had, in fact, been going off at weekends to write songs with another musician he'd found, and they were producing demos of the same unusable standard that we were hoping to transcend with our new facility, but it seemed that the allure of being a struggling artist was greater than working towards creating something that would instantly give him releasable music – it was just plain daft.

However, the many people in and around music whom we already knew had heard about Nagasaki Management's proposed facility, and they had all expressed a keen interest in using it. We would give them recording time in a top-quality facility which they could normally never afford, in exchange for our managing their careers and publishing, and securing them a recording contract.

Dave, the keyboard player from B.O.S., was one such possibility – he'd gone back to the Midlands and formed a very commercial-sounding and potentially promising pop band called 'MayDay', as well as Gene October, an old friend, a group called 'The Jackals', and several others – the future looked promising.

In the west end nightclubs, I'd seen a remarkable young singer who went by the name 'Beulah'. Her real name was Laura, and she was a big girl with an even bigger personality, and tremendous stage-presence. With our studio coming on-line soon, I foresaw great things for her under our management, and I began to make subtle advances in that direction.

The first recording sessions in our new studio went very well – it worked as it should, and the finished songs were strong and clear. One of the first projects was a song idea I'd come up with to coincide with the wedding of Charles and Diana, which we recorded with Polly Perkins, a delightful West-End nightclub singer, with Dave on keyboards and Lloyd Ryan on drums – the single was 'Diana', as originally recorded by Paul Anka.

Dave then joined a post-punk glam band called the Cuddly Toys, who were looking to record their next album, and he steered them towards us. They already had quite a following on the 'indie' scene, as well as a recording contract with small independent label 'Fresh Records', and they wanted management. Their music and image were unique and fascinating, not to mention often controversial, and we saw great possibilities for them, so we took them on.

They found an aspiring producer for the album, a radio engineer from New York, and when everything was agreed, recording began at Nagasaki Studio.

The album took a little longer than expected, what with some performance problems and visits to two other studios and arguments over the mixing, but we eventually ended up with a finished album– Trials and Crosses by Cuddly Toys – Nagasaki Management's (and the studio's) first product.

That's when the management proper began. They might well have a recording contract, but Fresh Records was so small that they couldn't possibly generate enough sales to make real money, so we set about raising their profile by taking them on mini-tours, speaking to radio stations and agents, and inviting influential people to gigs, in order to generate album sales, get airplay, get support slots for bigger bands on tour, and ideally a licensing deal which would see the album marketed and sold by a bigger record company. It was very much a full-time job, not least because – once again – managing so many young, egocentric musicians was like trying to herd cats.

One promising promo tour involved the Toys supporting chart-topping glam band Classix Nouveaux. We got the band well-rehearsed and made all the preparations needed for a tour, and on the first day when all the members turned up, Sean the singer began playing with a pair of handcuffs. As we were collecting the last bits and pieces from the garage, Sean invited me to 'test' them, and in a trice, I was securely manacled to a substantial bench vice. When I asked Sean for the key, he giggled and said he didn't have one!

I almost had a coronary – Peter would be livid! When everyone was in the van and about to set off, my absence was noted, and sure enough, Peter appeared. When he asked me why I was loitering in the garage, all I could think to say was, 'Don't look, dear – you won't like it!' I was in tears, and he was, as ever, entirely unsympathetic to my plight. It took him about 40 minutes to saw the handcuffs off, which is a very long time to be castigated for being stupid enough to allow this to be done to me! My wrist had only just healed-up by the end of the tour.

Now, anyone reading this memoir will be aware of a particular elephant in the room which has so far been successfully skirted – you can't talk about the eighties music business without talking about drugs. It wasn't that we ever indulged (apart from the occasional stiff double!), but they seemed inseparable from our musician friends – mostly dope and sometimes speed or other 'uppers' and 'downers'.

One day a musician told me he'd just had a very strange experience – another musician had arrived at the house, he'd gone straight to our fridge and retrieved a bottle he'd apparently secreted in there some time earlier. He opened the bottle and took a huge sniff from it, and then breathed out near the first musician, who said he'd nearly fainted from the fumes! I was horrified to hear that our fridge had been co-opted as a recreational drug storage unit!

Another event was more serious. After the Classix tour, we began a day as usual, and out of the blue, the drugs squad descended on the house – there were seven of them plus a dog. Roy was downstairs in the studio with a producer who was known to be a keen dope-smoker, and he had a lump of dope lying on the desk. After every room in the house had been thoroughly searched the dope had disappeared, but in a cabinet in a bathroom (to which everyone including visitors had access) they'd found a bag that had appeared to contain the tiniest residue of speed. Once it had been emptied, it must have been casually left there like a piece of litter by one of our musician 'friends', but with it being found by the 'Old Bill', it landed us deep in the proverbial.

As it was his house, Peter ended up being prosecuted for possession of narcotics, but as there were only traces of drugs in the bag the verdict was hardly punitive – he was fined £60. Nonetheless, as salacious gossip, it ended up in the Evening Standard. We suspect that it was no more than a witch-hunt designed to exploit Kendo's name and reputation, maliciously started by someone who didn't have so many interesting guests as we had, nor as much fun!!

It was a surprisingly heavy-handed operation considering we were just sociable innocents, although we had no idea what dubious connections some of our acquaintances may have had – it gave one pause for thought...

I wrote poems and limericks as a kind of therapy to deal with the madness, one of which was accurately entitled The Gladstone Street Asylum:

I live in a madhouse, of that there is no doubt,
I'm not alone, there's others here, lying round about,
Some just pop in, some come and go, and some seem here to stay,
I feel like spending half my life, hidden far away.
There's many things I try and do, whilst working from my home,
And most of them do not get done unless I'm on my own,
The music blares, the telly blinks, and still the voices shout,
Their fingers point, they moan at me and say the food's run out!
So many different people, so many different styles,

So many story tellers, so many crafty wiles,
They all live here, or seemed to do, 'cos they don't live no place other,
While I just cook and clean and write, and feel like Whistler's mother
They'll have to go, or so shall I, this ain't the price of fame,
If I don't see some action soon, I'll put them on the game!!

We also signed Laura to a management deal and got her into the studio, seeking to harness her impressive live presence on tape. It turned out that her voice was indeed strong, but she had some difficulty singing in tune; this was not insurmountable, but it meant that additional recording time had to be allowed for. Eventually, she too would follow the Toys on the same promotional merry-go-round.

We managed to book some impressive shows for the Toys through our friend Simon White who was a director of the organisation that ran The Marquee Club in Wardour Street. There, among others, they supported super-glam act Adam and the Ants, and also supported by a singer/songwriter called Howard Jones. He was very complimentary about us as managers, being present at the Toys' gigs and making sure everything ran properly, and he asked if we could manage him too. At the time, we couldn't as we were very busy with both the Toys and Laura, the former being on a promotional tour and the latter having new recordings under way in our studio – it was all pretty frantic. In any event, we hadn't been particularly impressed with him at the gig and didn't think we'd be passing-up anything important, so we declined. Soon afterwards Howard went on to great success, which was infuriating for us, having missed that opportunity.

We were disappointed to find, however, that even

though we were going through a sophisticated and refined process to take our acts to subsequent levels of success, it just wasn't happening. Influential people attended the gigs, but it didn't translate into signing our artists to production and distribution deals, nor did they give us prime radio-play slots, and while gigs did spread our artists' music around, this didn't happen enough to make sales increase dramatically. The fees for playing gigs covered costs, so we weren't losing money, but progress was frustratingly slow.

We stuck doggedly to our promotional regime, and gradually the Toys' profile began to rise, and they began to seem destined for success. It's essential to be ready when the 'big time' calls, so we scheduled a break in touring to begin recording their next album, so it would be ready and waiting in the wings. We'd been introduced to record producer Steve James, whose sound and approach the band and ourselves really liked, and he was very happy with our studio, so we began putting down the backing tracks, but then – catastrophe!

Sean's behaviour had become ever-more eccentric, and out of the blue he announced he was leaving the band. Unbelievable! We had a whole album of songs all arranged and rehearsed, the band was tight and well-coordinated, but suddenly we had no singer and front-man. This led to a frantic round of auditions, and we settled on a singer called Gadge Wonfer who had a melodic and soulful voice, but his sound was very different to Sean's plaintive angst, and it simply wasn't the Cuddly Toys any more.

Sean claimed he owned the name 'Cuddly Toys', so the rest of the band changed their name to the Crocodile Tears (keeping the initials), but, without the Toys' substantial glam legacy, they were effectively newcomers, who were no longer particularly charismatic. Without Sean's voice, the new album couldn't build upon whatever success Trials and Crosses had, so we shelved the recordings, and the whole thing just evaporated.

This had been yet another experience of a band being impossible to rely upon, so we decided to focus upon Laura, who's star had begun to rise.

While touring with Laura, we opened the studio up to commercial bookings, and we recorded and mixed some of the most significant 1980s indie-label bands, and – just like the gigs – the income put us in the black, but the 'big boys' were now going to bigger studios, funded by all the freely-available speculative money which was increasingly becoming widely available in the second half of the '80s.

There was still the occasional wrestling show thrown into the mix, as well as some TV appearances, such as Big Daddy's 'This Is Your Life' show. I'm afraid to admit that I over-indulged somewhat at the after-show party, and when we got back to Gladstone Street I ended up having a huge argument with Peter over absolutely nothing! He threw me out of the front door and down the steps, after which I created such a scene that the police advised me to stay away from the house that night! By the following morning, having sobered-up in the less than salubrious surroundings of the nearby Elephant and Castle shopping centre, I had no choice other than to swallow my pride and phone home, assuring Peter of my good behaviour thenceforth...

We were delighted that our perseverance with Laura began to pay dividends. She supported the dance troupe, Hot Gossip, for the first-ever gay night at the Hippodrome, which quickly became their most successful nights. She was soon a big name on the Gay scene, appearing at the Hippodrome sixteen times in the first year, five times headlining.

At one of her shows she was supported on stage by a lion, which caused even more of a stir than she did. It came up on the stage lift, but as soon as it got to the top it dragged its keeper across the stage and jumped into the audience. It wasn't much more than a cub but it was big enough to be bloody wary of, and I've never seen so many terrified queens scatter so quickly in my life. There were shrieks and yells and a huge panic, and it made headlines in the Evening Standard, which Peter Stringfellow was very happy with. He'd also reaped the rewards of setting off fireworks from the roof of the club without getting a permit – no-one had known, and in a nearby restaurant, Princess Anne ended up being dragged under her table by her security men when the bangs went off. As the old saying goes, you can't buy that sort of publicity.

Laura was signed to Record Shack records and released several singles produced by hi-energy producer Ian Levine, she then headlined all the major gay venues in London, including Heaven. Outside London, her many country-wide tours continued to raise her profile, and we could feel things accelerating. The 'big time' was still a step away, but we'd got plenty of air-play and done a great many interviews, and the singles sold more than well enough to cover our costs.

Laura's gigs were almost invariably spectacular, but very occasionally, there was a night to remember for the wrong reasons! One gig at major West End gay nightclub Heaven promised to be the expected festival of camp glamour, but it actually began quite differently... With the venue lights flashing and a triumphal soundtrack blaring, Laura appeared on a litter being carried to the stage through the audience by four muscular guys. She was every bit the 'Queen of Sheba' until they reached the middle of the venue, when something went wrong... One supporting corner of the litter disappeared, and Laura plummeted to the floor, rolling to a dishevelled halt among an astonished audience – lights still flashing and music still blaring. She had to scramble to her feet and get to the stage and then perform her entire set as if nothing had happened.

The show did indeed go on, but she was furious with Peter and I, who had assured her that nothing would go wrong!

There was also an occasion in which a misunderstanding ended up infuriating Laura. She'd had a few records released and quite a lot of promotional press, so she did occasionally get spontaneously recognised. Once, on a promotional tour supporting Divine, the outrageous and generously-proportioned drag-act, we were flying to Copenhagen on the same aeroplane as Divine, whom the Monarch Airlines staff knew would be flying. At check-in, one of the staff approached Laura and asked her for her autograph. She was as magnanimous and regal as any mega-star, but when she handed the autograph back, the 'fan' looked terribly puzzled at what had been signed – she had been expecting Divine's autograph, and had thought that Laura was him! Sadly, she didn't take it as a compliment...

Coincidentally, an excellent opportunity for Laura came up involving Divine, who had recently had a chart hit with 'Walk Like a Man'. Having got to know Laura while supporting him on tour, he wanted to record a duet with her – the song 'Big Girls Don't Cry'. Peter and I immediately saw the commercial potential of this, but Laura didn't like the idea. She'd occasionally held unwise views regarding what might be good for her career, but we'd always managed to persuade her to see sense, and we went ahead and booked the studio time. This time, however, Laura dug her heels in – she didn't turn up for the recording session, and we couldn't find her anywhere. This time she got her way, by completely sabotaging the recording session – we were furious with her.

Sadly, only six weeks later, Divine passed away – 'Big Girls Don't Cry' would have been his last-ever recording, which would have really put the spotlight onto Laura. It was only then that she realised the opportunity she'd thrown away.

Then, another aspect of the music business reared its very ugly head – treachery. We had seen that, sometimes, powerful people exercise their might just because they can, and just for the amusement they can get from it. This now happened with ourselves and Laura. John Reid, then Elton John's manager, began telling her how much he could do for her, and how we at Nagasaki Management were not doing her justice, even to the extent that we were actively mis-managing her. Laura was street-wise, but still only in her mid 20s, so she soaked all this up, and then fired it back at us. There was nothing more that we could have done for her, and she had sabotaged the 'Divine' recording, so the only poor decisions about her career had been her own. The acrimony dragged on, and it broke my heart; Peter has never forgiven Laura.

We definitely made the most of Laura's talent, bringing an impressive new gay icon to the stage, but ultimately, she seemed unclear about her direction. (As a post-script, following an unremarkable appearance opposite Madonna in the film Evita, Laura's closest contact with the creative arts was reduced to becoming an agent in Los Angeles, handling, among other stars, Superman.)

Despite all our valiant efforts and more than a little understanding of show-business, the 'music biz' hadn't made our fortunes. It's been said that to succeed in music, you need the right thing, with the right people, at the right time; we'd done everything possible to satisfy all aspects of that at all times, so perhaps the equation itself is incomplete. We came to the conclusion that musicians and music business people are fundamentally different to wrestlers and wrestling folk, and that there was much more luck than judgement in becoming successful in the former compared to the latter;

certainly, we'd found that many of those who'd 'made it' in the music business had simply been in the right place at the right time, but apart from that fluke, had possessed none of the skills needed to actually work their way there.

So, since demand for Kendo had never diminished we decided to return to that field, where everything we did always worked. Kendo had been the right thing at the right time, a time that had never actually gone away, so we went back to an arena in which we'd already had considerable success.'

I was disappointed that our music venture didn't work out, especially when we seemed to have everything going for us. I'd sold Chequered Flag, the Riley Crescent houses, and White Lodge before moving to London in 1977, but there continued to be a sprinkling of car dealing going on throughout that time. We found cars for the group Japan and for their manager, Simon Napier-Bell, first a Jaguar XJ6 and then a Bentley T1. I drove whatever was coming and going, including a Bentley S1 and a several XJ6s, and even a perfectly-restored early Morris Minor with the 850cc engine, a beautiful little classic even then. We even picked up a Cadillac Eldorado that Barry had borrowed from his father and abandoned, which was refurbished and sold, paying the monies owed to Geoff, and a Pontiac Firebird also came and went.

My connection to Blackpool kept cropping-up. An old friend called Steve from whom I used to buy cars in Stoke opened a small hotel there; he still sold cars, and when I went to look at one he told me that the site of the former Ribble Bus Company in North Shore was for sale. He felt it would make an excellent car site, not least because it already had planning permission for vehicles, so we went to see it and decided to buy it to open a car site. It was quick and relatively easy to set up in the old offices and sell 'bread and butter' cars like Ford Sierras, and it did respectable business.

After Laura, we came to the decision not to manage any more acts, which meant that our in-house studio effectively became redundant. Whilst it had been perfect for our acts to develop songs and record demos, it wasn't a commercial studio and couldn't compete in that market. We did get some mixing work of 'indie' singles and albums, and, at the invitation of engineers and producers who'd worked there, Roy began being offered engineering gigs in London's bigger studios, so I was glad to see that we had at least launched him in the career he'd so much wanted. For George and I, after all the problems with Geoffrey, the Cuddly Toys, and Laura, we came to the conclusion that the music business was uncontrollably volatile, which was why I diversified into the Blackpool car site and began looking for other opportunities, and one did indeed arise.

By 1985 Yvette and I had become very close friends, and we'd been speaking more about her big old house. It was in dire need of attention and I'd found woodworm in some of the furniture, and we began considering what we could do with it. An idea that Yvette liked was to have a bungalow built for her in the grounds and convert the big house into flats, which could then be sold. Percy and I began exploring all the possibilities, and this new project seemed to gain a momentum of its own.

Then something happened which surprised me, but also felt just right – Yvette asked me to marry her. How very modern of her! We were spending a lot of time together and we enjoyed each other's company very much, so I thought, 'Yes – we should!' It made absolute sense; we already had the kind of affinity and friendship that the best marriages are made of (nothing like poor Uncle Norman had with Aunt Ida!), and I wanted to look after her. Apart from Edith, who was by then becoming quite infirm, Yvette was alone, but there was something more – this was something she wanted, and I was more than happy to make her happy, which our quiet but elegant ceremony really did.

There was an amusing aside to our wedding. One of the guests was a close friend of Yvette's called Annette, about whom Yvette had told me that she'd found ladies underwear at their home. At first she thought her husband was having an affair but after confronting the issue it turned out that he liked to wear ladies underwear. She raged to Yvette that she was going to divorce him but wiser heads prevailed when Yvette told her not to be so silly! Ultimately the marriage survived and this highly respectable and austere couple ended up as guests at our wedding; I couldn't help wondering what was beneath the husband's very formal suit!

Yvette wanted to make me happy too, and one of her attempts turned out to be most amusing. She had never cooked – that had always been done by Edith – but one day Yvette decided she would prepare a meal for me. She knew I liked fish, so that was the plan and she set about it with great determination...

One evening, after I'd been at the house and waiting for quite some time, she emerged from the kitchen and presented me with a plate which was inhabited by two fish-shaped objects and some warmed-up tinned peas. The fish had been grilled to within an inch of its life – well, far beyond actually – and now closely resembled durable cardboard shapes. She knew they weren't quite right, but it was the thought that counted, so I made a determined effort to consume as much as I could. She forgave me for leaving some, because she was, after all, a compassionate woman!

Yvette's driving kept me entertained too. One day, she somehow managed to reverse her Ford Escort onto a rockery in Dulwich Park. The police couldn't persuade her to get out of the car until I arrived. On another occasion, after being taken out in Yvette's car, George came home ashen-faced, and shakily said, 'Never again, dear!'

Eventually, after she drove (slowly) through a pedestrian crossing with the lights on red while being observed by the police (who then engaged in a short low-speed pursuit), Yvette was advised by the court that she shouldn't drive again. It was a sad development, but everybody, including innocent by-standers, was much safer as a result...

When we began exploratory work on the Clarence Avenue house, a locked door off the master bedroom was found. When asked about the mysterious room on the other side, Yvette said she'd never been in it. Edith said it was a room which Yvette's mother kept locked and never opened, and it had remained that way even after her death – no-one else had ever had a key. I forced the door open and found a room packed absolutely full with World War II provisions. It was so full you couldn't even get in – lots of emergency rations had to be taken out before there was any access at all to the room. It had remained secluded and completely untouched for over forty years, and it was all eventually sold to a museum, which regarded it as a treasure-trove.

By the late eighties we had built Yvette's dream bungalow and we moved in, with Lawrence taking over from Edith in looking after things. I sold Gladstone Street, recording studio and all, and invested into the conversion of the Clarence Avenue house into flats. We'd given the music business ten years which seemed to have gone by in a flash, and as it had wound down we'd found that Kendo's influence had returned to our lives and was once more rising, so we gladly returned to serving him.

Chapter 27

The Comeback

As Nagasaki Management and the recording studio were winding down, out-of-the-blue we had a phone call from Brian Dixon. He told us that his shows were going to be televised, and that there were plans to re-launch wrestling with a new image. He asked if we'd like to go to a show at Croydon where everyone involved was going to see how he did things; the TV people would be there, and having George and myself there too wouldn't do any harm to his credibility. The meeting took place at the Fairfield Halls' 'Green Room', the hospitality area for theatre people.

Brian introduced us to a chap called Mike Archer who'd been engaged as the executive producer for the re-launch of wrestling. He explained that they intended to revamp the whole business, which included a new canvas, new titles, the brand, and the image all being upgraded, and Brian would be one of the promoters at the centre of it.

As Mike and I were chatting he mentioned how interesting he'd found some of Kendo's matches. He said, 'The unmasking was sensational. Who thought it all up?'

I smiled and replied, 'Kendo, of course.'

'It was really good, it's one of the biggest ever highlights of TV wrestling.'

Looking me up and down he said, 'You don't look that old – in fact, you don't look any older than some of the lads that are getting in the ring. Why aren't you wrestling?'

I think at this time I was about forty-four. I said, 'You could be right, there are a few old crocks in the business!'

Archer laughed and asked, 'Would you ever consider coming back to it?'

That took me by surprise; 'I hadn't considered it, no. What are you suggesting?'

Archer explained that having Kendo on the bill for the grand re-launch show would be another big plus, and, giving me his card, he said, 'Have a think about it; if it's something you'd like to do, give me a call and we can meet up.'

George and I talked about it, and we decided that it would be interesting to find out more about what Archer was offering, so we did indeed call him.

He invited us to lunch in the artists' dining room at London Weekend Television, overlooking the Thames. Cilla Black was there and Mike introduced us; there were a number of other current TV stars there too but I couldn't put names to the faces – George said they were mainly soap stars.

Over lunch he outlined his plans for the big launch – a total revamp, bringing the world of wrestling right up to date; I liked the sound of his ideas. It was still in planning and perhaps three or four months from completion, which to me was plenty of time to get behind the project and work with it. My weight was around thirteen or fourteen stone – not my fighting weight, but if I was to wrestle I knew I could be ready in time.

I told Mike that I felt the launch should take place in central London, somewhere spectacular, not just an ordinary wrestling hall, and that's when I suggested the major West-End night club, The Hippodrome. The club had something like a million pounds worth of lights, so it should be possible to stage a really spectacular event.

Everybody liked the idea, and I agreed that if it was going to be done that way, Kendo would indeed make a comeback. I proposed a disco ladder match and described how I saw it working.

Before we came away, Mike gave us some videotapes of the latest thing on the block – American wrestling.

As soon as I saw them I was immediately worried and I phoned Brian right away. I asked him, 'Have you seen this?'

"Wrestlemania'? Yeah.'

'Don't you think you ought to be worried?' I asked.

'Oh, no,' he said, 'They're only showing one a month. The rest of it will be ours – one of mine and two from Joint Promotions every month.'

I tried to put across my concerns. 'Brian, if they start showing this, our wrestling won't last five minutes. As far as entertainment is concerned, this is streets ahead.'

He wasn't having it; 'No, no, it's only going to be on once a month, we'll be okay,' he assured me.

'Not with what I've seen on these tapes we won't.'

At that moment I realised that re-launching British wrestling back onto television meant there was only one way to do it successfully – start thinking like the Americans.

I stressed to Archer and Dixon that if they were serious, they would definitely need The Hippodrome. It was Peter Stringfellow's club, whom I knew because we'd been instrumental in launching their gay nights with Laura, who'd appeared there many times. I spoke to Peter and he agreed to host the event.

I took the entire production team to The Hippodrome three times and wined and dined them. I'd already planned-out the whole launch show and told them what they needed to do; they agreed and said they understood. They said that a month before the show was due to air, they would advertise it on TV, stating that it was at The

Hippodrome and that entry was free, which should guarantee a great house.

I told them that to make a show as spectacular as the Americans they needed a proper director. 'You need somebody who understands performance and drama. You can't just put this thing on and hope that the people in the ring will pull it off,' I stressed. I recommended Mike Mansfield, the pop video director we'd known for years and who had made the video for our first group, Burnt Out Stars. His career had gone from strength to strength, and at that time he was in charge of Elton John's videos. I knew Mike well enough to propose it to him, but Archer and his team didn't go for that, so I had to trust that everyone involved had the necessary skills and vision and would do their parts properly.

The plan for the Disco Challenge Match was that at the moment the winning wrestler actually got hold of the disc, that's when the lights show would begin and music would play, right at the climax of the headline match. We even decided to run the show under American All-In Wrestling rules – no rounds, more freedom for the wrestlers to engage and challenge each other, and fighting outside the ring was allowed – that should get the crowd going, and with a million pounds worth of motorised lights show, it should be very spectacular indeed...

However...

The first problem was that they never actually advertised the event on TV, so they couldn't fill the venue.

Then, the camera angles were wrong; in the background there was no crowd, such as it was, and all you could see behind the ring was a bar and some PA equipment. I'd arranged for the wrestlers to get to the ring via the club's two spectacular staircases from the restaurant to the dance floor, which would have made a brilliant shot, but the cameras were set up to look in the opposite direction! Instead, the wrestlers crept up to the ring from a fire exit door at the side – a brilliant image wasted.

Those who had come to see the show weren't properly managed– they were allowed to scatter wherever they wanted to in a two thousand capacity venue, instead of being led to seats by the ring, which would have helped it look busier. But, as I've described, the seats were out of shot, between the invisible staircases...

Then the billing was wrong. For the main supporting match, Brian put his top villain, Mark Rocco, on with Chic Cullen, who, although he was a baby-face, was tough enough to take villains to task. Rocco did his spectacular villain thing, completely flooring Cullen, who, instead of selling the hits, jumped up like he'd had a dose of Epsom Salts. Rocco's villainy didn't have enough impact for the audience to hate him, and Cullen's toughness meant the audience couldn't be sympathetic to him – their match had no clear sides.

On top of that, Dixon put Kendo on with 'Ironfist' Clive Myers. When I'd discussed it with him, Brian said, 'He's the best man for that job – he can work the match.' Myers had come along while Kendo had been out of the business and we'd never worked together, so I talked to him beforehand and told him what should happen and he seemed to understand. Dixon should have known what his wrestlers were capable of, so I took his word for it.

However, when Kendo and Myers got into the ring, everything fell apart.

The bout began with only the sound of the sparse crowd in the background, so you could hear there was virtually no-one in the place, and then the absence of a proper director really became apparent.

The lights show started forty seconds after the match began, accompanied by loud fanfare-style music – that wasn't supposed to happen until the winner grabbed the disc.

The ring had been set up in the middle of the dance floor

but the lights hadn't been reconfigured from a dance-venue set-up – the whole place was lit up by downwards spotlights which revealed the thin audience.

The TV director even had shots of the lighting rig cross-fading against the ring, which took the focus off the wrestling. It looked like Top Of The Pops, and the wrestling was made to look like 'filler eye-candy', like on-stage pop dancers against flashy lights – was he drunk?

The music only distracted from the action in the ring – and after three-and-a-half minutes, it stopped – silence! Kendo tried to motivate the crowd, but thirty seconds later, gay disco music began and carried on for the rest of the bout – completely and utterly the wrong atmosphere for wrestling. The audience didn't know whether to get angry at Kendo or dance around their handbags, so they did neither – they just gawped in uncomfortable confusion, as the TV audience must have done too.

Against Kendo, Myers was very poor. It turned out that he was only good at being himself – his show consisted of getting beaten up and then doing a comeback with chops and kicks – anything complex was beyond him. After the lights and music began he was even worse – he wasn't where he should have been, he didn't react properly to the moves, and he didn't know how to work with Kendo – the action was stuttering instead of dynamic. When Kendo finally went up the ladder for the disc, Myers should have been fiercely challenging, but he was feeble and he let Kendo reach it far too easily. Dixon's recommendation had been disastrously wrong.

Amazingly, as the lights show began Kent Walton had announced what he called '...the disco part of the performance...', so he must have known what was going to happen, but it was nothing like what had been agreed. Even with Myers, if the lights and music had come on at the right time it could have been a decent match with a spectacular climax, but as it was it was a ridiculous, farcical shambles – and it was televised!

I knew it had been bad, but I didn't realise just how bad it was until I watched it on TV myself. It must have been one of the worst shows ever seen – in the worst venue for it, if you made a mess of it. I wanted to shoot everybody and drown myself.

Everyone involved had agreed to every suggestion, but their contributions had been piss poor. They thought they could go to the Hippodrome, turn the cameras on, and it would all run like clockwork – but it couldn't, not without proper direction by someone like Mike Mansfield. I'd trusted Mike Archer and his team, but it seems they either didn't have a clue, or didn't give a damn – I think it was most likely to be the former.

Afterwards, I learned that the TV director's experience was limited to generally static sports like snooker, darts, and golf, and even ordinary wrestling shows – he had none of the preparation, vision, or experience needed for something as dramatic and theatrical as this American-style wrestling re-launch spectacular. All of Archer's team had similar outdated experience, and were therefore similarly out of their depth; they could no more re-launch and upgrade the image of wrestling than levitate.

I should have smelled a rat when Archer's team insisted that for the comeback, George should have a sober, business-like look. He wore a suit and Bowler hat and carried an umbrella, which wasn't him at all, but ironically, that was probably the only decision that helped make Kendo look credible – if George had been wearing a gown and make-up, he would only have amplified the tragic, ridiculous camp of how it was directed.

The show was so bad that it opened the door to Mick McManus to become a real busy-body at subsequent televised shows. He already had an office at London Weekend Television as manager of quality control, but after the Hippodrome, he ended up at every televised show, poking his nose in everywhere to ensure there were no more such disasters. He could have vetoed anything he didn't like the look of before it went to air, but fortunately he never came near me.

After I'd had time to think about it all, I spoke to Dixon about the bad billing. 'You totally missed this, Brian. Kendo should have been on with Rocco – he and Kendo can work well together.'

Brian said, 'He doesn't want to work with Kendo.'

'Why not?' I asked.

'He thinks Kendo will use him as a knock-off.'

'That's ridiculous. Why didn't you tell me that? I could have had a word with him.'

Eventually I managed to speak to Rocco.

His reasoning was, 'Kendo's just come back after being away, I'm a full time professional – this is how I earn my living, but Kendo might be gone again tomorrow. He'll want to bump me off (meaning win), and I'll be left with nothing but a loss. Kendo will just go back to where he was, because he's not really bothered about wrestling.'

'You're wrong,' I assured him, 'Kendo's here to stay as long as wrestling's here. He doesn't want to bump you off – he wants to work with you.'

I wanted to make the business successful, especially since we were up against the Americans and Max Crabtree, and I felt that that Rocco could work well with Kendo.

On reflection, from Dixon's point of view, Kendo had come back after ten years away from wrestling and thirteen years away from him, and gone in straight at the top, immediately elbowing him and Rocco, his top villain, aside. Brian had been working all these years to get his shows on TV, and as soon as he got it, Kendo parachuted in and immediately took over from them both. Having worked together for so many years and become close friends, Dixon and Rocco must have commiserated and discussed how to salvage something for themselves from Kendo's take-over, and that's why they'd put together the bill we'd had.

Dixon should have had the vision to see past his feelings and got us together to discuss things – of the wrestlers on the night, Kendo versus Rocco should have been the headline match.

I managed to persuade Rocco that it was a good idea for us to work together, and we could repeat the theme of the Big Daddy matches. I said we should tag-up to start with, and a couple of shows in, he would pull the mask off. We did exactly that – Rocco tried to save Kendo from having the mask pulled off by Dave Taylor, but it was him who ended up with the mask in his hands. George immediately got into the ring and called Rocco a scoundrel, and the resulting feud between Rocco and Kendo went on and on. From the next match onwards, holding a mask aloft, Rocco would shout, 'Every time I'm on with you, I'm gonna take one of these home!'

Now that Kendo was back, Brian and I worked well together. We had a long series of shows around the country with Rocco and Kendo, just as Daddy and Kendo had done. They were packed out – everyone wanted to see if Rocco could pull the mask off again.

They were great tactics that always worked well – that's what the audience at the Hippodrome thought they were going to get, and should have got. It certainly wasn't an easy journey recovering from such a bad start to the 'comeback'.

However, some time later, I came up with an idea that was to be talked about for years afterwards – the hypnotising of Robbie Brookside.

I'd found that there weren't many wrestlers to do singles matches with, so I decided to get into tag matches. I was told about a wrestler who would be a good tag partner for Kendo – Blondie Barratt, 'The Rock'n'Roll Express.' Dixon said it sounded like a good idea, and he put us together against 'The Liverpool Lads', Robbie Brookside and 'Doc' Dean.

The Liverpool Lads were young and all the girls loved

them, especially when they were getting smacked around by Kendo. Blondie was in his thirties and was a good partner for Kendo – he was always a villain, known for crowd-infuriating tactics as much behind the ref's back as in front of him. They were very good matches and became a successful extended run around the country.

Then a controversial idea came to me – I felt it might be exciting if Kendo appeared to put someone under his spell.

By this time I'd got to know Robbie Brookside quite well, and I discussed it with him – he liked the idea. He was good to work with, and we were both sure that it could be put across very well in the theatre of wrestling. When it happened, live on-air, it really was sensational.

It happened a long way into a tag match between Kendo and Blondie Barratt versus Robbie Brookside and Steve Regal. It had been a hard-fought match, so much so that Blondie had been counted out, which left Kendo alone facing Brookside and Regal. They both ended up in the ring against Kendo, and they battered him – at one point, they both drop-kicked him together, which the crowd loved. Kendo was left stunned and Brookside dragged the mask off him – the audience was delighted.

But suddenly the tables were turned; a de-masked Kendo recovered and got hold of Brookside, staring into his eyes and then making a hand gesture which instantly put him into a trance. Kendo grabbed the mask back from an immobile Brookside and put it back on, and then he made another gesture which made Brookside turn and attack his own tag partner. Instead of tagging Regal back in, Brookside punched him in the stomach and hauled him over the top rope into the ring. Kendo then threw Regal into the corner post before knocking him out with a Kamikaze Crash, as a dazed Brookside stood and looked on.

Kent Walton was genuinely astonished – he said, 'That is a brand new one – that is a first!' Kendo released

Brookside from the trance as Regal was counted out. The win was announced for the Nagasaki/Barratt team as Brookside and Regal argued over what had happened. Brookside grabbed the mic to complain that Nagasaki had '...done something to him, compelled him to do that...', and George got into the ring to say the time-honoured words – 'I warned you and I warn every other wrestler – there's more to Nagasaki than meets his eye!' The audience were genuinely stunned – they hated seeing baby-faces Brookside and Regal defeated by Nagasaki, but seeing it done by a mysterious power made Kendo into an even bigger and more dangerous villain.

Robbie was brilliant – he'd gone along with the idea despite pressure not to do it from Steve Regal and Dave Taylor – they both told him they felt it would make a fool of him. But he'd seen the theatrical potential of it and really rose to the occasion.

In later matches where Kendo's 'mysterious power' was used, he would take Brookside to the ring at his side, then work the magic with the hands, and Robbie would fall into a trance. The girls would all shout and scream, 'Don't look at him, Robbie! Look at us! Listen to us!'

After the shows, Brookside's fans – women in particular – used to crowd the stage door, shouting, 'Don't go with him, Robbie, don't go with him! We know what you're up to, Nagasaki. Don't go with him!' God knows what they were thinking!

The reality was much more mundane – Robbie was usually dropped off around the corner for somebody else to pick him up and drive him home.

Despite being one of the most talked-about wrestling matches ever, and the one that actually made him famous, Robbie's still a little embarrassed about it. I don't think it did him any harm – it got him noticed and talked about, and it was very successful – it became a whole series of shows throughout the halls. By then, he was so involved in the storyline that he couldn't escape anyway.

Years later, I was having dinner with influential art dealer Charles Cholmondeley, who has always been fascinated by wrestling – so much so that he was to buy a portrait of Kendo by renowned pop artist, Peter Blake.

I explained to Charles that a lot of wrestling was, in fact, show business – that for a match to be sensational, as well as skill it requires a level of showmanship. As I regarded him as a friend, I tried to be honest with him, but Kendo's mystique proved far more powerful than reason; as we neared the end of the meal he suddenly glanced up and said, 'What about the match when Kendo hypnotised Robbie Brookside?'

I realized then that it didn't matter what I said about the wrestling business, he wanted to believe it. It showed that Max Crabtree's original premise remained true and crossed all levels of society – everybody wants to believe in magic.

Chapter 28

Losing George

After the Hippodrome show, George gradually began to feel less and less well, and as time went by it became clear that he had some sort of persistent illness. Eventually he had to go to the local hospital for a minor treatment, but when I went to visit him, to my surprise I was directed to the private patients' section on the top floor; I found him in a single room with a sign on the door saying, 'Contagious Disease'. This was most alarming.

I went in and could tell straight away that he was putting a brave face on something serious; he told me that he had the HIV virus. In the late '80s this was a horror story, with high-profile sufferers like Liberace and Rock Hudson dying from it; I was suddenly faced with the prospect of this disease possibly ending George's life.

He'd been told everything that was then known about HIV and he enlightened me – that there could be certain complications, and that it might or might not develop into full-blown AIDS. I immediately hoped for the best, of course – that it wouldn't develop, that it could be treated, and he would get well.

About a week and a half later George came home, but he felt very weak and was clearly worried. He went into a programme at St. Thomas's Hospital for people with HIV, and I always went with him, not only because he didn't drive, but I also wanted to give my very dear friend every possible support.

After a few hospital visits with George the medical staff accepted me as his next of kin, so whenever they had an update or something to explain, I was included. I think this was helpful to him because it meant that he didn't have to repeat what he'd been told about his condition, which made it easier for him to maintain a sense of dignity.

This went on for a little over a year, during which time George's health continued to decline and he got a lot thinner, but then the experimental drug AZT came into play and the clinic decided to try it on him. He started to feel a bit better and his condition did improve, and because he felt better he engaged a bit more with things.

We continued doing wrestling events, no more than about two a week, and one evening, someone in the audience shouted, 'The Manager's got AIDS!'

When we left, a dejected George said to me, 'Well, the writing's on the wall...' He was sadly conceding that his gaunt appearance was becoming a liability for us in the wrestling business.

At the time, there was a fear that you could get HIV or AIDS from drinking from the same cup as someone who'd already got it, and with the wrestling business being so very physical and involving so much bodily contact, such concerns put me in a vulnerable position. I was the one in the ring with the other wrestlers, so if the Manager had HIV or AIDS, the next assumption might be that I had it as well.

I had, in fact, been tested, and was all-clear. We never responded to any suggestion that George might have AIDS, and nobody we knew was indiscreet enough to ask about it, but to explain George's gaunt appearance, I confided in a few people that he had cancer, which was accepted.

Eventually George ended up back in hospital and I continued doing wrestling shows, supported by Lawrence, who, alongside George, had been my personal assistant. However, George being in hospital meant that Kendo didn't have his traditional manager persona with him, which detracted somewhat from the spectacle of his arrival and departure at the beginning and end of matches, and appropriately winding-up the audience.

Our friend Lloyd Ryan came to a show at Walthamstow and he asked where George was. I told him he was in hospital and I suddenly said, 'How would you like to be a manager for the evening?'

He said, 'I'll give it a go!' Lloyd is quite a bombastic person, and could be quite 'bolshy', so he was very much the right kind of character for that role; he did that first show very well, albeit in a much more abrasive way than George's eloquent impudence towards the audience.

On one of my later visits to see George in hospital, I bumped into Lloyd who was on his way out from visiting him. We exchanged pleasantries and concerns over George, Lloyd left, and I went in to see him.

George was furious! With anger glittering in his eyes, he hissed to me that Lloyd had said, 'Your job is safe with me!' He was furious! As he told me this, he had to reach for an oxygen mask!!

After another stay in hospital George came home, but he never made enough of a recovery to go back to being Kendo's Manager. Lloyd ended up taking on the role as a result of George's enforced absence, and he did it well, although with a very different style and atmosphere to 'the Gorgeous one'.

George's health continued to decline and he had regular bouts of becoming quite seriously ill, during which he had to go back into hospital. His condition left us in no doubt that he was dying; he knew it too, and that his time was becoming short.

After one particularly bad episode, he told me that he

wanted to see the stage play, 'Phantom of the Opera', and he wanted to see it on Broadway, in New York. We'd been to Canada, of course, but never America, and he wanted to see The Big Apple. We found that there was a special package trip, to fly to New York on Concorde, see 'Phantom of the Opera' on Broadway, and fly back, all in three days.

Because you flew faster than the earth turned, time-wise, you arrived before you'd left, so we got there early enough on the first day to do some sight-seeing and we took a trip on the Hudson River. In the evening, the hotel put on a meal – it was the Marriott Marquee on Times Square, and it was spectacular – the lobby was on the second floor, and you could look up forty-four floors to a revolving restaurant, which had views over all of New York.

The second day included a helicopter trip around Manhattan and the Hudson Bay, including flying past the Statue of Liberty, followed by seeing 'The Phantom of the Opera', and we were taken to the theatre by horse-drawn carriage. In the evening there was a special meal for those on the tour in the revolving 'Restaurant in the Sky', but sadly the helicopter trip and going to the theatre had tired George out too much, so he took to his bed. I went to the gala meal myself, but I didn't stay long because I was so concerned about him, but he seemed to benefit from the rest.

On the third day, we had the morning to ourselves; we'd planned to go up the Empire State Building, but George wasn't well enough, so we just packed and took the Concorde flight back. It was clear that he'd really enjoyed the trip, but it had completely exhausted him and he had to take to his bed for a while when we got back.

A little while later, George mentioned that he'd seen a ring he'd really liked, and he wanted to buy it. It had been in the window of Cartier's in New Bond Street, London, and while I couldn't imagine how he'd seen it or when, we decided to go and get the ring for him. It was about £5,000 – not that that matters, because it was what he wanted, but unfortunately, when we got there we found that the ring had been sold.

They showed him another similar one with two rubies and a diamond, which he also liked, and he decided he'd have that one. When George tried the ring on, it fell off straight away because it was too big for him, but Cartier were very helpful and said they could see that the gentleman wasn't very well, and they could re-size it for him in a few minutes if we went and had a cup of coffee. We did, and when we went back the ring fitted perfectly and we bought it – George was delighted with it.

As I was coming out of the shop, the salesperson mentioned to me that if I wanted to have the ring size changed later, I could bring it back and they would gladly do it. I understood that this offer was made so that I could wear the ring to remember 'the gentleman' after he was no longer with us; on one level this was a considerate thought, but on another it brought me face-to-face with the fact that the day was coming, and it didn't look like it would be far off. I pushed the thought out of my mind.

George wasn't able to leave the house much after that outing; he spent most of his time in bed, and was cared for by us in the house and the nurses who would come in every day. He always remained dignified and optimistic throughout his difficulties; he was under no illusions about the seriousness and inevitability of his illness, but he always looked forward to the next thing, the next outing, the next meeting with friends, and in this way he helped those around him stay optimistic too.

One January morning in 1989 we found that he had passed away peacefully in his sleep, which was at least merciful.

I'm very glad that we were able to go on the 'Concorde-Phantom of the Opera' trip and buy him the ring he so much liked, because these things made him happy during a time which was sad and difficult for us all, particularly him.

Those who saw George on television will never forget his uniquely eloquent and compelling presence, his outrageous dress-sense, and his complete professionalism as Kendo's Manager. Those who knew him personally knew these things magnified a hundred-fold, but also his warmth, his wit and skill as a raconteur, his sensitive reflections on life and human nature, his prodigious ability to drink and create merry hell, as well as his infectious, uproarious laugh.

George was unique, gifted, special, profound, fun, jovial, and the consummate social butterfly, all turned up to eleven tenths; he is dearly missed, and never has it been more truly said that '...we shall not see his like again.'

...but he left us some fantastic memories...

George was a central character of 1960s and early 1970s Earls Court – absolutely everyone across all levels of society knew him, and wherever there was something sensational happening, he'd be at the centre of it.

One evening George was in the Boltons, having an argument with a young man with whom he was most enamoured, who eventually said he'd had enough and walked out. George slammed his drink down and stormed out after him, but by the time he reached the street, his friend was already some distance away. George wasn't going to chase after him so he found a stack of crates with empty beer bottles in them and he grabbed one and attempted to hurl it down the street after his friend. He might have had the heart of a lion but he had the muscles of a mouse and the crate barely travelled any distance, but as soon as he'd let go of it the back doors of a Black Maria (a police van) burst open and several policemen piled out and jumped on him and hauled him straight into the back. It had been parked right there and I'll never know why George hadn't seen it – perhaps because he was so wound-up – but as it sped off it struck me that his capture had been so slick it could have been choreographed.

While he was being held at the police station there were loads of his gay friends outside chanting, 'We want mother! We want George!' One of the policemen inside asked, 'Who's this "mother" they're all asking for?' George answered, 'Erm, – it may well be me!' Later, When he went to court and the police evidence was presented, the judge asked, 'Mr. Gillett, are you a practising homosexual?' to which George replied 'To be honest, your Honour, I'm a bit out of practice at the moment!' That was frowned upon and George was found guilty of behaviour likely to cause a breach of the peace, for which he was fined thirty shillings.

On New Year's Eve 1973, something more dramatic happened. We were in Earls Court's Masquerade club when someone got rather violently thrown out by the doorman, Scots John. The man had to go to hospital to have a cut stitched up, which meant the police had to get involved, so they went to the club looking for Scots John. They arrived after hours so the place should have been closed, but in the underground restaurant part of the club there must have been upwards of thirty people still having a get-together. We suddenly saw five policemen coming down the stairs, one of whom appeared to be an inspector; they stopped the music and demanded to know where Scots John was but he'd already left. The police were quite heavy-handed in their questioning of the guests, and this was actually quite common back then; earlier that year they'd been heavily criticised for their rough approach to patrons of the Coleherne who'd been drinking outside the pub in the sun, which had resulted in a headline-making riot all up the street.

Suddenly I saw George in front of me facing the police inspector; he'd had a drink or two to say the least, and he began complaining at the police's tactics. He clearly wasn't happy with the responses he was getting so he clumsily tried to slap the inspector, missing him by miles, but the inspector then knocked his own hat off and shouted, 'You hit me!' Several policemen leapt on George and dragged him feet-first up the steps to ground floor level, and then they threw him back down the stairs. I wanted to help George but another copper told me to go and sit down. They dragged George back up the stairs and threw him into a Black Maria, and then one policeman claimed he'd found a knife on the floor where George had been and they said he was probably carrying it; he was arrested for assaulting a police officer.

The following morning at 10 o'clock he appeared in the local magistrates court, stood beside Scots John whom they had tracked down. The police inspector was also there, with a theatrically-large plaster on his head. In the public gallery was a large number of George's gay friends, who were outraged at this further episode of police heavy-handedness. The charges were read out and pleas asked for; I'd spoken to a lawyer, but as it was first thing on New Year's Day he hadn't been able to get to George, so he'd told me to try and get a message to him to plead 'Not Guilty'. They wouldn't let me see him so he never got the advice, and he ended up pleading guilty.

The judge said, 'People who strike a police officer do so at their peril.' In front of the judge would have been George's previous conviction for throwing the beer crate, which meant this subsequent sentence wouldn't be quite so lenient – this time he got three months in prison. The public gallery erupted, all the queens shouting, 'It's not fair! He didn't hit him!' One of them shouted, 'Make him take the plaster off!', referring to the inspector, and it became a chorus, but he wasn't going to do that because everybody knew there was nothing underneath it...

George only served about six weeks time and he had no choice but to be philosophical about it – he was, at least, one of the most popular and flamboyant members of an oppressed minority.

I was out with George one evening and we were driving through the West End when he suddenly leapt out of the car and went rampaging down the street, furiously swinging the metal liner of a public litter bin into shop windows and yelling, 'I'm as much a man as any of you!' Fortunately he didn't break any windows, but as I slowly drove after him, he suddenly turned and glared at me with this metal bin still in his hands. I instantly knew that he was going to throw it at the car so I sped off to a safe distance. He thought I was going to leave him there so he put the bin down and ran after me, and when I saw that I waited for him and let him in. Such volatility was rare, but could be dangerous.

Once in Wolverhampton, George, myself, and a friend, Mick Roberts, went to the Silver Web, a gay club. George was being his usual loud and boisterous self and one of the owners, Betty, came over and asked him to be a little quieter. Mick saw this as an opportunity to wind George up to even louder boisterousness, which resulted in Betty coming across again. She said, 'George, I've asked you nicely – if you don't keep the noise down you'll have to leave.' George had a half-finished glass of brandy in his hand, and he stood up and slowly and carefully poured it over Betty's head. She froze, and several large lesbians emerged out of the shadows and formed a ring around George. He was man-handled to the exit without too much protesting, but when they got him to the door, Betty said, 'Right! You're barred for life!' Then George broke loose and gave Betty a mighty shove and she shot backwards, disappearing into the club. The lesbians got somewhat more forceful at this point and got him to the bottom of the stairs and Mick and I followed, never to return to the club again.

One New Year's Eve we were invited for an early evening meet-and-greet in the restaurant on the top floor of the Hilton hotel on Park Lane, by an 'ideas' man who thought that Pal Toys could be persuaded to do a doll of Kendo Nagasaki. However, George got drunk and the hotel staff felt he was being too boisterous – once again. They decided he should leave, but he refused and hotel security was called. They also asked him to leave and again he refused, so they got him by the arms in a way that made it look like they were helping him rather than man-handling him out. They got him to the lift and I followed, and they got him all the way through the foyer to the motorised revolving front door, which was where the fun started. Every time the doors revolved past the exit, George managed to stay in the revolving part for at least three revolutions before the security men managed to shove him out into the street, after which they stayed there to stop him trying to come back in. We ended up seeing the New Year in somewhere in nearby Leicester Square.

When we lived in Wolverhampton, George liked to shop at the up-market town-centre department store, Beatties. He particularly liked what they had in their Food Hall, as they had nice little meals for one. One day, he was accosted by store security as he left. They insisted he had something of theirs, and he correctly pointed out that he had a carrier bag with their produce in it, for which he had a receipt. However, George did have his 'shushing coat' on. It was a three-quarter-length fur-fabric jacket with two large inside pockets; he'd developed a lightning-fast sleight of hand that would deposit anything that took his fancy into these pockets unnoticed. But that didn't seem to have happened this day. Beatties' security persisted and hauled him back into the store, at which point he confessed and produced from the coat a single frozen portion of duck in orange sauce. Hardly the Crown jewels, but he ended up being prosecuted for it. He had no excuse – he had money – I think he was just falling back on the habit he'd developed when he was living in bed-sits in Earls Court.

It was inevitable that interesting episodes followed George into wrestling too. One of the wrestling lads was called Kelly (not his real name), he was married and bisexual. He was a man of large stature and he had a thing for George. His normally deep, strong voice would go all soft and soothing when he was anywhere near the object of his affections, cooing such things as, 'Ooh, George..!' We were all in the dressing room one day with Mal Kirk and Albert Wall when Kelly grabbed George and pushed him up against the wall and kissed him. Kirk and Wall, both true 'salt of the earth' types, looked at each other and shrugged their shoulders, then Kirk said, 'What's t'fuckin' job coming to?', and they walked out.

The next time George and Kelly met I said, 'Go on, George – give your uncle Kel a big kiss!' George went all shy and retiring, then Kelly grabbed him, lifted him off the floor and kissed him.

When we were alone, a surprisingly serious George cautioned me; he said, 'Don't encourage him, dear – that fuckin' queen is taking this seriously and your mother's going to get into a lot of trouble with him one day!' I didn't do it again...

Once, after a particularly 'hot' show with a very wound-up audience, George managed to get back into the ring but the angry crowd surrounded it. I said to him, 'I'll get out, you follow immediately behind me, and we'll make a run for it.' I jumped off the apron and before my feet had hit the floor George also jumped out – straight onto my head! I wasn't prepared for his extra weight on top of me and we ended up sinking vertically down to the floor, like some kind of odd statue sinking into the sea. Fortunately, that de-fused the situation – everyone broke out laughing, which was a huge relief compared to their previous fury – we wouldn't be lynched after all...

At Hanley, George once did a magical disappearing act, completely by accident. At that venue there's a big, high stage, and the ring has to be set up in front of it.

There was usually a gap of about nine inches between the stage and the ring so you could step down off the front of the stage and onto the ring's apron, but on this occasion it had been set up about a foot further away than normal. The dressing rooms are behind the stage and they used to have ranks of audience seats on it, with a space at the front for the acts to make their entrance from the wings. Usually, we'd come onto the stage and face the main hall and George would hold Kendo's hand aloft, then we'd turn and acknowledge the audience in the seats on the stage. After that, we'd turn around and walk to the front of the stage and step down to the ring.

This time, while I was still facing the on-stage audience, George turned around and went to the ring, but he clearly hadn't seen the extra gap and he walked off the stage and shot down between it and the ring. I turned round ready to step onto the apron to find that George had vanished – I couldn't believe my eyes. Then his head popped up at the front of the stage and he had to shuffle along the gap until he was clear of the ring, and get to the steps to the stage, rubbing his bashed knees. Fortunately, he didn't hurt himself and we resumed the show – only George could have thrown such an unexpected surprise into our entrance that day.

Also at Hanley, George once wore a djellaba, a kind of slim kaftan, which was to cause unintended hilarity. We did our usual Hanley entrance, this time with George twirling a parasol and really camping it up, but before we got to the front of the stage to step onto the ring apron, George turned to me and said, 'I can't get into the ring, dear.' I said, 'Why?' He didn't answer but looked at me with a pained expression and glanced down and pointed towards his feet. I didn't understand the problem and I certainly couldn't see one through the kendo helmet, so I just said, 'Get into that fuckin' ring!' He obeyed immediately.

It turned out that the bottom of the djellaba was so

narrow that it would prevent him from lifting his legs over the ropes to get into the ring. Before I knew what was happening, George had hitched it up to his waist, revealing legs elegantly clad in ladies' stockings with garters, and boots with Cuban heels...

The audience erupted into fits of laughter, then George stepped onto the apron and through the ropes. He did his speech but then had to hitch up the djellaba and reveal the stockings and Cuban heels again as he got out. After that I had to get the audience back to a state of anger at Kendo, which took at least a round and a half. When it came to the end of the match and George approached the ring to do his usual triumphal speech, I said to him, 'Don't fuckin' get in – you'll ruin the finish!' I didn't want to see those stockings and Cuban heels again; he didn't get in.

He was sometimes a bit playful with the other wrestlers. Mike Marino had a slight wall-eye and scar-tissue above his left eyebrow. If it got hit during matches it would open up and bleed, which was always good for dramatic effect. The scar used to make him wince on that side – we used to refer to it as 'the old glad-eye' – and when Mike would wince, George would wink back at him. Mike complained to me, saying, 'Lover, tell George not to give me the old glad-eye in the groin!' 'The groin' was a nick-name for the wrestling ring, but as soon as I told George to cut out the winking he did it all the more, winding Mike up something rotten.

I'd like to leave the last word about what wonderful company George was to the man himself, in his own reflections of those whose company he enjoyed.

I've had the pleasure of knowing some jolly interesting characters whose good company has greatly enriched my life.

A man who knew the value of entertainment was the manager of Rod Stewart, Billy Gaff. I've already mentioned that our paths first crossed many years ago, but they re-crossed again during the eighties.

It was New Year's Eve. I was passing the time in a non-too-glamorous small drinking club. The Bacardi wasn't bad, but the company was – all the best people might have been tempted elsewhere.

In any event I was settling down to see in the New Year in solitary fashion with just my fur coat and a bottle of Bacardi for company. Then in through the front door swept Tony Toon, an old friend. He had improved his status over the years, having twice been P.A. to Rod Stewart, and moving rapidly through a social circle that was still occasionally out of our reach. He had with him a small group of assorted people. It transpired that he was actually out on business, looking for a suitable cross-section of people to take on to a party at Billy Gaff's house. As someone who usually knew where to find such a cross-section, and still having the entree into scenes and places that Tony was now too busy or to successful to be seen in, I was immediately co-opted to help find those people.

Naturally, a combination of wit and charm on my behalf, and the prospect of free booze plus whatever else might prove to be on offer, soon helped us to round-up a posse delectable, off we cruised through the slush to party away the night.

It was such a good night that I don't have many memories of it after the first hour or so, but I do remember Billy having gold records hung up in the lavatory, which I thought was a pretty appropriate place. Inevitably, when it was time to go, I collected my fur and the remnants of my wits and wandered off into the morning.

Billy lived off Fulham Road then, and the nearest underground station was Earls Court, or so I thought, so I made off in that general direction. There was however, one major, and completely unpredicted problem –

totally unbeknown to me throughout the duration of the party heavy snow had fallen, so there was virtually no traffic, and in a drunken stupor, one white and ghostly street looks very much like another.

It took me about an hour to reach the underground, by which time I felt incredibly ill, and took all my strength and resources to force myself on the first train to arrive. I then naturally fell fast asleep and arrived not at my destination, but at Cockfosters. Almost as naturally, I then sailed back along the entire length of the Piccadilly line, only to return once more to Cockfosters, by which time, even my befuddled brain began to think the whole thing was getting a trifle out of hand.

A good nine hours after I'd left the bloody party I finally arrived home. It should have taken an hour. So whatever Rod Stewart might have said about Billy Gaff in their counter-suits against each other, he'll never be able to say he doesn't throw a damn good party – he does.

Simon Napier-Bell, who signed Burnt Out Stars, wasn't the very first rock manager that Peter and I ever met (that had been Billy Gaff), but by the time we launched the band to a general wave of apathy, he was the first one we actually worked with.

His own book gives a very reasonable account of the way he entered the music business, and he makes no bones about his own attitude to musicians and record companies. In many ways they are to be seen as the enemy – people who are on permanent self-destruct (in the case of musicians) and equally permanent in the case of A & R executives. Even to dignify them with the name of executive is in the majority of cases a gross overstatement of talent or position.

Simon would freely admit to being more than a little deft at picking the pockets of record companies in order to promote his own ventures, and as a result he has ample companies and bank accounts scattered around the world to paper entire suites of offices. Simon was very much an eighties version of Larry Parnes or Brian Epstein – a high-profile manager/wheeler-dealer whose personality and attributes were as famous – if not more so – than those of his artists, with the possible exception of George Michael and Wham!, whose considerable successes only served to raise his profile even higher.

One of my enduring memories of Simon is he and I crying on each other's shoulders in the middle of the dance floor of the Hippodrome over the sad demise of Steven Hayter, the owner and manager of the Embassy Club, who had just died of AIDS.

Though emotional and gregarious, Simon always managed to hide his real self behind an invisible wall. At an age when most pop managers were beginning to look distinctly haggard and pale, he constantly looked tanned, fit, and trim, and although his love of a good time and good drinks has never diminished with the years, he has never allowed either to inflict injuries on his body.

The same could not be said for Kit Lambert. Peter and I unfortunately only got to know Kit after his best days were over. He was no longer the manager of The Who, and the hell-raisin', room-wreckin' days were simply ghosts that forever rose out of a misty past to haunt him. If ever there was living proof of the fact that some people really do have a self-destruct button then it was Kit. There wasn't a way known to medical science of distillers of how to gradually kill oneself that Kit didn't know about, or hadn't tried.

Kit was still operating in the music business right up to the time of his death, trying to produce some tracks with the punk-rock band Chelsea. Their lead singer and founder, Gene October (known better to his friends as John O'Hara, and the music press as '...that well-known bender...') confided to us that the whole proceedings rapidly descended into a farce. Kit apparently was reaching the two-bottle of spirits a day stage, plus whatever else he was snorting, shooting, or swallowing, and was in no state to handle the then-present-day sophistications of a recording studio.

Things must have been really bad if Gene thought so. We'd known him for around thirteen years – he once slept on my floor as a very young vagrant – and he liked a good time just as much as the rest of us.

One of Kit's most unfortunate habits, and indeed it could well have turned out to be a fatal one, was in the manner of the company he chose to pick up to share his bed and board with. Rough trade wasn't the phrase, and anything was grist to the mill of his unending, stupefied wanderings. His life was rambunctious and spirited, and his personality was by turns outrageous, bombastic, and cruel. His manner could be formal, intimate, cutting, or affectionate. The changes of his mood were mercurial, and his nature had been totally perverted by the self-destroying quantities of alcohol and drugs that he fed into his system on an hourly basis.

It's not that surprising therefore that his death should have been as bizarre as his life. He was apparently involved in a fracas in a Kensington nightclub, which must have been as much an embarrassment for the owner, a friend of his – and ours. It's never quite been ascertained whether he was persuaded to leave the club, thrown out, or left of his own accord. He had however already been subjected to quite a good thumping. His assailants undoubtedly followed him outside, and repeated their beating as he was stumbling his way homeward. He evidently did arrive home, and his body was found some time later at the foot of the stairs. It was apparent that he had fallen down them and died of his injuries. His aged mother, however, was profoundly convinced that he was murdered.

Murdered or not, it is eminently conceivable that he

was pushed. Even after two skirmishes, it is not impossible that Kit would have invited either his assailants, or even someone he picked up after, back to his house. It is certainly in-character to believe that he perhaps had one of his lightening mood changes, and might well have imperiously ordered someone out of his house, even trying to physically force them out. I don't believe he was murdered. I think he was pushed, not with the intent to kill him, but as the tragic end-result of another of his mind-games and the befuddled state of his reflexes and emotions.

In that way at least, Kit kept his reputation right up to the end, and left this mortal coil in a way compatible with the way he had lived - uproariously and dramatically.

Another interesting person was someone called Rachel, which was not her real name – there were deep-seated physical reasons for that, because Rachel was a fella – just. Peter and I were in one of the late-seventies classier watering-holes, Maunkberrys, late one night in a party of liggers, and amongst others we were chatting to Rachel. Although she was dressed very fashionably and was entirely feminine, we both guessed that underneath there might well be quite another tale to tell.

She was however, very amusing company. Eventually, as we all spilled out onto the pavement at around 3.00 am, we decided to go on to another club, a 'Shabeen' this time. A Shabeen is an illegal drinking den, of which there aren't as many around as there used to be, but they are still very much in evidence if you know where to look.

After the Shabeen eventually closed, Rachel invited us – and I think two other guests – to join her for breakfast at a top London Hotel. There are not that many top class London Hotels that keep a restaurant open all night, but this one did, and it was quite a popular haunt for club and music people.

We dined and chatted and drank our coffee, but most of all we laughed. Rachel was hysterically funny in a

Valium-induced way, and was quite happy to sit at the breakfast table eating her way through a whole bottle full of pain-killers while entrancing us with tales of New York, from where she hailed.

Many years ago Peter and I had met the likes of Cherry Vanilla and Jayne-nee-Wayne County of the Warhol/Underground set. Rachel knew the same people, came from the same background, and was in fact particularly friendly as it turned out with Lou Reed. She didn't really make much of a secret of the fact that she was not quite what she seemed, although she didn't – at first that is – reveal whether she was a transvestite or a transsexual.

It was by now around 7.30 or 8.00am, it was well past time to call it a day. The bill was asked for and received. Rachel dove into her handbag and paid the bill with a cheque. We got up to leave. The waiter came over. We sat down.

He said, 'I'm sorry madam, but I cannot accept this cheque.'

Rachel replied, 'Why the fuck not?'

He shrugged and said, 'Unfortunately it would appear you have given us one of your husband's cheques by mistake. The name on this cheque is undoubtedly a man's.'

Around this point in the proceedings, Rachel started to rise rather ominously out of her chair, and when she spoke, her voice had risen rather more ominously, so that she had the completely undivided attention of a room-full of American, middle-aged breakfasters.

'That's my cheque book, you motherfucker, I'll show you what I am – nobody, but nobody, fucks with Rachel.'

Simultaneously, Rachel had stood up to her full height, and had begun to raise her skirt to reveal all for the hypno-horrified masses, and after a clattering of dropped cutlery, you could have heard a pin drop. Those two or three seconds seemed to take all eternity, and the rest of us suddenly felt exactly the same religious experience as what passing-over must really be like.

Peter swiftly decided to take a much-needed hand in the proceedings and pushed Rachel down into her seat, at the same time as he engaged the waiter in conversation. He pointed out that as the restaurant had never asked for proof of identity, and made no mention of credit cards or the like, they were duty bound to accept the cheque. They disagreed, and he told them they should call the police to give a verdict, as by this time a senior waiter had arrived on the scene to impound the cheque-book, and he refused to give it back.

The Police most certainly arrived, and Peter left the restaurant with the head waiter to talk to them while the rest of us played the game of keeping a – by now – very stoned Rachel amused until we knew what the hell was happening.

Happily, the police agreed with Peter, that as the hotel had initially accepted the cheque in all good faith, they had to keep it, especially as they made no mention anywhere on their premises that cheques might not, under certain circumstances, be acceptable. Furthermore, it was totally illegal of them to even try and impound the cheque book – it was not their place to try and define whether it belonged to the person holding it or not.

So Rachel had already won hands down. She got her cheque book back, which she desperately needed, as she was flying out to New York in a matter of hours, but she still played one final wicked stroke. The bill had come to around £140, and Rachel made the cheque out for £160, so that she could have a little petty cash, and she didn't leave a tip. She then sailed gaily out of our lives off to collect a banker's draft from Lou Reed at a post office, then on to The States.

Burt Shevelove became a friend of ours in the last couple of years of his life, and in that short time gave us a veritable treasure trove of anecdotes.

Burt was a writer, producer, and director. He had

many Broadway hits to his credit, and was often associated with the composer Stephen Sondhiem. He wrote the libretto for one of the most successful Broadway shows ever, A Funny Thing Happened to me on the Way to the Forum, and even up to the time of his death had started to direct the West End smash hit musical Windy City. He lived in a penthouse flat off Hyde Park for periods of time in each year, and it was a place literally overflowing with rare books, theatrical memorabilia, and collections of photos and posters of all kinds of freaks and tattooed people.

I believe it was probably a mutual friend, the actor, Victor Spinetti that first introduced us, and we were all immediately charmed by Burt's style. He couldn't help it, but he looked rather like a benign old frog. His glasses were either up on his forehead, or perched on the end of his prominent nose, thus enlarging his already somewhat bulbous eyes. He would sit, almost completely still, with his hands resting on his stomach, and talk in a deep, gravelly, New York Jewish voice, which had a wheeze running through it from time to time. The wheeze was caused partly by the heart condition from which Burt suffered, and eventually died of.

Burt played an immobile host to countless friends and acquaintances, and seemed to have an ever-open door – that is, if he felt you were an interesting enough person. He never suffered fools, and had reached both a position and an age where he felt he could express himself pretty freely, without worrying too much whether or not he offended anybody. As long as he thought you were fun, he didn't much care what you did or where you came from, if you were a good listener, or told a good tale, or even better, played a good game of backgammon, you were welcome, otherwise...

...you might hear the following line with which he greeted Peter and I one night as we stepped out of the lift that led directly into his penthouse's hallway: 'Gee, I'm

glad to see you, I've got a roomful of the most boring people in London.'

We went in. He did indeed have just such a room-full, and now they all knew it. As the hallway led directly into his lounge they must obviously have heard every word. Quite understandably under the circumstances, they soon made their various excuses and departed off into the night. Burt didn't seem to notice.

A story that Burt told was that in New York during the second world war, they also suffered power blackouts, when the Americans thought the Japanese were about to jump down their collective throats. That might be all very well for safety reasons, but it didn't do a lot for a short sighted Shevelove pursuing an elegant sailor he'd spotted from some distance.

As he followed the sailor along a series of dark and dingy brownstone streets, Burt slowly drew a little nearer to his quarry, who suddenly turned round. In his haste to appear nonchalant, Burt stopped and leaned on what he thought were railings, but they turned out to be a gate, which obligingly flew open causing Burt to plummet about twelve feet down into the open basement area of one of the tenement buildings.

He hadn't actually broken anything, but there were more than enough cuts and bruises to go round. Apparently the sailor heard Burt's shouts and came back, lit a lighter, and was greeted by the non-too pretty sight of him spread-eagled beneath his flickering gaze. A rescue was somehow affected, and the sailor, who had once been the rather distant object of Burt's projected attentions, had to turn into an instant medic to patch him up and send him on his way.

I'm sorry to say that there are not a lot of Burt Sheveloves left in the world. His humour and intelligence will both be sadly missed, and his death reminds me of the futility of doing as he did – collecting books and other things to the tune of well over one million pounds, only to have to leave it all behind. Death is the greatest of all levellers.

Poignant words indeed.

There are countless more wonderful stories of George's crazy activities, but the foregoing shows that he crammed an astonishing amount of life into his all-too-short 48 years.

Chapter 29

Wrestling Comes Off TV

Brian Dixon's All-Star Wrestling and Max Crabtree at Joint Promotions both had TV shows in competition with each other, both with big main attractions – while Brian had Kendo and Rocco, Max kept building up Big Daddy.

The tag team of Kendo and Blondie Barratt worked quite extensively together against Rocco and various tag partners, including Clive Myers, Dave Taylor, and even Fuji Yamada. During this time, as part of Kendo's 'Victory at any price' notoriety, we developed the theatrical side of our matches, with routines which were quite controversial and very successful at enraging the audience.

In one scenario where Kendo was doing a singles match, if he got into trouble, his partner from his tag matches was supposed to rush from the back of the hall and act as a distraction to his opponent or the referee, so Kendo could seize the moment and gain the advantage. As a variation on this, while I was tagging with Psycho Stevens (before Blondie became my tag partner) I once persuaded him to hide under the ring and wait for his cue to appear and rush to Kendo's aid; I even talked him into taking some sandwiches and a drink – after all, he'd be hiding there for quite a while, from before the audience came in until the middle of the bill.

In the match, Kendo and Rocco ended up fighting outside the ring; as Rocco was getting the upper hand, Kendo was about to throw salt in his face but it was knocked out of his hand. Just as things looked bad for Kendo, Psycho appeared from under the ring like an avenging angel. The outraged referee yelled at Psycho to clear off, while behind his back Kendo retrieved the salt and gave Rocco a face-full. Kendo got back in the ring followed by Rocco, but he couldn't see because of the salt. He complained to the referee who said he hadn't seen the salt-throwing and announced, 'Wrestle on!' A half-blind Rocco would try his best, but would soon be beaten by Kendo. The audience was stunned when Psycho appeared from under the ring, outraged when Kendo salted Rocco behind the referee's back, and furious when Kendo won through such dastardly tactics – it was perfect theatre, and had the audience at fever-pitch.

While the routine worked extremely well, I couldn't persuade Psycho to do it again – he wasn't happy about being trapped under the ring for nearly four hours! He said, 'No way! All I had for company all that time was a bloody tool-box!'

Kendo throwing salt into his opponent's face became quite a frequent occurrence, and one day, Brian came into the dressing room and said, 'The punters are calling the shots,' which means they were expecting salt to be used. He said, 'See if you can come up with something different tonight...' and he went away leaving us to think about it.

When he came back to ask us what we'd worked out, I said, 'Double salt!'

Brian said, 'Oh, fuckin' 'ell – no!' and he left the dressing room mumbling to himself. However, he wouldn't get more of the same, he'd get an entirely new twist...

In the match, as Kendo was knocked to the canvas he knocked the referee down too. Rocco went to pull Kendo off the referee and pick him up. Kendo got up first and produced a bag of salt. Rocco saw what Kendo was doing and kicked him, knocking the salt out of his hands which Rocco then picked up. The referee had recovered enough to see that Rocco had the salt in his hands so he demanded it from him, to pass it out of the ring. As he handed it to the MC, behind his back Kendo produced another bag of salt, but Rocco saw it and grabbed it, and the referee turned back just in time to see him throw a generous handful of salt into Kendo's face. The referee disqualified Rocco so Kendo won the match, but Rocco was the hero, getting one over on the dastardly Nagasaki even though he'd lost the match.

By this time, the audience was on fire, and they carried Rocco shoulder high from the ring. Brian's reaction had gone from 'Oh, no!' to thinking that double-salt was just brilliant. While the audience may have been expecting salt to be used, they couldn't possibly have expected what actually happened...

Sometimes other devices were used to inflame the audience. At one match, Lloyd slandered Tony St.Clair's ability so badly that he publicly challenged Lloyd to compete against him. He couldn't back down so he had to accept, and he was billed as Kendo's tag partner in the following grudge match.

However, when that match came, Lloyd appeared with his arm in a plaster cast, so he couldn't wrestle; the audience was disappointed because they'd wanted to see Lloyd get his come-uppance. Conveniently, Blondie had come along to support the team from ring-side, so even though he wasn't billed, he took Lloyd's place as Kendo's tag partner and Lloyd retreated to the back of the hall.

In the match a point came where Kendo was tagged-in and Blondie was on the apron, from where he grabbed Tony and held him against the ropes as Kendo battered him. On the opposite side of the ring, Tony's partner stormed in to try and help him, but the referee saw him and went over to insist that he got out. While the referee was so preoccupied and had his back turned to Kendo, Lloyd came from the back of the hall and got onto the apron and bashed Tony on the head with his plaster cast.

At that precise moment, Tony's partner got out of the ring and the referee turned back to Kendo, but by this time Lloyd was off the apron and gone. Tony was so dazed from the hit on his head that Kendo easily got a fall on him. The audience was fizzing with fury, but the referee hadn't seen what they'd seen, so his ruling stood. In the next round we try to repeat the same skulduggery, but...

Once again, Blondie grabbed Tony and held him against the ropes so Kendo could batter him, and this time Lloyd got into the ring. As the referee turned to him to insist he got out, Tony broke free from Blondie and back-elbowed him off the apron, then he hit Kendo so hard that he knocked him out of the ring too, leaving him in the ring with a frightened-looking Lloyd. He grabbed at Lloyd to put him in a hold and as he did, he pulled the plaster cast off – it was a fake! Tony clobbered Lloyd with the cast and knocked him down and caught a glimpse of Kendo getting back onto the apron so he rushed over and swung the cast at him, hitting him on the head so hard that it shattered, scattering bits of plaster everywhere.

As a dazed Kendo tumbled off the apron, Tony turned back to Lloyd who had got to his feet, and he immediately slammed him into a fall, which the referee allowed – after all, Lloyd was on the bill! The audience was delighted – they'd loved seeing all the skulduggery reversed and turned against the villains, just as it looked like it would win them the match. Kendo & Blondie refused to get back into the ring, giving the excuse that they had to look after Lloyd and his broken arm, protesting that Tony had broken all the rules. For refusing to return, they were disqualified, and Tony and his partner were hailed as heroes.

Audiences never knew what to expect from any match with Kendo, and his tag partnership with Blondie, irritatingly introduced by Lloyd, was to run and run...

But then, out of the blue, Brian suffered a big setback. It was discovered that Rocco had a heart condition which was so serious that he had to immediately stop wrestling, his twenty-two year career suddenly cut short. Fortunately, Brian already had the Liverpool Lads as very popular headliners, and he later brought Haystacks back into the All Stars fold once more.

Brian had first promoted Haystacks back in the early seventies when I was his partner in All Stars Wrestling Promotions. Before Kendo ever faced Haystacks Brian had told me that he didn't want to work with Kendo because he was concerned that Kendo would either hurt him or he would 'out-villain' him. Consequently, we sometimes appeared on the same bill, but we didn't work together while either of us was with the Opposition.

One of those early shows involved several wrestlers going to do a show in Dublin where Haystacks was billed as the Irish Champion; over there he wrestled under his own name, Luke McMasters. Normally the whole team would take the boat from Holyhead, but on this particular morning we missed it. There was a general panic until Brian remembered that there was an RAF base nearby; we went there and tried to borrow one of their 'planes, but unsurprisingly, we were unsuccessful. They did, however, arrange for us to hire the 'plane that Vernon's Pools flew their pools winners around in.

There was only one problem – the 'plane was strictly a ten-seater (including the pilot), and there were nine of us, plus baggage. That might have been bad enough, but one of the nine was Haystacks, who at the time was bigger than two average men. We didn't think the pilot would take very kindly to this, so we hid him in a hanger until the first eight had boarded. When Haystacks sheepishly shuffled out from inside the hanger and climbed up the steps to the plane, the look on the pilot's face was priceless.

We managed to get to Dublin and back, but we never tried it by light aircraft again.

Haystacks later went to Joint Promotions and after a while Kendo did too, and it was with Joint's that a match was finally agreed.

That first match was in Huddersfield, and it was televised. Haystacks grabbed hold of Kendo by the head and ripped the mask across the top, pulling it down; the audience could clearly see the hexagram tattooed on Kendo's head, but the mask didn't come completely off. Kendo jumped up and hit Haystacks in the face, cutting his eye, and he continued to batter that area before the referee stopped the match. That led to a series of follow-up matches, which were very popular.

Kendo fought Haystacks from time to time up to Mark Rocco's departure, but in 1988, something drastic for wrestling took place – the end of television coverage. I believe that the Hurst Park Syndicate and Jarvis Astaire got wind of the decision well beforehand, and they decided to sell the business and salvage what they could. They'd made plenty of money and now they wanted to make a bit more by selling the carcass of the business they knew was doomed.

They asked both Brian Dixon and Max Crabtree if either of them wanted to buy it. Max was running the Hurst Park Syndicate side of things on TV and Brian was running his, so they were the ideal candidates to sell to.

Brian and Rocco attempted to raise the money but they didn't manage it. I found out later that they'd approached several people about raising the funds but they never spoke to me. This seemed strange because I was the only person they knew who had the money, but I think they steered clear of me because both Brian and

Rocco were afraid that I'd take control and marginalise them both; I wouldn't have – I didn't particularly want to promote shows.

However, Max did. I don't know what the final figure was but I believe it was quite high – many thousands. He ended up with what was left of Joint Promotions, but his coup turned out to be very unlucky because very soon afterwards the plug was pulled and wrestling disappeared from the nation's TV screens. I heard that Max had mortgaged his house to raise the money but had only ended up with a business with a very bleak outlook.

After the TV contract had gone, to keep people coming into the halls, Brian and Max agreed not to stand in each other's way, and they allowed their bigger names to work for the other promoter.

Max asked me, 'How do you get on with Haystacks?'

'We just about manage,' I said, 'But it's not brilliant. You know what he's like.' By this point, Haystacks's mobility wasn't so good.

Max said, 'I'd like to get you on some of our shows – the punters want to see it.'

I had my doubts, but I said, 'I'm sure we can work something out.'

Before the first show Max appeared in the dressing room and said, 'Kid, I'm keeping you apart. I've got him over in another room.'

'Okay,' I said, '...but why?'

'He's moaning about you. He says he's fed up with you spoiling his gimmick and turning him into a baby-face.'

I laughed and said, 'How do you turn a forty-stone monster into a baby face?'

Max said, 'I don't know, but it seems like you're doing it.'

'But that's the show we've got. The punters always regard me as a villain. You can't go against the flow of things.'

'No,' agreed Max, 'Of course you can't.'

Next thing I knew, Max had brought Haystacks in and we managed to organize a match; we made the best of it, but it was – frankly – bloody hard work.

Kendo continued having to make the best of Haystacks, because that's what people wanted – it was a crowd-puller, and they worked quite a lot round the halls during this time. Haystacks and Kendo didn't always do tag matches; it was felt that they were a big enough attraction in the ring as a solo match, but it wasn't as good as we'd hoped.

In fact, there was virtually no-one else left standing. Most of the other lads had either retired or were no longer interested. If you wanted a top-of-the-bill and something from the old school, the only choice left was Kendo versus Haystacks; it was attractive on paper, but not in reality.

Haystacks had become very heavy, very awkward, and very grumpy, and as a result he could be very difficult – he didn't want to get in the ring, and was obviously fed up with what he was doing. He didn't talk much, and if he said anything at all he'd just say, 'Let's go.' I think he was extremely uncomfortable physically.

The shows were, in all honesty, farcical. They consisted of Haystacks managing to get into the ring, Kendo doing his ritual with the salt, and then somehow trying to make an interesting match.

Ninety percent of the time it ended up with Kendo leaving the ring and Haystacks left there screaming for him to come back. Done that way, we would get another shot at it, but really, without trying to knock the business, it was weak. I really didn't think it did either the business – or the audience – any justice. It wasn't the way I would have liked to have seen Kendo's career wind down; it wasn't a good time.

At one of the matches I went into the dressing room and approached Haystacks and asked, 'What do you want to do?'

He wouldn't even speak to me. We went into the ring not knowing the result – I wasn't sure who was going to win or if one of us was going to drop dead in the ring.

In the event, Kendo did a few bits and pieces and Haystacks made a comeback by hitting Kendo on the top of the head, which he continued to do even when the referee told him to stop. Kendo went to the canvas and Haystacks told the referee to disqualify him. Kendo got back to his feet to find Haystacks leaving the ring.

'What's going on? What have you done?' I asked.

'He told me to disqualify him,' replied the ref.

'Why? You shouldn't have done that – it's a lousy decision! We're only a few minutes into the match!'

'What would you do?' pleaded the ref. 'I'm not going to argue with him – have you seen the size of him?'

'Of course I have,' I said, 'I've got to wrestle him!'

Eventually, Haystacks wasn't happy being out-villained by Kendo so he began to pull away from the arrangement, but he was to confront Kendo in the ring for what turned out to be an important TV show – more about this later.

Some time later, Kendo was in Morecambe for Max. Shirley Crabtree was in the dressing room, which made it a double top-of-the-bill – Shirley with one opponent and Kendo with another. It was holiday time, so it was a very good house.

Shirley was sitting in the dressing room – in carpet slippers, of all things. I hadn't seen him to talk to for years, not since the time we had a run when he became Big Daddy, around 1977.

We started talking and Shirley was very complimentary about Kendo. He said, 'I always tell everybody about Kendo and the Big Daddy thing, when I pulled the mask off on TV.' We reminisced about it all and Shirley proposed the idea that we could work together again.

I said, 'I don't see why not, Shirl.'

'But you know I can't do what I used to do? I'm a bit

limited now.'

'I appreciate that – we're all getting a bit older, aren't we?' I laughed. 'But I'm used to working the same concepts with Haystacks so I'm sure we could work something out.'

We left it at that. I'm not sure which one of us went on first that night, but we did our shows and said our goodbyes.

I believe that was the last time I ever saw Shirley Crabtree. It wasn't long after that I'd heard he'd finished wrestling altogether – I think it was on health grounds. Although I never saw him again, I didn't hear that he'd died whilst I was still wrestling.

Kendo struggled on with Haystacks for a few more matches before I decided that enough was enough and I left the business.

As we all know, Haystacks eventually contracted cancer and sadly died. I went to his funeral, which was only the second wrestling funeral I had ever attended. The other had been Count Bartelli's – two very iconic people in Kendo's wrestling career.

I was to find that I'd been right about the conclusion I'd come to after watching the tape that Mike Archer had given me – British wrestling was indeed finished; within eighteen months of seeing that tape it was gone. Max Crabtree's focus on Big Daddy hadn't helped, but the real death knell had been the appearance of the Americans. Their shows were so much better, the choreography was excellent, and in every respect it was far more entertaining.

The American wrestlers were Kendo Nagasaki-type characters, they were comic book heroes – larger than life. They were all on steroids, all had terrific bodies; the ones who didn't were outrageously ugly and big, Andre The Giant being one. Hulk Hogan was a six feet six steroid man in the California mould, and he looked terrific. As a result, they intrigued the younger generation

– they were the new up and coming fans. They'd seen the American comics – Flash Gordon, Captain America, Superman. The next thing you knew, films were being made about them and the fans could go and see them in the wrestling ring.

Sky TV picked up the American wrestling contract and it grew into a multi-million dollar business; I think they sold out Wembley Stadium in ten hours when they brought Wrestlemania over here.

We couldn't put on shows that were anything like that. We still had an ardent British fan base but it wasn't enough to make a living – it became a fringe/cult attraction, out of mainstream entertainment. Haystacks and Big Daddy really just became iconic; they couldn't do anything that resembled wrestling – in fact, they could barely get themselves into the ring. Those two belly-butting each other wasn't a patch on the American action, and neither were the Billy Howes and Les Kelletts of this world, however hard they were. If you were to put any of the British wrestlers in a suit they could have been anybody, but an American wrestler in a suit still looked like a super-hero. It really was no contest; it was like comparing British black-and-white television with an American blockbuster like Star Wars – the entertainment was on an entirely different level.

I foresaw all that from watching one tape.

As before, the time had come for Kendo to leave wrestling, at least until a new challenge came along...

Chapter 30

Attacks from Outside the Ring!

Kendo Nagasaki has always evoked strong feelings in his audiences. A poll was once taken at Belle Vue to find out who was the most hated and who was the most respected wrestler – Kendo came first in both categories. However, some reactions have been genuinely extreme, and have led to an astonishing range of attacks on Kendo – physical, legal, and even involving 'fake news'...

Very early on in Kendo's career he was wrestling at Liverpool Stadium and during the match he felt a dreadful stabbing pain in his back. He looked round but couldn't see anything, so he carried on wrestling.

In the dressing room I said to Billy Best, the promoter, 'What the hell's wrong with my back?'

He said, 'You've got something stuck in it.'

'Well, what is it?'

'It looks like the end of a pen, but it's pretty well-embedded.'

Somebody in the audience had stabbed me with a fountain pen, and the nib had broken off and lodged in my back. I had to go to the hospital and have it removed. It's left me with a strange sensation there ever since; I can still feel it – I know exactly where it was. I get an itchy feeling and I have to scratch it – I think it must have damaged the nerves. I'd obviously been injected with ink as well, because the whole area was black. The doctor had a right job cleaning it up, and then it needed stitching.

At another show in George's old stomping ground, Kettering, Northants, as Kendo came out of the ring during a match, a punter sitting in the front row jumped out of his seat and came running up in rather a ungainly fashion and tried to kick him. Anyone who knows anything about martial arts or self-defence knows that if you're going to throw your feet in the air and try to kick someone, you need to be very careful how you do it. You're only standing on one leg – the other is in the air. The wrestler, or the martial arts man, can easily grab the airborne leg and take the other from underneath you – which is exactly what happened. Kendo grabbed the leg the punter was trying to kick him with and swept the other one from underneath him, landing him on his backside on the floor. He then climbed back into the ring and thought nothing more about it.

The day after, we received a telephone call from the police and Kendo was summoned to answer for his actions, which were now being called an assault.

I, of course, said that Kendo didn't assault anyone; I said that the punter had fallen over, which – technically – had happened while he was trying to assault Kendo. I said I didn't know what they were talking about, or my accuser. The police insisted there was much more to it than that, and they were going to prosecute.

We were living in Wolverhampton at the time, and George and I had no choice but to traipse all the way back to Kettering for the evidence to be presented; I took my local solicitor, Mr. Smith-Dawson, with me.

Eventually the case came to court. The punter got into the dock and presented his case. He said he was sitting in his seat, and he never left that seat until Kendo Nagasaki dragged him out of it. He said that Kendo had leaned over the top rope, plucked him out of the seat, lifted him into the ring, and then flung him back out of it.

Have you ever heard anything so preposterous in your life? Smith-Dawson and myself were completely bemused by this outrageous statement. He rose and took up the challenge.

He said, 'We accept what you're saying, but have you any idea how far the first row of seats is from the ring?'

'No,' replied the punter.

'Well I can tell you,' replied Smith-Dawson, 'It's at least five feet. And have you any idea how tall the wrestling ring is?'

'No.'

'I can tell you that it's about nine feet off the floor. Now if you add those two distances together, unless my client has some sort of extendable arms, how does he manage to reach you in your seat, pluck you into a wrestling ring, and throw you back out?'

No answer was forthcoming.

Smith-Dawson said, 'I put it to you that what you've told the court is simply not physically possible. My client could not do that.'

The ensuing silence spoke hugely embarrassed volumes.

I can only assume that the punter had never told that story to the police – I honestly believe it came as a complete shock to both parties, the prosecution in particular. The magistrates looked aghast; they all went into a mumbling huddle, with the lawyers from each side. The whole ridiculous case was immediately withdrawn.

Another, more messy, story concerns a plumber called Noakes.

Max Crabtree told this tale in the book 'The Wrestling' by Simon Garfield, but he told it incorrectly. He said that Noakes was called to fix a leak in the bathroom at my house in Wolverhampton, and that when he got into the house he saw George talking to a person that he assumed was Kendo Nagasaki. That's an absolute fabrication – Noakes was never in the house.

At that time I was driving a Jensen Interceptor, an expensive and unusual car. It was parked in my front drive in Wolverhampton. I believe Noakes had driven past the house, seen the car, and then worked out how to get a photo of Kendo getting into it – without the mask, of course.

It was possible to see the front of the house from some distance away, across the intersection of two roads, so he could have parked with a camera without being noticed. I assume this is how Noakes ended up with a somewhat unclear photograph of a man getting into the Jensen, which he then used to try to expose me as Kendo Nagasaki.

He had a lot of copies made, including the words 'Kendo Nagasaki' and an arrow pointing to the (unmasked) man in the picture. When Kendo appeared at a match he would turn up at the hall and give them out.

This went on for some time, and to give Max Crabtree his credit, whenever he spotted Noakes at matches he'd grab him and take the photos from him and tell him to leave – sharpish.

However, that didn't stop him. His next ploy was to put an advert in the local newspaper whenever he found out that Kendo was appearing somewhere, announcing that Kendo Nagasaki was Peter Thornley, as well as giving my address. He actually had the cheek to send the bill to me! He'd somehow persuaded the newspapers that I'd put the advert in.

This happened on about three occasions. When we traced the ads back – which wasn't easy because he hadn't used his own name (he'd used mine) – we discovered it was Noakes. In 1974 or '75 it was much easier to get away with that sort of thing than it is now, but we finally managed to stop the ads.

Still not satisfied, he then persuaded his nephew,

who was about thirteen or fourteen, to go to a show at the Wolverhampton Civic and accuse Kendo of hitting him when he left the wrestling ring.

That fiction was reported to the police, who came round and spoke to George and myself. The police had statements from witnesses, the lad, and one from Noakes himself, who'd happened to be there and seen it all – surprise, surprise! They asked me what I had to say about it.

I told them, 'As far as I'm concerned it never happened. We (George and Kendo) left the ring and went back to the dressing room. Nothing happened.' We even had a number of fan statements to that effect.

However, the police charged me with assault. At that time, Kendo had very high profile, so it was bound to end up in the press.

Bill Abbey, Jack Dale's brother (Abbey being their real surname) spoke to us about it. He said an assault charge on a thirteen-year-old would be very messy, and if they made it stick, it would be bad for the job – we'd have all sorts of claims coming out of the woodwork. They took it so seriously that they decided to get behind me and they paid for a barrister to come from London to represent me in Wolverhampton.

The time came for the case. We were all sitting in the outer part of the court when the other side approached and said, 'I don't think this is going to go ahead.'

'Why not?' asked my barrister.

'The lad's mother's arrived with him to give evidence and she's told us that her son has been up all night, distressed and crying. He's told her that it's not true, that his uncle has made it all up and persuaded him to say it.'

Although the case would not go ahead, there was now a new case for perverting the course of justice and wasting police time. The difficulty with that was that the police would have to prosecute both Noakes and his nephew, which meant that we would have to return for the case and I would have to stand in the dock and be Kendo Nagasaki, and they would have to put this lad in the dock and grill him about what had happened; we didn't really want to do either.

Everyone concerned had a conversation – Bill Abbey, myself, George, and the barrister, and we decided that all the case would result in was bad publicity, so we let it go.

Another time, Kendo was leaving the ring at a show somewhere in the north. A woman was standing in the middle of the aisle blocking the way to the dressing room. She didn't seem anything to worry about – all she had with her was a handbag. I thought, even if she smacks me with it, it's not going to hurt.

She suddenly swung this bag from somewhere near the floor and cracked Kendo right across the head with it – stunned, he nearly went to his knees.

Kendo grabbed the bag from her and ripped it apart. Along with all the usual bits and pieces, half a brick fell to the floor. Kendo could hardly retaliate against such a vicious assault, so he just went to the dressing room with a sore face.

Another incident happened for Jack Atherton in Nelson. Kendo jumped out of the ring and there was an old guy blocking the way, on old-fashioned wooden crutches tucked under his arms. Once again, he didn't seem likely to cause Kendo any problems – an old man on crutches wasn't likely to be dangerous, was he? He could hardly stand up.

Kendo walked up to him and when the distance had closed up to about three or four feet, his right-hand crutch came off the floor, swung round and bashed him in the face, just above the eye.

By the time Kendo realized what was happening, the crutches were back under the old guy. Kendo wasn't sure what to do; ramming the crutch up his arse would have been one choice, but that didn't happen. He continued back to the dressing room before a trip to the hospital for three stitches.

Then there was the incident involving a partially blind man who used to go to a lot of shows locally and to televised ones, where he used to perform a little at the side of the ring. The joke going round the wrestling business was that he used to bang the canvas with his white stick and shout, 'I saw that, referee!'

On this particular day he was lurking around the ring and Kendo hadn't noticed he was there. Suddenly he felt a stabbing sensation in his backside. Kendo saw the stick and grabbed it, brought it up to head height and snapped it in half. It was only then that he noticed it was a white stick. Realising that was a bit of a shock – he could hardly give the useless bits back to the blind man, so Kendo chucked them onto the floor.

On live television, Kent Walton said, 'Kendo Nagasaki has just snapped a blind man's cane!' He left out the fact that Kendo had just been jabbed with it...

A few days later we were at the DeMontfort Hall in Leicester. When we walked into the foyer a woman came up to George and gave him a right old smack round the face and shouted, 'That'll teach you to break a blind man's stick!' George was aghast! He hadn't done it, but the woman had clearly felt he was fair game, and she clearly didn't want to have a go at Kendo.

During the 1980s, the so-called gutter press began attacking high-profile people, particularly celebrated gays, many of whom George and I knew, and Kendo was a prime target. After George's own vile portrayal in the press, it was only a matter of time before they came after Kendo.

A spectacularly slanderous article about Kendo appeared in the News of the World. In the mid-1980s many high-profile people were being targeted by tabloids in precisely this way – the article about Kendo was almost a carbon-copy of fictitious allegations made against Elton

John by The Sun newspaper, the story of which was eloquently de-bunked by Washington Post writer Glenn Frankel in his October 1989 article. Elton sued The Sun seventeen times and ended up with the (then) biggest ever libel settlement in Britain of one million pounds sterling.

The article about Kendo purported to be the story of a gay man who claimed to have had a sexual relationship with Kendo, during which he had been sadistically beaten with a stick. He said he was a wrestler himself, and he wanted to get his own back on Kendo by giving him a good thrashing in the ring. Ironically, we knew this 26-year-old man, as he had asked Kendo to train him, but he turned out to be un-coordinated and completely lacking in the required abilities, but, just like the discredited sources of The Sun's articles, he too was susceptible to being bought by 'cheque-book journalism'.

At that time the newspapers could find any number of unscrupulous people who would say practically anything when money was waved under their noses, and because it was so expensive to issue libel proceedings, the newspapers felt able to print any tissue of lies they could concoct. Most of the people targeted – and most tabloid readers – regarded the stories as salacious low-brow tittle-tattle, but it was nonetheless an assault in print which they couldn't get away with now.

When the article appeared I was training at a local gym and it gave all the regulars a good laugh, but I was disappointed that the man behind the article would stoop so low – a couple of weeks later we heard that he'd taken to jumping onto car bonnets so he could claim compensation from the hapless drivers – I think this spoke volumes about the credibility of his story.

Within two weeks of the News of the World article, another appeared which attacked me more personally. It said that my wife, Yvette, was disabled and I kept her locked in just one room and wouldn't let her out. Once again, I was portrayed as a cruel tyrant when nothing could have been further from the truth, and Yvette was deeply hurt when the article glibly described her as having to wear 'cripple shoes'. She had arthritis and did have to wear orthopaedic footwear, but there was no justification for such a cruelly harsh portrayal of such an innocent, kind, and benevolent person.

Another spectacular example of audience interference – and its consequences – took place at Walthamstow during Kendo's second phase, after Lloyd Ryan had taken over as manager.

Kendo was in a tag match, partnered with Blondie Barrett. We were well into the match and Kendo suddenly realized that someone had jumped on his back. At first, thought nothing of it, but he soon realized it couldn't have been one of the other wrestlers – Blondie was behind him and he wouldn't jump on Kendo, another wrestler was in front and the fourth member was on the apron, so it had to be a punter.

Kendo managed to shake him off. He was around forty years of age, not particularly well-built and, in Kendo's opinion, not someone to be concerned about. So he grabbed him and chucked him out of the ring, as efficiently as he could. We continued wrestling.

That however wasn't the end of it. I noticed a police presence appearing in the hall just as Blondie leaned over and said, 'What are they doing here?'

At the back of the hall, almost from one side to the other, was a line of policemen. There must have been fifteen or twenty of them.

It turns out that about an hour earlier there had been a football match in Walthamstow, and they'd had a riot. The fans had attacked each other and about fifty or sixty policemen had been drafted in to separate them all. When they got a phone-call from the venue to say that someone had been assaulted, they thought that the football fans had managed to get into the wrestling hall and had started assaulting people, so they arrived in force.

It was nothing like that. The punter who had invaded the ring had accused Kendo of assaulting him, but he hadn't called the police – someone else had. Once the police arrived they decided they were going to arrest me.

Three of them jumped into the ring and said, 'We're going to arrest you.'

I said, 'No you're not.'

They said, 'Yes we are.'

'No – you're not,' I repeated.

Surprisingly enough, they got out of the ring and went to the back of the hall; I watched them carefully. They all huddled together and then came back and one said, 'Yes – we are.' You couldn't make this up.

By now, I was thinking to myself, 'They probably are...' There was no way Kendo was going to fight the police so the match was stopped. I returned to the dressing room; the police accompanied me but they didn't touch me.

In the dressing room one of the coppers said, 'You've been accused of assaulting one of the audience.'

'I didn't assault him,' I said. 'He jumped into the ring and got on my back. What was I supposed to do?'

One of them replied, 'Well that's not what we've heard. It's alleged that you knocked him about and then chucked him out. You'll have to come to the police station. He's coming as well, and we'll take statements.'

'Well I'm not going like this,' I said, 'I'm all sweaty. I'm going to have a shower and put my street clothes on.'

'If you're going to have a shower we'll have to come with you and stand by the cubicle,' said a policeman.

'You can do what you like – get in with me, if you want.'

I had my shower and got changed and went to the police station with Lawrence (my PA), and Blondie went with us as well. We were all sitting on a bench in the lobby while the police were in another room talking with my accuser.

As we were sitting there a policeman came through and spoke to the desk sergeant. Once he'd left, the sergeant glanced over to us and said, 'Do you lads want a cup of tea?'

A little surprised at this light tone I replied, 'I wouldn't mind.'

'I don't think you're going to be here much longer,' he said.

'Why – what's happening?'

'That bloody fool in there has just told my lads that Jesus told him to get into the ring and drag you off the other wrestler. Like I said, it won't last much longer. We'll get him out of the way, but there's quite a crowd outside, so we'll have to get rid of them, and then it'll be all over for you lads – you can go home.'

We had our tea and about an hour later we went home, no charges brought.

In recent years the internet has proven to be the perfect platform for cheap-shots and unsubstantiated slanders. In 2010, a particularly unpleasant neighbour decided to trespass on my land, and when I started legal proceedings to restrain him, his family began posting insults and falsehoods on Facebook and their own ranting conspiracy-theory website. There was a persistent campaign to link me with Jimmy Savile and his vile misdemeanours, but in fact I never met him. The insults and slanders continue, but no-one takes it seriously – the author's petty malice only contributes to the low tone of so much of the internet these days.

In February 2017, the Daily Star Sunday newspaper inadvertently but obligingly lifted the veil on something that has always puzzled me – the drugs raid that had been carried out on Gladstone Street during the 1980s.

Firstly, two journalists turned up at my home and

asked to see me, but Lawrence fended them off and told them to phone us with their questions. They did, and were persuaded to put their allegations in an email, and they turned out to be astonishing. They claimed that an un-named former under-cover narcotics detective had told them that during the 1980s he'd been part of a team that had investigated Kendo for supplying cocaine to Princess Margaret!

They phoned back a couple more times asking for a comment, but we never gave one, so they went ahead and printed the article but without mentioning Kendo or my name. In the article, the 'former under-cover narcotics detective' explained how Scotland Yard investigated their intelligence before passing it into the 'corridors of power'; the raid on Gladstone Street must have been part of that process, and the Star's 'mole' may have been on the team. They apparently believed there was intelligence linking 'the sportsman and the royal black sheep', and he described how they would have been 'amused at the prospect of arresting a royal as her dealer turned up.' Now – as then – the story was front page news.

Thinking about it, when I looked at all the people we knew and how they connected with each other, I can see how the connection could be made...

All these occasions added to my first-hand experience of how easy it is to sensationalise alleged 'evil' and ignore any good works. I'll concede that some of the press Kendo has had was entirely positive, such as the 'healing' write-ups in Psychic News and Radio Times, but they were dwarfed in number and viciousness by the slanders attributed to the villainous wrestling presence. Kendo always was an easy target, but his shoulders were always broad enough to shrug off sticks and stones, as well as the rantings of the petty and vicious.

The powerful reactions that Kendo has always caused in audiences, individuals, commentators, and even journalists has always shown that he's extra-ordinary, challenging, and thought-provoking. Given his high profile, all the attacks were probably to be expected in one way or another, and, as George often said, quoting Oscar Wilde, 'There is only one thing in life worse than being talked about, and that is not being talked about.'

31 Gladstone Street, London SE1. There was another floor on top at the back which was George's domain, and the studio (below) was under the garage. This view is from the drum booth.

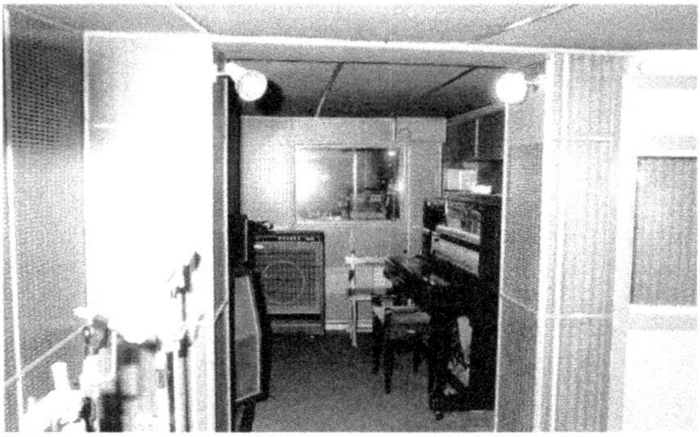

We're in the music business now! Two dynamic executives out on the town...

Below, the cover of the single that our first band released; even for the 80s it was a bit much, so perhaps we shouldn't have been surprised when their recording contract wasn't renewed.

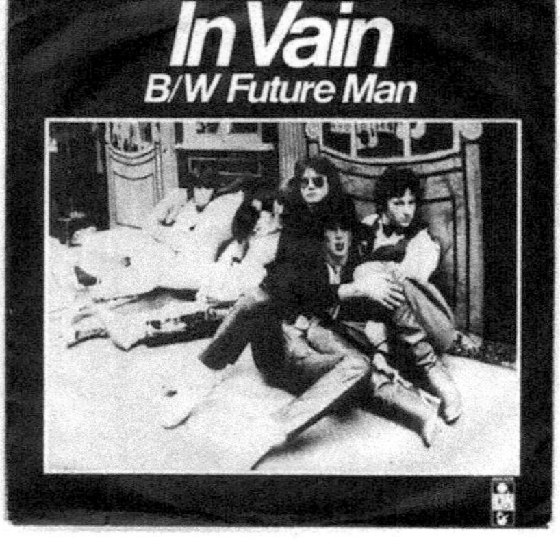

Two promotional shots of the Cuddly Toys, taken at Gladstone Street. The shot below was taken in the garage with paper screens surrounding the group. Paul, the bassist, is in a bad mood because he'd tried to cut his own hair the night before, and had to be almost scalped to make him presentable - the band tortured him all day.

In the studio... Above, I'm discussing 'the biz' with producer Steve James, son of 'Carry On' actor Sid James. Below, Cuddly Toys guitarist Terry Noakes is setting up to record another blistering solo. In the background is the Ampex 2" 16-track recorder.

Above, George's winning smile, snapped before a Cuddly Toys gig (minus handcuffs!)

As work in our studio wound down George and I toured with the Toys. Roy (below) worked in other studios and toured with the acts he recorded.

Even during the music business years the occasional wrestling engagement cropped-up. The unmasked Kendo appeared like this back-stage.

In the background, just visible wearing the hat is the legendary Jack Atherton.

Above, Yvette - as the 80s progressed, we became ever-closer.
Below, George and me as we signed Laura to Record Shack records.

Right, a crew for a wrestling trip to Israel. Left to right at the back are Dave Taylor, Steve Regal, Psycho Stevens, myself and Lawrence are top right. Klondyke Kate's in the middle, Mitzi Mueller and Brian Dixon flank George. Below is a promo shot for the re-launch show at the Hippodrome, with a very sober-looking George - that look didn't last!

As the music business wound-down and we returned to wrestling, this promotional shot was taken at the Clapham house.

After the 'Comeback', the late-80s saw the arrival the tag team of Kendo Nagasaki and 'Blondie' Barratt, the Rock 'n' Roll Express.

As George became less able to be Kendo's 'Manager',
Lloyd Ryan and Lawrence took charge of things on the road.
Below, George on our trip to New York.

'Masters of the Canvas' central characters, Paul Yates, Kendo, and Sir Peter Blake.

The film crew with Paul and Kendo in my Excalibur, outside Moor Court Hall.

A collage created by the pupils of Cheadle High School and residents of Moorcare was hung with Sir Peter Blake's work at the Tate Gallery, Liverpool. Pupils and residents are pictured with Sir Peter and Kendo.

Kendo horse-riding around Moor Court for Masters of the Canvas.

Kendo, Lloyd, and Lawrence being filmed arriving at Sir Peter Blake's studio.

The master of his canvas at work...

Kendo and a masked Sir Peter in the ring as shots are set up.

Here we're holding the 'Masters' director, Mary Dickinson, aloft.

Above, Trades Hotel, which I bought in 2004. It's capably managed by Neil Cropper, who went on to manage Kaos Bar too.

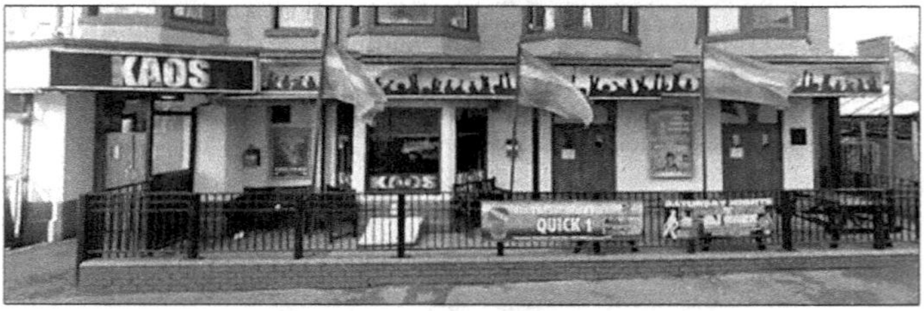

Kaos was bought at the end of 2005 to complement the hotel. It opened in time for Blackpool Pride 2007 under the name Trades Bar, but research of the club market suggested it would be more popular re-branded as Kaos Bar. It's gone on to become the central attraction at Pride events, hosting a spectacular and very popular street party to this day.

Above right, an LDN Wrestling poster for the ladder match at Hanley in September 2008, which was Kendo's penultimate match. Above left, Atlantis looking fearsome!

Below a picture of the Sword of Excellence, which the ongoing feud revolved around, shot outside Moor Court Hall in 2008.

The Nagasaki Retreat, photographed from the south lawn, and a view from the terrace across the lawn itself and the pastures can be seen beyond. The gazebo in the picture below is set up for a Nagasaki Event ceremony in front of the enormous 'Tree of Souls', a huge and spirital Atlas Cedar tree.

One of the Nagasaki Retreat's hidden gems - a Zen garden in the shape of the bay of Kamakura, the city from which Zen for the people began and spread world-wide.

Kendo has a traditional Japanese tea room nestled among the trees close to the Zen garden. Here he's meditating before performing the tea ceremony.

In October 2017 the Lee Rigby House opened on the Moor Court estate, a very proud day for us all. Here, Lyn and Ian receive a donation cheque from the Mayor of Rochdale, amidst lots of press and TV coverage.

Below, Lyn and Ian pictured with Kendo, as the Lee Rigby Foundation and the Kendo Nagasaki Foundation joining forces attracts yet more press coverage.

Chapter 31

Granada TV's Double-Cross when a Stunt Goes Wrong

As a major regional television company, Granada Television provided a wide range of programmes, from news to soap operas to investigative documentaries, and their roster always included interview shows and live debate programmes with an audience of members of the public. One such programme was called Upfront, which was shown in the early evening once a week, hosted by charismatic presenter Tony Wilson.

For one episode in October 1990 they decided to discuss whether or not professional wrestling was 'real', and they invited pro wrestlers Mick McManus, Pat Roach, Blondie Barrett, Marty Jones, and Kendo Nagasaki for the debate.

We sat on podiums with Blondie and Kendo on one side, Marty, Mick, and Pat on another, and a third podium in the middle for the presenters. There were gym mats on the floor in front of us, and a small barrier had been erected between the mats and the audience of about two hundred.

Unbeknown to the professional wrestlers, Granada had arranged for a number of amateur wrestlers to sit in the audience, and for them to challenge the professionals on camera. They'd also arranged something that wasn't disclosed publicly or to their wider staff, which was that some kind of on-screen falling-out would occur between Kendo Nagasaki and Marty Jones. Brian Dixon had been in the loop, and he communicated to us what Granada wanted, along with the requirement that it should remain secret.

We were told that we would receive some sort of cue when they wanted things to flare up – the timing had to be right so that the program didn't finish with two of the wrestlers missing, because following the fallout, Kendo was supposed to leave the stage (and in fact the studio) in disgust just as the program ended.

The debate started, and the amateur wrestlers chimed-in straight away to challenge the professionals. It appeared that Granada had placed mats on the floor to act as an opportunity for the amateurs to start rolling around with the professionals so they could make fools of us, but we weren't that stupid – we would never have let that happen.

Eventually, an argument developed whereby Marty Jones said that Kendo Nagasaki was a disgrace to the wrestling business. Blondie defended Kendo, who sat there impassive but threatening, as usual. Pat Roach was a gentlemanly voice of reason, encouraging us all to be professional about each other and calm down.

The programme proceeded with appropriate strong opinions and arguments from both sides, and although no-one had been told what the cue for the scuffle would be, it finally came from Tony Wilson. He said, 'You've heard the debate. Marty, you've levelled some accusations at Kendo and Blondie, and they've come back with their positions – you've got thirty seconds left to tell us exactly what you think...'

There it was – the cue.

Marty fired up again with his accusations and criticisms, and Kendo jumped out of his seat and set off across the mats toward him, and he got up too. Tony Wilson stood up and tried to step between us, but Kendo shoved him and he flew backwards out of the way. Marty and Kendo linked up and had something of a professional tussle on the mats – nothing out of control, and nothing that would incite the amateur wrestlers to join in.

We pushed and pulled briefly and Marty managed to get hold of Kendo's mask and pull it off, after which Kendo stormed off the set with Blondie close behind.

Before the show a stage-hand from Granada had shown me a gangway from the studio floor to the dressing room area which he'd said Kendo should use, so he did, and he and Blondie went to the dressing room and slammed the door, making it clear that we were livid about the whole thing.

Job done! Upfront had exactly what they'd wanted.

After a few minutes Marty Jones came into the dressing room and said, 'What happened with that bird you've knocked over?' (back then, 'bird' was a slang term for a girl or woman.)

'What do you mean?' I asked, 'What bird?'

'They've had to get an ambulance – she's out cold on the floor and they're saying you knocked her flying.'

'I never knocked anybody flying,' I insisted.

'Well, that's what they're saying,' replied Marty.

'It's a load of bollocks. I didn't knock anyone over – there was no-one between the stage and here.'

The discussion pretty much ended there and Blondie and I got changed and left.

On the way home I phoned Brian; he told me that Tony Wilson thought the show was fantastic – the fact that he'd been knocked down gave him a bit of glory and would be great for ratings. I asked him about what Marty had said regarding a woman who'd been knocked over, and his reply was unsurprising – nothing fazed Brian! He said, 'Oh, yes, I saw some ambulance men there, but don't worry about that – it'll just go away.'

Within two days, the police in Manchester contacted me saying they wanted to speak to me about what had happened on the Upfront set; they wanted to interview me. I had no choice but to go, and as soon as I arrived they arrested me for assault and battery!

'What the hell are you on about,' I demanded, 'What assault and battery?'

The arresting officer said, 'The victim claims that you ran off the stage, called her a fucking bitch, grabbed her by her breasts, lifted her in the air, and threw her against a wall.'

'Rubbish!' I protested. 'Absolute rubbish. Who has said that?'

'A woman called Lois Richardson who is the head of make-up for Granada Television.'

'I never touched anyone as I left the stage and I certainly never assaulted anyone in the way you've said,' I countered.

'OK – tell us what went on?'

I said, 'Beyond what had been arranged, nothing else went on. Marty and Kendo had a falling-out and Kendo left the set via the gangway which he was told to use.'

'That's not what we've heard. We're going to charge you.'

Sure enough, I ended up with a charge of assault and battery and had to find legal representation.

Fortunately for me, as I've mentioned earlier, I'd met a lady called Bertha Barr whose husband was one of the Fathers in the print union and a Freemason. I'd previously been invited to a couple of their gatherings, and I'd also been invited to become a freemason, but I'd declined. I called Bertha's husband and told him the predicament I found myself in. He said he knew someone who could put me in touch with solicitor John Carden, who represented

The Jockey Club, and he also ran a stud in Manchester where he bred horses. He only dealt with a handful of celebrity clients and had previously defended Ken Dodd and Lester Piggott, so Kendo Nagasaki fitted his client profile perfectly.

John Carden then called me. After a brief discussion he said, 'Come over and see me.' I went and explained the charge against me.

He said, 'What have you said to them?'

I said, 'Nothing. Basically, I told them I didn't do it.'

'You haven't said anything else to them?'

'No.'

'Okay, tell me exactly what happened.'

I ran through it all for him: Brian Dixon had spoken to myself and Marty Jones some weeks before the show and told us that Granada wanted us to do this stunt, and he'd said that it was all stage-managed. For Marty and I to do what we were asked we didn't need mats, so when we saw them on the night it was a surprise, but it seems they'd put them out for us to fight the amateur wrestlers.

I told him that if he looked at the footage of the show he'd see that Blondie Barrett and Marty Jones were wired up with mobile microphones. Kendo had no microphone because he doesn't speak, and Mick and Pat had wired microphones because they weren't going to get up. All this meant that the planned scuffle could be done without cables getting in the way.

If you watch the footage and slow it down, Pat Roach did actually jump up to calm things down, but when he left his seat he dragged the microphone cable with him.

I also explained to John Carden that when I went in I was shown exactly where Kendo could make his exit to run out, and I naturally thought that the gangway would be kept clear.

'So Granada wanted you to do this?' John asked.

'Yes. They told Brian Dixon what they wanted and asked him to arrange it with us.'

Granada were explicit in their denials over any such arrangements. The Daily Express of Saturday 6th October 1990 described the incident and wrote that UpFront's executive producer, Charles Tremayne, had said to them, 'This is the last thing we wanted or expected to happen.'

John did his homework and prepared for the hearing, which took place at Manchester Magistrates Court. He told me that it was serious enough to possibly end up in front of a jury at the Crown Court, but he said that if we defended it vigorously at the Magistrates court, we had a good chance of nipping the case in the bud before it came to that. He seemed pretty confident of a good outcome.

On the day of the criminal case there were lots of press at the court so Kendo had to arrive in the mask. As we walked up the steps to the court I realised that Ms. Richardson was half-way up them, supported by some kind of walking aid and a man at her side. He saw me and alerted her to my presence, at which point she grabbed hold of the man and screamed, 'Daddy! Daddy! Daddy!' It crossed my mind that Ms. Richardson must have been a frustrated actress...

In fact, her portrayal of terror in my presence was so convincing that the Crown Prosecution Service gave her a private room, instead of having her wait in the corridor outside the court, as plaintiffs and defendants normally did.

When she came into the courtroom, she was supported on either side, clearly unable to walk without a lot of help, and her makeup was stunning – she'd applied all her professional skills to making herself look haggard and very ill – when I saw her I thought I'd get ten years.

When we got into the courtroom, the Crown Prosecution Service lawyer invited Ms. Richardson to the stand and asked her to tell the court what had happened – she made the episode sound dreadful. Her position was that I made a bee-line for her and was determined to attack her. John Carden then cross-examined her – brilliantly.

'Tell me, what do you do at Granada?' he asked her.

'I'm a make-up artist.'

'What do you actually do on the set? Why were you there at that time? I thought make-up took place off the set, in another room – is that not the case?'

'Oh, no,' she said, 'I have to be there so I can touch-up people's makeup – they tend to sweat under the lights.'

'How do you do that?'

'I've got a case with all my things in,' she replied.

'Where was the case?'

'Just behind me.'

'Just behind you?'

'Yes.'

Then John changed tack. 'My client is quite a big fellow, isn't he?'

'Yes.'

John said, 'Can I ask you something? If my client came running towards you, what would you do?'

'I'd try to get out of the way.'

'But you can't, because there's a case behind you.'

'Well, it wasn't there.'

'But you've just told me it was,' replied John.

After a short silence, John continued. 'Can I suggest to you that my client didn't pick you up by your breasts and throw you into the air? I agree that you were startled – my client was running toward you, rushing off the set – but I put it to you that you fell over your own case.'

'No,' she said, 'That wasn't what happened.'

John Carden also challenged her assertion that I chose not to use a clear exit from the studio floor but instead chose to attack her specifically, but she had no answer.

'No more questions,' said John. Ms. Richardson stepped down.

He then put me on the stand. I clearly explained how it had all been arranged, how we'd been told exactly what Granada had wanted, and when he had finished, I was cross-examined by the Crown Prosecution lawyer. In my initial statement to the police, I said I didn't knock Ms. Richardson over, but John Carden had advised that I shouldn't call her a liar but accept that I might have done, and make that my position. The lawyer tried to highlight this as me changing my story, so-to-speak, but I rebutted this and many other assertions of wrongdoing.

Then a spokesperson for Granada's took the stand; he claimed that they hadn't arranged any of it – he said they'd had no idea there was going to be any kind of confrontation or anyone rushing off the set.

'What were the mats for?' asked John. 'Why were they there if Granada didn't expect someone to fight?'

'We thought the amateurs were going to wrestle the professionals,' replied the Granada spokesman.

'So you did want a fight?' John asked. 'You clearly wanted someone to fight on that set, whether it was my client and Marty Jones, or the amateurs and the professionals – is that not so?'

No answer came so John continued: 'Let's say you got a fight between the amateurs and the professionals, what would you expect to happen? Didn't you think that it might get out of hand?'

Silence.

'Didn't it occur to you that if that happened, someone might run off the set? Did you take any precautions? Did you organise any safety measures? Did you tell Lois Richardson and any other staff that you were going to organise a fight?'

Again, no answer.

In fact, no-one from Granada had any answers for any of John's questions – from that point on their case fell apart. The Crown Prosecution lawyer realised that John Carden had whipped the rug away from under them and they asked if they could have an adjournment – it had suddenly become glaringly obvious that Ms. Richardson and one executive from Granada was insufficient and they desperately needed more witnesses. However, the magistrates told them that they'd had more than enough time to prepare their case and it should continue, and it ended up being dismissed.

The case went away, but Lois Richardson didn't – she had three years off work and took a further five years to think about how to put together a claim for damages, and eight years after the original incident, she put together another case. In collaboration with her union they decided to sue Kendo Nagasaki and Granada TV for her injuries and loss of earnings – they sought damages of five hundred thousand pounds.

As the criminal case had been dismissed, this one would be heard in civil court – here we go again, back on the litigation merry-go-round.

It was a huge endeavour. We had to gather all the evidence together once more, Marty Jones, Pat Roach, Blondie, and Brian Dixon all went to court to give evidence.

By this time I'd lost John Carden. He was a man of around fifty and had decided to enter a seniors horse race, during which, unfortunately for him, he fell from his horse and broke his neck. He ended up a paraplegic, confined to a wheelchair, so I had to find a new lawyer.

I managed to organise a new legal team and eventually it went to court, with myself and Granada as co-defendants. My barrister's opinion was that even if they didn't find Kendo entirely responsible for Ms. Richardson's losses, there was a possibility that he could be found partially responsible. He recommended that Kendo and Granada TV come to some joint arrangement to settle, and not to let it go to trial.

My barrister said, 'It's likely that the court will find both you and Granada jointly liable for the damages.'

'Well, what do you think my proportion would be?' I asked.

'It could be fifty percent, it could be as low as thirty-three percent; I think a reasonable approach would be for the co-defendants – yourself and Granada – to make an offer to settle of three hundred thousand pounds, of which you should contribute one hundred thousand pounds, plus a proportion of her costs.'

I was shocked. I actually laughed at that figure. 'How much???'

'Yes,' he said, 'If it goes badly, you might be looking at two or three hundred thousand.'

I had no choice. My barrister was experienced and had seen all manner of cases come and go and he clearly knew what the best and worse case scenarios could look like. What else could I do but bite the bullet, and agree?

My barrister then spoke to Granada's lawyers, who liaised with the company executives, and they rejected any offer to settle – they said they'd rather go to trial.

Our side got our case together, and this time, Ms. Richardson had a stronger case. It emerged in court that when Granada had been arranging the stunt, a man in the office had overheard a conversation between the producer of the program and Brian Dixon, making the arrangements for the scuffle. He'd left Granada by this time but had been co-opted to support Ms. Richardson's case.

That was the last thing Granada expected – or wanted – to hear.

They countered where they could, but not very effectively. The question over why the wrestlers who would scuffle or leave the set were given wireless microphones arose again, and Granada called their sound man to explain. He said that he'd miked-up the wrestlers in the way he did because '...they'd run out of hard-wired microphones...', but the judge was sceptical – his daughter worked for Granada, so he knew a little about TV. He'd have understood that a media company as big as Granada would always have plenty of microphones in reserve, wired and wireless, and once a judge has little doubts like that, the credibility of the whole case is called into question.

Brian Dixon gave evidence of the way Granada arranged the scuffle with him, including a devastating allegation – he said that part of the 'package' was for the host of the show, Tony Wilson, to be pushed over. Brian said that when he'd explained it to me, I'd asked him, 'Will he be ok? Can he take a bump?', and he assured me that it would be fine, because Tony had done it before, as part of charity wrestling matches.

When it came to be Tony Wilson's turn to give evidence, he was asked about getting pushed over – he said he hadn't been told it would happen. The judge himself asked him whether arrangements could be made that the host wouldn't know about because it could be more spontaneous and amusing that way, and he said, 'Yes – that sort of thing could happen.'

Of course, I was required to give evidence and answer questions. I made the point that over the previous 34 years I'd left hundreds of wrestling rings and safely made it back to the dressing room without ever knocking anyone over, let alone attacking anyone, even when surrounded by extremely hostile audiences, many of whom wanted to attack Kendo! Therefore Ms. Richardson's contention that I attacked her completely contradicted all those years of stage exits without incident.

Granada's barrister picked up once again on the difference between my initial statement to the police and my later conceding that I may have inadvertently knocked Ms. Richardson over. He worked very hard at trying to portray me as the kind of person who would say whatever suited the circumstances – their barrister tried again and again, until the judge intervened and told him that he was satisfied with my answers, and counsel for Granada should be too.

During my time on the witness stand I was able to do something that my lawyer had advised me would be a very positive move. I said, 'Can I please take this opportunity to apologise to Miss Richardson, if I did hurt her or cause her any distress?' I was intrigued to see that as we were on the way into court the following day, Ms. Richardson held my gaze for a moment longer than before and she had a suggestion of a smile – I think by then she'd decided (or had been advised) that in her pursuit of compensation I was less of a viable adversary, and Granada now looked the most promising target – we were approaching being on the same side.

Once everything had been presented by all the parties, the Judge told the court that he wouldn't be able to deliver a verdict for some time, as he had a murder trial to deal with; we had to wait what seemed like an endless three months before it came.

Finally, we returned to court to hear the verdict of judge Brian Walsh QC; we were cautiously optimistic... Immediately before the trial the judge had offered to recuse himself because his daughter worked for Granada, so he was required to inform us of that fact and if we didn't want him to preside over the case, he would appoint another judge. My barrister asked me what I thought.

I said, 'Isn't he obviously going to swing toward Granada? What do you think?'

'I don't think it will work like that,' he replied. 'He's more likely to swing toward you so as he doesn't look biased. I think he's the right man for the job. And to be honest he's known to be very fair.'

Once again, my barrister was right – the opening line of his summary was, 'There's no business like show business...' I was astounded!

He found absolutely for Kendo. His summary was extremely detailed and encompassed every aspect of the evidence given, including the claim about Granada running out of microphones – he mentioned that he was incredulous at that assertion. He said, 'I prefer Mr.

Thornley's explanation of what went on. It's obvious to me that Granada not only knew what was going to happen, but they also made arrangements for it to happen. It's clear to me that Granada didn't exercise their duty of care towards Mr. Thornley or their employee, Ms. Richardson. I find for Mr. Thornley and against Granada.'

He granted me all my costs, and Lois Richardson was awarded £327,000 in damages for loss of earnings and loss of career. She was also awarded all her costs. I was told the whole thing cost £750,000.

I believe that one of the main ways that Granada undermined their own case was by using footage of the scuffle to advertise future programmes, suggesting that this was the kind of action you could see on Upfront. We'd found that footage and had it shown in court, which they found more than a little embarrassing – it suggested that they'd counted on having such footage to use for promotional purposes, so it was more likely to have been arranged.

At the end of the case, in the foyer of the court, in front of my lawyer and myself Lois Richardson actually said, 'Now we can write the book.' Those were her very words.

I said to her, 'Write the book? Don't you find the whole thing a bit weird? I'm sure somebody at Granada must have known about it.'

She said, 'Oh well, we all knew something was going to happen – we were talking about it beforehand in the make-up room.'

Throughout the trial she had denied all knowledge.

After Ms. Richardson had left, my lawyer said to me, 'Do you know what she's just done? By admitting that she knew all along that something was going to happen yet denying any such knowledge, during the trial she perjured herself.'

I was later told that Ms. Richardson's boyfriend had been an executive in Granada's Coronation Street experience, so a cynic might assume that he would have known how to advise her on her case, but in any event, we decided that following-up on this revelation wasn't our fight!

But to my horror, the case still wouldn't go away – about a week later, Granada decided they were going to appeal the verdict. It would be heard in the High Court in London – the nightmare went on and on!

Whilst I'd won my costs back in the verdict (which amounted to ninety thousand pounds), they hadn't yet been paid, and they wouldn't be until the appeal was resolved, and now my lawyers wanted me to find another ten thousand pounds up-front for the appeal.

That hearing had been scheduled three months ahead, so I had another drawn-out period of sheer hell, thinking, 'What's going to happen next?'

However, two days before the hearing, Granada capitulated. I received a cheque for all my costs and Ms. Richardson obviously received her settlement.

Lois Richardson's initial claim put me through a lot of stress, which was repeated when she sued civilly for damages, and I really could have done without the additional three months of worry caused by Granada's decision to appeal the verdict. It was a terrible time.

I genuinely don't remember Ms. Richardson being there or knocking her over, but the judge of the second case accepted that I might have done, and he believed Ms. Richardson – he never asserted that she was lying, that she didn't somehow fall on the set, and that she hadn't suffered a back injury, which was ultimately why he awarded her the damages. The truth is in there somewhere, but I'm certain that I was blameless, and being dragged through the courts for so long was a truly harrowing experience.

I would advise anyone who has anything to do with television – get it in writing. That was my mistake – there was no documentation anywhere which acknowledged that I was going to do that stunt, which would have demonstrated Granada's knowledge of and responsibility for the scuffle, as well as their need to exercise a proper duty of care for everyone concerned.

I believe that corporate structure played a part in how Granada defended themselves. The programme-makers were prepared to take risks in order to make sensational viewing, whereas senior management wanted success without risks. When the stunt went wrong, the programme-makers panicked about repercussions from above and denied responsibility, and senior management denied any knowledge, but both levels of the corporation had the perfect scape-goat – the villainous wrestler. Kendo is the kind of character to whom it's easy to attach allegations of wrong-doing, but that's just the public perception of the wrestler – the reputation of the character gets in the way of the truth about me, which is that I am an entertainer, not a violent criminal.

It was disappointing that the police couldn't see that before they charged me, and that Granada latched onto Kendo's reputation to hang responsibility for Ms. Richardson's damages on me. The fact that I was able to defend myself in court with the required clarity and eloquence must have come as an unpleasant surprise to them, particularly when the Crown case was dismissed and Granada were found wholly liable for the damages and costs. They really should have had the courage to make an early offer to settle with Ms. Richardson, but that would have meant admitting liability; instead, by choosing the path they did, it probably cost them more than ten times as much, needlessly dragging me through the courts in the process.

I've always known what it's like to find myself the subject of unfounded allegations of wrong-doing, and this case showed the level to which it could rise, based on nothing more than questionable allegations and Kendo's reputation in the theatre of wrestling.

Chapter 32

Masters of the Canvas

Ever since October 1975, the BBC has made and broadcast a remarkable arts programme called Arena. It has been described as one of '...the fifty most influential television programmes of all time...', and one of its most admired episodes featured Kendo Nagasaki having his portrait painted by celebrated 'pop' artist Sir Peter Blake.

The episode was called 'Masters of the Canvas' and it evolved from an article which appeared in The Sunday Times Magazine in March 1987 called 'The Chain of Envy'. The premise of the article was that 'No life is so perfect that it cannot gain from others...', and it described a series of individuals who, despite their own successes, admired the life of someone else. The 'chain' began with a doctor who wanted to be a painter, in particular, Sir Peter Blake, who, in turn, wanted to be a masked wrestler, specifically Kendo Nagasaki.

Sir Peter gained world-wide success after creating the astonishing life-size collage which was used for the album cover of The Beatles' 'Sgt. Pepper's Lonely Hearts Club Band' in 1967, but he'd been painting a series of 'fantasy' wrestlers since 1961. He went to his first wrestling match in 1947 at the age of 15 and loved the spectacle; he said that in those early days, wrestlers, masked ones in particular, fascinated him because they existed '...on the fringes of entertainment...' – not a widely-seen main attraction, but something away from the mainstream, existing in a surprisingly dynamic and exciting twilight zone.

In the Sunday Times article, Sir Peter said that Kendo was the most capable, extraordinary, and professional masked wrestler he'd ever seen, which was why in his fantasy world he'd want to be him. Perhaps surprisingly, Kendo Nagasaki claimed that he admired the life of Sir Richard Branson, because of the ways in which he strove to break all sorts of extreme world records, such as covering vast distances in record time by hot air balloon and speeding across oceans in speedboats.

When the Sunday Times article was printed it was read with great interest by a television producer called Paul Yates, who, coincidentally, had also been a very big Kendo fan for many years. Paul later told me stories of the ways in which he'd sought to emulate Kendo, the most extreme of which was when he found himself as a young man in college, practising Kendo's signature Kamikaze Crash with a punch bag over his shoulders, to see what it felt like. He said that when he did it he couldn't work out how it could be done without hurting himself. I had to point out to him that he probably couldn't – it's a highly specialised move, and even with a great deal of training and experience there was always a certain amount of risk in performing it.

Paul also said he very much admired the spiritual side of the Kendo phenomenon, and even claimed that he understood some of what was going on 'under the surface', so-to-speak; he said he could see aspects of Japanese Kabuki theatre in the Nagasaki presence, which I thought was quite insightful, as Kendo has indeed used wrestling as theatre to hold a mirror up to aspects of life.

To Paul, Sir Peter and Kendo were each the masters of their respective canvases, and he had the idea to bring them together for a television programme which showcased both their particular skill-sets. If Sir Peter were to paint a portrait of Kendo, he would add to his series of masked wrestlers, but this time he would paint the real, live masked wrestler whom he most admired. Paul also envisaged Kendo being filmed in the environment where Sir Peter most admired him – in the wrestling ring. He contacted Sir Peter, who apparently didn't take much persuading, and then Lloyd Ryan, who was by then 'managing' Kendo, and described the idea to him, and Lloyd relayed all this back to me.

I thought it sounded like a most intriguing project so I told Lloyd that he should research it a bit more, and if it looked genuinely promising then we'd get back to Paul Yates.

Eventually I suggested that Paul and Sir Peter should visit me at my home in London. The main picture in the Sunday Times article shows Kendo standing in front of the living room fireplace, and it was in that very room that we discussed the idea of the programme – Paul recognized it immediately, and I'm sure he muttered something about destiny. I knew he was genuine when he told me that he'd tried to write a story about a masked wrestler, but he wasn't happy with it because, as he said, 'It doesn't matter how I write it, I cannot improve on Kendo Nagasaki.'

After several discussions we all agreed that the programme sounded like an excellent idea, so the next step would be to find a television company – Paul already had a way in, as he worked for Ulster TV.

He persuaded them to seriously consider the project and we went to Ireland for further discussions, but ultimately Ulster TV said they could only fund a half hour programme. Paul wasn't happy with that – he said it would need to be a whole hour to create the right atmosphere and intrigue, so discussions were broken off and he looked further and wider to get the programme made.

Eventually, the BBC agreed to make the programme as a 'Special Episode' in the Arena series of documentaries. They particularly liked the fact that Sir Peter was already committed to the project and would play a major part – he was very much sought-after as an artist and his work was perfect material for an Arena programme.

They had many further discussions, during which some concerns over Kendo arose – the BBC felt he was elusive and hard to get hold of, not to mention the fact that he never spoke; could he be got hold of, and could he be communicated with? How could a director possibly work with him? In selling Kendo's exclusivity and enigmatic nature, Paul had almost made him unusable! However, he back-tracked appropriately and assured them it would work. Furthermore, as Arena programmes usually contained plenty of dialogue, they wanted more than Sir Peter's narrative alone...

Since the making of the programme seemed to hinge on definitely getting some input from Kendo, we assured them that they would get an interview. With that matter settled it was written into the script, which evolved into a very interesting journey...

The story centred around the search for Kendo Nagasaki, and, if and when he was found, persuading him to meet Sir Peter and sit for him to paint his portrait. That then opened the door to hearing about Sir Peter's fascination with wrestlers in general and Kendo in particular, and then, whether Sir Peter's wish to be Kendo, as described in the original Sunday Times article, can be realised, even if only for a moment. Whilst we'd agreed to an interview, the programme wouldn't make it obvious that there would definitely be one, so it would be necessary to create an atmosphere of suspense around Kendo and Paul's pursuit of him – if it could be made to work, we all felt that it could be quite special.

The director was to be a lady called Mary Dickinson,

who'd directed several Arena programmes and episodes of other TV series for the BBC. Mary and the production team were initially quite apprehensive about the project because they'd heard quite a lot about how awkward Kendo was. The truth of the matter was revealed when they finally met the man behind the mask – I told them 'Of course I'm going to co-operate – Kendo being difficult is part of the story, but it's not the reality of dealing with me!' There were sighs of relief all-round!

I was immediately impressed at Mary's quick thinking and insight, and we got on very well straight away. She and I were to develop a very positive and productive relationship as the script was shot – she understood very well what would put Kendo across properly as well as how to make sure that all the scenes stayed 'on-message' and consistent with the mysterious atmosphere we sought to create.

Of course, Mary met Paul Yates very early on in the process, and she was very intrigued by his fastidiousness and business-like intensity; she thought that he would make the perfect enquirer after the Kendo Nagasaki phenomenon, and she suggested that he actually play that role. While Paul had come up with the basic idea for the programme, he was a producer and didn't usually appear on camera and he was actually quite nervous about the suggestion. However, everyone deferred to Mary's experience and Paul did indeed turn out to be the perfect foil for the other characters, with an earnest on-screen intensity and professionalism as he searched for Kendo.

It was Mary's idea that at the start of the programme, Paul should unpack his case and set his possessions out to show that he was the kind of man who would embark on a meticulously-planned quest to find the mysterious Kendo Nagasaki, and who would know about Zen Koans – her vision in this – and other ways – worked extremely well.

A shooting script was finalised so we knew what to

film and where, and we visited various locations over six to seven weeks, including Moor Court Hall in Staffordshire, London's Knightsbridge, Sir Peter Blake's own artist's studio, and, of course, the Fairfield Halls in Croydon for the wrestling segment. At that time, Kendo was still wrestling for Brian Dixon but not doing many shows.

Arena told high-profile photographer Terence Donovan about the project and he came on board to do a specialised photo-shoot of Kendo. He had photographed a huge range of celebrities and even the British royal family – only two weeks before Kendo's photo-shoot, he'd done a series of shots of Princess Diana in front of a striking blue back-drop, which he also used for Kendo.

Terence turned out to be a BJA third Dan and he had an interesting story which contributed to the project. You may recall that when Kendo visited Japan in 1968 to wrestle, he'd gone to the Kodokan in Tokyo, the main centre for judo in Japan, to practise. Terence said that he was also in Tokyo that year, and whilst there he too visited the Kodokan where he saw an Englishman who was missing a finger practising with Dutch judoka Gesinc, who had become the first Heavyweight Olympic Judo Champion in 1964 when everybody had expected a Japanese to win. He was pretty sure that it was Kendo Nagasaki practising with the Olympic champion.

He brought the British and Commonwealth Heavyweight Judo Champion along to the shoot. This man said he'd only taken up judo in the first place because he'd seen Kendo on TV, and when he heard that Terence was taking the photos, he asked if he would introduce him.

The photograph was stunning, and Sir Peter went on to make a silk-screen print of it, to be sold as a limited edition of one hundred – he gave me number 001 of the autographed prints, and it hangs in my office to this day.

When Kendo sat for Sir Peter to paint his portrait, he remarked that it was a very different experience from usual portraiture work. He was later to remark that he had difficulty with portraits because he couldn't easily disengage from the eyes of the subject – he said they tended to distract him from being objective about the work he was creating, and instead made him feel subjective about the subject. When he painted Kendo, however, he said it was a lot easier for him because Kendo was so completely still, almost as if he wasn't present at all. I had, in fact, gone into the deep mindful state I always use so that Kendo can express himself – Sir Peter was absolutely correct that I wasn't present, Kendo was, and his aura is indeed deeply still and powerful. I was delighted to see that Sir Peter's portrait shows Kendo's inscrutable power extremely well.

Lloyd effortlessly carried-off the role of the no-nonsense manager who was very protective of his charge

When it came time to film the proposed interview, I suggested that it should take place where mysterious and secretive meetings are traditionally conducted – a multi-storey car park late at night. Mary's assistant Annie was essential to organising all the supporting equipment for the entire shoot which she did very efficiently, and she found the perfect long wheelbase Daimler limousine for Kendo to arrive in and have the interview conducted in. As the set-up was being done, no-one from Arena knew that I had a surprise in store for them – this was not going to be the one-to-one interview with Kendo Nagasaki that the BBC thought they were going to get...

At the last second, in typical Kendo style, we moved the goalposts. The first thing I told them was it was not going to be an interview with Kendo Nagasaki – it would be with me, the man behind the mask. Furthermore, while it would be filmed in the back with me, there would not be any microphones near me – they would only be allowed to record it through the partition of the limo, which would completely muffle my voice.

They knew nothing about the idea until they were in

the car park and my car finally made an appearance. I jumped it on them. I didn't want to tell them too soon because of the aggravation of them trying to persuade me to do it another way. For that reason, I've found that it's better if you leave such radical ideas to the last minute.

Mary was not sure what the producers at the BBC would say now that they weren't going to get one of the major points it all hinged upon. But, as has been seen so often in the most imaginative and unexpected ideas in wrestling, like George Relwyskow expecting an unmasking and then not getting it, they frankly didn't have a choice, but in the same way, I knew it would work spectacularly well.

They had to do it my way and make the best of it, and it went exactly as I'd planned. They did indeed make the best of it – Mary rose to the occasion and directed the interview brilliantly from the most unusual vantage point – lying on the floor of the limo, at my feet! By this point in proceedings we'd become quite good friends, and we both found this off-camera situation quite amusing.

As it turns out, it was one of the best ideas of the programme, and one of the highlights that people picked up on. Although the BBC were initially very sceptical, once they had it edited Mary called me a few days later and said, 'I think it's going to work.'

The final shots were filmed at the Waddington gallery in Cork Street, London. Amidst an impressive gathering of celebrities, Kendo walked in wearing his full regalia and drew his sword with a flourish, and an awed silence fell. The shot cuts to Kendo in street clothes as he walked to the portrait and regarded it with an intense scrutiny – the viewer is left wondering what will happen next... The shot fades and a head in a Kendo mask comes into frame, a hand missing an index finger descends and removes the mask, revealing – Sir Peter Blake; his fantasy realised.

Perhaps the most haunting shot comes right at the end of the programme when Kendo returned to the gallery at night and, in Shinto style, cast salt over Sir Peter's iconic portrait, honouring it and everything it stood for.

Once it was – as they say – 'in the can', everyone was very enthusiastic about the finished programme. Mary said, 'I think we've got something special here!' Even the BBC executives were excited, so much so that when they held a special series launch event which previewed the programmes that were coming up during the forthcoming year, of all the programmes Arena had filmed over the past year 'Masters of the Canvas' was first, launching the next series. It was attended by many celebrities, actors, and influential people – Ian McShane respectfully asked if he could join Kendo in holding his sword, which made an interesting pose.

Prior to a programme being transmitted, the press had a preview. Several of the quality newspapers wrote it up as one of the most interesting stories they had seen for a long time. Subsequently, I was told that it was sold worldwide and won a number of awards. Mary and I kept in contact, and many years later she said to me that Arena later used our episode to train new programme makers, to show them how to create an experience and hold the drama.

On the night of the original Arena transmission, art dealer Charles Cholmondeley contacted the gallery and bought Sir Peter's portrait of Kendo. I later found that he kept it for quite some time and wouldn't have let it go, but another big arts buyer insisted that it be included in a multi-work purchase. After I'd got to know Charles, he told me that he'd never have sold it if he'd known me at the time.

Arena made a special programme to celebrate and showcase forty years of its innovative arts documentaries, and in it they showed excerpts from 'Masters' three times. The only other episode that received more air-time was about David Bowie, because he'd recently passed away.

Sir Peter Blake was to do two further portraits of Kendo – firstly, the screen-print of Terence Donovan's photo-portrait, and secondly as part of a large collage-style mural in the Royal Albert Hall, showing all the famous faces who have appeared there. Kendo is front-and-centre – as he should be, having appeared at the venue some twenty-two times.

Kendo returned to the Royal Albert Hall a twenty-third time in 2016 as special guest at a Lucha Libres wrestling tournament, following an invitation to an art gallery which featured a photo-portrait of Kendo as captured by celebrated art photographer, Katinka Herbert. Both at the art gallery and the Royal Albert Hall Kendo gave the new portraits the same Shinto blessing as he'd given Sir Peter's original painting in Masters of the Canvas.

In November 2017, the oldest cinema in the country, the Regent Street Cinema, held a 25th Anniversary screening of 'Masters', and a question and answer session followed afterwards. It was well-attended, the audience comprising some ardent Kendo fans and many media and film people. On the stage alongside Kendo to answer questions were Sir Peter Blake, Mary Dickinson, and Kendo's current spokesperson, Roz MacDonald. The questions were varied and intelligent, and it was good to hear Sir Peter and Mary explaining their fascination with, and roles within, the project, both revealing some insights that I hadn't heard before. Sadly, Paul Yates didn't attend.

We ran out of time – many more questions seemed ready to be asked, but the cinema had to close. The evening ended with Kendo and Sir Peter side-by-side in the bar area, posing for photos and signing autographs on copies of an original picture from the programme that we'd taken along, showing Sir Peter holding his portrait with Kendo in the background – they were so popular that we ran out of copies. The organisers, Heavenly Films, said it was their best attended and most successful night ever.

Masters of the Canvas remains an excellent and timeless arts programme; it most effectively takes its audience on a mysterious journey of discovery and it tells several fascinating stories. I continue to be impressed at the talented contributions of all involved and how such a successful synergy emerged, almost as if it was meant to be. Perhaps Paul Yates was right about the destiny aspect, but I've never doubted it.

Chapter 33

Moor Court Hall

After I moved into the bungalow in Clapham Park I was able to more easily indulge a pleasure I couldn't when I lived in SE1 – horse-riding. I already had some horses which I kept on Wimbledon Common and used to ride out to Richmond Park early in the morning.

However, what I really wanted was a place in the country with its own stables, and I found such a potential place for sale in Oakamoor, Staffordshire, called Moor Court Hall. It had been built in 1861 and had around six acres of formal grounds and a feature that particularly interested me – nine acres of pasture.

I knew many people in London who'd mentioned they'd like to have their own weekend countryside retreat, and the Hall seemed like a viable candidate for such a project; it would comfortably accommodate six luxury flats and a principal residence which I would keep, including the reception rooms, a library, drawing room, day room, dining room, and 'games room'. It seemed like a sound and potentially lucrative project so I sold the Blackpool car site and the last Clapham flat and bought Moor Court Hall in late 1988.

However, as the aftermath of the financial crisis rumbled on I suddenly found that the Hall was worth less than I'd paid for it, and the people who'd initially wanted apartments could no longer afford them. It seemed I had two options: either do something with the Hall or sell it at a loss, and as no other uses were immediately apparent I concentrated on trying to maximise its value and find a way of leveraging my investment.

It was daunting looking at the Hall knowing that I no longer had an 'end-game'; there wasn't a single room that didn't need attention, it had a vast and complicated roof which had numerous leaks, and we were to find that it had dry rot from the cellar up to the third floor. I'd have to front all the refurbishment costs – just like the music business, changing financial circumstances beyond my control had stalled my hopes for the project.

As I became increasingly involved with the restorations, a friend, Alan Moss, joined me in the project. He has an astonishing range of skills and is a tireless worker – the perfect business partner; he's been here ever since.

Because the grounds included pastures I reasoned that the Hall's value would be enhanced if it also had a stable block, so we built one with five stables and a tack room, and I brought my horses up from Wimbledon Common. I began hacking-out in the valley where there are some beautiful rides, which I enjoyed very much; although the Hall hadn't (yet) fulfilled its promise, I was at least now able to enjoy the pleasure that had led me to find it.

We took on some trainees to work in the stables and the grounds, and the mother of one worked at a place called Stallington Hospital, which cared for people with learning disabilities. He told me how such a facility worked, which planted a seed in my mind that a place like the Hall would be an ideal place for people with those types of difficulties. He referred me to his mother, Heather, who in turn put me in touch with her sister, Yvonne, who was a clinical nurse specialist who'd run wards at Stallington. A few days later Yvonne came over to talk.

I'd been at Moor Court for around seven months, and now that the place was a little tidier my wife, Yvette, moved in and we sold the Clapham bungalow. Yvette, Alan and myself met with Yvonne, we chatted, and all got on really well. She told us that Stallington was closing and that she'd like to start a home for people with learning disabilities herself, but while she had the knowledge and qualifications she didn't have the money. After many further discussions, the four of us all felt that we had a viable plan and we decided to go ahead with this new project.

Already on the Moor Court site was a nineteen-bed residential care home for the elderly. It and other properties had been built on the site in the 1950s when the last member of the Bolton family moved out and the Hall and its grounds were bought by the Home Office and turned into a women's open prison. There had been a Governor's House, other smaller houses for senior staff, and a large dormitory block for the wardens. The prison closed in 1984 and all the properties and land were parcelled-up and sold privately, but the lawyer who'd done all the conveyancing bought the dormitory block – the biggest building on the site after the Hall – and opened the care home, calling it Moorside Lodge.

By 1989, it wasn't running well. Only fourteen of the nineteen bedrooms had clients because it was too isolated, it needed a major re-vamp, and none of the rooms were en-suite. We thought it would make a better building in which to start our care facility than attempting to set up such facilities in the main Hall, so we approached the people who owned it and they agreed to sell it to us.

We ran the care home for several months during which we consulted with the local authority to assess the residents so they could be re-housed, and then we closed it so that the four of us (plus Heather) could refurbish and extend the building. We re-opened it in 1991 as a residential unit for people with learning disabilities, keeping the name and calling our company 'Moorcare'.

To start with we were hampered because we had no track record. Social workers visited with a view to placing clients with us, many of whom knew Yvonne and her good reputation within the Health Authority, but she hadn't managed a care home in the private sector so there was reluctance to place clients in an un-tried facility. Eventually, Yvonne's reputation, the quality of what we offered, and the need to place residents overcame that artificial reservation.

But a whole, expensive month passed before our first client came; we had to be fully-staffed to the level of accommodating twenty residents before the local authority would consider sending us a single one, and all the wages and upkeep costs still had to be met – it was a worrying time. However, after that, things snow-balled, and within six months we were full.

The feedback we received was so positive that the local authority encouraged us to consider extending our services. A couple of the other residential properties on the estate came up for sale, which we bought and made into semi-independent living houses, one with six beds and the other with five, and because demand kept growing, eventually the Hall was adapted and included. We ended up with about sixty people living on the site and employing well over a hundred staff – it was a very successful and continually-expanding business.

Sadly, during the final stages of developing the Hall, Yvette passed away, which left us all reeling. She'd had circulatory problems and had gradually become less able and progressively weaker. I got her all possible support but I couldn't avoid the conclusion that the outlook wasn't good. She stayed at the Hall for as long as she could but eventually she had to go into specialised care, where she passed away.

After meeting Yvette I hadn't been prepared for how

she made me feel – there was a 'rightness' about how we got on, how easy we were with each other, and how much we laughed. Of the relationships I'd had I'd never felt inclined to commit myself to marriage, but Yvette had been the one – the right one. We'd only been married for nine years but had made each other very happy, and I feel very fortunate to have had our time together.

Demand for residential care kept increasing so we looked again at expanding. In Uttoxeter there was a complex called Highfield Hall that had twenty-six bungalows for learning disability and mental health residents, as well as a nursing home for the elderly. Yvonne and I regularly went back and forth to it in connection with referrals from there, and we eventually heard that the man who owned it had had enough and decided he wanted to sell. We subsequently bought it and closed the elderly care side, turning it all over to learning disabilities, adding another eighty residents to our clientele. We ended up as one of the largest providers for learning disability care in Staffordshire, employing well over three hundred people, and the business ran very well for fourteen years.

Of course, car buying and selling continued in the background during this time. I started a company called Moorcourt Cars so that I could acquire, drive, and sell-on cars that I liked, which included a couple of BMW 7-series, Lamborghini Diablo SV, an Excalibur, a Chevrolet Corvette Ruby Anniversary, an Aston Martin DB7, a BMW 850i, a Mercedes Benz E55 AMG, a 1964 Rolls Royce Silver Cloud III (celebrating the year of Kendo's debut), a couple of Rolls Royce Silver Shadows, a Ferrari F355 GTS, and another, rare, open-headlight four-wheel-drive Lamborghini Diablo VT.

Out of the blue, there was a change of Government policy which suddenly regarded places like Moor Court Hall as being too isolated. The Uttoxeter site was favoured because it was only half a mile from the town centre; residents could walk there with a member of staff whereas that wasn't possible at Moor Court. The lanes have no pavements and are not suitable to walk down and it's a three-mile walk to the nearest town, so trips to local library or the swimming baths required transport – in Uttoxeter, there was no such need.

We were encouraged to consider either shutting the Moor Court site and moving residents to Uttoxeter, or finding another site. We gradually moved all the Moor Court residents out, some to different facilities and others to Highfield Hall (which we continued running), but then a very large national provider which had several care homes throughout the country offered to buy it. We didn't really want to sell, but the sum they offered was simply too good to turn down.

Alan and I kept Moor Court Hall and all the related properties in the grounds, looking to eventually develop them ourselves, so the Moor Court estate was kept dormant, but this was later to change when Kendo Nagasaki suddenly sprung back into our lives.

Chapter 34

Goodbye Roy, Hello Roz!

I was sorry to see the Gladstone Street house be sold, as it had been the focus of such powerfully positive influences on my life – besides being a lot of fun and the origin of my international music recording career, it seemed to have been a place of powerful catharsis for me, like those mythical locations where ley-lines cross and create a focus for healing and evolution. However, there was no denying that all its energy flowed from Kendo, through Peter.

As I've mentioned, you couldn't wish for a better house-mate than cheerful, witty, profound George (with the possible exception of his huge fried breakfasts, punctuated with two or three cigarettes!), and I think he was happy to pass on the positivity he'd gained from his association with Peter – whom I reasoned was also passing-on what he'd learned from his 'sensei', and that was a lot.

I was also inspired by something that Peter said – he liked 'hungry fighters'. It had been while we were building the fabric of Nagasaki Studio, as I marvelled at his joinery skills and many others, that I came to find out about his basic and challenging origins. It had been as a result of them that he had been just such a fighter, and he appreciated working with people who were equally ambitious. Even though I'd begun from a position of being disabled and unemployed and thoroughly disillusioned with life, he'd given me hope that I could make the most of my potential, as he had, and I was by now sure that he was on an unspoken 'tough-love' mission to help other 'fighters' do the same – as I was later to learn that he had done with George.

Something else I was to continue reflecting upon was a Buddhist principle he'd told me about which was fundamental to everything at Gladstone Street: nothing and no-one was judged at face value, in-and-of itself; instead, people and actions were considered in terms of motivation and outcome. It was a wonderfully refreshing approach that involved not indulging in disempowering judgements of yourself or others, but instead seeking to make the most of all people and opportunities; it was to help me in all my problem areas.

Gladstone Street had been the perfect environment to help me with my non-existent self-confidence. I'd never have thought it possible, but I'd come to believe in my own abilities and that they could have a positive expression, after which I felt that absolutely anything was possible – even resolving my gender identity problem. I still couldn't yet see when, but I felt that my earlier indecision and confusion had evolved into a positive momentum, thanks to that amazing place.

Peter had helped me with another disorienting problem too – my near-death experience, my 'NDE'. It had been genuinely other-worldly and had shown me a completely unfamiliar dispassionate objectivity about my own human condition, and I had no idea what to do with it other than shut it out of my mind. I felt that I should try to make some sense of it – I was inclined to believe that I'd been shown it for a reason, and I wanted it to become something positive for me, as opposed to just being damned confusing. Peter told me that hypnotic regression could be dangerous, and the safe way of achieving a higher level of vision was through meditation. He told me about 'Kyu Shin Do', which was a way of looking at everything objectively, and by combining the two, I gradually began seeing the world and all my problems in an objective and dispassionate way, and my NDE came to fit into that vision. I was delighted at the sense of calm strength and understanding that meditation gave me, and I'll always be grateful to Peter for showing it to me.

George had been helpful to me too, by listening and offering his counsel, but also as only he could – he knew a vast cross-section of London society which included some trans-gender people, and he'd introduced me to some of them, and I had also been greatly emboldened by his 'Fuck it, dear!' attitude – he encouraged everyone to be who they truly were, regardless of the consequences! I began to feel that if he could be so confident, why couldn't I?

As my work had become more wide-spread in London and then international I'd moved out of Gladstone Street but I kept in touch with Peter and George and we met-up as often as we could. I was saddened that our little studio hadn't led to greater things for us all, together, as I would have dearly loved to have shared my success with its spiritual architects.

The last time I saw them together was at the Clarence Avenue house. I'd known that George had become unwell and I continually hoped for the best for him, but I knew things were looking difficult. I was working in Berlin when he passed away, and, as usual, as soon as I got back I spoke to Peter and he told me the sad news; I went to see him and we shared many fond memories of our dear old friend. Only a few months after I'd first met him, George had said he was certain that I had a future in the music business and he'd turned out to be emphatically right, a visionary in that as in so many other ways.

However, my success had delayed the resolution of my gender identity problem – whilst I'd been empowered by freedom from negative judgements in Gladstone Street, the outside world was still full of them. Changing genders was still a very controversial thing to do in the late 1980s, and being a freelance music producer-engineer had no innate security or guarantees of fair treatment – anyone with any negative attitudes towards trans-people could simply choose to exercise them with no repercussions, and I saw every prospect of never getting work in the music business again if I went ahead with my transition. The prejudice of the outside world was therefore enforcing a choice on me – carry on working in my chosen creative sphere, or be myself, but both seemed far from possible.

Once again, Peter reminded me that these circumstances simply meant the time wasn't yet right, and I should continue to meditate on how to proceed when it came. He also pointed out that I shouldn't forget the problems of attachment – I should be completely prepared to contemplate letting my enjoyable and satisfying career fall away; he said I shouldn't abandon it, but its existence shouldn't block envisaging other possibilities which may be more beneficial in a bigger picture.

Then, tragedy struck. Only eight months after George had passed away, my mother took her own life. Unsurprisingly, it stunned the whole family right to its most extended members, but it affected me very deeply; I'd been particularly close to my mother, as we'd supported each other in our violent and abusive household. I'd been able to escape when I went to London with Peter and George, but my mother simply had to prevail, and, being keenly aware of how difficult it was for her, I'd spoken to her at least once a week for the next ten years, from wherever I was in the world. I'd just got back from Brazil and had phoned her to arrange my next visit, to which we'd both been looking forward, but she clearly hadn't been able to carry on and chose to escape, courtesy of my father's .357 Magnum.

Her death and the manner of it was a huge and tragic loss in its own right, but it also brought back all the trauma I'd experienced while growing up. When I went to see Peter he could see that I was putting a brave face on things, but that I was really struggling.

He counselled that I approach the whole experience as a Zen Koan. He said that under such emotional pressure it was inevitable that the dominant responses of my (unpleasant) formative years would come to the fore, so I'd be awash with recriminations of myself and others and it wouldn't be possible to see past recent events until I set them aside. It was to be perhaps the biggest possible test of my faith in how meditation could help me, but I had no idea what else to do with my huge and complex emotions, so, not without some difficulty, I let them fall away, and a benevolent understanding did begin to emerge.

Then, as if to test me in the most extreme possible way, an additional and cruelly ironic complication added to my problems – three months after my mother's suicide, my father had a stroke, following which he needed caring for. Despite having been on the receiving end of his cruelty all my life, I couldn't leave him to his own devices, so it would be up to me. I knew it was the right thing to do, but at considerable emotional cost, and it caused me a whole new mountain of internal conflict.

It was inescapable that I'd have to quit the music business to care for my father, but following Peter's advice and my meditations, I found myself curiously at peace with the decision. I found I had a hint of the feeling I'd had when I'd first gone to London with Peter and George, of being prepared to commit myself to an unknown but right-feeling future, so I put one foot in front of the other on the road to a positive somewhere...

As I settled-in to becoming a carer I also began to feel the beginnings of momentum towards the resolution of my gender identity problem. Peter suggested that I should visit Moor Court to meditate in the grounds, which I did, and the way ahead gradually revealed itself. It was to take seventeen months; achieving such a thing requires a great deal of preparation, not least of the people I would continue to encounter such as neighbours, and those with whom I had friendships that I wanted to survive my self-realisation.

But – how to broach the subject? I decided that a factual approach was best. I put together a single-page document that as concisely as possibly described the difference between physical gender and a person's gender as they understand it, and that sometimes they didn't match. I also pointed out that changing the gender in which a person lives is the only way to resolve the conflict, after which they can get on with their life, freed from that conflict. I wanted to give people the opportunity to become informed before reacting from a position of knowing nothing, and I was pleasantly surprised at how well many of them responded. Sadly I did lose some friends who simply stopped taking my calls, but the people I was most surprised and disappointed by were family.

Apart from my favourite uncle, my entire extended family of seven uncles and aunts, eight cousins, and one grandfather completely shunned me. I'd hoped that because they were family they could see past any misgivings born of unfamiliarity with the problem, but they didn't even try – they just instantly reacted negatively. Even twenty-four years later my brother reported that they only spoke of me as a bizarre curiosity – they had absolutely no interest in me as a person. This is now known as 'trans-phobia', and overt displays are regarded as examples of 'hate' which is illegal, but packaging it up as a concept and giving it a name didn't diminish the hurt and betrayal I felt when I suddenly found myself reviled by people I'd always regarded as decent, and whom I thought would support me particularly because they were family.

I'd known for many years that many gay people had found themselves similarly reviled, and during my time in Gladstone Street I'd heard of some whose lives had been devastated by such betrayals by their loved ones, but if they were lucky they'd find others in their own community who would support them; I'd found that community in Gladstone Street, and ever since.

However, knowing that I had a support structure even without my family, particularly one as strong and philosophical as Peter, I put my hurt and disappointment at my family behind me and pressed on. Finally, on a sunny May morning in 1993 in Beverly Hills, California, Roz was born. Peter had been with me throughout the journey and he'd characteristically kept my focus on horizons well beyond that single end – he ensured that my acutely subjective journey should fade into insignificance after that phase of it was completed, so that the new me would be a productive member of society.

The only regret I have is that my mother never got to know the real me – Roz. She'd known of my gender identity problem since I'd first mentioned it to her when I was four years old, and I know she'd worried about what it would mean for me. She'd also known that I'd struggled-on through all the years in which resolution hadn't been possible, so she'd have worried about me until she'd died. She loved Peter and she knew he was the kind of strong character who would help me make the most of my life, for which she was very grateful to him, and I wish I could have shown her that with his help, I'd resolved things well, I looked forward to a fulfilled future, and that I was finally happy, all of which would have made her happy. In her memory, I try to be the kind of person and live the kind of life that she would be proud of.

Having guided me through the surreal imagery of my near-death experience, Peter had revealed that I had a 'feel' for psychology. To keep my 'monkey-mind' occupied in my early days at Gladstone Street, he'd encouraged me to study western mysticisms and consider how metaphors from them could be used to understand lessons from Zen. It had indeed kept me occupied, and I found that fifteen years later, such images were becoming clear. To deepen my understanding and help visualise the 'bridges' between knowledge and 'being', he suggested I do a degree in psychology. Of course, I had no A-levels, but I was by now a committed believer in anything being possible! I did an Access to Nursing and Health Studies course which qualified me for university entrance, and after they'd secured support for my learning disability I went on to get a Bachelor of Science in Single Honours Psychology, two-one class degree. I'd never have thought myself capable of such an achievement before meeting Peter and I was grateful beyond words.

It wasn't to end there, though – further opportunities opened up for me. I needed to get away from the academic microcosm for at least a while, and as soon as I graduated I was offered a job in IT. I'd bought my first ever computer with my last ever music business royalty cheque, and – fortunately, as it turned out in a bizarre way – it had been faulty! This meant that right from my introduction to IT, I'd had to learn how to analyse and fix computer problems, which, for a natural nerd such as myself, was fascinating! I'd carried on with computers, building them for my friends at university, and coincidentally, just as I graduated, the company I'd bought the parts from needed someone to build lots of them.

Peter had told me of how doors had seemingly magically opened for him, and having followed his philosophy and having faith in my future, the same appeared to be happening for me. I studied the prestigious Microsoft Certified Systems Engineer course and ended up becoming a 'Solution Provider', moving on to Systems Administration in industry, then first-line technical support at a software house, then I became a freelance IT consultant – all achievements I'd never have believed possible before I met Peter.

Then, another dramatic change came along – my father passed away.

Once again, I saw Peter at Moor Court and he helped me put everything into perspective. A whole lot of new challenges arose, including refurbishing my father's house and selling it, after which Peter said he had an opening for someone with my skills. After knowing him for twenty-six years and being helped by him to completely transform my life for the better, joining him once again was a foregone conclusion! Thanks to him, I was now at peace with my past, I'd become the person I should always have been, I was academically accomplished despite my awful early educational experience, I had some highly saleable skills, and I had strong foundations in Zen.

I was delighted to re-join the fold; I still had much to learn and I looked forward to continuing to grow and contribute wherever I could. Knowing Peter, it would be a journey towards yet more and deeper understandings, and not without challenges!

I did, however, have a worsening problem that dated all the way back to before meeting Peter – the broken ankle from my motorcycle accident was becoming so arthritic that I could barely walk on it. The degeneration had been so gradual that I did what anyone would do – I'd just put up with the pain and carried on, but it was now becoming impossible. I was almost taken aback when Peter matter-of-factly said, 'You'd be better off without that!' He meant my entire foot!

Actually, I had done extremely well with such a badly-compromised leg. Originally, the fractures wouldn't unite, despite six operations to try and persuade them to. Peter had told me that I had nothing to lose by walking on it, which I had done, and magically the fractures did unite – finally I was out of plaster casts (there had been ten) and free from pins through my shin-bone.

Then there were other problems – there was a lot of nerve damage so I had foot-drop and the other muscles were very weak, and the way the fractures healed made it three-quarters of an inch shorter than my good leg. Peter gave me many sessions of 'interferental' treatment, which strengthened the plantar-flexing muscles and helped a lot with pain-relief, and he told me how to compensate for the shortness and foot drop and make my walking more natural.

Sadly, however, now that the arthritis in the ankle had got so bad, radical treatment was needed. I learned all about my options, which boiled-down to arthrodesis (fusing the ankle) or amputation. Peter said that arthrodesis wouldn't necessarily be the best solution because the stresses of walking would be passed-on to other joints in my foot which would then become arthritic themselves, but amputation seemed so radical... As he had done with so many other projects, Peter told me to just get on with researching everything – but he kept me madly busy with work too, so I had no time to dwell on things! Typical of him, he just steered me to the most practical and efficient route to resolution.

I saw consultants and went through all the other requirements, and found myself working late into the night on the day before I went into hospital to have my right foot amputated – I think if Peter hadn't kept the pressure on me, I may have too much time to think and worry, and indecision may have crept in. Two weeks after my amputation he had me back at work! So much for the thirteen weeks off that most people get after such surgery!

It had gone very well, and so did my recovery, once again thanks to Peter. He had always trained at least three times a week, and for the six months before my amputation, he had asked me to join him. He gave me a program of exercises on various machines which gave me good fitness and general strength, which had been excellent preparation for the surgery. I practically stormed through rehab, but I needed a revision surgery eleven months later when the acute pain was diagnosed as being caused by nerves that had been left in the incision scar. After that, my progress was rapid, and I was alarmed to find that Peter had a new role for me...

I was to become Atlantis Chronos Goth, Kendo Nagasaki's spokes-person at wrestling matches! He was delighted that I had a characteristic as unique as my metal leg, but I was now more able than I'd been since I was twenty so there was no physical reason why I couldn't do it. I'd never performed publicly before, and the thought of facing a rowdy wrestling audience was terrifying! However, I was thoroughly coached as to how to fire-up Kendo's audiences and alarmingly dressed for the role, and I was also personally motivated to do justice to George's excellent supporting mouth-piece role for the masked marauder. It was a somewhat terrifying experience but it became great fun too, but sadly it ended prematurely when LDN Wrestling lost their television contract.

Eighteen months later, Peter moved me to Moor Court Hall to begin the preparations for Kendo's next phase – the Nagasaki Retreat. I greatly looked forward to the project – I'd been absorbing Peter and Kendo's wisdom for thirty-one years and it had revolutionised my life, and the least I could do would be to be part of sharing it with others.

There was, of course, no rest – being close to Peter is like living on an anvil – he's always firing challenges at people that test them to extremes, hammering them into a newer and better shape. It's not always a pleasant experience, but – as he has done with himself – it's made the most of me, more than I could ever have imagined, especially considering my own disadvantaging early-life difficulties.

Chapter 35

Blackpool Revisited – but This Time it's Gay!

My attention had been drawn back to Blackpool once more, through the same connection with whom I opened the car site there in 1985; he told me about a hotel that could make an interesting and profitable project.

It comprised five terraced houses that had been knocked-through to make one premises, and the owners wanted to sell. I found that the local authority were happy to have such properties returned to private houses, so I decided to buy the Highlands Hotel and do that conversion. We never intended to be hoteliers, but we ran it for a short while, re-naming it Rainbows Hotel, then we closed it and began the conversions.

As we worked on shutting-off and returning the first of the five houses to residential use, I learned of another interesting hotel. It was extremely popular with a single client group – gay men only – and it was coming up for sale at a price that was open to negotiation. I went to see it, and was very impressed at how busy it was (it actually had an 80% occupancy throughout the year – an astonishingly high rate that most hoteliers would kill for), but it was clear that much of it was now in disrepair, so it would be a project in the true sense of the word. When I heard that it was probably the best-known gay hotel in the country, I decided to buy Trades Hotel and raise its game.

I was also to learn of another small hotel in Blackpool that just needed tidying up and selling, so I bought that too and turned it around relatively quickly.

I was also interested in pursuing the possibilities around something I'd heard more and more about from the clientele of Trades – a men-only nightclub. There was a candidate nightclub coming onto the market, and once again, I hoped to be able to refurbish and re-brand it, and satisfy the clamour for a night-spot for those who went to Trades, which couldn't possibly house a dance-floor. In late 2005 I bought Club Rendezvous with the aim of making it into Trades Bar, a companion venue to the hotel.

Ever since meeting George all those years ago in London I'd appreciated how essential it is for people to have places they can go where they can feel safe and able to relax without being judged, and I was pleased to be working towards helping extend such facilities in Blackpool.

Suddenly, therefore, I had one minor and two major refurbishment projects going on at the same time – Trades Hotel continued operating but with rooms being closed on a rota to be done-up, the house on one end of Rainbows Hotel was finished and sold so we began on the other four, and the club venue needed gutting and completely refurbishing. As things were expanding, I was delighted to be joined in Blackpool by Roz, who'd become an accomplished and experienced computer expert, so the team now comprised her, Lawrence, the current manager at Trades Hotel, Steve, and myself.

When we looked more closely at what was to become Trades Bar, we were horrified – behind the sparkly paint and tinsel was a building about to collapse. Like so many of Blackpool's hotels it was essentially three terraced houses knocked-through to create a single venue. It had been owned for some thirty years by one man who had torn everything out on the ground floor to put a restaurant there, and he'd had the worst, cheapest, cowboy-builders' job done. There were two floors of flats above the ground floor space we were leasing for the nightclub, but they were barely supported at all – their floors had taken on alarming angles and virtually all the upstairs plumbing leaked into our space.

When an inspector from building control came to see what we'd found, he literally ran out of the building and instantly condemned it, insisting that the residents of the flats be moved out immediately, and for no work to be done until many tons of structural steel beams were professionally installed to properly support the building. I'll never forget his face when he said that the cracking in the upstairs walls was '...horrendous.' He said it was a miracle that no-one had been killed in the building, either by an unsupported chimney-breast collapsing onto them (of which there were at least seven), or – horrifyingly – from a total internal collapse of the building!

At the same time as the property developments, we were becoming more involved with another aspect of Blackpool – its gay scene. Trades Hotel had visitors from all over the country, but the town didn't have its own Pride event, and setting one up would provide another attraction for gay people and greatly boost tourism, which would be good for us all.

We spoke with several people who'd begun discussing a Pride event, specifically a man called Mark Seargent who had taken a central role and was to become the manager of our men-only nightclub. We collaborated with him to hold Blackpool's very first Pride in 2006 – it was held on the station car park in North Shore where we organised a wrestling show which was so well-received we decided to do the same thing the following year. The Pride was a great success and we all looked forward to the next one.

We were determined to have Trades Bar open for the 2007 Pride, and we threw ourselves into the rebuilding, redesign, and fitting-out of the club. Even with the structural steels in place, we discovered many more woes – there were rotten joists and rusted-out RSJs everywhere, and even the utilities had been botched – literally everything had to be reinstated from the ground-up. This meant brand new designs for everything – electrics, plumbing and heating, fire alarm system, and then the new layout we wanted for the Bar itself; I lost count of the schematic drawings we had to prepare.

But we did it – the final fittings were being installed at Trades Bar on the morning of Blackpool Pride 2007, and it was to open that day for a truly memorable weekend.

We completed converting Rainbows Hotel back into houses and sold them off as they were done, and we finished all the refurbishments and refinements in Trades Hotel, but as any hotel owner will tell you, it's a non-stop, ongoing process keeping the standards up. Our team was enhanced with the addition of Neil Cropper, who became an extremely able manager of Trades Hotel.

By mid-2008, however, we'd discovered that a men-only clientele for Trades Bar wasn't covering its costs, so we opened it to everyone and re-branded it as Kaos Bar, and it remains one of Blackpool's best and most popular gay nightclubs to this day. For every Pride event since 2008, Kaos has been central to a fantastic street party.

It was a huge amount of work and included some alarming surprises along the way, but my latest and biggest investment into Blackpool has turned out to be a complete success. Some eleven years after joining us, Neil now has full control of both Trades and Kaos, and he runs them excellently.

The cherry on the cake, so-to-speak, was when the

Pride event finally achieved something it had been aiming for ever since the first one. They managed to get the rainbow flag flown from the Town Hall from the 2008 event onwards, but the owners of Blackpool Tower had always refused. Finally, they conceded that 'the pink pound' contributed too much to the town for it not to be acknowledged, and the rainbow flag now flies from the Tower at every Pride.

George would have been hugely proud, and I like to think he'd have appreciated everything we achieved in Blackpool, as well as enjoying himself so much that he'd have been happy being thrown out of either of our venues!

Chapter 36

LDN Wrestling

In mid-2007, one of the new-style wrestling promoters called Sanjay Bagga approached Lloyd Ryan to see if we would be interested in doing some wrestling shows. His promotions company was called LDN Wrestling, it was based in London, and was putting on shows around the south of England, but – interestingly – they also had a weekly television slot on The Wrestling Channel. Their shows were professionally put together and capably hosted, although the matches were in dire need of realism and 'oomph!', which I knew I could give them. I felt we could work with them.

At first, Sanjay asked for just an appearance by Kendo, but that didn't appeal at all; there's no point in going to an event and being treated as a legend – what are they? It's like the Wrestlers' Reunion – Kendo had been invited to the Reunion for many years, but he couldn't go and be just another wrestler – if he went at all, he had to be there as an iconic figure.

There followed a couple of meetings with LDN, during which they seemed very eager to do everything to secure Kendo's participation, and after some thought, I was guided to put together a contest which would be called 'The Kendo Nagasaki Sword of Excellence'. Initially, Kendo would judge a match or two, but if the right people came on board and everything worked out, it could lead to him getting back into the ring, and therefore back on TV, which would be infinitely more impressive than just an appearance. I discussed it with Robbie Brookside and he was up for it.

I decided that for the first match there should be a knock-out tournament for the Sword, with Brookside and Phil Powers ending up in the final. Kendo judged the match from ringside with the sword on a table in front of him, but he wasn't just a passive observer... Late in the match, Powers knocked Brookside down and jumped out of the ring to grab the sword, but Kendo hypnotised him and sent him back into the ring, where he attacked a recovering Brookside, who suddenly did his signature throw and got the winning fall on Powers. However, Kendo made the controversial decision that even though he'd won, his performance wasn't good enough to deserve the sword, and he refused to award it to him.

After the show, Brookside went ballistic – he stormed out to the foyer where Kendo was signing autographs, he up-ended his merchandise table and ranted about the injustice of Kendo's decision and threatened dire repercussions. Of course, Kendo serenely stood back and let Robbie get on with it, while the awed audience wondered what was going to happen next – it was a 'Watch This Space' moment – a good start to a new feud.

A week later, Lloyd Ryan went on LDN's TV show and made a statement, saying that Kendo had been wrong and Robbie should have been awarded the Sword. This disloyalty resulted in Kendo dismissing Lloyd as his manager, and a new 'mouthpiece' was appointed, Atlantis Chronos Goth, who then made a counter-statement and issued a challenge.

Atlantis was actually Roz, who had always taken a keen interest in Kendo, particularly the mystical side. She'd never performed in public in any way and was a little apprehensive, but I was sure she could do it, and before long, 'The Goth' was ready to wind-up audiences and glorify Kendo.

Atlantis's statement said that if Lloyd Ryan believed that Brookside deserved the Sword, then he should find himself a tag team to fight for it. He duly did this and came up with a team comprising his own son, Damian, and Robbie Brookside. Kendo's side would be Blondie Barratt and one of his trainees, the promising Jackie Steel.

The tag match was sensational, and LDN loved it – they said it was the biggest event they'd ever held, and it made a great episode of their weekly TV show. Once again, there was lots of uncontrollable out-of-the-ring action which resulted in angry protests by Brookside and Lloyd Ryan. When the Ryan team were winning by one fall, Damian Ryan was thrown through the ropes by Blondie who then attacked him outside the ring, which resulted in Brookside storming across to confront Kendo; Atlantis intervened and threw a fireball into Brookside's face, immediately followed by a huge handful of salt from Kendo. Brookside was blinded and unable to continue and Damian Ryan was injured so their team had to concede the match, which was followed by a furious tirade by both Brookside and Lloyd Ryan against Kendo. It had all worked extremely well – the audience was well and truly fired-up, awaiting the next instalment in the feud.

The fires were stoked quite literally when Brookside burned a life-sized image of Kendo, which was filmed and broadcast during LDN's slot on The Wrestling Channel, along with re-caps of all the bad blood between all the parties – this kept the feud's head of steam at full pressure.

The next match was at the Thurrock Civic Hall in Grays, Essex, with a six-man tag-team contest featuring Brookside partnered with Phil Powers and LDN's Yorghos Christopoulos, versus the team of Blondie

Barratt, Gregory Cortez and, back in the ring for the first time professionally in ten years, Kendo Nagasaki. For his return, Kendo's entrance music was the excellent 'Anthem for Nagasaki' by Jonathan Smeed, as edited by Roz.

Even before the match began there was controversy – following all of Lloyd Ryan's taunts, Kendo had approved a match which included Damian Ryan in the opposing team, but neither Lloyd nor Damian had turned up. At Kendo's direction, Atlantis dismissed Yorghos as an '...inappropriate substitute...', and said Kendo would choose who should be in Brookside's team. They protested that Yorghos was entirely worthy as he was the LDN British Heavyweight Champion, but Kendo wouldn't have it – he was booted out. They asked the LDN wrestlers from the supporting matches to come to ring-side, and the audience was kept in suspense – Kendo eventually chose Hakan.

The first fall went to Brookside's team when he pinned Cortez, which eliminated him from the contest. The dirty tricks soon began – Kendo threw Hakan through the ropes and slammed him onto the time-keeper's table, before overturning it and slamming it onto him and pounding it with a chair. Kendo then pulverised Hakan and threw him with a double underarm souplex followed by pinning him, which levelled the score and eliminated him.

Then a furious Brookside dragged Kendo over the top rope and attacked the mask, managing to pull it half-off. He threw Kendo who escaped from the ring under the ropes but in another out-of-the-ring scuffle he got thrown into the audience. Back in the ring there was a flurry of fighting which knocked the referee down; Kendo grabbed Powers and hypnotised him and set him against his team-mate, Brookside, who was knocked out, then Kendo salted Powers, blinding him, then body-slamming him for the winning fall.

After the match there was a furious and resentful rant from Brookside about how unfair Kendo was, and he demanded the chance to get his own back – it all made great TV.

Unfortunately, there was a falling-out between Brookside and LDN so he jumped-ship, then we had to re-establish the Sword of Excellence feud. Sanjay wanted to use his own wrestlers, who would cost him much less and also promote LDN, but none of them had any history of working with Kendo, so a good show was far from guaranteed. Eventually we arranged for LDN wrestlers Yorghos and Hakan to steal the Sword from Kendo at an autograph-signing session, and then Yorghos issued a challenge to Kendo on LDN's TV show, to take it back if he could, in a ladder match.

This match was held at the Victoria Hall in Hanley with tag teams of Kendo and Blondie competing against Yorghos and Hakkan for the Sword, which was suspended above the ring. The promotion of the feud on LDN's TV slot meant the show was well-attended, and it turned out to be as exciting as the Grays match, fought almost entirely outside any rules!

Yorghos and Hakan were typical of the new breed of wrestlers – they'd learned show wrestling which they put to good use – both of them gave Blondie a hard time, which he countered with dirty tricks, keeping the audience on the edge of their seats. However, they couldn't counter Kendo's villainy, particularly when he pummelled Hakan on the ropes behind the ref's back. Yorghos and Hakan did a spectacular double drop-kick on Kendo and Blondie, knocking them out of the ring, which gave Hakan time to retrieve the ladder from the back of the hall and set it up in the ring to try and get the sword, but Blondie knocked him off it.

The ladder ended up being thrown in and out of the ring, where Kendo battered both Hakan and Yorghos with it. After that, Hakan 'sold' his injuries and wasn't involved a lot more in the match. Yorghos set the ladder up and started to climb, and Blondie went up the other side. As they were going up Kendo pushed it over and they both fell to the ring. To the audience's delight, a 'salting' went wrong, where Blondie grabbed Yorghos and held him for Kendo to throw it in his face, but Yorghos ducked out of the way and Blondie got it full in his face. Yorghos made some strong come-backs against both Blondie and Kendo, and he almost retrieved the sword, but at the last second Kendo pushed the ladder over and Yorghos crashed to the stage outside the ring, dropping the sword in the ring, where Kendo grabbed it and claimed it, and the victory.

The audience was both furious and enthralled – Hakan and Yorghos had so nearly won the match and the sword – where would this feud go next? It was all building very nicely...

The series then went to the Civic Hall in Wolverhampton, and it had been building so well that the local press and radio and TV came to do features on Kendo's return to the venue, which was just down the road from where his career had begun, in Willenhall. They also attended on the day of the match and covered a controversial and brutal battle.

Once again, right at the start, Kendo switched things around. It had been billed as a singles match between Kendo and Yorghos, but Yorghos was marginalized by Kendo demanding a match for the LDN Tag Team Championship Belts, which were then held by Travis and Hakan. This fired-up the audience, who wanted to see Heavyweight Champion Yorghos have another go at Kendo, but they were denied the chance – it looked as if the devious Kendo was scared of Yorghos, which was what we wanted.

From the audience's point of view, Kendo was spectacularly brutal in this match. Firstly, he seriously softened-up Hakan before throwing him over the ropes outside the ring, where Blondie picked him up and held him so Kendo could hit him over the head with a chair. The crowd was incensed. Hakan was thrown back into the ring by Kendo, where he was mauled in the corner by him and Blondie while the ref was distracted trying to keep a furious Travis out of the ring, after which Kendo slammed Hakan and got the first fall of the match.

Then it was Travis's turn. Furious, he rushed into the ring against Blondie and chucked him about, until he was pushed into Kendo's corner and repeatedly forearm-smashed. Then he was thrown out of the ring and while he was on the floor, Kendo jumped out and picked up the time-keeper's table and hit him with it – hard. Kendo couldn't pull that attack or do it less harshly, because the audience was right there – he hit Travis for real. While Travis was stunned and Sanjay was trying to rouse him, Kendo picked up the time-keeper's bell and threw it full-force into Travis's stomach. He couldn't pull that either – he really hurt him, which took the audience over the top – they went wild.

There was a woman in the front row who was absolutely livid – her face was purple with rage. She yelled, 'You're fucking evil, Nagasaki! You're a fucking animal! You're nothing but a monster!' It was old-school brutality-theatre, so effectively staged that the audience seemed more shocked than entertained. So many had got to their feet in outrage that the MC had to ask them to stay in their seats for their own safety.

The audience saw Travis drag himself back into the ring so he could continue against Kendo, but he was clothes-lined by Blondie, then got a vicious straight-fingers to the throat from Kendo, before being slammed into a corner post which Kendo had already taken the cover off. After that, he was easily slammed and pinned by Kendo for the winning fall. Both youngsters had been cruelly demolished by Kendo – the audience wanted to see him get his come-uppance, but that never happened.

After the win, Yorghos stormed back to ring-side and gave an angry rant about Kendo's dastardly tactics and swore that he'd take the mask when they next met, which all the audience wanted to see.

However, a message came through the following day from Sanjay that Travis was hurt – he had very bad bruising around his ribs. He complained that Kendo had gone too far and he wanted things to be toned-down. Just as things were building well, LDN got cold feet.

Over the years it's been said that wrestlers don't intend to hurt each other – it's all put on and they're all friends, really. As I've explained, wrestling is theatre, but you have to be prepared to make sacrifices to make it a compelling spectacle – LDN's attitude showed how the business had changed, which seemed to be that today's wrestlers aren't prepared to make those sacrifices, take those knocks, and do what it takes for the business to look convincing.

In the old days, there were plenty of wrestlers who would go into matches with the intention of promoting themselves over others. I've already mentioned a number of examples with the likes of Billy Howes, Dennis Mitchell, Billy Robinson, Geoff Portz, and Les Kellett, who would do this – they weren't bothered if they hurt you, providing they came out looking like tough guys.

In Kendo's early matches, against wrestlers such as these, he fought at least as hard as them, and this was why the audience was never left in any doubt that the combat was real. Current wrestlers don't fight with anything like as much commitment, which is why most modern matches don't seem real – I believe this is why a sport as aggressive as MMA is quickly eclipsing professional wrestling. Kendo's visible brutality evaporated that vibe in an instant, bringing real old-school passion to the matches he was involved with – it's such a shame that LDN couldn't see that.

What should have happened next was a singles match

between Yorghos and Kendo, down south in LDN territory. Travis should have been there on the night, and Kendo was going to take control of him, make him a new victim of the mythical in-ring hypnosis, and use him in a similar way to Brookside, turning him against Yorghos.

Sanjay came back to us and said that Travis didn't want to do the match, and anyway, he was going on holiday with his family. In retrospect, I don't believe this came from Travis – I think it all came from Sanjay.

The finish of that match should have been that Travis's intervention meant that Kendo would get his hands on the Sword of Excellence and retreat towards the dressing room, as if he's making-off with it. Yorghos would follow him, and back-stage, he would be 'bladed', given an insignificant but impressive-looking cut, and return saying he had been attacked with the samurai sword. When this was proposed, LDN said that it was inappropriate because it was a family show, and anyway, Yorghos's real job was as a policeman, and he couldn't turn up to work looking brutalised. I'm convinced that Stu Hart and the Calgary Stampede would have loved this finish – he'd have said, 'Eh! What a great idea!'

It was infuriating. LDN had been struggling for ideas, interest, and a decent following; we'd developed something that was working well and attracting ever more interest and TV viewers, but they couldn't appreciate it. LDN couldn't have got either the Hanley or Wolverhampton venues without Kendo's involvement, and even if they had, they would have struggled to get above two or three hundred people in those venues. With Kendo involved, the audience through the door totalled around eight hundred, maybe nine hundred; if we'd had Brookside on-side and working properly with us, it might have been even bigger and better.

I felt as if I'd been here before – like the Hippodrome show; everything was set up for Kendo's return, but the people running it didn't get the point. In the old days, because Joint Promotions had control, this would never have happened; whatever the wrestling business had become, it wasn't even in control of itself.

It might have been possible to salvage something if LDN had seen sense, but then came a bombshell – they lost their TV contract. Without the TV shows, I couldn't see any point in Yorghos and Kendo going into a match where we just wrestled or faced each other off in the ring – it had to have a bigger dynamic than that, otherwise it would be a waste of everyone's time. At that stage we decided they could – putting it bluntly – stick it up their proverbial; we withdrew our services.

However, all was not lost. Because I'd co-promoted the shows with LDN, I had the rights to the video that they'd shot of the matches, and we used it to put together an interesting movie about Kendo, called 'Kendo Nagasaki: The English Samurai', which we sold from the Nagasaki website. LDN hadn't had the chance to edit the Wolverhampton show together for TV before their contract ended, so it was never shown. I included it in my movie in its entirety, including the build-up and recriminations after the match, and it makes compelling viewing. I was pleased with the finished product because that turned out to be Kendo's last ever professional wrestling match, and he finished as he'd started – devastating, uncompromising, and brutal, both hated and admired, and always iconic.

We also had a laugh when a reporter's arrogance got him into trouble. For the Wolverhampton show there was a lot of press and TV coverage, including a spot for the BBC's evening regional news show, Midlands Today, which was covered by reporter Ben Godfrey. I was told that during the run-up to the match while he did interviews for his piece he seemed quite interested in Kendo and his return to the Wolves Civic Hall, but after the match he came to the dressing room to do an interview and he was anything but respectful. As is usual, there were more questions than what made it into the final edit, but now he seemed to want to take the piss out of wrestling in general and Kendo in particular.

With his camera rolling, he asked, 'Now you're a pensioner Kendo, do you find it difficult to do the things you used to, to get into the ring?'

Atlantis's answer reaffirmed Kendo's high level of ability and fitness and that I trained several times a week, so he moved on to the next question, but I was irritated at Godfrey's attitude – he seemed very pleased with himself for asking such a cocky question.

The cheek continued; Godfrey then asked, 'Have you heard about one of Kendo's biggest fans – his name's Peter Thornley from Stoke on Trent?' His smirk was fucking sickening by this point, but Kendo remained impassive...

When the interviewing was finished, he wanted a shot of himself in a 'head-lock' which would form part of his piece to camera, but everyone in the dressing room knew what would happen next! In addition to Atlantis, Lawrence was there and so was Rob Cope, a long-standing ardent supporter and founder member of 'The Keepers of the Salt', a close group of Kendo 'super-fans'. Everyone knew that Ben Godfrey would now find out that Kendo was not to be taken lightly!

Atlantis tried to warn him that wrestling was not a joke and that Kendo didn't 'play' at combat, so he wouldn't like the experience of being in any of Kendo's holds. He then suggested that perhaps a pose with Kendo's sword might also work, but it was actually far more appropriate that he felt what it was like 'at the sharp end' so-to-speak, and he stepped forward to find out... Kendo put him into a front head-lock, not particularly hard, and he held it for a few seconds.

When he released Godfrey, he was a changed man! He staggered back and shook his head and in a somewhat strained voice and with a strained smile, he said, 'The sword is a good option! *(Cough! Splutter!)* I've always wondered how it was done!' Rob and Lawrence thought it was hilarious.

Godfrey was now much more respectful; he carefully took a couple of shots with the tag team belts that Kendo and Blondie had won that night, and they ended up opening his TV piece. Predictably, perhaps, he got revenge of a cowardly kind – his commentary on the finished broadcast was full of sarcastic and piss-taking quips.

The head-lock wasn't filmed for the BBC but we caught it as part of our own video-diary of the day – it makes great viewing on our You Tube channel, *Kendo Nagasaki 101.*

Chapter 37

The Nagasaki Retreat

When I found Moor Court Hall, the then owner, Peter Pinecoffin, told me that it had almost been bought by an Indian guru.

As I've mentioned, it had been my interest in finding a place in the countryside to have horses that had led me to Moor Court, but as soon as I pulled onto the drive, I knew there was more to it than that. As a practical person I'm not particularly fatalistic in my day-to-day life, but it was crystal clear to me that this beautiful, peaceful place would be important to Kendo. I somehow knew it wouldn't be immediately, but I knew it would definitely happen, so I decided then and there to buy Moor Court Hall.

At the east and south entrances to the estate are gate-houses called East Lodge and South Lodge respectively, and at that time a man called Graham Wagstaff lived in South Lodge. He was a follower of the guru in question, who he called Swami; Graham told me that he wanted a place like Moor Court to open an Ashram, a place of spiritual guidance.

Pinecoffin confirmed that the guru had already seen the Hall and put in a bid, and then gone off to America to collect the necessary funds, which had apparently been donated by a wealthy colleague at another Ashram. As the sale was more-or-less agreed, Pinecoffin had a figure in mind, but – ever the haggler – I bid him fifty thousand pounds less than the guru had.

'But I've had a bigger bid,' said Pinecoffin.

'Maybe,' I replied, 'But you haven't got it, have you?' I was playing the 'bird in the hand is worth two in the bush' trick.

I said, 'Look, Peter – I'm here today. I don't have to go to America to get the money – I'll buy the Hall and sign the contract today, but that's it. When I get in my car and go back to London, I'm not coming back, so it's make-your-mind-up time.'

The Pinecoffin family had a trust and he had to consult all the trustees, so this was hastily arranged, and they accepted my offer; they reasoned that Swami might not come back from America, and even if he did, he might not have all the money, but with me, a sale today was a sure thing. So, I bought Moor Court Hall in one day.

I later heard from Graham that Swami had returned from America and still wanted to buy Moor Court, and he wanted to know if I was interested in selling. I said no, but when the financial collapse came and I was looking for prospective buyers, Swami was no longer interested; clearly, it was meant to be mine.

Graham also told me something very interesting– he said that Swami had told him that it didn't matter who owned the Hall, because it was destined to be an Ashram. As that's what eventually happened, Kendo must have known that too, even then.

I didn't have the time to ponder the bigger picture when I got here because I was immediately preoccupied with renovations and refurbishments, then Moorcare sprang into being, then Blackpool and LDN came along – suddenly, twenty-two years after I'd bought it, I found that Moor Court Hall was my sole focus; the time had come for Kendo's Retreat.

Ever since inviting people into my Wolverhampton

home in the mid-1970s for treatment I'd known that Kendo would eventually have a place dedicated to helping others, and now it was completely clear to me what form it should take. By 2010 I knew the Hall and the grounds extremely well; in 1989 we'd only refurbished a few rooms before the need arose to adapt the majority of the remainder to residential care, but when that closed most of the facilities were removed and taken to Blackpool as part of the refurbishments there, and virtually everything had gone, including carpets, curtains, kitchens, sanitary ware, internal doors, even light fittings. In twenty two years, the Hall had been taken from being a wreck to a care home and back to a shell needing everything doing again, but it had become a blank canvas once more, onto which Kendo's vision could be created.

I'd been so busy with day-to-day practicalities that I hadn't consciously realised all the possibilities, but now that there was nothing else to worry about my intuition laid it all out for me. Like the Hall itself, the grounds had needed a lot of work when we first got here, but as they took shape, I walked in them more and more and began meditating there. The only sounds are the breeze in the trees and birdsong, which made it extremely easy to let everything conscious fall away...

The first impressions I got were of what Kendo wanted to provide. It went without saying that this would be a place of empowerment based on peace, but, in contrast to helping people one-at-a-time, here Kendo would help groups of people.

Facilities for meditation would be needed, but there are many forms and I needed to plan for several. The most accessible kind for those who hadn't meditated before was a guided type, and this would have to be written and recorded – Roz and I could put our music experience to good use there.

Having begun using singing bowls in meditation many years before, I now had a collection of thirteen which I regularly played as a meditation, and I was guided as to how Kendo could use them for groups of people. The key would be a mindful-meditative approach, being intuitively guided to which bowls to play or strike at any given moment according to what the person receiving healing needed; it would be an expression of Ai Ki Do, 'doing/not doing', and Kyu Shin Do, after sensei Abbe and his sensei, master Ueshiba.

I'd noticed that the phrase 'mindfulness' was becoming popular in the west, even though it had been known of for hundreds of years in the east, so it would make sense to let those who came to the Retreat practise 'Shakyo', the mindful-meditative Japanese art of tracing Buddhist sutras in Kanji.

The grounds would be of considerable value – not only are they beautiful, but there are many places which could act as symbols to help people make sense of their lives and take heart. For example, the huge Atlas Cedar at the bottom of the west lawn can be seen across it from the seats in the place we call the Pavilion, and this is a metaphor for life. As mortals, we can't take the direct route across the lawn to the tree that represents long life and success – instead, we had to take the stony paths around the edge and overcome the challenges that the stones represent.

There is an unassuming little stone bench halfway along the path between the Pavilion and the pond, which could represent success – having made it there and overcome all those challenges, those that lay ahead needn't seem overwhelming.

The pond itself had been filled-in, but it had to be brought back into use and populated with fish, so it could provide the same meditative peace as I'd found all those years ago, sat before Abbe's aquarium.

There is a stone seat facing directly east, which could be used to meditate on the healing of the rising sun and the fast-changing energies of Western Astrology's rising sign; this would become the Contemplation Seat.

The Atlas cedar itself is a hugely imposing expression of nature and forms an almost perfect triangular shape pointing upwards, symbolising aspiration to higher inspiration and the wisdom of our ancestors – this would become the Tree of Souls.

There was a secluded lawned space which was simply begging to be turned into a Zen garden in the shape of Kamakura, the Japanese city where Zen for everyone began, and to which I felt a strong connection. As I mentioned when describing the genesis of Kendo Nagasaki, I'd read about a samurai family called Nagasaki who had defended Kamakura, and I later learned more about the youngest warrior, Shin'Uemon, who lost his life at age fifteen. When I meditated on it later, I felt that he and Kendo Nagasaki were the same spirit, and this Zen garden would honour both the name and the warrior spirit.

There was the Hidden Garden which is natural and uncultivated and very reminiscent of the temple gardens in Japan, where nature expresses itself with no more intervention from man than keeping it tidy, where it's so easy to feel close to nature and how it expresses itself so simply and elegantly.

And finally there was the hilly north lawn, then featureless, but which would make an exquisite orchard; I envisaged it ringed with Japanese cherry trees, with fruit trees in the middle. It would be a place of natural beauty that would become ever more enchanting with time.

Everything that happened in the grounds fell under an overall principle of Kendo's that I felt was essential to get across; in our busy western lives, it's east to forget that we are part of the big picture of nature, and we need to re-connect with it. Kendo's perspective has always been a Buddhist one, and Japanese Buddhism incorporates their indigenous religion, Shintoism, which is similar to British Paganism in respecting everything in nature as having an in-dwelling 'spirit' – as do we. Pointing this out whilst surrounded by so many elegant 'spirits' of nature would be a powerful metaphor for those present, reminding them to surrender their egos and recognise their one-ness with nature. We set up several Shinto 'Torii' Gates in the grounds to mark particularly spiritual spaces.

I knew that Kendo would want to use the grounds to illustrate many powerful symbols and metaphors, so tours of them would be an essential feature for our visitors.

As regards the Hall, there was a huge amount of work to do. Not only did we have to make it habitable once again, installing new kitchens and bathrooms, but we also had to undo all the work that had been done to accommodate the care home, which had affected all of it apart from the principal rooms. I decided to dedicate the entire west wing to the Nagasaki Retreat, including offices upstairs and downstairs a Seminar Room, which would accommodate singing bowl performances and meditations, a Terrace Room to relax in, a Meditation Suite for guided meditations, and the conservatory for Shakyos. As we would prepare meals for groups of people we needed a new kitchen and scullery, as well as toilets. Lastly, as we'd begun selling Kendo merchandise on a web store, we decided to open a small store in the Hall for those who wanted a souvenir of their visit.

I knew the guided meditations would be very important, as they had to deeply relax those new to meditation as well as work for those experienced with it, so I decided to combine several elements of Kendo's classic relaxation techniques. There needed to be music at the start and end, sounds of nature, sounds of singing bowls, and the guiding narrative; I meditated for quite some time before coming up with a format, which Roz then recorded.

We did two different guided meditations, respectively called 'Empowerment' and 'Kyu Shin Do', which deeply relax the listener and then invoke either empowering affirmations or the Kyu Shin Do perspective on life, before bringing them back to full alertness. The meditations have worked very well, with all those who experienced them reporting deep relaxation and feeling refreshed afterwards, and we went on to sell them on CD from our web store.

As regards a singing bowls experience, I decided that the oak floor in the Seminar Room would make an excellent sounding-board, and I developed three ways in which Kendo could play singing bowls to relax participants – one just listening to a performance by Kendo, and two more where they lay on mats on the oak floor and felt the bowls resonate through them, from bowls either on a table above them or placed close to them on the floor. These performances were also accompanied by a sound-track of nature sounds, and music at the end to help bring people back to full awareness.

Once again, everyone was to report very positive experiences, either a complete emptying and 're-booting' of their minds from listening to a performance, or deep relaxation and refreshment from the lying-down sessions.

Of course, Kendo had been known as a 'healer' ever since the 1970s, but he had since evolved from giving individual people 'treatment' to meditating on their well-being, which meant that more people could be helped at the same time. They are told the time and date to perform a meditation, at which point Kendo would meditate with them, together visualising their wellness and strength. When we had an Event at the Retreat on the thirteenth of the month, those present would join Kendo in his meditative 'Distance Healing' ceremony; many were to find it a humbling and deeply moving experience.

I decided to structure the days so that the level of relaxation would get deeper and then shallower, finishing with a 'stick-burning' ceremony by Kendo. This is an ancient Shinto ritual, where thoughts, hopes, and prayers are associated with a small stick which our guests would keep with them, and at the end of their stay the sticks would be ceremonially cast into a brazier, releasing the hopes and prayers to the 'deities of nature', a final reminder of our one-ness with nature and the need for humility towards it.

It took two and a half years to do all the work on the Hall to prepare it for being the Nagasaki Retreat, including setting up a new website which described the foundations of Kendo's Buddhist 'strength through peace' approach. I was very pleased with how everything had turned out – it did justice to the wisdom that I'd gained from studying under sensei Abbe, including the essential philosophy of Kyu Shin Do, and everything I'd gained from my own mindful experience of facilitating Kendo's expression – he'd taught me a great deal too.

Our first 'Event' took place on the thirteenth of November 2013 – the forty-ninth anniversary of Kendo's debut, and in numerology, four plus nine equals thirteen – Kendo's magic number. Roz officiated, guiding our guests through the schedule and explaining what they could expect, and Lawrence supported myself and Kendo, as usual.

It was indeed a magical day – everyone there was deeply impressed at seeing the full out-working of the spirituality which Kendo's presence had long hinted at, and they appreciated the opportunity to be included in the practices and perspectives which had made him so strong and iconic, and a legend of the wrestling ring.

I was interested to find that everyone wanted to be photographed standing beside Kendo and his Lamborghini Diablo VT. I was happy to provide this – Kendo's success sprang from strength gained from meditation and Kyu Shin Do, and now these were being made available for people to experience first-hand, and there's nothing wrong with 'being the best you can be' and having that reward you with the finer things in life!

My approach to Kendo's participation was the same as it had always been – I meditated, I went into a deeply mindful state, so that all I was aware of was allowing Kendo to express himself, as only he could. He was the same as when he wrestled, absolutely focussed, at peak performance, and unspeaking, an example of the diligence required to get the full benefits of meditation. I found that our guests held him in the same esteem as they had when he'd wrestled, but I was very pleased to see that those coming to the Retreat weren't necessarily wrestling fans – many of the fans' wives began coming and they too described considerable benefits from the meditations, and I was delighted that Kendo's empowering practises were finding a wider audience on their own merits.

The November 2014 Event was the fiftieth anniversary of Kendo's debut, so we made it a special celebration – we put an open invitation on our website and narrowed the responses down to fifty, ten of whom read their special tributes to Kendo. Long-term tag-partner Blondie Barratt also came with his wife, Wendy.

The Anniversary Orchard of fifty trees had been planted, each one commemorating a year of Kendo's spectacular career, and in the evening we had a commemoration ceremony with a candle lantern hung from each tree – all the points of light stretching up the hill into the distance was an enchanting sight, and that evening's Stick-Burning Ceremony had a special atmosphere as it was performed in the orchard.

Having begun holding Events throughout the year and receiving universally positive feedback ever since the first one, we decided to become incorporated as a Charity. Of course, there were costs associated with holding Events which we asked those coming to help towards by paying a small fee, and as we wanted to increase the number of events and extend their reach to those who couldn't afford a fee, Charitable incorporation made sense as we could raise funds from donations and put them towards costs. 'The Kendo Nagasaki Foundation' was awarded Registered Charity status in March 2015 as a Buddhist charity which helped people by introducing them to Buddhist practises. I couldn't be more proud that Kendo's empowering wisdom was now officially recognised.

Also during 2015 we set up a traditional Tea Room in the grounds, in a secluded place next to the Kamakura Zen Garden. The Japanese Tea Ceremony is a fascinating blend of art, precision, and mindfulness, and participating is a calming and inspiring experience. It was very popular with the samurai because it represented virtues that were at the core of their way of life, and after Abbe had performed the Tea Ceremony for me, I had learned it many years ago. The Tea Room we built had all the values of an authentic Japanese one – it's very small and simple, which encourages participants to leave their egos at the door, and it has that Japanese quality of 'Wabi Sabi', or 'elegant rustic simplicity'. It's dedicated to sensei Abbe, and allows one to step into another world. Guests have been very keen to participate in a Tea Ceremony as performed by Kendo, and whenever we've scheduled it, it's been fully-booked.

For the November 2015 Event, we had finally become able to provide overnight accommodation in a suite of rooms, complete with sitting room and kitchen. Those who stayed then and since have reported getting an immensely good nights' sleep at the Retreat, which we'd hoped for and were delighted to hear. The rooms were always booked as soon as an Event was announced so we planned to extend the accommodation, but those who still wanted to come for a whole weekend were so keen that they'd find accommodation in the local area; we were all delighted at how successful Kendo's Events were.

At the beginning of 2016, a new direction suggested itself to me. I'd always been fascinated at how Zen had begun; by the year 1247, the city of Kamakura, Japan, was a huge military garrison, and the ruling Shogun was showing signs of what we now call PTSD. He invited the founder of Zen, a monk called Dogen, to come to Kamakura to help him find peace of mind, which he did, very successfully. From that 'little acorn' moment, Zen spread throughout Kamakura, then Japan, then the world, and it was a revelation. Up to that point, Buddhism had been the province of the rich in Kyoto, but from that moment, Zen's simple approach to finding oneself and one's place in the universe was accessible to all. Zen must have helped countless samurai who'd previously felt lost, and this struck a chord in me.

PTSD was in the news much more, and I thought that our Foundation could reach out to forces' Veterans and offer them the chance to deeply relax, and see if that would help them. I was reminded of a nugget of feedback that had come back from some of our guests; one of the most frequent early questions was asking why Kendo had been so brutal as a wrestler. The reason was because Kendo was using the 'theatre of wrestling' to illustrate a fact of life: basically, it's not fair, and you need to be the best you can be to meet its challenges. It was explained that Kendo had represented both those things – the unfairness of life and the excellence required to triumph – and our guests appreciated this metaphor once they'd felt the strength that came from deep relaxation.

I reasoned that Veterans are already the best of us – highly-trained, well-disciplined, and motivated – and if they could be helped to let go of what was causing their stress, they could greatly contribute to a better society. I felt it was my duty to help this group.

As a result, we had a group of four Veterans to the Retreat, all of whom had experienced harrowing combat conditions, but were just about managing to function. They stayed for a weekend, and by the time they left, they were all much more relaxed, with two of them claiming to feel a great deal better. We were delighted to hear that one of the Veterans who had previously had very disturbed sleep was now sleeping so soundly that he sometimes overslept and found himself late for work!

We've had many Events since, which have included a mix of Veterans and civilians, and I decided that we'd cater for both groups – those who were interested in Kendo's Buddhist approach to relaxation and empowerment, and Veterans specifically. Interestingly, circumstances were to unfold that supported this idea.

The Nagasaki Retreat's Events continue to this day, usually being fully-booked within hours of being announced, and we look forward to growing and expanding the availability of Kendo's approach to peace, strength, and self-empowerment. The Retreat has turned out to be all I'd hoped it would, and it will continue helping people into the future, by sharing Kendo's uniquely accessible Buddhist wisdom.

Chapter 38

The Lee Rigby Foundation

In early 2015, a friend of ours, Chris, called and said he would be able to put us in contact with Lyn Rigby. In common with everyone else in the UK, we all knew about the murder of Lyn's son, Lee, in May 2013, and how devastating it had been for the Rigby family. Our first thought was how we could help them to heal from such a tragic loss, and we pursued the possibility of inviting Lyn and her family to the Retreat for a get-away break.

We heard that Lyn wanted to set up a Foundation to help families who had been bereaved; this sounded like an excellent idea, and I reasoned that she must have a particular insight into the problem based on her own experience – as the aim of our Foundation was to help empower people through peace, perhaps we could help Lyn with that too.

We invited Lyn and family to come to our Retreat, and she finally made it on 1st July 2015, accompanied by her husband, Ian, and daughter, Amy, as well as Rosie Dunn, her biographer. It was a lovely summer's day and Yvonne, Roz, Alan, Lawrence, and myself greeted them and, as always, the atmosphere was friendly and relaxing; they said it was very nice to get away from their Manchester home for a day out. As we chatted on the terrace, gradually they all visibly unwound and laughter broke out more and more frequently, which was very good to see.

Eventually, Yvonne took Lyn on a tour of the Moor Court site, and when they'd gone past the Willowview house and the Moorside Lodge building came into view, Lyn stopped and became quite emotional. Looking at the Lodge building, she said, 'That's what I want for Lee's legacy.' The building hadn't been used since 2005 when Moorcare had closed and it had been de-commissioned, but the exterior remained sound and, nestled among the trees, it looked every inch a potential haven for those who needed a peaceful, relaxing get-away; indeed, we had been planning to use it to extend the accommodation facilities for our own Foundation's Events.

When we all went back to the terrace for another cuppa, Lyn was more open about her experiences and motivations. She told us that the reason why she wanted to set up a foundation for bereaved families was because hers had received virtually no support since Lee's death; the army had kept in touch until Lee's funeral but there had `barely a word since then, and no organisation or charity had offered support of any kind, such as a get-away break. Lyn told us that because Lee had been married his parents and sisters were no longer considered to be immediate family, and the army and forces' charities only provided support for the immediate family of serving or deceased personnel. It seemed most unfair that a family in such need of support as the Rigbys had found themselves so marginalised by those whose mission was supposed to be supporting people just like them.

We also heard something quite shocking. Apparently, in the twenty-four hours following Lee's death, the public made donations of seven million pounds to Veterans' support charities, but not a single penny of it had been offered to support Lyn and her family. By then it had been three years since Lee's death, and I reasoned that if a family that had suffered such a high-profile and tragic loss as the Rigbys hadn't been helped-out even by Forces charities then something was indeed very wrong. Lyn said she knew many families in similar circumstances, and this was why she wanted Lee's legacy to be a force for good, supporting those who had been similarly overlooked.

I asked Lyn how plans for her foundation were progressing, and with a wry smile she said, 'Slowly...' She said she was involved with a few good people who had done the groundwork for setting up a charity to achieve her aims, but for various reasons progress had been very slow; her frustration was clear and in sharp contrast to her great strength and determination to make her son's life stand for something good, and at that moment I resolved to support her in any way I could.

She told us more about the book she was writing about her experiences, but whilst it had been completed it apparently couldn't be published until an appeal concerning Lee's murderers had concluded. It seemed grossly unfair that so much of what Lyn wanted to achieve was on hold because of forces beyond her control.

We had a lovely afternoon with the Rigbys and eventually bade them a cheery farewell, and I promised I'd think things over to see how we could help them.

I had no problem with Moorside Lodge becoming the home of the Lee Rigby Lodge – it would indeed make a perfect getaway for families in Lyn's situation, so it was time to consider the practicalities, and ultimately it all seemed to boil-down simply to finding the money. I reasoned that once the Lee Rigby Foundation was up-and-running, our two charities working together should be able to get the wheels in motion.

Lyn and Ian came to see us again in September 2015 to experience one of our Nagasaki Events, which they both seemed to enjoy, and afterwards we were able to chat more about how to move things forward. Lyn was as determined and optimistic as ever, but there still seemed to have been no progress and this was continuing to frustrate her. All we could do at that time was keep in touch and be ready to move on any opportunity to make progress.

We eventually discovered that the key people in the Rigby organisation were very spread out and almost never seemed able to meet and move things forward. We were included in an email group, and whenever we heard from them there seemed to be plenty of discussions and lots of enthusiasm, but there was no actual progress on fund-raising, publicity, or web presence.

As we'd already decided to throw our weight behind the Lee Rigby Foundation, the Nagasaki Foundation arranged an event that would have two purposes – to celebrate an important anniversary for Kendo, and raise funds for the Lee Rigby Foundation. The 5th March 2016 was the fiftieth anniversary of Kendo's spectacular match against Count Bartelli, when he defeated and unmasked the Count at the Victoria Hall, Hanley. For the anniversary, we decided to hold a wrestling contest between today's best newcomer wrestlers, donate the profits to both Foundations, and also video the shows and sell DVDs to raise more funds. We asked wrestlers to tell us about themselves and were inundated with applications for the contest. We were capably assisted by my old colleagues Marty Jones and Brian Dixon, who also did the commentary and prize-giving.

A nice touch was that we contacted a local couple, Margaret and Joseph Heath, who had been in the audience on the night of the Nagasaki / Bartelli match in 1966, and they came along as our special guests.

The matches were judged in two stages – the heats by Mr. & Mrs. Heath and our own in-house wrestling fan, Yvonne, and we wanted a celebrity judge for the finals. We were delighted that Lou Macari, the former football star and team manager who now runs his own charity to help rough sleepers in the Stoke area, joined us to support the Rigby Foundation's cause, and he sat on stage alongside Lyn and Kendo to judge the finals.

It was a great event, with excellent performances by all the newcomer wrestlers, it was capably videoed by our friend Roland Platt, and we included interviews with the wrestlers, the Heaths, and Lou Macari on the DVD, which was put together in-house; it's still selling from the Nagasaki Web Store, continuing to raise funds.

Soon afterwards, a welcome positive development was the granting of the charity number to the Lee Rigby Foundation in April 2016, so the organisation was at last legitimately set up as a charity and able to make progress with its aims. However, despite all the claimed enthusiasm from the initial contributors, there were only a handful of emails in the following five months, and when we heard that Lyn and Ian were by that point hugely frustrated with how things were going, we volunteered to take a more active role.

Our Foundation freed-up Yvonne and Roz, and at the beginning of September 2016 they went to speak with the key people. The timing was fortuitous, because one of the original trustees, Spencer Taylor, had found that his work commitments had evolved to the point where he was no longer able to devote time to the Lee Rigby Foundation, so he bowed-out. Another contributor was Glenn Millar at Source Design, a web development company which had put together a wonderful plan for an extensive website. Glenn was extremely helpful and allowed the Foundation to purchase the artwork and branding that Source had developed, so it was finally time for a brand new website, which Roz put together.

Yvonne's executive experience immediately shone through, and her no-nonsense attitude towards getting things moving soon earned her the nick-name of 'Top Dog' from Lyn, and things really did start moving.

All the essentials were set up, including new email

addresses and a social media presence, PayPal and JustGiving accounts, and we gave the Lee Rigby Foundation its own office space here at Moor Court, and we got a dedicated phone line in – by December 2016 it was finally a fully-functioning charity.

The first fund-raiser organised in-house by the Lee Rigby Foundation was put together for March 2017, a charity dinner at Manchester United football stadium, including after-dinner speaking by Lee Rigby Foundation patron Colin Maclachlan, and there was an auction compèred by the spectacular Miss Joanna Phuc, a drag queen from Kaos Bar. Some Kendo items were auctioned, for which Kendo himself appeared in full regalia, and amongst many other excellent items donated for auction, the other Rigby patron, Matt Croucher VC donated a certified replica of his medal, which was bought by a police officer to inspire everyone at his station.

All the tables were sold and the dinner just about broke even, but it acted as an excellent publicity vehicle for the Foundation, kick-starting many more fund-raising activities – things were now moving.

Whilst we'd originally discussed raising funds to refurbish the former Moorside Lodge building and open it as the Lee Rigby Lodge, another idea came to me. For the previous couple of years, Alan and I had been gradually refurbishing the Willowview house on the estate, but it seemed it would make an excellent focus for the Lee Rigby Foundation's work, and it would be achievable a lot more quickly than the Lodge project. It still needed quite a lot of work, but it was a single house as opposed to a 20-bedroom building, so we reasoned that it must be possible to galvanise donors to help with materials and trades to do the work. We decided to make the house available exclusively to the Lee Rigby Foundation, and the Lee Rigby House project was born.

It soon began gathering momentum – as the work progressed, many television and press features were done on the Lee Rigby House, and it greatly helped raise their Foundation's profile; we were astonished at the generosity of the donors, both individual and corporate, and we kept meeting more and more wonderful people whose hearts were very much in the right place.

One of the earliest to offer help was Keith Lawson of The Blind Company, who was a member of some Veterans forums. After he came to measure-up for the window blinds that his company would donate, he posted that we needed help, and before we knew it thousands of offers had come in. It took quite a while for our small team to go through them, but that's the right kind of problem to have.

Many companies also offered generous support, including donations of kitchen appliances, bedding, furniture, and flooring; they're too many to mention here, but they've all been recognised on the Lee Rigby Foundation website.

A group of tradesmen called Band of Builders was astonishing, rallying groups of decorators and landscapers and multi-skilled tradesmen to move the project forward literally in leaps and bounds – we're still in touch with them, and will always be deeply grateful to them for their generosity and skills.

While the project was under way, Lyn brought several prospective users of her Foundation's facilities to the House to visit, including bereaved mothers and Veterans themselves. We were delighted to hear from one mother of a soldier who'd been a friend of Lee's and had died in Afghanistan that the completed house would be the perfect place to come, to '...get away from all the reminders and questions...'. Also, one of the Veterans said that it seemed the perfect place to forget everything and finally get a good night's sleep – he said that's what he'd most needed when he was '...in a bad place.'

Another big step forward was achieved when Lyn and her family were able to move to Moor Court in August

2017. A house on the estate had become available and Lyn was very keen to be 'hands-on' in the office and become part of the on-site team working towards the completion of the Lee Rigby House, as well as meeting-and-greeting the families who would use the House when it opened. I was delighted to see how coming to live on the peaceful site of her Foundation helped her to relax and focus her energies on her wonderful project.

The Lee Rigby House formally opened on 9th October 2017. We had two hundred guests for the opening day party, including the Mayor of Rochdale who presented a donation cheque for over £10,000. BBC and ITV television covered the event, as did the press, and it's had continuing press coverage since. The house is now booked throughout 2018 for families to come and have their relaxing get-away breaks.

It's been very gratifying to see the combined efforts of our Foundations recognised in the press – a lovely article appeared in the Sunday People on Christmas Eve 2017, a double-page spread which described the collaboration of our Foundations. I'm delighted that we've been able to help the Rigby family and their cause in this way, and I look forward to our Foundations together helping many more bereaved families and Veterans feel the same.

As ever, we look to the future; the next project – once again, more immediate and therefore accessible sooner than the big Lodge project – which is to convert a wing of Moor Court Hall into an accommodation area specifically for Veterans. It will have four bed-sits and another four bedrooms (making a total of eight) and its own kitchen and sitting room, and we'll be getting various leisure facilities in place too, such as re-commissioning the therapy pool and setting-up a gym and art areas, as well as getting the greenhouse and planting-out area up and running again.

We're hopefully taking the Foundation to Parliament to present it's evolving vision to MPs and other influential people, whilst also announcing an extension to the support it offers. In May 2018 on the fifth anniversary to the day of Lee's passing, there was the terrorist bombing at the Manchester Arena. Lyn was back in Middleton at the time, sharing the sad anniversary with family, and such an event on that particular day shook her deeply. So many families losing children in such a tragic and indiscriminate way vividly brought back Lyn's own loss five years earlier, but typical of her she responded in a positive way, deciding to extend the support of her Foundation to civilian victims of terrorism and their families. I continue to be impressed at Lyn's strength and resolve to heal wounds, and I will continue to support her in every way possible.

Lyn and her Foundation's trustees have kindly recognised the support that my own Foundation has given them, and they have recognised our collaboration in their Foundation's name – The Lee Rigby Foundation has become the Lee Rigby KNFoundation, or the Lee Rigby KNF. We are honoured.

The whole supportive community approach is the ideal out-working of the Zen principles I learned so long ago, and I am grateful that the Lee Rigby Foundation has given me the opportunity to put them into real, tangible practice. I believe we are building something that will stand as a beacon of hope and healing long into the future.

Epilogue

Whatever Happened to Brian Stevens?

The circumstances of my birth set me on a certain path, and as soon as I was able to recognise that, I worked very hard to get off it.

My ambition was severely frustrated by my dyslexia, which, in the middle of the 20th century would normally have condemned me to a life of manual labour.

I was also plagued by nagging doubt about who I was and where I came from. After being told in primary school that my father 'wasn't my father', it came up again at secondary school when one of the few friends I had – also called Peter – told me he'd been warned-off hanging around with me by his grandmother because I had 'Polish blood.' That was all he could tell me, and fortunately he didn't avoid me, but it deepened my sense of being an outcast.

When I was eighteen or nineteen I asked my Aunt Ida about it, and she said, 'Don't give it a second thought – you're a Thornley.' I knew that wasn't really the case, but I was grateful for her unconditional commitment to me.

The same was true of my father; although he seemed

distant, he always supported me without question. When I was in my early twenties I was talking to my step-mother and mentioned my adoption. She reacted surprisingly – she said, 'Ooh – how do you know about that?' I said that I'd known for years, and she said, 'Whatever you do, don't tell your father that you know – it would break his heart.'

So, even though I knew I had unconditional support I had no answers, but the fact that I was adopted seemed to be something shameful, not to be spoken about.

On the evening before my father died and I was at his bed-side, he didn't realise it was me and he spoke to me as if I was someone else; he said, 'I've just been talking to my lad; he's done so well and he's always been very good and looked after me.' The sort of affection that came over from him at that moment, and Ida before she died, they could not have expressed before due to their Victorian backgrounds and the traumatic disappearance of their own father. It was clear that, given the circumstances, both he and my Aunt did their very best for me.

I never saw my adoption papers until after he died – my step-mother found them amongst his papers and said to me, 'Well, I suppose these belong to you.' She'd respected my father's confidence until his death, by which time I was thirty seven years old, which showed how much he'd wanted to shield me from what he'd perceived to be the stigma of adoption. That was also the first time I ever saw my birth mother's name.

I found growing up under this cloud as oppressive as the stigma of being illiterate, but there was another aspect of my existence that caused me a great deal of confusion and anxiety in my early life – I am bisexual. This might be regarded as the 'Easter egg' of my story, a revelation that's perhaps the most closely-guarded aspect of my private life as a consequence of such relationships being illegal until I was 26, and the stigma that remained attached to them for years after that. These days no defence is needed – a person's sexuality is a celebrated aspect of their individuality, and today's members of the LGBT community are fortunate to live in such enlightened times. Whilst never feeling drawn to the 'scene' and avoiding the spotlight of publicity – until now – I have done my bit for the gay community, providing a stage for the glittering Gorgeous George and taking pride in my hotel and nightclub in Blackpool's gay village. I am glad to have had the opportunity to contribute positively to these parallel walks of life too.

In light of my early difficulties I am fortunate to have had the natural skills I had, and to be able to exploit them to achieve the 'good life' that Ida and The Count had showed me. My success was hard-won, against the odds, and I felt I deserved it. I allowed myself to be self-indulgent, particularly with expensive cars, but influence of sensei Abbe went deep, so meditation and contemplation came increasingly naturally to me. From first meeting the sensei I was aware of a slower, deeper 'Kyu Shin Do'-type evolution growing beneath the surface; I haven't felt it was right to go into too much depth about it in this book, but this powerful, simple, and accessible philosophy has done so much for me that I feel I must share it in future writings.

Self-indulgence is, of course, ultimately meaningless; we are all participants in the quality of our society and should do whatever we can to elevate it. For me this began with giving treatment and sharing Zen principles, but it's been particularly since meeting Lyn Rigby that I want my success to benefit others who haven't been as fortunate as I have. I'm hoping that writing my story will inspire anyone who feels stigmatised in the ways that I did (and others) to strive for better things and ultimately have a strong enough sense of completeness to give back to the world around them. I want to shed light on the things I feel deserve whole-hearted support, and to leave a legacy that everyone who's helped me on my journey would be proud of.

One of the happiest times of my life was when I was helping people with learning disabilities. That has been surpassed by my present situation, where I am involved with the meditation and mindfulness work of my own charity, and supporting the Lee Rigby KNFoundation in all its admirable aims.

It's taken me a life-time to arrive at these perspectives, and I hope that following my journey in the short time it takes to read my book can show how adversity can be turned into self-empowerment and the will to do the best for others. As the vehicle for sensei Abbe's philosophy, Kendo Nagasaki has helped me do just that, and I hope his message reaches far and wide and helps countless others too.

www.ingramcontent.com/pod-product-compliance
Lightning Source LLC
Chambersburg PA
CBHW052026090426
42739CB00010B/1803
* 9 7 8 1 9 0 8 3 4 5 4 5 5 *